Published in the United Kingdom in 2017 by DC Thomson and
Co. Ltd, Albert Square, Dundee, DD1 9QJ, and written by staff
and associates of The Courier, 80 Kingsway East, Dundee,
DD4 8SL.

This book was edited, designed and produced at Kingsway,
Dundee, by Richard Rooney and Roland (Gus) Proctor.

DC Thomson

Foreword: By **Paul Hegarty**

Our fans showed what fair play really means

It was only later in life that the players came to realise what a great achievement it was to take a club like Dundee United to a major European final.

For professional footballers, the game is all about winning and we felt the only way to make the season really special was to claim trophies.

But if you're going to lose you've got to do it graciously, and the fans certainly made sure we did that…

For a while we couldn't get past the first hurdle in Europe but we started to make progress from the late 70s and by the mid-80s the nucleus of the team had a lot of European games under our belt and we felt comfortable there.

The team was like a clique. If you came into the club and you couldn't handle us, and the laughing and joking, you were binned. But it wasn't a clique of two or three — it was 14, 15, 16. That's how strong we were.

If you could handle us you were brought into the fold and it was easy because the guys at the club were different class. Just good, down-to-earth people who wanted to work hard to make a living in football and support their families.

We stood up for each other and everyone knew their job. That's what Jim McLean was great at: as a coach and tactician, and he got you so fit.

And we played very much like foreign teams: soaking up the pressure and catching sides on the break. The foreign teams couldn't understand how a Scottish team could do that.

Even when it came to the massive games like Barcelona we were fortunate because we had beaten teams like Borussia, Werder Bremen and Monaco in recent years so we had sampled the big time already. There were no superstars but we always fancied ourselves to do well.

Could it have happened without Jim McLean? Probably not. He got the whole team together. The team was in transition and he brought players in to fit the jigsaw again and it worked.

I'm sure in later years he wished he'd enjoyed his success more than he allowed himself to but he has to take enormous credit for getting so much out of his resources.

But today's players couldn't handle two minutes of

Paul Hegarty (front, second from left) with other United players days before they headed to France to play RC Lens at the start of what would become their most famous European campaign.

wee Jim. He was so intense. So you also have to praise the players for being so mentally strong.

And we can now look back and be proud that we gave a lot of pleasure to a lot of people. Supporters work hard to follow the game and if you send them home with a smile on their face you're doing your job as a footballer.

I didn't realise it at the time, but I found out later that even former players would come to Tannadice and pay at the turnstiles to watch our European games.

When fellow pros are making the effort to come from across the country to watch how you handle European competition, you realise it must have been a special time.

But the fans have got to take the greatest credit of all for what they did in the final.

People staying back after watching their team being beaten and applauding the away team lifting the trophy on their own ground? That's something we had never seen.

UEFA must have been rubbing their hands. They've spent years talking about respect, but what the United fans did that night — that was respect at its highest.

They went to another level.

With all of Europe watching, they showed a Scottish team and the Scottish people in the very best light.

Paul Hegarty salutes the Dundee United fans after the second leg of the UEFA Cup final against IFK Gothenburg.

contents

Changing for the better?

By 1986, Dundee United are expected to advance in Europe.

While no side sent out by Jim McLean would ever be allowed to be complacent, United had not failed to reach at least the third round of European competition since 1981 and had appeared in the European Cup semi-final only two years earlier — meaning anything but progress would represent a major setback for the Tangerines.

However, United's European campaign gets under way at a time of major change for the club.

McLean's assistant Walter Smith has left to join Graeme Souness at Rangers in the summer, long-time talisman Davie Dodds has joined Neuchâtel Xamax and other club stalwarts, including legendary keeper Hamish McAlpine, have moved on after years of loyal service.

With the season only weeks old, United's squad is weakened further when international defender Richard Gough leaves to join Tottenham Hotspur.

With injuries also ravaging what is left of his line-up, and with limited success in the transfer market, McLean is forced to rely on a mix of youth and trying players in new positions.

However, the surprise signing of a somewhat reluctant Iain Ferguson from city neighbours Dundee will later prove a master stroke — even if he is ineligible for the early rounds of the UEFA Cup.

Despite United's apparent frailty, they start the season in spectacular style, racing to the top of the league and leaving Lens' sports director, Romain Arghirudis, worried.

After watching United beat New Firm rivals Aberdeen, he is full of praise for their performance in general and Paul Sturrock's in particular, paying the ultimate compliment of describing him as "very French in temperament".

Nevertheless, Sturrock and the rest of the United team are frustrated when they suffer their first defeat of the season, losing 1-0 in France.

They are also dumped out of the League Cup by Rangers, and can only draw against Hibs in the league in the days leading up to the second leg versus Lens — meaning McLean needs to get his men back in the right frame of mind.

The Courier reminds readers that "Eight seasons have lapsed since Jim McLean's men last fell at the first hurdle in Europe" and the manager challenges his players to record another Tannadice turnaround, reminding his players that European football "is the icing on the cake, it gets the adrenalin going."

It works, and goals from Ralph Milne and Tommy Coyne set United on their way.

No new signing before U.E.F.A. deadline

Dundee United have failed to beat the European signing deadline (reports STEVE BRUCE). The Tannadice club had offers for three players rejected within the last few days as they sought to strengthen their squad before the deadline which expired last night.

Jim McLean, who has cash from the transfer of Davie Dodds and Alex Taylor to spend, has made inquiries about players both sides of the border, without success.

United remain keen to sign a goalscorer, but if they are successful in that quest, he will not now be eligible for the U.E.F.A. Cup first round tie with Lens.

Meanwhile, the Tannadice manager is refusing to comment on a report that Richard Gough will play his last match for the club at Ibrox today before leaving them for Spurs.

"A disgrace"

"I'm not getting involved in speculation but it's a disgrace, the upset we've had to contend with during preparation for matches," was all he would say on the subject.

Continuing speculation over Gough's future is also likely to be handicapping United's bid to bring fresh faces to Tannadice, with other clubs upping prices for players in the belief United will shortly have plenty of cash with the sale of the Scotland star.

Close-season signings Dave Bowman, Jim McInally and Chris Sulley were all signed from English clubs and it's odds on any fresh additions to the playing staff will also come from down south.

Continuing his stated policy of "freshening" the team from game to game, manager Jim McLean is planning alterations to the side that drew 0-0 at Clydebank in midweek.

Added to the 13 on duty for that match are Dave Beaumont and young striker, Kevin Gallacher, who made such an impact on the first team scene last season.

Dave Beaumont . . . added to pool.

The difficulty of attracting players to Tannadice would be a feature of the coverage throughout the season. And while United struggled to recruit, they suffered the blow of losing international star Richard Gough only a few weeks into the new campaign.

United impress Lens boss

United impressed visiting Romain Arghieuais, manager of U.E.F.A. Cup opponents Lens, with their display against Aberdeen on Saturday (reports STEVE BRUCE).

"It was a very good game and Dundee United's performance wasn't very reassuring for my team," he commented.

"They played very solidly and I particularly liked Sturrock, who seems very French in temperament.

"I was also impressed by United's amazing physical strength and, although I noted a few weak points, I don't know if that'll really help us."

Arghieuais, whose side have drawn their first two matches of the French season, is returning to Tayside on September 6 to take in the Dundee derby.

United meet Lens in France in the first leg on September 17, with the return scheduled for October 1.

Only place

"Ibrox is the only place in Scotland that we've never done ourselves justice at," said manager Jim McLean.

"I cannot believe we only took one point from there last season, the way we played.

"Given an improvement in our finishing, I'd settle for a repeat of those displays," he added.

United from—Thomson, Holt, Gough, Malpas, Hegarty, Narey, Bannon, Milne, Sturrock, Clark, Redford, Bowman, Coyne, Gallacher, Beaumont.

Gough goes to Spurs for £750,000

Richard Gough showing the ability and determination that he will take to White Hart Lane.

Richard Gough, Dundee United's Scottish international defender, signed for Spurs yesterday for a fee of £750,000.

Gough agreed personal terms with Tottenham secretary Peter Day yesterday afternoon after the two clubs had settled on the fee. He has passed a medical examination.

He will be joining the Spurs party which flies out to Spain today to play in a tournament with Barcelona, A.C. Milan and P.S.V. Eindhoven.

The versatile 24-year-old is expected to make his First Division debut at Aston Villa next Saturday.

Gough made his farewell appearance for Dundee United in the thrilling 3-2 win over Rangers at Ibrox on Saturday.

Rangers' new manager, Graeme Souness, had been keen to sign Gough, but Dundee United were understandably reluctant to sell to another Scottish club. Souness turned his attention to Ipswich and England centre-back Terry Butcher, ironically the top summer target for Spurs.

Spurs, who had earlier failed in an attempt to lure the highly-rated Steve Bruce away from Norwich, were outbid by Rangers.

Ample compensation

But the arrival of Gough at White Hart Lane is ample compensation for missing out on Butcher. He is three years younger than Butcher and can play in a variety of positions.

Capped 26 times, Gough played in all three of Scotland's World Cup games—and clearly impressed new Spurs manager David Pleat, who was out in Mexico.

He made his international debut against Switzerland in March 1983 and scored the winning goal against England at Hampden Park in May 1985.

Born in Stockholm, of a Swedish mother, Gough was brought up in South Africa. He came over to Scotland in 1980 and signed for Dundee United after being turned down by Rangers. He will be the second member of the Gough family to play in London. Father Charlie played for Charlton.

Gough still had one year, plus a three-year option, to run on his contract with Dundee United but was keen to join a bigger club. He put in two transfer requests since returning from Mexico—both were turned down.

But United knew they had to sell if the price was right, and Spurs have beaten off competition for Gough from Manchester United, Everton, Arsenal and Chelsea.

Spurs lacked a top-class defender last season and Gough, who has signed a long-term contract, will undoubtedly strengthen their bid for the league title.

Pleat has already signed full-back Mitchell Thomas from his old club, Luton, for £250,000.

CHAIRMAN'S STATEMENT

In a brief statement after the news of the Gough transfer finally came through, Dundee United chairman George Fox told "The Courier" sports editor, "We are sorry to lose him, naturally, but you can't have a discontented player in the team. The people I am sorry for are those who have been refused transfers and have soldiered on, but we hope to recompense them."

Right decisions

— By THE SPORTS EDITOR —

Dundee United were RIGHT not to sell Richard Gough to Rangers. They were also RIGHT to try and make him stay for the length of his contract, even though, big money being what it is, they had to sell in the end.

There is a mistaken impression in some quarters that United somehow did something wrong in not giving the 24-year-old (whom they had a lot to do with making the outstanding player he is) his way as soon as he wanted a move.

That is based on the assumption that the Uniteds of this world shouldn't be allowed to build teams, but should merely be "feeders" for big city outfits.

No club, however big, has a God-given right to the best players and success based on them.

If a club like United can create a successful team, so be it. If they can keep their players, and in the process win honours, again, so be it.

Had Gough been on the opposite side at Ibrox on Saturday, he might have scored a winner against United.

As it was he was important in United's excellent victory. Is that somehow wrong? Of course it isn't.

Now, United have money to spend—BIG money. But on which player and for which position?

They have, in Jim McInally, a possible immediate replacement for Gough and the way Dave Beaumont performed on Saturday, problems at the back aren't all that apparent.

Another scorer is a must—and, already, the club has found that even the hint they were to become rich has upped prices for that already pricey commodity all round.

But United have sold before, dating back to Andy Gray, Ray Stewart and the like and up-dating to Gough, Davie Dodds, Billy Kirkwood and Stewart Beedie. And what has happened? They have become one of Scotland's top teams and had league and cup success on the way.

They'll look after themselves again all right . . . and become even better? Only time will tell, but I wouldn't bet against it!

Ferguson bombshell hits Dundee

Rangers last night ended their loan arrangement with Dundee and recalled striker Iain Ferguson to Ibrox (reports STEVE BRUCE).

The move follows Ferguson's rejection of two approaches by Dundee United.

Rangers and United last week agreed upon the £150,000 transfer of Ferguson to Tannadice, but the 24-year-old player declined, saying he wanted to remain "on loan" to Dundee in the hope of attracting the attention of an English club.

Since then, however, it is understood United increased not their bid, as that was already acceptable to Rangers, but the personal terms on offer to Ferguson. He again said no to the move.

The big-spending Glasgow club, keen to recoup some of the £200,000 spent on buying Ferguson from Dundee two years ago, were clearly upset at his vetoing the transfer (securing a move for the player was, after all, the

reason he'd been placed in the "shop window" at Dens) and promptly called him back to Ibrox, where he looks like once more being consigned to reserve football.

The terms offered Ferguson by United are understood to have been excellent.

Innocent victims

Innocent victims in this are Dundee.

Ferguson scored twice in three appearances for them and manager Jocky Scott had been hoping that, given a bit more time, he might raise the cash necessary to make the move permanent.

Although Rangers' efforts to "sell" Ferguson through the loan system have failed, they haven't been put off employing it again.

Yesterday they agreed to lend former Aberdeen midfielder Doug Bell to St Mirren. Bell will play against Dunfermline tonight.

Lens create a good impression

Dundee United manager Jim McLean turned up only an hour before kick off at the Dundee United-St Mirren game (reports THE SPORTS EDITOR).

He had been watching U.E.F.A. Cup opponents Lens the previous night and did a France-Belgium-England-Scotland dash in a few hours, starting at 5.30 a.m.

His impressions of Lens? They lost 1-0 but are a good team.

He confessed to being an admirer of French football and made the point that it was the nearest thing in Europe to the Scots game, where everyone has to work hard yet there are considerable skills.

The first leg, in Lens, is on September 17.

While United built up for the first-leg match against RC Lens, they finally found success in the transfer market. Although Iain Ferguson would not be available to feature in the early UEFA Cup rounds, he would later make his mark in the most dramatic of ways.

Ferguson agrees to join United

Iain Ferguson

Iain Ferguson will today formally join Dundee United for a £145,000 fee, with Tannadice manager Jim McLean last night emphasising, "His terms are the same as those discussed earlier with the exception that the length of contract is slightly less."

The sequence of events involving the player, Rangers, Dundee and Dundee United over the past few days has been—

1. He was "farmed out" to Dundee to put him in the shop window and scored two goals in two games for the Dark Blues;

2. Dundee United made a bid for him, but club and player failed to reach agreement;

3. Rangers recalled Ferguson to Ibrox;

4. Dundee made a bid "in the six-figure bracket" but it wasn't acceptable to Rangers;

5. Dundee United moved in again and, yesterday afternoon, Ferguson agreed to join

By THE SPORTS EDITOR

them. Only a few formalities have to be completed this morning.

"Very pleased"

Emphasising again that the terms were the same as originally discussed, manager McLean said last night, "I am very pleased that he wants to play for Dundee United.

"That really was my problem today—that he could convince me of that fact.

"Knowing what it has been like for me this past few days, I can appreciate how extremely difficult it has been for the player.

"He has been bought for £145,000 to replace Davie Dodds, for whom we got £170,000. And he is only 24—four years younger than Dodds.

"We have players who can make us play well. What we need is players to put the ball in the net.

"He likes to shoot every time he gets around

the box and likes scoring goals, whereas many of our players are thinking on linking up, on setting up moves.

"His biggest asset is his determination to get in shots and his record of hitting the target from these shots is why Rangers bought him and why we are buying him.

"I would like to emphasise that it is a Rangers player we have bought, not a Dundee player.

Welcome

"I would hope that our supporters on Saturday make him feel welcome, help him to settle quickly," the manager added, after confirming that Ferguson would be in the pool for tomorrow's game with Hearts at Tannadice.

Then, broadening his theme, the manager went on, "The most important thing to me is that the players here deserve more good players and that the supporters are given a team worth watching.

"This is not the end of our search for fresh faces, but it will hopefully take the pressure off a little."

The only flaw so far with the Ferguson signing is that it has come too late for him to be used in United's early U.E.F.A. Cup ties. Had United got him when they originally moved in he would have been eligible.

But he is clear for all domestic competitions.

Ferguson joined Rangers from Dundee in May 1984 in a double swoop by the Ibrox club involving him and Cammy Fraser.

Ferguson's fee was finally set by a tribunal at £200,000.

In his first season he played 33 games, scored 11 goals; last season he played three games and didn't score.

That the ability to put the ball in the net which he showed in his years with Dundee is still there was proved by his two goals in two games during his recent brief return to Dens Park.

Jim's selection problem with a difference

I doubt if Dundee United manager Jim McLean has ever had a harder job with a pool of players than he is having for the U.E.F.A. Cup tie against Lens in France on Wednesday night (writes the Sports Editor).

And although injuries are holding up the selection of the pool until this morning, it isn't only that.

With the departure of so many players in the relatively recent past, only one room-sharing partnership, Paul Hegarty and John Holt, is left on the present staff!

It used to be Paul Sturrock and Davie Dodds, Dave Narey and Hamish McAlpine, Maurice Malpas and Derek Stark, Ralph Milne and Richard Gough, Eamonn Bannon and Billy Kirkwood.

Now, all the second named have left Tannadice and a new list is necessary.

Ian Redford is having intensive treatment on bruising above the ankle after Saturday and the delay in his case might also be because he has scored no fewer than four goals in four European starts and is a very important figure in planning for the Lens game.

"He has a good chance of being fit," is the McLean comment.

John Holt is an experienced European campaigner and the manager also wants to check his fitness this morning.

"New" team's display excites Jim

BY THE SPORTS EDITOR

The normal Jim McLean approach to any performance by his team is to make sure you don't think he is being too complimentary. Good points are mentioned, but it could be said he emphasises problems more.

Yesterday, however, he was genuinely excited over the display of his "new" team in the Skol Cup quarter-final against Hibs, which they won 2-0.

"The performance last night was by far the best this season," he began. "No, I'll go further. It was one of the best in recent years in passing, positional play and confidence on the ball.

"And I'm going to do something I don't normally do—single out a couple of players. Dave Beaumont and Gary McGinnis were outstanding."

He concentrated first on Beaumont. "He was playing against a winger for the first time and he hardly gave Joe McBride a kick at the ball.

"I'm delighted at the way he is playing because he has always been a good player but has lacked the devil and arrogance you must have.

"Don't forget, either, that he has played mostly as a centre-half and is now at full-back. I doubt if he has played more than half-a-dozen games there.

"Astounding"

"It was an astounding performance, never a kick or a header out of place.

"I got on to him about not getting forward enough at half-time in the game against St Mirren. So what did he do? Went forward and laid on our opening goal for Kevin Gallacher.

Then, to McGinnis. "It's a tremendous feeling to see him playing like this after the nightmare injuries he had. He was immaculate."

A third player to come in for praise was Iain Ferguson. The ex-Dundee and Rangers striker has had a quiet start in many ways at Tannadice—but he is now on the five goals in four games mark and you can't do much better than that as a scorer.

"Against Hibs he linked better than he has been doing and, of course, got the goals," was the McLean comment.

"At Ayr, he looked tired—he still isn't at peak fitness—and I was about to take him off. But he went and scored two goals!

Long time away

"Don't forget he has been a long, long time away from regular first-team football, yet he has already scored all these goals.

Then, looking at the overall showing against Hibs: "We had one passing spell in the second half when we strung ten together one after the other.

"If it had been a continental team we'd have been cheered off the park."

Next, the only criticism of the evening—and even that wasn't

Gary McGinnis.

too harsh. "Kevin Gallacher and Paul Sturrock played well, but not as well as the rest of the team. Mind you, I'm judging them on their own tremendously high standards."

It is a long time since I have seen Jim McLean as excited over anything as he is over this "new" team.

"One million pounds worth of players have gone, we have spent nothing even remotely like that, but the whole place is buzzing. It's great."

● Jimmy Rimmer, the former Manchester United, Aston Villa and Swansea 'keeper is "in attendance" for a fortnight, coaching United's three 'keepers—Billy Thomson, Scott Thomson and Mike McAdam. The invitation originated through his friendship with former United (and Manchester United) favourite Frank Kopel.

● The reserve game due tonight has been postponed until Monday because Dundee have injury problems. So have United. John Holt is still getting treatment, Paul Kinnaird has an ankle knock and Brian Welsh has been withdrawn from the under-19 squad for Tuesday night's game against West Germany at Paisley.

Dave Beaumont.

13

Injured Redford fails to make French trip

By THE SPORTS EDITOR IN LENS

As we bump-thumped our way down through thousands of feet of rain-filled cloud into Lille airport late yesterday afternoon, the thought occurred that these European trips weren't the jaunts some imagine.

When we stepped off the plane it was to be met by rain being driven out of a slate grey sky by a fierce wind. Not so much case of "UP wi' the bunnets o' Bonnie Dundee" as "ON wi' the bunnets . . ."

Also, news that tomorrow night's UEFA Cup opponents, Lens, had been beaten 3-1 by Lille in their latest game.

The main news from the United party was that John Holt had made the trip, but Ian Redford and John Clark were missing, the latter suffering from flu.

It looked at the weekend as if Redford, scorer of a goal a game in his Euro excursions so far, would be making the journey fo France.

But further tests yesterday morning showed unsuspected ligament damage above the ankle, so it is treatment back home from Dundee physiotherapist Eric Ferguson ("we are immensely grateful for the co-operation," said manager Jim McLean) instead of match action for the midfield man.

Iain Ferguson is also left behind, of course. He is ineligible for the early rounds in Europe, but is also suffering calf muscle bother following a kick on the muscle on Saturday.

Sprint training

"It is not connected with the injury which caused us worry last week," said the manager. "That was in the thigh."

While we are here, Ferguson will be training at Tannadice, including sprints with coach Stuart Hogg.

John Holt is on duty because, though he may still not be fully fit after his long lay-off with severe bruising of both ankles, he is an experienced Euro campaigner and United are running a wee bit short of them right now.

The manager's problem is whether to use John from the start, then take him off, or put him on the bench ready to go on later in the game.

Normally, I'd reckon on his playing the 90 minutes, but you must be 100 per cent for that and he obviously can't be after such a long spell out of action.

Change of tactics

One thing United didn't do at the weekend was check on Lens, and that was a deliberate change of direction by manager McLean.

If you fancy having a wee competition before manager McLean names his 11 plus five subs, this is the list of players here: B. Thomson, S. Thomson, Malpas, McGinnis, Beaumont, Hegarty, Narey, Milne, Gallacher, Bannon, Sturrock, Coyne, Bowman, McInally, Sulley, G. McLeod, Holt.

You could perm a few elevens from that lot!

Obviously looking at the magnificent comebacks against Rangers and Celtic already this season, he told me yesterday, "I have made up my mind more than ever recently that it is all about what we do.

"If you worry about the opposition you give players an excuse for not going out and playing to their real form.

"That's the background to why I didn't watch Lens at the weekend or send anyone."

So, as we settle into our hotel here in north-east France, the next question after what will be a strenuous training session today is, "what will be tomorrow's line up?"

Search on for a new "midfield anchor"

By THE SPORTS EDITOR IN LENS

No team from Dundee United manager Jim McLean until this morning, only hours before they trot out on to the Stade Felix Bollaert for the start of their 1986-87 venture in the UEFA Cup.

Not that there are any deep worries, although Gary McGinnis picked up a slight knock in training yesterday morning, which physio Andy Dickson thinks should clear by today and there's still a doubt in the mind of the manager over the fitness of John Holt.

Jim McLean is, however, more worried about this season's Euro campaign in general.

Reason? The absence of Billy Kirkwood in particular.

"I have got to see everyone in action soon," he said yesterday, "because we have to sort out a replacement for Kirkwood.

"We definitely can't play now the same way as has gained us considerable success in Europe. That's down to people like Kirkwood.

Praise

"We have received great praise for our defensive abilities in Europe and, certainly, that is partly due to people like Paul Hegarty and Dave Narey.

"But a lot of that success stemmed from midfield, where Kirkie was brilliant at marking out the opposition danger man.

"He was the midfield anchor and, as a bonus, got us vital goals. Trouble is, only the players and people like myself appreciated him and the way he pulled the strings in midfield alongside such as John Holt and Eamonn Bannon.

"If we try man-marking against the French tomorrow night we will be torn apart, but, hopefully we will be progressing to later rounds and will have to cope with man-marking again.

"That's why I am seeking a Kirkwood replacement—one, too, with more confidence in himself—and why I have to see all first team pool players in action.

"It hasn't been easy to chop and charge much so far this season because vital games have piled up. But there is no way the same team will play at Hamilton on Saturday as will play against Lens.

"Freshen up"

"It is in no way showing disrespect to Accies, but we will have to freshen up after four days away in Europe and in freshening up I may get the chance to spot that man who could be vital in Europe."

If I had to bet on it, I'd say that right now Dave Bowman is edging into pole position.

I used to think him a bit one-paced, even a touch slow with Hearts, but a couple of times lately he has proved me wrong with forward thrusts at speed.

So it was interesting to learn that the newcomer is one of the fastest men on the books—and

---

United are hoping to improve on a pretty impressive European record tonight.

They have played 66 ties, won 28, drawn 18 and lost 20, with a goal difference of 101 for, 65 against.

---

that is official from the manager.

Mind you, there's also Chris Sulley and Jim McInally to consider. They haven't been able, for one reason or another, to mount a challenge so far, but it is coming if their effort and enthusiasm in a brisk work-out yesterday on a superb training pitch is anything to go by.

Cracking shot

There was another aspect of training yesterday which impressed. The scoring prowess of the striker in the team playing upfield.

The goal he took in the opening minutes was a gem—a cracking shot in to the corner of the net.

The scorer's name? Gordon Wallace.

When I asked him about it he made the point, "You'll have noticed the goal came early on. The pitch seemed to grow in size after that!"

There is no truth in the rumour that he will make a comeback tonight, but it would be nice if a few of his type of goals are tucked away!

As a final point on that training session, I have never before known such a relaxed atmosphere in a Dundee United party.

There was speculation about the future when so many people left in such a short time recently, but I would say that, if anything, team spirit is better than ever.

I admit a winning streak like United are in is a great thing for "lifting" people, but there is more to it than that.

Tough games against Dundee and Celtic in the week leading up to the Lens tie meant United faced serious injury problems in France. The need to replace the under-appreciated Billy Kirkwood was also weighing heavy on McLean's mind.

'Hard luck' stories too true for Lens

Never read too much into stories of woe and gloom when you meet foreign opposition. It's their old-fashioned way of trying to lull British opponents into a sense of false security (writes the SPORTS EDITOR).

However Lens really are having problems on the eve of the game against Dundee United.

First, a 3-1 defeat by nearby Lille at the week-end has bitten deep. Like all derby's it's a "downer" for the losers.

Then, Lens are ninth equal in the French first division with

The game tonight is in the Stade Felix Bollaert in the centre of Lens. United weren't allowed to train on the pitch yesterday as there has been heavy rain recently.

Capacity is 51,000 with 40,000 under cover and considerable seating.

eight points from nine games—a much poorer a start than anticipated.

On top of that there are the injuries.

Not expected to play tonight

are Uruguayan Venancio Ramos (midfield, wing) thigh knock;

Who says Dundee aren't in Europe? Passed a bill on the way to training yesterday which stated that tonight's game is Lens v. Dundee!

Cesar Tobollik (left wing) thigh knock and Didier Senac (centre-half) suspended.

Senac is the biggest blow to Lens. He was rated by former Aberdeen striker Eric Black as possibly the key figure in the Lens line. His replacement is likely to be Deplenche—but whoever it is there won't be any surprises for United boss Jim McLean.

When he was over watching Lens recently, he actually saw both the first team and reserves in one afternoon.

"I heard they were playing at different times on the same day

It's pretty flat country around here, with the exception of massive pit bings—with a difference. Along the side of one is a long, multi-coloured painted strip and others have also been decorated with various forms of art.

and wasn't going to miss a chance like that," he said.

"I have a good knowledge of their players and their tactics, though I still say it is mostly about how we play."

If United were struggling to put out a fully-fit side, they were fortunate to face a Lens side dealing with their own problems. Although the campaign began with a slender defeat, the Tangerines were happy to be in the tie with a home leg to come.

Vital break eludes battling United

LENS 1, DUNDEE UNITED 0

Dundee United are going to have to do it the hard way after this defeat in the Felix Bollaert Stadium last night.

Not that entry into the second round of the UEFA Cup is beyond them. They didn't play to their best form last night, but are still only a goal down with the home leg to come.

Lens were a good team, but not an outstanding one, though in Njo-Lea and Carreno up front they have the type of players who can turn games in a split second—as they proved by combining for the winning goal.

United's defence deserves almost full marks, though newcomer Chris Sulley found the going tough at times and it took time for Maurice Malpas to settle fully into his middle of midfield role.

When he did in the second half, United came alive as an attacking force, without getting the goal that mattered.

Full marks, too, to Eamonn Bannon throughout and Billy Thomson, who made vital saves when it mattered.

After the game the verdict from manager Jim McLean was, "Disappointed in our first half performance, but we were a lot better second half. We have left ourselves a lot to do but we are capable of getting a result and going through."

Noisy fans

The 50,000 capacity ground was about quarter-full at the start, with several hundred United supporters having made the trip.

First incident of the game was in four minutes when Lefebvre put in a nasty tackle from behind on Narey, who limped for several minutes afterwards.

Sturrock mounted United's first threat with a cross which bounced off the face of the crossbar but fell badly for Milne, who managed, however, to turn the ball back for Beaumont. The youngster's shot lacked power and was easily cleared.

Late decision

With both teams springing the offside trap there were frequent hold ups, but the danger of that game was almost exposed in 12 minutes when Sturrock slipped clear. The linesman made a very late offside decision—just before he whipped the ball into the net.

When Carreno broke on the right, he sent over a wicked cross headed down by Oudjani and well held by Thomson as he was falling.

United's reply came from a Beaumont free kick, touched on by Bannon's head. Milne swept in to send a powerful shot just over the bar.

This led to a quick counter-punch by Lens. Thomson again did well to get to a bending drive by Oudjani.

Lens were proving a fluid team in the best French traditions of building attacks from deep positions but United's experience in Europe was showing as they coped well at the back.

When Carreno burst through from right back

he got in a low cross which the dangerous man in Lens' No. 9 shirt, Njo-Lea, got on the end of to fire a wicked shot past the left hand post.

A tackle on Carreno, deep in the Lens half, saw Sulley's name go in the book and the winger needing treatment.

Beaumont's increasing maturity was shown in the 40th minute when he made a tremendous tackle on Carreno to clear up a surging Lens raid,

By THE SPORTS EDITOR IN LENS

but the pressure on United's defence was suddenly building tremendously as Lens moved up several gears—and it told in the 41st minute.

Njo-Lea got in on the act again to send a low ball inside the box to Carreno. He was on to it in a flash to steady and lash a great shot high into the net above the helpless Thomson.

These two had been the danger men, so it wasn't surprising that they broke the deadlock.

There were no changes as the second half started. United had been hit by a first class goal and had to respond with a repeat of the Rangers-Celtic comebacks.

Flashing run

An early corner—fruitless—and a piece of Gallacher trickery set things off on the right note, and it was Gallacher again who opened the door to Huard with a flashing right wing run.

His cross, however, was just too far ahead of Sturrock. The striker did get in a shot in the 53rd minute, but it was easily taken by Huard.

After a spell, of midfield play, the game exploded into action in the 60th minute.

Sulley was comprehensively beaten for pace by Njo-Lea and Thomson had to time his run out of goal to perfection to take the ball away from the striker with a wonderful tackle that would have done Hegarty or Narey proud.

He again proved his quality with a great save low down from Carreno.

United were showing more like their real form now, though, and in the 62nd minute Gallacher had the ball in the net, only for offside to ruin the move.

As the rain started to pour down, Hanini went on for a none-too-pleased looking Oudjani.

United immediately forced three corners in succession. Bannon took all three—two left one right—and all were cleared, with Gallacher left lying prone after the third.

He recovered after treatment and immediately United were on the attack again, with a Beaumont shot going just over.

From another Bannon corner Hegarty did get a header in, only to be injured and stop the next attack by being unable to get back from an offside position.

Compact defence

The game had turned completely round, but United just couldn't get that vital break . . . in fairness, mostly due to compact defence by Lens when it mattered.

And it could all have been so costly with three minutes to go. Hegarty hesitated in defence, sub Hanini was through in a flash to send a tremendous shot blasting off Thomson's right hand post.

The ball rebounded to Njo-Lea, but he was a fraction too far forward and couldn't take advantage of a nearly empty goalmouth.

Krawczyk was booked in 88 minutes for a foul on Milne.

Then another moment's hesitation in defence by Sulley and Hanini was through to send a great shot just past the right hand post before the full-time whistle.

Attendance—11,330.

Lens—Huard; Sikora, Catalano, Deplanche, Gillot, Krawczyk, Lefebvre, Dewilder, Njo-Lea, Oudjani, Carreno. Subs—Fajal, Dubois, Hanini, Lagrange, Gardie

Dundee United—B. Thomson, Malpas, Sulley, Beaumont, Hegarty, Narey, Bowman, Gallacher, Bannon, Sturrock, Milne. Subs—Holt, Coyne, G. McLeod, J. McInally, S. Thomson.

Referee—M. Losert (Austria)

15

United's first failure to recover lost ground

By THE SPORTS EDITOR

"The same thing has happened all season. Only a couple of times, against Hearts and Aberdeen, have we scored first half and last night was the first time we haven't been able to retrieve the situation."

Manager Jim McLean was looking back yesterday at the 1-0 U.E.F.A. Cup first round, first leg, defeat by Lens the night before.

"What the result has done, though," he went on, "is set up a great game for the home leg.

"The result might have been better, could have been worse, but if we had played all through like we did second half it would definitely have been better."

The manager reported injuries to Paul Hegarty, who developed hamstring trouble just after the start; David Narey, an ankle problem after a vicious tackle from behind early on; and Gary McGinnis, who

couldn't be considered after aggravating a strain during a training session in France.

There are also, of course, Ian Redford, left behind for treatment, and Iain Ferguson, who can't play for a couple of U.E.F.A. rounds yet, but who was also receiving treatment at Tannadice.

Key pair

The main problem is those "anchor men" Hegarty and Narey.

It seems almost unthinkable for a United team to line up without them, they have been for so long key figures.

But the manager makes clear his thoughts on that score when he says, "It's going to be a worrying couple of days before the Hamilton game. We are definitely short of experienced central defenders."

His Lens Man of the Match was Maurice Malpas, in the position United have been trying to play him for a long time

now—in the centre of the midfield three—and he also singled out Eamonn Bannon and 'keeper Billy Thomson for praise.

Malpas told me yesterday, "It was the same as when I played there for Scotland against Holland.

"I didn't play first half, the game seemed to be racing past me. But I settled second half and got involved. I really enjoyed myself then."

Mistake

The manager admitted that, in the case of John Holt, he might have erred in taking him on the trip.

"He might have been better staying behind having treatment and training after his long lie-off," he said.

But the Holt absence, and that of McGinnis, let in 25-year-old Chris Sulley for his first game for United and his first in a European competition.

"I played in friendlies with Chelsea and Bournemouth," he told me, "but this was completely different and a great experience.

"I honestly wasn't satisfied with my performance, however, and hope to get the chance to do better."

More needed

Summing up the first Euro excursion of season 1986-87, manager McLean said, "There is no way we are out, no way we are through. But we have to have 90 minutes positive play, which we aren't getting at the moment."

Lens coach Joachim Marx said he rated the tie 50-50 before it started. With the second leg due at Tannadice the week after next he reckoned it 70-30 in Lens favour now.

I can imagine a few Tayside betting men who wouldn't mind him offering them those odds!

Tribute to travelling fans

Dundee United boss Jim McLean yesterday paid a belated tribute to the 500 supporters who followed the club to Lens for the midweek U.E.F.A. Cup tie (reports STEVE BRUCE).

"I would like to thank all those who travelled to France and gave us such tremendous backing over there," he said.

"Our failure to acknowledge the supporters at the end of the game was due to the fact that the players felt sick at the result.

"I must apologise to the fans, for they deserve terrific praise for the backing they gave us."

Dave Narey.

United set for stage two of "difficult" tie

The Lens squad arrived on Tayside last night in preparation for the next step in what manager Jim McLean described as "the most difficult first round tie we have picked for a long, long time."

The Tannadice manager also thought United may well require the entire 90 minutes, and possibly some extra time, to make things go their way tomorrow night.

Lens lead the Tangerines by 1-0 after the first leg of the U.E.F.A. Cup tie.

"They have exceptional pace up front, but all we need is one goal to set ourselves up," said the manager.

There is still no news regarding Dave Narey and Jim McInally's inclusion in the team to face the French side tomorrow night.

Manager Jim McLean said yesterday both were "very doubtful" but indicated that their appearance or otherwise could well be an eleventh hour decision.

Headache

"I hope both will be fit and I hope they will both make it into the side.

"Normally, we have to expect injuries but everyone knows how important these two are so it's left me with a bit of a headache."

Looking back to Saturday Mr McLean seemed satisfied with the performance of his team against Hibs—during the second half at least—and was also pleased with the progress of some of the younger players at the club.

He also pointed out, "I've used 20 players so far this season alone, that's more than I used in the team that won the Premier League title!" he said with a smile.

Jim McInally.

Lens next on "hit-list"?

United went into the return leg with a proud recent record of turning around European ties at Tannadice, and did so again to reach round two.

Dundee United tonight aim to add another name to the list of clubs who have visited Tannadice on European business and lost the tie despite holding a first-leg lead.

Borussia Munchengladbach, A.I.K. Stockholm and Rapid Vienna each had an advantage to defend on Scottish soil and failed. This evening, United and their fans hope R.C. Lens follow suit.

Manager Jim McLean yesterday voiced respect for the talented French side but is convinced the task confronting his team is within their compass.

"I rate Lens highly, particularly in view of the fact they had several key men missing in the first game," he said.

"Although they aren't as experienced as us in Europe, their record away from home is exceptional.

"We missed a chance in France because their best players were out, but our record at home in Europe is a good one and we can definitely do it. The players are confident and so am I."

While winning the Premier League—which, of course, they currently top—is United's No. 1 target this season, European competition holds a special place in the hearts of the players and management of the club.

"Europe is the icing on the cake, it gets the adrenalin going,"

By STEVE BRUCE

was how Jim McLean summed up the platform on which his side has enjoyed many of its greatest moments.

As regards this match, their 68th in Europe, the manager will demand his men make a better start than in recent games and play for the full 90 minutes. He is also looking for the fans to show patience.

United's line-up is being kept under wraps until just before kick-off time because of the Dave Narey-Jim McInally situation.

News of the injured duo is that one definitely looks like making it and there is increasing optimism over both being ready.

"Getting these two back would enhance our chances, therefore they'll be given as much time as possible to recover," said Jim, adding that Narey and McInally will both play if available.

A replacement for ineligible striker Iain Ferguson has also to be found. Young Kevin Gallacher looks the obvious choice, but the more experienced Ralph Milne's excellent record in Europe also gives him a claim.

Ian Redford is another with an impressive Euro pedigree having scored four goals in last season's U.E.F.A. Cup campaign and as the former Rangers man missed the first leg, he might be a successful secret weapon.

Darrel Carreno, Lens' scorer in the first leg.

Cards are being kept close to the chest in the Lens camp. It is understood they still have fitness doubts over Uruguayan international Venancio Ramos and winger Cesar Tobollik who were absent a fortnight ago but centre-half Didier Senac, suspended from the first game, is expected to return.

Jim McLean certainly has no doubts over the importance of this trio to the French outfit. "Lens being without these three would be like us playing without Hegarty, Narey and Sturrock," he opined.

Tonight's tie could well prove to be a real nerve-jangler with Lens—who need only draw to be guaranteed passage into the second round—rated very dangerous on the break and United obviously needing goals.

Eight seasons have elapsed since Jim McLean's men last fell at the first hurdle in Europe and they have the experience to maintain that fine record.

Dundee United from—W. Thomson, Malpas, Sulley, Beaumont, Hegarty, Narey, Gallacher, Milne, Bannon, Sturrock, Redford, Coyne, McInally, McGinnis, Clark, Bowman, G. McLeod, S. Thomson.

● There will be no segregation at Tannadice this evening with home fans able to use any turnstile except gate 12.

United are off and running again

DUNDEE UNITED 2, LENS 0 (agg. 2-1)

Two hands prove better than one head as Ralph Milne is beaten to the ball.

European maestros Dundee United did it again last night. Set the task of retrieving a 1-0 U.E.F.A. Cup first leg deficit without the services of veteran defender Dave Narey and against a talented French side, they responded magnificently.

Two goals in four minutes early in the second half did the trick for the Tannadice men. Ralph Milne, the club's top scorer in Europe, found the net for the 15th time on this platform to set them on their way and then provided transfer seeking Tommy Coyne with the ammunition for a second.

In Paul Sturrock United had the Man of the Match. He was magnificent, although Jim McInally ran him a close second with an excellent performance.

Victory was more than deserved for the home side, who dominated the 90 minutes and for the eighth season running moved in to the second round of a European competition.

By STEVE BRUCE

United boss Jim McLean commented afterwards, "That is probably the most inexperienced side I've fielded in a long time. That was the most pleasing aspect for me, and it was a splendid result."

The Tannadice manager reckoned Jim McInally, who played with three stitches in an ankle wound, to be the best man afield, while he also praised the contribution of Sturrock, Milne and substitute Bowman.

Early chance

Coyne was presented with a great chance in six minutes from a Redford cross, but instead of bringing the ball down he tried a header, which was easily gathered by Huard.

The Lens keeper was more seriously tested when Sturrock drilled in a low shot, but he held it.

The French gave early warning of the punch they packed on the break when Lefebvre beat Malpas on the right and swung in a dangerous cross which Hegarty dived to head clear.

Ralph Milne drives the ball home for his 15th goal in Europe.

Lefebvre was again in the thick of things moments later, testing Thomson from 20 yards, then from a similar distance at the other end Malpas sent a volley dipping narrowly over.

United continued to do the pressing, with Lens looking dangerous on the break. Jim McLean's men had a let-off when Oudjani just failed to connect with a Lefebvre centre, but in 20 minutes they came within inches of taking the lead.

Ian Redford's powerful 25-yard shot from a Coyne pass looked net-bound, but Huard produced an excellent save, turning the ball on to his bar.

Though cracks were appearing in the French defence, United couldn't quite force the breakthrough. Huard was under pressure but coping admirably.

That said, Billy Thomson was the home hero three minutes from the break, saving first from Deplanche then knocking the ball away for a corner as Carreno seemed certain to score.

United began the second period with a flourish. Coyne broke down the left, but his intended cross for Sturrock was knocked behind by Gillot, and the resultant Bannon corner flew across the face of the Lens goal untouched.

Sturrock moves in

Almost incessant Tangerine pressure finally paid dividends in 55 minutes.

The move began with a poor ball from Bannon down the left touch line, but quick as a flash Sturrock sprinted to take possession.

He hurdled the advancing Huard and crossed for Ralph Milne, who from 12 yards brought the ball under control and smacked it into the net.

United might have had a penalty shot right afterwards when a Milne cross hit the hand of Senac, but the referee waved away the claims. However, the second goal though duly arrived in 59 minutes.

Lens' use of the offside trap had proved a source of frustration all night, but Milne caught them out on the right and crossed for Tommy Coyne to bundle the ball home.

The French were livid, claiming Milne had been offside, and after consultation with his stand side linesman referee Claudio Pieri ordered Lens coach Joachim Marx to the stand. There was considerable delay before the French official complied with this instruction.

Thereafter United's grip on the game, which had been so tight earlier, began to slacken, and although never in serious danger it was an anxious run-in to the final whistle for both home players and supporters.

Having said that, a third goal almost arrived six minutes from the end when Paul Sturrock raced onto a Thomson kick from hand, but could only flick it into the arms of Huard.

Attendance—11,645.

Dundee United—Thomson, Malpas, McGinnis, Beaumont, Hegarty, McInally, Coyne (Bowman), Milne, Bannon, Sturrock, Redford. Subs—S. Thomson, McLeod, Gallacher, Sulley.

Lens—Huard, Sikora, Catalano, Senac, Gillot, Krawczyk, Lefebvre (Ramos), Deplanche, Diewilder, Oudjani (Hanini), Carreno. Subs—Pagal, Nzo-Lea, Gardie.

Referee—C. Pieri, Italy.

Rewards in "Rumania"

With RC Lens safely despatched, it is back to league business for United in early October and three wins out of four sees their confidence building.

Indeed, the good run of results in what he regards as the toughest quarter of the season even prompts the normally super cautious Jim McLean to predict United will "definitely win the Premier League" if they can continue to accrue points at the same rate.

This spell also brings the first of what will be many tributes to the United fans throughout the UEFA Cup campaign.

Against the backdrop of the English football hooligan problem, the French national newspaper L'Equipe carries an article praising fans in Tangerine for the way they welcomed RC Lens supporters to Tannadice.

However, it is not all good news for the Tangerines.

Ahead of the draw in Switzerland, McLean is asked for his preference for a second round opponent, and answers: "Firstly, we like it as easy as possible, secondly to be playing away in the first leg and lastly involving little travel."

He gets none of that.

The draw instead pairs United with "Rumanian" (not a spelling mistake, it was The Courier's house style back then) side Universitatea Craiova, and means a home tie before a trip behind the Iron Curtain in the second leg.

With an almost total absence of video footage to aid their research, Gordon Wallace is sent to Craiova to watch the team in action.

October also sees one of what would be a series of direct pleas to United's wider fan base to support the team's efforts to bring more silverware to Tannadice.

McLean also raises the highly controversial issue of whether the city of Dundee is big enough to support two competitive teams.

"Until this is a one club town it will always be an uphill struggle financially," he says.

Thirty years on, it is a question that still regularly resurfaces as United and Dundee FC battle to compete in a game that has become much more global in nature; one where would-be fans are now more likely to stay at home to watch Europe's biggest clubs on TV than turn out to watch their local club — ensuring the greatest riches continue to go to a small number of elite clubs.

And while supporters today would jump at the chance of just seeing United competing in Europe, it seems success on the Continent was no guarantee of greater financial health in the 1980s.

Speaking openly about the costs incurred in recent European adventures, McLean reveals reaching the next round could often cost United £10,000 a time.

With the big pay days only coming later in the competition, it is no wonder then that the manager expresses such obvious pride in his injury-ravaged squad's performance in Craiova.

With an average age of just 24, the United players battle hard in the intimidating atmosphere of a 35,000-plus crowd at Stade Central — with many more watching from outside — to claim their place in the third round draw.

Iron Curtain tie for United

Dundee United—celebrating their 20th season in Europe—face a nightmare trip behind the Iron Curtain in the U.E.F.A. Cup second round (reports STEVE BRUCE).

Yesterday's draw in Switzerland paired them with Uni Craiova of Rumania, the first leg to be played at Tannadice on October 22 with the return scheduled for the 40,000 capacity Stade Central on November 5.

It was exactly the draw United didn't want.

Craiova reached the second round with a 3-2 aggregate victory over Galatasaray. They won the home leg 2-0 but went down 2-1 in Turkey on Wednesday night.

The Rumanians have a fair European pedigree. In season 1981-82 they reached the European Cup quarter-finals, only to be eliminated by Bayern Munich.

The following year they lost a U.E.F.A. Cup semi-final to Benfica on away goals, having disposed of Fiorentina, Shamrock Rovers, Bordeaux and Kaiserslautern en route.

League winners

On the domestic front, Craiova have won their league title on three occasions and the cup four times.

Last season they finished third in the table behind champions Steau Bucharest, who beat Barcelona in the European Cup final.

"Though lacking the glamour of big name clubs, there is no doubt that high calibre football is being played in some Eastern Block countries," commented United boss Jim McLean.

"This is obviously a difficult draw with the first leg at home and a lengthy journey and travel problems confronting us for the return."

The Tannadice manager pointed out, however, that last season his men successfully defended a home leg advantage against Vardar Skopje in Yugoslavia.

Previous visit

United have visited Rumania on one previous occasion. That was in the 1974-75 Cup Winners' Cup when they were paired with Jiul Petrosani.

Though they lost the return 2-0, a 3-0 advantage established at Tannadice took United through.

The trip was a memorable one for on the journey from Bucharest to Tirgu Jiu, the team coach ran off the road in heavy rain.

An inspection of the bus tyres the next morning revealed them to be treadless!

Changes for return to league business

By STEVE BRUCE

Though delighted with his side's midweek UEFA Cup performance, Jim McLean is promising changes for tomorrow's clash with Falkirk at Tannadice.

Iain Ferguson, Britain's leading goal scorer, appears certain to be restored to the team but Kevin Gallacher looks unlikely to return.

The United boss sprang a surprise in selecting Ralph Milne and transfer-seeking Tommy Coyne ahead of the talented teenager against Lens but his decision paid off with Milne and Coyne grabbing the goals that took the club into today's second round draw.

Yesterday Jim McLean explained why the player had been rested against Hibs and Lens.

"Kevin carried us up front at the beginning of the season and has done a tremendous job but he has shaded off recently and, it must be remembered, still has a lot to learn."

"The longer I can keep the boy sitting on the bench champing at the bit the better it will be when he does return."

Milne was also occupying the thoughts of his manager in the wake of the European match.

"Ralph's attitude has been very good this season and he is now getting what he deserves," said Jim.

"He needs a run of games and the supporters' backing to help rebuild his confidence."

Another aspect of Wednesday night's game that particularly pleased the United manager was that the team he fielded had an average age of only 25.

"In terms of our play when the other team were in possession I rated that one of our better European performances," he praised.

"The players worked hard against Lens and none more so than Dave Bowman who in a short substitute appearance did a great job.

"However we haven't turned the corner yet, we need to work on being more aggressive," he added cautiously.

On the injury front Dave Narey is a major doubt for tomorrow because of the back problem which has forced him to sit out the last two games, and defensive partner Paul Hegarty has a tight hamstring.

Ralph Milne . . . good attitude

The injury that has been dogging John Holt for the past few weeks has now been diagnosed. He has a stress fracture in his leg and will have to rest for around a fortnight.

EUROPEAN CUP

REAL MADRID (Spain) v. JUVENTUS (Italy).
VITKOVICE (Czechoslovakia) v. PORTO (Portugal).
ROSENBORG (Norway) v. RED STAR BELGRADE (Yugoslavia).
BAYERN MUNICH (West Germany) v. AUSTRIA VIENNA (Austria).

ANDERLECHT (Belgium) v. STEAUA (Romania).
CELTIC v. DYNAMO KIEV (Russia).
BRADSBY (Denmark) v. DYNAMO BERLIN (East Germany).
BESIKTAS (Turkey) v. APOEL NICOSIA (Cyprus).

CUP WINNERS' CUP

LOCOMOTIV LEIPZIG (East Germany) v. RAPID VIENNA (Austria).
REAL ZARAGOZA (Spain) v. WREXHAM.
VITOSHA SOFIA (Bulgaria) v. VELEZ MOSTAR (Yugoslavia).
TORPEDO MOSCOW (Russia) v. STUTTGART (West Germany).

KATOWICE (Poland) v. SION (Switzerland).
BENFICA (Portugal) v. BORDEAUX (France).
NENTORI TIRANA (Albania) v. MALMO (Sweden).
AJAX (Holland) v. OLYMPIAKOS PIRAEUS (Greece).

UEFA CUP

GRONINGEN (Holland) v. NEUCHATEL (Switzerland).
BEVEREN (Belgium) v. ATLETICO BILBAO (Spain).
RANGERS v. BOAVISTA (Portugal).
WIDZEW LODZ (Poland) v. UERDINGEN (West Germany).
LEGIA WARSAW (Poland) v. INTER MILAN (Italy).
ATLETICO MADRID (Spain) v. VITORIA GUIMARAES (Portugal).
FEYENOORD (Holland) v. MOENCHEN-GLADBACH (West Germany).
GHENT (Belgium) v. SPORTUL STUDEN-TESC (Romania).

RABA ETO GYOER (Hungary) v. TORINO (Italy).
DUKLA PRAGUE (Czechoslovakia) v. LEVER-KUSEN (West Germany).
BARCELONA (Spain) v. SPORTING LISBON (Portugal).
HAJDUK SPLIT (Yugoslavia) v. TRAKIA PLOVDIV (Bulgaria).
TYROL (Austria) v. LIEGE (Belgium).
GOTHENBURG (Sweden) v. BRANDEN-BURG (East Germany).
SPARTAK MOSCOW (Russia) v. TOULOUSE (France).
DUNDEE UNITED v. UNI CRAIOVA (Romania).

Matches to be played on October 22 and November 5.

What Jim McLean wanted he normally got — but not this time.

A first leg at home followed by a long trip to Romania was the opposite of what he was hoping for.

Optimistic mood at Tannadice

"Nineteen points from the first quarter of the season. If we have anything like that from the next three quarters we will definitely win the Premier League—especially as I think the most difficult quarter is past."

A surprisingly optimistic comment from the man noted more for his caution than his forecasting—Dundee United manager Jim McLean.

He rates the key to the current great run, which has seen United top the league for the past six weeks, as his bringing into the scheme of things in a coaching capacity senior players Paul Hegarty, Paul Sturrock and Eamonn Bannon; the hard work of Gordon Wallace and part-time coaches Doug Houston and Steve Murray and the way newcomers like Iain Ferguson, Dave Bowman and Jim McInally have fitted in.

"There is also, of course, the bonus of Dave Beaumont, possibly the biggest plus of all the way he has taken over from Richard Gough and Dave Narey since he has been injured.

"The Hegarty, Sturrock, Bannon move has strengthened the family feeling within the club.

Give more

"After all, there's nothing a young player likes better than working with his heroes.

"On match days, people like Hegarty and

By THE SPORTS EDITOR

Maurice Malpas have been asked to give more and have given it.

"Choosing a team this year has actually been more difficult than it was.

"I had about 12 players. I got stale because every player here knew where he stood with me.

"There's a freshness now. I've been freshened up and so have the players who are battling to prove they are first choice.

"I have always said that if a manager doesn't move he must move players in the interests of the club.

Paying off

"We have moved players, brought in fresh faces and, right now, it is certainly paying off."

There is one unusual thing the manager thinks could affect the club's championship challenge—segregation.

There were only 290 fans in the Arklay Street end, reserved for Motherwell supporters, on Wednesday night.

Before the game, United chairman George Fox appealed to the police to allow United fans in there.

The appeal was refused.

"How are we to bring sanity back into the game if football followers aren't allowed to mix?" queried manager McLean yesterday.

Fence

What United hope to do when clubs with small followings visit in future is have a type of segregation fence which would keep the two sets of supporters apart, but allow United fans into the Arklay Street end.

What they have had to do to achieve this, however, is add to their toilet and canteen facilities at that end so that the visitors have these facilities available.

"I feel kicking into the almost empty end on Wednesday saw us lose a bit of form at the start of the second half," summarised the manager.

"The lack of atmosphere could cost us points and, in the extreme, the league title. There is nothing worse than a lack of atmosphere for a team."

Meantime, the injured Dave Narey is training again and is hopeful for tomorrow's game against Aberdeen; Iain Ferguson has a groin strain and is doubtful and John Holt is out, though he might play next week.

● The reserve game due tonight against Aberdeen has been cancelled as Aberdeen cannot raise a team. Possible alternative date is November 10.

Pat on the back for United fans

Dundee United supporters have been given another pat on the back for their exemplary behaviour both at home and abroad—this time from a French national newspaper.

After the tie at Tannadice Park on October 2 between Dundee United and Lens, an article in "L'Equipe," entitled "Hooligans—Never Heard of Them," commented about the behaviour of the home fans.

It read, "There was a pleasant atmosphere—good-natured, you may say—at Tannadice Park, Dundee, for the Dundee United v. Lens match. Far, far removed in any case from the trouble sometimes encountered in the English grounds. Here in Scotland the supporters of all ages, when they told you that United would win 3-0, did so with a smile on their faces. For these fans the match was more of a party . . ."

The paragraph was sent to Dundee United with the "best regards" of a Mr Ron Langlands, of Monaco, so that the compliment could be passed on to the fans.

Mr George Fox, chairman of United, said they had been "delighted" to receive the remarks of the French paper.

"We are accustomed to our fans being well behaved, though," he added. "Our supporters are a credit to the club."

Mr Bobby Cargill, president of Dundee United Social Club, pointed out that United fans had also been praised for the way they acted on the first leg in France.

"In Lens we were received very well," he said. "We even went out with them after the game, and the French fans were singing United songs and we ended up singing the French national anthem at the end of the night!

"There was no animosity at all, and we gave them the address of the social club here. Some of their fans came up after the game at Tannadice for a drink as well.

"There was a great atmosphere at both games. Since the social club opened, there have been two foreign teams playing in Dundee—Bohemians from Dublin, and Lens. We struck up a very good relationship with them, and there were no problems at all.

"We're very happy indeed to have this said about us by a French newspaper."

Craiova may keep it tight

"They have four internationalists in their team— Negrila, Ungureanu, Irimescu and Geolgau— and it would be five if Lung wasn't suspended after being sent off in the previous round.

"They have been in Europe for seven or eight of the past ten years. It isn't going to be easy."

A summing up by Dundee United coach Gordon Wallace of United's UEFA Cup opponents Craiova, whom he saw beat Cluj 2-1 in a Rumanian league game a few days ago.

Gordon continued, "Having played against Leeds United, Shamrock Rovers and in Germany, they know what to expect from us in a general sense.

"Their team reminds me on Vardar Skopje (who United beat 2-0 at Tannadice and drew 1-1 with over there last season).

"I anticipate, from their formation, that they will play it tight here, open out a bit over there.

"Ungureanu played against Scotland and England last season. He is a left back, small, but comfortable on the ball.

"Rumania failed to qualify for the World Cup from the same section as England and Northern Ireland, but it was close, and the Craiova players were involved in the international series, so it isn't as if they won their honours years ago.

When the Rumanians arrived in Dundee last night their party was found to be not the expected 25, but a rather larger 37!

Ticket "snub": McLean replies

By THE SPORTS EDITOR

Allegations that former Dundee United striker Davie Dodds had been "a victim of an astonishing snub" by United were answered yesterday by manager Jim McLean.

Replying to the story that Dodds, now with Aberdeen after a brief, unhappy spell with Swiss club Neuchatel Xamax, had been refused complimentary tickets for United's recent UEFA Cup tie with Lens at Tannadice, the manager commented, "First thing I want to say is that Davie Dodds was told to stay away from Tannadice after Hearts' 3-0 league victory here on April 12.

"The reasons building up to this involved our UEFA Cup tie with Neuchatel on December 11 last year. We went there without Paul Sturrock, injured, and defending a slender 2-1 lead."

The manager then went on to say that Dodds had a slight injury worry before the trip, "which seemed to clear up according to both himself and the physiotherapist."

In view of this, the team to face Neuchatel was announced to the players. But, on the morning of the game, after a light loosening-up, Dodds reported that he was feeling the injury. The team had to be changed.

The manager claimed that on the Tuesday night in Switzerland the agent responsible for taking Dodds to Neuchatel appeared in their hotel.

"Some time later, on the eve of our game with Dundee, it was announced that Dodds was going to Neuchatel. The Dundee game is one on the eve of which we would least like upsets, for obvious reasons.

"As we were still interested in both the Premier League title and the Scottish Cup I, wrongly, I now believe, took no action and continued to use Dodds in our team.

"There were several performances below the standard Dodds himself had set and the situation climaxed after the Hearts game at Tannadice.

"I telephoned Dodds that weekend and told him to stay away from Tannadice.

"Coming up to date, Aberdeen did phone for two tickets for Dodds for the Lens game. When I found out I told our secretary to phone back and tell them there were no tickets for him.

Davie Dodds comes off worst in this tussle with former team-mate Dave Beaumont.

"Davie Dodds will not be allowed tickets as long as I am involved with Dundee United."

The manager stressed that Dodds was "a model professional for any manager" up to the time he went to Switzerland.

"Dodds is entitled to his opinion of me, but, equally, I am entitled to my opinion of him and of the situation in general.

"It has also been said that Alex Ferguson made a heated phone call to me about the situation. In fact, at no time did he phone me. I phoned him because of our friendship and fully explained the details to him."

Yesterday Dodds said he wished to make no comment other than to emphasise he had not started the publicity about the ticket situation.

While McLean was being uncharacteristically upbeat in reviewing his team's form so far, a row involving former player Davie Dodds saw the manager taking to the pages of The Courier to set the record straight.

21

Hegarty unlikely to make Euro line-up

Dundee United skipper Paul Hegarty looks unlikely to win a place in their line-up for tonight's U.E.F.A. Cup second round, first leg, tie with Universetea Craiova at Tannadice.

As the hours tick away towards kick-off Hegarty (32), a veteran of so many continental campaigns, is losing his fitness fight.

Remarkably, it's exactly 11 years ago to the day since United's captain last missed a European tie.

Manager Jim McLean yesterday said, "Obviously we would love to have him because of his vast experience and goal threat at set-pieces, but it looks like we are hoping against hope."

United's captain, sidelined since suffering a groin injury against Aberdeen on October 11, is still being troubled by the damaged area in his left thigh. Either John Clark or Dave Beaumont will deputise.

Clark proved an able replacement against Falkirk on Saturday and with the Rumanians reportedly lacking height, his aerial power would add another string to the Tangerines' bow but Beaumont also did well against Lens in the second leg of the first round tie when called upon to step into Dave Narey's boots.

The news of Paul Sturrock and Ralph Milne however, is better, with both expected to be available.

Sturrock looks certain to pass a morning fitness test while Milne has exceeded expectations in training since casting off his plaster on Monday.

"With Milne its a question of whether I play him and Kevin Gallacher or stick one of them on the bench," revealed Jim McLean.

By STEVE BRUCE

Though furnished with an extensive rundown on the opposition by coach Gordon Wallace and having personally viewed a video recording of Rumania's World Cup qualifying tie with England, featuring three of the Craiova players expected to line up tonight, the United manager admits he would have preferred greater knowledge of the opposition.

Apprehension

There is also the matter of this first leg being played on home soil, which Jim McLean feels is a disadvantage. "Apprehension at losing a goal is always greater when the first leg is at home," he claimed.

"In these circumstances you have to try to establish a two-goal lead for the return, at the same time feeling extra apprehensive about being caught on the break."

"Our expectations are such that we would be looking to get through this tie, but to do so will require a good or very good performance both here and in Rumania," he continued.

"In the modern European game you cannot afford a bad leg, we've gone out in the past because of that and only just went through against Lens following a poor half in France."

Universetea, who, like United, are in the process of rebuilding their side, have recently undergone a managerial change.

Paul Hegarty

Only last week 64-year-old former national team boss Constantin Teasca was appointed in place of Silviu Stanescu, "demoted" to the position of coach.

Team news is that international right-back Nicolai Negrila has recovered from injury and plays, while in goal Racoltea takes over from the suspended Silviu Lung.

Tonight's match is a virtual step into the unknown for the Rumanians. Jim McLean might wish for more detailed information on Universetea but his opposite number is even more in the dark.

While the Tannadice boss is able to formulate his plans, assisted by the fruits of Gordon Wallace's spying trip, Teasca in contrast is having to rely on videos of United to plot their downfall.

The ineligible Iain Ferguson will be missed and the loss of skipper Paul Hegarty would be a blow, but United are well capable of establishing a sufficient first leg advantage to take behind the Iron Curtain in a fortnight's time.

United from—W. Thomson, Malpas, McGinnis, McInally, Clark, Hegarty, Narey, Beaumont, Bowman, Gallacher, Milne, Kinnaird, Bannon, Sturrock, Coyne, Redford, Sulley, S. Thomson.

Taking a break from the build-up to tonight's match at Tannadice, this quartet took a computerised look at how United are doing in the league. Under a sponsored incentive scheme, United will receive a bonus if they reach 62 points, and are currently well on target. Left to right are Maurice Malpas, Dave Narey, Paul Hegarty and Paul Sturrock.

As United battled yet more injury troubles, McLean made a direct appeal to occasional supporters — and repeated his controversial view that the city of Dundee would struggle to sustain two top teams.

McLean's message

In last night's programme Dundee United manager Jim McLean had this to say about United's support—

"Our last three home games have attracted gates of 5957 (Falkirk), 5740 (Motherwell) and only 5314 against Clydebank on Saturday.

"All I can say is attendances like that make it very frustrating and make you wonder if it is really worthwhile trying to maintain a side capable of challenging for honours.

"I'd like to make it quite clear that I have absolutely no complaints concerning the loyal 5000 or so, every one of them deserves to see a trophy-winning side. However it is depressing that a city the size of Dundee cannot give us greater support at the turnstiles. If it continues at that level the books just will not balance and we will always be forced to sell.

"Now and again I dream of the side that could have been paraded at Tannadice had they all still been here. Richard Gough, Raymond Stewart, Andy Gray and Davie Dodds would all have been formidable assets. If what we have achieved at Tannadice had happened at one of the Edinburgh clubs, that dream might have come to fruition.

"I have repeated, probably to the point of boredom, that Dundee as a city cannot compete trying as it does to sustain two clubs. Until this is a one club town it will always be an uphill struggle financially.

"Although we have lost quality players, men like Iain Ferguson, Jim McInally, Dave Bowman, Kevin Gallacher and Billy Thomson are high-class replacements.

"The directors here are doing a magnificent job in running the club. The wages paid to the players here have matched the best in Scotland but it becomes more difficult each season.

"I am only too aware my comments will be taken as grumbling but it is certainly not directed at those who do turn up each week.

"Drawing a parallel is the fact almost 12,000 came to watch our last European tie, more than twice the number at any of the last three home league games. Just where do the other half go?

"I appreciate the financial implications of two games a week, but no doubt some who appear for only the glamour games are the loudest critics when we are forced to sell players or when trophies are not won . . . . "

Late double opens the door for United

DUNDEE UNITED 3, UNIVERSETEA CRAIOVA 0

Dundee United gave themselves a great chance of reaching the UEFA Cup third round with a late, late show at Tannadice last night. With only nine minutes of this second-round first-leg tie remaining, Jim McLean's side had only a scant 1-0 lead to take behind the Iron Curtain in a fortnight's time, but two late strikes changed everything.

Much of the credit for this result lies with Ian Redford, who maintained his remarkable Euro scoring record.

The former Dundee and Rangers man, who had scored in all but one of his previous European outings since moving to Tannadice, did it again, notching a brace.

The other came from man-of-the-match

By STEVE BRUCE

John Clark, who proved a more than able deputy for injured skipper Paul Hegarty.

This was yet another successful chapter in United's European history.

The signs weren't good for them at the interval with the scoresheet blank and an excellent goalkeeper in opposition but once more the Tangerines came up trumps with three second-half goals, thus surely establishing a sufficient advantage to take them through.

Shock for United

There was an early shock in store for home fans when Universetea came desperately close to taking the lead.

Only two minutes had elapsed when Adrean Popescu intercepted a Malpas pass and unleashed a 25-yard thunderbolt which beat Billy Thomson. To United's relief the ball came back off the crossbar, but the danger wasn't over, for it struck the keeper and ran loose to Raja, whose low drive was well saved by Thomson.

Confidence boosted, the Romanians tried their luck from a distance again, with Irimescu firing a 40-yard free kick wide and Bicu shooting over from the edge of the area.

United hit back, and Paul Sturrock had a close-range effort blocked by Racolta after Redford had just failed to connect with a Bannon cross.

But in 17 minutes the danger warning was again sounding at the other end when Bita was given a clear look at goal from 10 yards. To the relief of the Tangerine legions, stand-in centre-half John Clark got in a telling tackle to thwart the visiting striker.

United began to settle. Racolta was called upon to fist away a dangerous Milne cross and Sandoi had to whip a clever Redford pass off the toes of Sturrock.

Brilliant save

Only a brilliant save from the Craiova keeper prevented Paul Sturrock opening the scoring in 27 minutes. Ralph Milne created the opening with a terrific burst of pace down the right and his powerful cross was glanced goalward by Sturrock, only for Racolta to fist the ball away.

Twice in a matter of minutes full-back Gary McGinnis had chances, but skied the first after Redford had headed on a Bannon centre, then had an aerial effort saved by Racolta.

John Clark fires in a low ground shot.

A mistake by Sandoi presented Sturrock with a scoring opportunity as half-time approached, but the ball flew wide.

Breakthrough

United began the second period in determined fashion and might have struck almost immediately.

A Milne cross was knocked down by Redford for Maurice Malpas. However the full-back was unable to get the ball under control to shoot and Sandoi stepped in to clear.

John Clark burst into the action with a 30-yarder well held by Racolta, then blotted his copybook when play moved upfield by conceding Craiova their first corner of the evening.

In 53 minutes the breakthrough finally came for United and Clark was in the thick of things.

Rising majestically, he nodded down a Milne corner for Ian Redford to turn the ball home.

Moments later an identical move almost had the same outcome. This time, though, Redford was unable to connect.

The screw was tightened but two magnificent saves from Racolta denied United.

A well-placed Redford header from a Malpas cross looked certain to be rewarded but the keeper dived to his right to turn it away and in 67 minutes he bettered even that stop, somehow twisting

in mid-air to touch over a powerful Dave Bowman shot.

Another aerial effort from Redford dipped just over the cross-bar, then with 13 minutes remaining United made a double substitution, sending on Coyne and Gallacher for Sturrock and Milne.

The second

Four minutes later came the second goal United so desperately needed.

The build-up began with a John Clark free-kick from 25 yards which was deflected for a corner.

Eamonn Bannon fired the flag-kick into the near post and there was Clark to send a header glancing past Racolta.

With just 90 seconds remaining, their worries for the return eased considerably when Redford struck again, heading the ball into an empty net after Racolta had parried a Maurice Malpas drive.

Attendance—10,728.

Dundee United—Thomson; Malpas, McGinnis, McInally, Clark, Narey, Bowman, Milne, Bannon, Sturrock, Redford. Subs—Thomson, Beaumont, Gallacher, Sulley, Coyne.

Universetea Craiova—Racolta; Negrila, Sandoi, Ungureanu, A. Popescu, Raja, Bicu, G. Popescu, Bita, Irimescu, Geolgau. Subs—Sinescu, Cioroianu, Manaila, Cirtu, Bica.

Referee—D. Kreknak (Czechoslovakia).

Ian Redford turns the ball home for United's first goal.

Patience rewarded

Afterwards, manager Jim McLean said it was a great result but added, "We will have to be alert over there as they are a good side."

He singled out Clark and McGinnis who did a "tremendous job at the back."

He made the point that McGinnis had been faced with a difficult situation because of the way the opposition played but had coped extremely well.

Clark's use of the long ball was particularly noted by the manager and he was obviously delighted that the player got his reward with his goal "which made them more jittery and made it possible for the goal that followed as well."

He explained that it hadn't been because of substitutions that the result had gone the way it did, after all Milne and Sturrock had barely trained beforehand.

McInally was another mentioned by the manager as was Redford, whom he admitted didn't have a good first half but who, of course, got his two goals after the interval.

Although disappointed in the attendance the manager said those who were there were "magnificent compared to a year ago." The point he was making was that they, like the players, had shown the necessary patience in a European tie and had been rewarded with the late goals.

23

Gate receipts will only cover flight

As I reported yesterday, manager Jim McLean expressed his disappointment in the Tannadice attendances in the programme for Wednesday night's UEFA Cup tie against Universetea Craiova (writes The SPORTS EDITOR).

Yesterday, he spelt out the financial facts behind his comments.

"The gate receipts from last night (note—attendance 10,728, 37,130 fewer than at the Celtic-Dynamo Kiev game) will cover the cost of the charter plane for the second leg and nothing else," he said.

"On top of that we have to find £3597 for the referee and two linesmen from Czechoslovakia (travel, hotel and spending money), and money to pay gate checkers, the police and so on.

This doesn't take into account, either, the players' win bonus if we do finally go through to the next round.

"We want to be in Europe as we have been for many seasons now because we want success, but every time we go in it can cost us around £10,000. The only ties from which we made money were against Manchester United and Roma.

"I see Rangers saying that they want a good run in Europe this season so that they can do what Liverpool do, buy an expensive player with the proceeds.

No TV fee

"That most certainly does not happen with us! I wish it did.

"People will have noticed, too, that we weren't on television and therefore had no TV fee for our game.

"We are on the screen on a regular basis in normal games, but when it comes to the crunch we are left out.

"I remember when we were in the European Cup the television cameras were at a Cup Winners' Cup game and we weren't on the screen."

He didn't add "that hurts." He didn't need to!

Inexperience

Harking back to the game against Craiova, the manager drew attention to the youth and relative inexperience in the United team.

Average age was 25, which dropped to 23 when Kevin Gallacher and Tommy Coyne replaced Ralph Milne and Paul Sturrock.

"Although Maurice Malpas, Dave Narey ("they had great games, as had Gary McGinnis and John Clark, but internationalists are expected to have that!"), Eamonn Bannon, Ralph Milne and Paul Sturrock are very experienced in Europe, some of the rest are a long way short of that, yet I wasn't unhappy with any one of them."

Three goals should be enough to see United through, but it is interesting to note—and no doubt everyone at Tannadice HAS noted—that in 24 European ties at home Craiova have once scored four goals and five times three, mostly against good opposition; Olympiakos (Greece), Monaco (France), Weiner SK (Austria), Fiorentina (Italy) and Shamrock Rovers (Eire).

● United reserves play Hearts at Tannadice tonight at 7 p.m.

While the glamour games of rounds to follow would provide United with much-needed pay days, early European progress came at a price.

TV, and the effect on finances, is an issue we'll read more of later.

Final decision today on Hegarty's fitness

By STEVE BRUCE

Dundee United's hopes of having skipper Paul Hegarty in their line-up for the U.E.F.A. Cup second round, second leg clash with Universetea Craiova tomorrow night hinge on a fitness test this morning.

The veteran defender did enough in a running session at Tannadice yesterday prior to United's departure for Romania to convince manager Jim McLean it was worthwhile taking him, but there was no guarantee he'll be able to make his 52nd appearance in Europe tomorrow.

"Paul has cleared the first and easiest hurdle in making the trip, but now comes the hard part, turning and kicking the ball, which he hasn't done so far," said the United manager.

Safe arrival

The Dundee United party arrived at their hotel on time last night, but the accompanying Press party did not have such a smooth time, being delayed at the airport for 2½ hours before being cleared by Customs and security men.

The first leg of this tie, which United won 3-0, is one of five matches Hegarty (32), has missed since receiving a groin injury against Aberdeen on October 11.

"Big test"

The player himself confirmed "kicking the ball will be the big test.

"The groin is fine at present, running doesn't pose a problem, but I was in the same position a fortnight ago and it went when I started turning.

"I'm desperate to play, but even if I don't I've no worries over us being able to get through, for the lads have been magnificent in my absence."

Jim McLean is adamant he will not take a major gamble over Hegarty's fitness.

Plaster removed?

"We would be prepared to take a slight risk with him but there is no way we can afford to be without Paul for a further three weeks."

Narey—an absentee from this one with a knee injury—is to visit a specialist on Thursday, when he may have his plaster cast removed.

Certain to play against Craiova is Paul Sturrock, although he is still being troubled by a toe problem, while John Holt, recovering steadily from a stress fracture of the leg, could make the bench.

"This is not the best position we have ever been in, because of the injuries, but the lads who have been playing have done well, the character and graft from them has been magnificent," said the manager.

Still suspended

The Romanians have a fitness doubt over international midfielder Irimescu and will again be without keeper Silvio Luing.

Luing, who missed the first leg through suspension, is again marked absent, for it has emerged that his ban from U.E.F.A. is for four matches.

Racolta, who impressed at Tannadice, once more deputises.

Universetea are also contemplating a tactical change, with Cirtu coming in for Ficu.

Dundee United pool—W. Thomson, Malpas, Sulley, Beaumont, Clark, Hegarty, Holt, McInally, G. McLeod, Gallacher, Milne, Sturrock, Redford, Bowman, Bannon, S. Thomson, McGinnis and Coyne.

Paul Hegarty (left) hopes to get the thumbs-up today after a fitness test, while Paul Sturrock is already certain to play tomorrow.

United rely on youngsters

Dundee United appear set to field a reshaped defence, average age under 23, against Universetea Craiova in the UEFA Cup second leg in Romania today.

For if, as seems likely, skipper Paul Hegarty is missing, the back four will comprise Gary McGinnis, John Clark, Dave Beaumont and Maurice Malpas, surely the youngest and least experienced defensive unit United have ever fielded in European competition.

Hegarty spent most of yesterday morning's one hour training stint at the

—By STEVE BRUCE—

match venue, working with physio Jim Joyce, and afterwards reported he was still experiencing slight difficulty with his groin injury.

"We'll check him again tomorrow morning, but it looks like Paul will be missing," said a disappointed Jim McLean.

"Losing Hegarty on top of the absence of Dave Narey would be a tremendous blow.

"However, the other lads have done well for us in different games and the only way we'll know if they are ready for this is by playing them, anyway we have no option," he added.

Partly because of his defensive headache, the United boss is demanding his players go for a goal to put this tie beyond the Romanians.

"We have to make sure we are not pushed back into trying to defend the three goal first leg lead," he commented.

"We must go out to try and score, and that is why I will field a 4-3-3 formation when I would otherwise have opted for 4-4-2."

The midfield and forward areas are also posing Jim a slight problem as he has to choose between seven men— Dave Bowman, Jim McInally, Ian Redford, Eamonn Bannon, Kevin Gallacher, Paul Sturrock and Ralph Milne—for six places.

Sturrock, Bannon and McInally

> **Jim McInally** will miss the Premier League clash with Celtic on Saturday week following his booking against St Mirren. McInally has picked up a one match suspension after amassing 11 disciplinary points.

appear certain to play, thus reducing his choice to three from Bowman, Redford, Gallacher and Milne.

Of those four, the first two named are likely to go through on the final ballot, Bowman for the fact he'll add steel to the midfield, and Redford having demonstrated his goal threat in the first leg when he netted twice.

The Stade Central pitch is six yards longer and six yards wider than Tannadice, thus affording Milne and Gallacher ample space in which to utilise their pace.

It will be difficult for the manager to choose between this pair, but Milne could get the nod on the strength of his greater experience and scoring record in European competition.

He is after all the club's top marksman in Euro ties, and with 15 goals to his credit stands only one away from equalling Jimmy Johnstone's record for goals scored by a Scot for one club in continental competition.

The composition of United's subs bench will be determined by whether or not Hegarty plays, but one certain incumbent is John Holt, who is considered capable of managing a 30 minute appearance if required.

Universetea's international midfielder Mirca Irisescu appears to be winning his fitness battle, and the Romanians certainly haven't given up the ghost.

Manager Constantin Teasca said yesterday, "We have a chance, despite the severe first leg score line."

The match, which kicks off at 11.00

> **Good news for United is that today's referee, Monsieur Delmer from France, is rated one of the top three whistlers in Europe.**

a.m. British time, will be played in front of a capacity 50,000 crowd.

It is likely to be a test for the Tannadice side, but the club can proudly point to the fact they have never lost a European tie in which a three goal first leg lead had been established—a record they can maintain today.

United from—Thomson, McGinnis, Malpas, Hegarty, Clark, Beaumont, Bannon, Redford, Bowman, McInally, Milne, Gallacher, Sturrock.

McLean really proud of them all

UNIVERSETEA CRAIOVA 1, DUNDEE UNITED 0

(United win 3-1 on aggregate)

Dundee United jetted back home last night, their place in tomorrow's U.E.F.A. Cup third-round draw secured.

The Tangerines produced a superb performance in Craiova's Stade Central yesterday afternoon to see themselves safely through.

Never at any time during the 90 minutes did Universetea look likely to haul back the three-goal lead United had established at Tannadice a fortnight earlier.

The young players drafted in for injured veterans Paul Hegarty and Dave Narey did a magnificent job in defence.

Indeed, Jim McLean's men might have returned home the first Scottish club side ever to have won on Rumanian soil in European competition. They had chances.

The manager, never a man to issue praise where it isn't due, paid glowing tribute to his players.

"I am really proud of every one of them," he said.

"The workrate was incredible; the young lads at the back tremendous, particularly when you consider Maurice Malpas, at 23, was the oldest amongst them."

"This was a test for these lads and they came through it."

The average age of the 13 players used yesterday was only 24, which must augur well for the future.

Thomson tops

Man-of-the-match had to be keeper Billy Thomson, whose display provided backing for those people calling for his restoration to the international team.

"If I had to single out one individual, it would be Thomson," agreed Jim McLean.

"He settled everyone and the Rumanians knew they had someone to beat in our keeper."

Three times during the goalless first-half Thomson produced the goods, clutching a powerfully-struck shot from Adrean Popescu, racing off his line to block a Geolgau effort, then a minute from the break turning a difficult Rada shot round the post.

During the second period he again did the

By STEVE BRUCE

needful to deny Bicu (twice), on the second occasion after a bad back-pass by McGinnis had let the Craiova player in, and, as time ran out on the Rumanians, clutched a tricky grounder from Cirtu.

The one occasion on which Thomson was beaten owed much to bad luck.

It was a mistake by centre-half John Clark—who otherwise hardly put a foot wrong—which led to the goal in 59 minutes.

His tangle with McGinnis, when trying to clear a ball, left George Bita in possession.

Dave Beaumont came to meet the Rumanian inside United's area but slipped, and although Thomson managed to push the ball upwards, it bounced into the net.

Universetea were clearly a disappointment to their fans.

A fiercely partisan crowd of 40,000 had packed the stadium, with others standing six deep on the roofs of nearby multi-story buildings just for a glimpse of the game.

Evidence of their passion was provided just before kick-off when police tried to remove three banners from the perimeter fence and were promptly pelted with bottles, rolls and various other objects.

United might well have found themselves in front long before Craiova struck.

With only 12 minutes gone, Paul Sturrock beat keeper Racolta with a lob, only to see it cleared off the line, and from the loose ball Eamonn Bannon shot narrowly wide.

Then 16 minutes later, only the woodwork denied Bannon.

A Sturrock free-kick from the right picked out the World Cup man who beat Racolta with a downward header, only for the ball to take a severe bounce off the bumpy pitch and strike the bar.

The Universetea goal, in fact, came against the run of play, and a merited draw might well have been earned after it.

Midway through the second period, Bannon nodded down a Clark free-kick for Redford, who beat Racolta to the ball only to fire wide. Substitutes Kevin Gallacher and Tommy Coyne were both off target when they could have done better.

There were three bookings in a match well handled by French official Alain Delmer.

Dave Beaumont for fouling Cirtu, Eamonn Bannon for shoving Rada, who had almost strangled him, and the Rumanian himself for hacking down Ralph Milne.

Craiova—Racolta, Negrila, Sandoi, Ungureanu, A.Popescu, Rada, Bicu, Bita, Geolgau, G.Popescu, Cirtu.
Dundee United—Thomson, Malpas, McGinnis, Beaumont, Clark, McInally, Bowman, Milne (Coyne), Bannon, Sturrock (Gallacher), Redford. Subs—S.Thomson, Holt, Sulley.

Glad to be back in Dundee last night after yesterday's match in Rumania were (from left)—Maurice Malpas, Ralph Milne, Eamonn Bannon, Billy Thomson and Paul Hegarty.

25

Fans Split on United's form

If United went into the second round on a wave of confidence, the atmosphere changes markedly in early November.

A series of average results culminates in a heavy defeat in a Tannadice derby against Dundee — bringing angry complaints from a small section of the home fans and an even angrier response from manager McLean.

Incensed by seeing a scarf thrown on to the pitch, he declares: "Our supporters have been spoiled."

Reminding the minority that player departures and injuries have tested United's resolve to the fullest, he adds: "They had better realise right now that we are re-building and there will be more bad results to come."

It's a theme continued in letters to The Courier's sports editor, with a Mr A. Holt of Lorimer Street writing: "If it wasn't that the club needs the paying public to turn up in large numbers, I would rather the moaners stayed at home on a Saturday afternoon, allowing the players to get on with what they are all very good at — keeping the real supporters happy."

But Tim Cairns of Hill Street hits back, asking just how "United are going to remain one of the big guns when it would appear we are running out of bullets." He goes on to advise McLean to stop picking men "who simply are not good enough".

The UEFA Cup third-round draw again sends United east, this time to face Yugoslavia's Hajduk Split. However, the destination is not McLean's chief concern: he is more disappointed to be playing at home again in the first leg.

McLean also laments United taking another financial hit for their on-field success, revealing that getting past Craiova had meant another £10,000 loss for the club.

Meanwhile, Hajduk are also struggling for their best form and their manager Sergjei Kresic makes it clear that United's recent European achievements have not been lost on him.

"Bannon is very skilful ... Sturrock is excellent and Milne is very, very dangerous in European football," he says.

McLean also seems prepared to accept his team are the favourites, saying: "If we play as we can over both legs we'll definitely win through."

The second leg against Hajduk is also notable as the first of United's UEFA Cup run to be shown live on TV.

With a kick-off time of 3.30pm in the UK, fans across the city no doubt come up with some imaginative reasons for finishing early on December 10.

Round Three also sees the start of what must be some of the best competition prizes The Courier has ever offered.

In conjunction with United's main sponsor VG, the newspaper offers the chance to fly to Yugoslavia on the team flight and enjoy the match in VIP surroundings.

The wordsearch contests will be repeated throughout United's campaign, giving eight Courier readers memories to last a lifetime.

We reproduce the puzzles in this book but, unfortunately, the prizes have long since been claimed!

No Euro gold for United

By the Sports Editor

Europe has never been exactly a pot of gold for Dundee United—and this season is proving no different.

In fact, Dundee United manager Jim McLean reported yesterday that his club had lost a "five figure sum... over £10,000" in their tie with Universetea Craiova.

Now he is hoping for a third home tie, "not too far across the water, with the second leg at Tannadice," in today's draw.

What he is delighted about in particular is the form of the midfield in the away game in Romania in midweek.

He rated Dave Bowman as "magnificent" and put Eamonn Bannon, who on this occasion played a front role alongside them, in the same class.

"They protected those behind them and got those in front of them going," he said.

All-round ability

"McInally is proving a tremendous asset with his all-round ability and Bannon was involved in everything.

"Unfortunately, he has been sent home today feeling 'fluey.' We definitely don't want to be without him.

"He is the most consistent player we've had at Tannadice since I came here. You can depend on him to go out there in midfield or at full back and churn it out every game—which is what winning teams are made of.

"Frankly, we don't have enough players with that degree of consistency."

Taking an over-all look at things, the manager went on, "As far as the league is concerned it is a handicap being in Europe and we cannot expect to keep doing well in the absence of the quality of player we are having to do without at the moment.

"I was sitting thinking about freshening the team for Saturday and it suddenly struck me that all we have available with experience are two forwards in Tommy Coyne and Kevin Gallacher."

Clark's role

"If John Clark hadn't taken a tumble to himself and decided centre-half was his role, what kind of state would we have been in with Paul Hegarty and Dave Narey absent as they have been this past week?

"Dave Narey had the plaster off his knee today and is a good bit better, but it will certainly be a wee while before he is fit... maybe the end of the month.

"He certainly won't be available for the local derby with Dundee, nor will John Holt, who is again finding his leg, which was stress fractured, painful.

"Paul Hegarty did full training this morning and should be fit to return, if selected, but Paul Sturrock is feeling the toe he staved against Aberdeen several weeks ago still sore and will miss Saturday.

"We have to get back down to earth for this one. A derby is always a difficult game and this one will be no exception."

● News of two United reserve games. On Monday, Aberdeen reserves visit Tannadice. A week on Monday (November 17) it is the "wee" local derby against Dundee at Dens Park.

Another draw, another McLean wishlist — and another slice of bad luck as United were handed a long trip east to Yugoslavia. Meanwhile, Rangers were drawn against German giants Borussia Moenchengladbach. More on them later...

Tangerines head east once again

By STEVE BRUCE

The UEFA Cup third-round draw, made yesterday lunchtime in Switzerland, did Dundee United no favours.

Fresh from their success over Romania's Universetea Craiova, the Tannadice side again have to travel behind the Iron Curtain to tackle Hajduk Split of Yugoslavia.

It's the third time in five Euro ties that United have been paired with an Eastern Bloc country. In last year's second round they met and defeated another Yugoslav side, Vardar Skopje.

Just to rub salt into the wounds, the first leg is to be played in Dundee on November 26.

"Playing at home first is definitely the biggest problem," said a disappointed Jim Mclean.

"We haven't had much luck in the draw recently but cannot complain because over the piece we've not drawn too many teams from behind the Iron Curtain.

"And let's hope we do the same to this Yugoslavian side as we did to the last one we met."

Hajduk are currently lying fourth top of their league which is headed by Vardar.

Nine times champions, seven times cup winners on the domestic scene, they have also recorded some fine results in Europe in recent years.

Last season they beat Metz, Torino and Dnepr (U.S.S.R.) to reach the UEFA Cup quarter-finals before losing to Waregem.

Two years earlier, they lost to eventual winners Spurs in the semi-finals of the same competition having disposed of Universetea Craiova, Honved, Radnicki Nis and Sparta Prague enroute.

Hajduk have defeated OEI Crete of Greece and Bulgarian's Trakia Plovdiv to secure this meeting with United.

They have four players in the current Yugoslav national side—which meets England at Wembley on Wednesday night—Miljas, Bursac, Perozovic and Deveric.

That representation would have been six strong but for the fact twins Zlatko and Zora Vujovic were transferred to Bordeaux during the close season.

Hajduk play two league fixtures between now and their trip to Scotland.

Rangers face a difficult challenge in their UEFA tie against West German cracks Borussia Moenchengladbach but their assistant manager Walter Smith at least knows the set up of the West Germans— and already has a European victory over them.

Smith was assistant at Dundee United in season 1981-82 when the Tannadice side lost in Germany 0-2 but turned the tables with a sweeping 5-0 win at home.

Said Smith, "Borussia are always involved at the very top level but we showed in the last round that we could handle the pressure of being at home in the first leg.

"They have three matches before we meet them and we will be watching them in each one."

UEFA CUP DRAW

DUNDEE UNITED v. HAJDUK SPLIT (Yugoslavia).

GHENT (Belgium) v. GOTHENBURG (Sweden).

GRONINGEN (Netherlands) v. VITORIA GUIMARAES (Portugal).

DUKLA PRAGUE (Czechoslovakia) v. INTER MILAN (Italy).

SPARTAK MOSCOW (Soviet Union) v. TYROL (Austria).

UERDINGEN (W. Germany) v. BARCELONA (Spain).

TORINO (Italy) v. BEVEREN (Belgium).

RANGERS v. BORUSSIA MOENCHENGLADBACH (W. Germany).

Ties on November 26 and December 10.

27

Some fans' attitude saddens United boss

By the Sports Editor

Hurt at the sight of a supporter throwing away his scarf after last week's defeat by Dundee and by critical phone calls made to the club since the

Jim McLean.

defeat, manager Jim McLean said yesterday, "Our supporters have been spoiled.

"They had better realise right now that we are re-building and there will be more bad results to come.

"This season I have been as proud as ever I have ever been as manager of Dundee United in the progress we have made.

"If anyone had told me that after 27 games we would have been defeated only three times that matter I would have been delighted—and that would be even with our team having its full complement of international players in action.

"I am not lambasting all our fans. The great majority know and appreciate our problems. I am fully aware that I am talking about a minority, but the reaction of this few still depresses me.

"I have a mass of videos available and was watching one or two for specific reasons the other night.

"One clip was of our 4-2 home win over Celtic as recently as January 4 this year.

"Do you know that no fewer than six of that team are either no longer here or out because of injury?

That is a tremendous turnover in so short a time. It is bound to have an effect."

When I asked for news on the visit to Parkhead on Saturday, the reply was "the team will be whoever is fit!"

He continued, "I thought there would be 14 available yesterday. But that included Gary McGinnis.

"He didn't train today because of an ankle knock and is added to the "doubtful" list.

Forwards aren't the problem, it's defenders.

Up front Tommy Coyne, Iain Ferguson, Paul Sturrock, Kevin Gallacher and Ralph Milne are available.

But without the suspended Jim McInally and the injured Paul Hegarty, Dave Narey and John Holt, plus, now, McGinnis,

things are extremely complicated further back.

A very late decision on the line-up is likely.

United have now been officially informed that no player registered from now on will be eligible for the next round of the U.E.F.A. Cup against Hajduk Split. This is because, even though he is on an "S" form, Mike McAdams is considered to be on strength.

As he is only 16½ now, it is more than likely a defender will be substitute goalkeeper for both legs of the tie—perhaps John Clark, with the additional possibility of Dave Bowman who actually played once AGAINST United for Hearts when Henry Smith was injured.

● Celtic striker Mo Johnston is expected to be fit to face United tomorrow. Johnston took an ankle knock early in Wednesday's international against Luxembourg and that caused his Parkhead manager David Hay some anxiety.

Anxious wait for McGinnis

Dundee United full-back Gary McGinnis will undergo a fitness test today before manager Jim McLean names his side for the top-line game against Celtic at Parkhead.

The verdict on McGinnis, who has an ankle knock, could prove vital to a beleaguered defence, which is rapidly running out of alternatives.

Already Hegarty, Narey, Holt and versatile midfielder Jim McInally, who could have filled in at the back, have been ruled out.

The situation has become so desperate that youngster Billy McKinlay will be called into the pool if McGinnis fails his test and may even find a place on the subs' bench.

With few real defenders to choose from, United's back four will probably consist of Malpas, Sulley, Beaumont and Clark, with McGinnis taking over from Sulley if fit.

Jim's pool is—Thomson; Malpas,

And anger over £9500 loss

McGinnis, Clark, Beaumont, Sulley, Redford, Bannon, Bowman, Milne, Gallacher, Ferguson, Sturrock and Coyne.

Uppermost in manager McLean's thoughts yesterday, though, was the loss—approaching £10,000—that his side made in their successful completion of the latest round of the UEFA Cup.

The manager was seeing red over the cost of Eastern-Bloc officials for their home game against Romanian side Craiova, which amounted to £3797.

This contributed heavily to the club's overall deficit for the two legs of £9548.

"We will be complaining about the cost of officials to the S.F.A.," he said.

"It's a strange situation that as far as European competitions are concerned, Scottish, English, Welsh and Northern Irish teams are treated separately, but referees' nationalities are lumped together and they are considered British.

"In one of our ties in Eastern Europe the match referee lived just over 30 miles away. It would certainly make things easier for us if we were able to use English officials, for example.

"We have complained on numerous occasions to the S.F.A. but it always seems to fall on deaf ears."

Meanwhile Celtic will include Tony Shepherd and Alan McInally against United this afternoon, with manager Hay pointing out that he has not beaten the Tannadice club at Parkhead since taking over as manager.

He said yesterday, "United usually play with a lot of flair but I will not be surprised this time if they are much tighter because of their injuries."

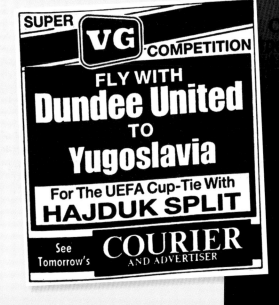

Gary McGinnis

Despite United pushing hard at the top of the league, advancing in the Scottish Cup and reaching the third round of the UEFA Cup, a derby loss at home was enough to anger some fans. Jim McLean, still frustrated by some of the game's red tape, was only too willing to respond.

29

Serious setbacks for Hajduk

Dundee United's U.E.F.A. Cup opponents of Wednesday night, Hajduk Split, lost 4-1 to Partizan Belgrade on Saturday (writes THE SPORTS EDITOR).

They also collected a couple of injuries—to central defender Jerko Tipuric and striker Stjepan Deveric.

Meanwhile, from Tannadice, the reports are—Dave Narey back and rarin' to go; John Clark probably o.k. even after three stitches in a leg wound; John Holt playing tonight in a friendly against Brechin, after which his chances will be assessed.

Mostly it is good news, but there is still worry over the stubborn toe injury which has bothered Paul Sturrock for five or six weeks now.

Manager Jim McLean gave a strong hint that young Billy McKinlay could be in the line-up on Wednesday night.

"We only took him off to give Ian Redford a run," he said of McKinlay's substitution five minutes from time. "He is ready and the Hibs game will have done him the world of good.

"Mind you, we didn't get him on the ball enough first half and not at all second half."

The manager summarised, "We need more goal threat from midfield in Europe and you can take it again that it won't be the same team on Wednesday, as it was today."

Money can't cure all United's ills

By THE SPORTS EDITOR

"If the directors were to give me two million pounds right now there is no way I could replace what we have lost in the recent past . . . Richard Gough and Davie Dodds transferred, Dave Narey, Paul Hegarty and Paul Sturrock injured."

Dundee United manager Jim McLean laying on the line his problem as he faces up to a spell in which injury has destroyed the balance of his team.

"A supporter phoned me and asked why I couldn't buy Craig Levein," he went on.

"My answer was, 'do you think we haven't tried?'

"But do you really think, even if we offered a million pounds, that Wallace Mercer would sell such a player to us?

"There was nothing spiteful in us not selling Richard Gough to Rangers. It was common sense not to sell to rivals in the same league.

"So why should other clubs in the Premier League sell to us?

"There's another aspect, too. Say we had been successful with a huge bid for Terry Butcher. Do you think he would have

come to Dundee United? Never!

"It isn't only a question of being able to afford the player. It's a question of his terms and the stage you are offering him to play on.

"Even a big club like Celtic haven't been able to buy and we will be continuing to try and develop the way they are doing—by rearing our own players.

"The current problem is that most of our international players are around the same age.

"Gough and Maurice Malpas, at 23, would have been perfect to step in as the senior men when they finished, but 50% of that plan has gone!

"The bright spot is that we do have some excellent talent on the way—for example Brian Welsh, Gordon Macleod and Billy McKinlay, all in the 17 to 19 age group."

The additional "X" factor with United, of course, is that, though they got a huge sum of money for Gough, for instance, nothing like all of it is available for a player or players.

There is a simple reason—the frequent 5000 gates at Tannadice.

It doesn't take a genius to work out that big fees are gradually frittered away keeping the club going from week to week.

Though no figure is forthcoming as to what average gate it would take to see the club "break even," financially I'd bet on it being a whole lot more than 5000 . . . probably double that at least.

What the manager had to say to "true United supporters" was, "My statement is, right now, we need you more than we have ever needed you. We have problems and your encouragement would help us solve them."

He rounded off by adding, "I have made bad buys and I have made good buys.

"What we will not be doing is making panic buys."

Obviously, then, if the right player at the right price doesn't turn up—and I know for a fact the net has been cast far and wide even though the manager is playing his cards very close to his chest on details—the present staff have the task of keeping domestic and European challenges going while the two, three, or even four-week wait for strengthening with the return of injured key men passes.

No plain sailing on Gordon's "spy" trip

Gordon Wallace.

The joys (?) of football travels in Europe were fully explored by Dundee United coach Gordon Wallace at the week-end.

Gordon arrived in Yugoslavia with the brief to watch United's opponents of tomorrow night, Hajduk Split, play Partisan Belgrade in a league game in Belgrade.

His plane landed in Zagreb, but instead of hopping on to another plane

By THE SPORTS EDITOR

for the capital, Gordon was informed that fog had cancelled his flight and that he would have to travel by rail.

He duly caught the appropriate train at 11 o'clock on Friday night and it was, to use his own description, "like an over-booked Wembley special for the England-Scotland game."

In fact, until an attendant arrived on the scene to sort out the seating, Gordon spent two hours standing.

Finally he arrived in Belgrade—at 7 a.m. on Saturday. Understandably, he went straight to bed, after first meeting his Yugoslav hosts, who had been combing the country for him.

What he saw after a brief but welcome rest was Hajduk losing 4-1 in the afternoon, "but there is no way they deserved that," he said.

"It was 2-1 until seven minutes from the end, then Partisan got a penalty. Trying to hit back quickly, and just after they claimed for a penalty, Hajduk were caught on the break and lost another goal.

"They are a good side in the Yugoslavian style, which can be very effective. They lie second equal in the league."

The result wasn't the only problem for the Yugoslavs.

Central defender Ivan Tipuric and striker Stjepan Deveric suffered hamstring injuries, with both going off.

They are already without suspended Zoran Vulic and Stjepan Andriejeseric and there are other injuries which will need treatment before tomorrow's game.

Injuries also feature in United's approach to the match.

Here, with Dave Narey having made a surprise comeback on Saturday and involved in full training yesterday and with John Clark fit despite three stitches in a leg wound—he will play with a shinguard protecting the injury—the news isn't as bad as it might have been, but it isn't all good.

A persistent toe injury is again troubling Paul Sturrock and there is a doubt over his appearance tomorrow night.

There will be no Paul Hegarty or Gordon McLeod in the starting line-up—"though both did a lot of hard running and could be available for selection at the week-end," according to manager Jim McLean.

Goalkeeper Scott Thomson went to hospital yesterday with expectations that his ankle break would be put in a walking plaster.

It didn't happen and the youngster will now be on crutches for at least another week.

Which is where Paul Hegarty comes back into the picture.

This early, the club don't want to have him throwing himself about in goalkeeping practice with his groin injury just about cleared, but if he gets a try-out tomorrow morning and comes through it satisfactorily he could be on the bench on Wednesday night—as substitute goalkeeper to Billy Thomson!

"He is the best substitute 'keeper we have," said the manager, "but, in view of his injury, if he does play, John Clark will take the goal-kicks."

Incidentally, with typical thoroughness, United have been checking back on a slight loss of form by Kevin Gallacher.

It is now believed he is suffering a reaction to a car crash in which his vehicle was written off early in the season. Dates of this and a change in form coincide.

● The Hajduk party arrived in their St Andrews hotel last night

feeling the strain after a 12-hour trip from their base via Zagreb, London and Edinburgh.

A light training work-out in the hotel grounds was followed by an early night.

Today it's training and shopping followed by a visit to Tannadice for another training session beginning at the same time as tomorrow night's game.

Manager Sergjei Kresic said it was too early to talk about a team, making the point that he, like United, has injury problems.

Dundee United striker Tommy Coyne has withdrawn his transfer request, "and I am very pleased," said manager Jim McLean yesterday. "I now hope the crowd will encourage and help him. What is wrong with him is that he tries too hard to please. In all my time in football I have only known two players who didn't need 'winding-up' before a game—rather the reverse. One was John Reilly, whom we transferred to Motherwell, the other is Coyne. If he could just relax and go out there and play as he can I'm sure he would be a success."

I couldn't agree more after watching Coyne in practice games several times (writes THE SPORTS EDITOR). There, with the pressure off, he attacks defences, especially down the left, and leaves good players wondering where he went. He is also a good finisher.

Now, as he says himself, "It is up to me to make a place for myself."

Kresic keeps calm

Hajduk manager Sergjei Kresic, polite and extremely knowledgeable about football, is philosophic about his injury and suspension list (writes THE SPORTS EDITOR).

"It is part of the game," he says with a slight shrug of the shoulders, recalling that, in the previous round, he had to call in three 18-year-olds because of injury and that they did very well.

He has seen United once "live," against Dundee a few weeks ago, once on television when they played Radnicki Nis ("but they have changed so much since then that I do not consider that important") and

has two video tapes of them, taken, we were informed by another member of the party, when they played Celtic and Dundee, "by a friend of ours in Glasgow."

The videos have been well studied and are with the party here now for further assessment.

But what does he think of United?

He chose to refer to the game against Dundee first when asked this.

"They play fast, aggressive football. They don't stop for a second.

"I was most impressed with them in the last five minutes against Dundee. They were losing 3-0 yet they never gave in and in fact created three chances in the last five minutes.

"They have a very high morale and character."

Did any individuals particularly impress him?

"Bannon is very skilful, Gallacher showed pace and skill when he went on. Sturrock is excellent and Milne is very, very dangerous in European football. We know all about the many goals he has scored."

And what did he consider would be a good result?

No messing here. "Victory!"

With Scottish teams now finding it so hard to compete in Europe, it's easy to forget how much respect clubs like United commanded on the Continent in the 1980s. Names like Bannon, Sturrock and Milne were clearly well known beyond our own borders.

Third time lucky this time?

By STEVE BRUCE

Dundee United attempt to end a three year wait against Hajduk Split in the UEFA Cup third round, first leg clash at Tannadice tomorrow.

For not since their marvellous run to the semi-finals of the European Cup back in season 1983-84 have the Tangerines reached the latter stages of a Euro competition.

United's progress in continental competition during the two campaigns since has been ended at this third round stage, last year by Neuchatel Xamax of Switzerland and twelve months earlier by Manchester United.

Manager Jim McLean set the scene for this evening's home leg, declaring, "This is the tie in Europe you most want to win.

"Getting past this stage gives you a breather until March and dangles the carrot of a quarter-final place and the financial reward that brings.

"For us there is also the added bonus that by then Iain Ferguson would be eligible to play."

Over-confidence is never a danger in United's camp, but the manager has no doubts over his side's ability to secure an interest in the resumption of this competition.

He said yesterday, "If we play as we can over both legs we'll definitely win through," then added cautiously, "If however we only play for half a game, as we sometimes do, we'll go out."

There was mixed news on the injury front. Striker Paul Sturrock is expected to play, but Paul Hegarty is ruled out and looks like being joined on the sidelines by John Holt.

Sturrock's troublesome toe injury is settling down sufficiently to suggest he'll be leading the line as usual.

However, plans to name Hegarty as back-up keeper have been abandoned as the club captain isn't as close to resuming playing as had originally been hoped.

"Being without Hegarty is a blow, but having a fully fit Dave Narey back is a big, big boost," commented the United manager.

Holt played the full 90 minutes of Monday's friendly with Brechin, but is currently being bothered by a stomach complaint. He isn't listed in a 16 strong squad for tonight and will only be considered if his condition has improved by this morning.

That pool consists of 15 outfield players plus keeper Billy Thomson. If anything happens to Thomson, centre-half John Clark will take over in goal.

The absence of a goalkeeper from the subs bench however isn't particularly troubling the manager, for as he pointed out, clubs find themselves in the same situation week-in-week-out on the domestic front.

Jim McLean isn't revealing his line-up, but indications are that teenager Billy McKinlay could well retain a midfield berth.

"Although I've not decided about McKinlay yet, the odds are in favour of him playing," he said.

It will be interesting to see just what sort of crowd Tannadice gets this evening, with Aberdeen and Celtic meeting on Premier League business less than 70 miles away.

By tradition, these European occasions have attracted supporters of other clubs, and United are a little annoyed at the sanctioning of this rearranged domestic fixture.

"It is disappointing this match is going on at the same time, for some Aberden and Celtic fans would otherwise have been looking for a game to go to," claimed McLean.

From those thousands who do attend this evening, United are as usual looking for patience and backing.

"A repeat of the 3-0 scoreline from the home leg of our last round tie would do nicely, although the fact goals come, rather than the timing of them, is what matters," he said.

Hajduk are without the banned Zoran Vulic and Stjepan Andriejeseric, and have injury doubts over regulars Jerko Tipuric, Stjepan Deveric and Dragi Setinov.

United from—Thomson, Malpas, Sulley, McInally, Clark, Narey, Gallacher, Milne, Bannon, Sturrock, Redford, Coyne, Beaumont, McKinlay, McGinnis, Bowman.

● There will be no segregation arrangements in force at Tannadice this evening.

However, supporters entering by gates 1-11 on Tannadice Street and 37-42 on Sandeman Street are reminded they will have to leave by exits located in the same areas of the ground.

Hajduk Split have been given the lowdown on United by one of their own players.

Midfielder Dragi Setinov was a member of the Vardar Skopje team that lost to the Tannadice side in last season's competition.

Here's hoping the men from Split are better disciplined than their countrymen. United fans well remember the Tannadice leg of the clash with Vardar when the Slavs had two men ordered off, three booked and their coach sent to the stand.

Setinov participated in that match but is considered doubtful for tonight's game because of injury.

Where did it go? Paul Sturrock has a weighty problem to deal with as he tries to reach a cross ball.

Lifelong fans win trip with United

Two lifelong Dundee United fans are the winners of the Courier/VG competition to follow their favourites to Yugoslavia next week and see at first hand United's attempt to reach the quarter-finals of the U.E.F.A. Cup.

David Wemyss (34) and Graeme Dunbar (27) will fly out next Monday with the United squad and spend three days with the team in Yugoslavia, taking in the crucial third round second leg U.E.F.A. Cup tie against Hajduk Split.

In addition, they will also receive a VG Christmas food hamper and an autographed copy of the 1987 Dundee United calendar.

David, of 12 Lintrathen Gardens, Dundee, has been a United fan since an early age, but his commitments to amateur football in Dundee recently have meant that he sees his favourites rarely.

"I was hoping to get along to the first leg last week, but unfortunately I'm doing a refereeing course at the moment which takes up a lot of my spare time," said David, a bricklayer with Dundee District Council's public works department.

"However, I've seen Hajduk before," he revealed. "When I was on holiday in Dubrovnik last year, Hajduk played the local team in a pre-season friendly and I was quite impressed by them.

"I enjoyed Yugoslavia and am looking forward to going back—particularly with the exchange rate with the dinar being so good at the moment!"

The hamper is consolation for David's wife Wilma for the loss of her husband for a couple of days.

Graeme, of 24 Kilbride Place, Dundee, a self-employed painter and decorator, is a regular attender at Tannadice games and in the past has followed United into Europe.

"I haven't been to many away games since I got married and I've certainly never travelled with the team," said an elated Graeme. "I've been a United supporter since my dad first took me to a game when I was nine—and when he was a Dundee supporter!"

Graeme saw the first leg at Tannadice last week and while feeling United did not play as well as they can, is still confident that they have plenty in hand for the second leg.

"I never believed that I would be seeing both legs of the tie and I'm really looking forward to it," he added.

Meanwhile, the news has one small setback for Graeme—his wife Alison demands that he finishes decorating their home before he is allowed away!

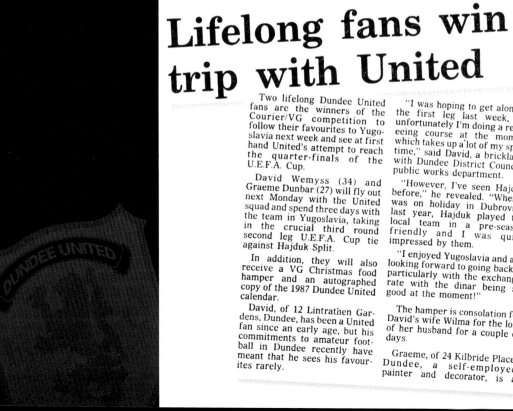

The Yugoslav keeper punches clear, under pressure from Eamonn Bannon, who was injured in the collision and later had to go off.

McInally and Clark set United up

United face a tricky trip to Yugoslavia in a fortnight's time, following their UEFA Cup third-round, first leg clash at Tannadice last night.

Goals from Jim McInally (his first for the club) and John Clark established the kind of lead these seasoned Euro campaigners are capable of progressing on, but the return will be no formality.

Hajduk, when throwing off their defensive shackles, showed enough to suggest they will make it tough in Split on December 10.

Frankly, United were disappointing. The effort and application were there, but they lacked the

By STEVE BRUCE

sparkle which has characterised so many of their finest performances in Europe.

They should make it into the quarter-final draw, however, and by way of a bonus, young Billy McKinlay, on his Euro debut performed well.

Paul Sturrock as usual worked tirelessly and big John Clark—who gets married today—turned in another fine display.

Billy Thomson was called into action early on, clutching a 20-yard grounder from Asanovic.

United retaliated quickly, however, with Peruzovic doing well to block a dangerous Sturrock cross from the bye-line after good work by Milne.

The same combination linked outside Hajduk's area in eight minutes, but this time Pralija gathered Sturrock's centre under pressure from Redford.

Twice in the space of 90 seconds hot-shot John Clark was provided with opportunitie to demonstrate his striking prowess at free-kicks, but on both occasions the keeper was perfectly placed to save.

Clark's first attempt from 30 yards was held by Pralija at the base of his right-hand post and the second, from just outside the area, was also gathered on the line.

In 21 minutes the United centre-half provided Sturrock with a chance when a low shot was deflected by a Yugoslav boot. Sturrock beat Pralija to the loose ball, but the keeper saved his shot and Bannon fired the rebound wide.

Three minutes later Redford and Clark lined-up for another United free-kick, but this time

DUNDEE UNITED 2, HAJDUK SPLIT 0

Clark was a spectator as Redford had a promising crack which the keeper was once more well placed to hold.

In 28 minutes, though, Pralija was finally passed and the blame for United's goal rested squarely on his shoulders.

The big keeper failed to cut out a low cross from Sturrock on the left and Jim McInally was on hand at the back post to turn the ball home.

Four minutes later, just after Hajduk's Asamovic had been booked for dissent, the Yugoslavs had a great chance to equalise when an unkind break of the ball of Beaumont allowed Deveric to take possession and advance on the United goal.

Fortunately Thomson advanced from his charge and bang on the 18-yard line blocked a shot from the winger.

Spurred on by the breakthrough, the Tannadice men stepped up the pressure with Bannon having a header from a McInally centre saved by the keeper and Redford not far off target with another aeriel effort.

Within 90 seconds of the restart, they were two ahead.

The build-up began with Pralija touching over a powerful Redford left-foot volley. From the resultant corner, a Sturrock cross was missed by McKinlay, but not by big John Clark who let rip with his left-peg and the ball flew into the roof of the net.

Hajduk sub Adamovic, who had replaced the injured Cakic during the interval, had his name taken shortly afterwards for running on with the ball after the referee had blown his whistle.

Then United lost the services of Eamonn Bannon with a hip-injury, his replacement being Kevin Gallacher.

Surprisingly the second goal sparked off Hajduk's best spell of the game and on the hour mark they might have pulled one back when Asanovic and Deveric combined to provide Bursace with a header which Thomson did well to save low to his left.

Though well behaved, the visitors had a third player cautioned in 68 minutes when Jarni had his name taken for fouling Gallacher.

United began to re-establish their grip on the game and Malpas was desperately unlucky to have a close-range shot blocked by Pralija after Gallacher had cleverly chipped a Sturrock pass, into his path.

The young substitute tried to find Milne with a cross, but his team-mate was surrounded by four defenders and even when the ball broke kindly, Milne could not connect.

In 75 minutes, Sturrock found himself with only Pralija to beat, but his strong, and seemingly well-placed shot from an angle, was brilliantly turned over by the keeper.

With five minutes remaining, Malpas was booked for fouling Adamovic and, before play could restart, United sent on Coyne for Milne.

Attendance 11,596.

DUNDEE UNITED.—Thomson, Malpas, Beaumont, McInally, Clark, Narey, McKinlay, Milne, Bannon, Sturrock, Redford. Subs—Coyne, Bowman, Gallacher, Sulley, McGinnis.

HAJDUK SPLIT—Pralija, Miljus, Setinov, Jernilnov, Jarni, Celic, Cakic, Peruzovic, Bursac, Asanovic, Deveric. Subs—Varvodic, Drazic, Adamovic, Mije,Veber.

Referee—W. Foeckler (West Germany).

"Ordinary," says McLean

Jim McLean admitted afterwards, "The overall performance was, in my view, ordinary.

"We still have a lot to do over there but 2-0 is a good score, it leaves us slight favourites and the task is within out capabilities."

The Tannadice boss went on reveal he had made a mistake in replacing the injured Eamonn Bannon with Kevin Gallacher. "No disrespect to Gallacher, but I should have sent on a midfield player."

Hajduk coach Serije Kresic commented, "We still have a chance, I think we will win in Split, but whether or not it will be enough to take us through remains to be seen."

"United deserved to win but from my point of view, five of our players were less than 100% fit and we can definitely play better."

Yugoslav sub Zdenko Adamovic will miss the return through suspension thanks to his booking last night.

Hajduk's keeper brings off a flying save to stop a net-bound Sturrock shot.

A home win, no away goals conceded, and well on the way to the quarter-finals. However, that wasn't necessarily enough to satisfy the mercurial manager. Through modern eyes, "ordinary" never looked so good!

Ignore the "experts"

Sir,—Having watched Dundee United for a number of years, I have come to the conclusion that many of our "supporters" know very little about the game of football.

The people concerned do not appreciate the contribution of players like Redford, Milne, Coyne and also Billy Kirkwood, who suffered years of harassment from the "experts" on the terraces and in the stand.

Consequently, Mr McLean should pay no attention to these people, who cumulatively know much less about the game than he does, and he should take comfort in the fact that those of us who do know something of the game, appreciate the effort that he and the players are putting in, to keep a team which is crippled by injuries, on the winning trail.

If it wasn't that the club needs the paying public to turn up in large numbers, I would rather that the moaners stayed at home on a Saturday afternoon, allowing the players to get on with what they are all very good at—keeping the real supporters happy.

Mr A. Holt.

15 Lorimer Street,
Dundee.

Dundee and District Sports Council won the David Narey Trophy in the Dundee United F.C. Supporters Club last night. 60 teams took part in the sports quiz, which was organised as part of the Dundee United and Scotland player's testimonial year.

Sir,—I, it would appear, am one of the United "supporters" Mr Holt reprimanded for daring to criticise certain United players.

Having been a supporter for many years, travelling all over this and other countries supporting my team, I surely have the right to criticise if I see certain players who have not, and will not, reach the high standard to which all United supporters are entitled to expect.

If I happen to think that one of our forwards could not strike a match off a wall (and I do) then I will certainly continue to make my feelings known.

I am indeed glad that Mr Holt thinks he knows something of the game, and look forward to hearing him inform the "supporters" who are obviously not up to scratch just how United are going to remain one of the big guns when it would appear that we are running out of bullets.

Are we to persist in playing men who simply are not good enough, or is it not time to give some younger reserves, in particular Kinnaird, Welsh and, best of all, a born winner, Billy McKinlay, their chance.

Come on, Jim McLean, give these lads a chance—the only way to get experience is to play in the first team and, as far as this supporter is concerned, there are vacancies now!

Tom Cairns.

Hill Street,
Dundee.

Unlucky Hegarty faces a long lay-off again

Injuries continued to plague United as the season reached the halfway point. However, an optimistic McLean was hoping the bad luck would soon be over — and he still had Celtic and the league title in his sights.

"Our injury situation is horrendous," said manager Jim McLean yesterday when disclosing that skipper Paul Hegarty, taken off injured after less than half-an-hour against Motherwell at Fir Park on Wednesday, has a torn groin muscle and could be out of action for six to eight weeks.

Hegarty was, of course, returning after a nine-game absence—apart from a substitute appearance against Dundee—in place of John Clark, who has been in tremendous form since settling down at centre-half.

Why was Clark missing? He was injured—it would be easy to add, of course!—with ankle trouble which also makes him doubtful for the home game against Aberdeen tomorrow.

"Last season we had a back four of Richard Gough, Paul Hegarty, Dave Narey and Maurice Malpas who, between them, missed only six games," said manager McLean.

"This season Gough only played three before departing for Tottenham Hotspur, but Narey (10), Hegarty (12) and Malpas (1) have—at exactly the halfway mark—totalled 23 absences."

Hegarty first suffered groin trouble against Aberdeen. In his comeback as a substitute against Dundee five games later, he over-stretched and the problem recurred. Now it has happened again, with rest the prescribed treatment.

"People say clubs take players back too quickly, but when do you do it?" queried manager McLean.

"Hegarty had stretched and tackled in a try-out, but, in a game played on a very heavy pitch, he first stretched, then had to clear the ball hurriedly and the injury happened.

"The past two games have been played on heavy surfaces and this might have been partly responsible for some of our problems."

By THE SPORTS EDITOR

Maurice Malpas also went off at Fir Park, but, because this was done so early after his thigh knock, he is a possible for the Aberdeen game.

Into the very doubtful category come Eamonn Bannon with a severely bruised hip bone and Paul Sturrock with tendon trouble.

Long-term injury victims Gordon McLeod and John Holt will be in the first or second team pools tomorrow, depending on day-to-day progress with their injuries.

As Hegarty and Malpas went down on Wednesday and substitutes Dave Beaumont ("he had a great game") and Kevin Gallacher ("he looked really sharp") had to go on, manager McLean cracked to two policeman standing in the tunnel, "You had better get yourselves loose!".

"They had a good laugh," he said, "but it really was getting serious."

A bonus for the club has been the sudden emergence—or should it be re-emergence?—of 22-year-old Jimmy Page on the scene.

It was only his third start in the first team last night, but he couldn't have set the seal on that with his first goal for the club at a better place.

He trotted out there on April 28, 1984, with a wonderful future opening out in front of him. Within a minute of the start his leg had been broken.

Since then, other injuries and glandular fever have held him back, but his form against Falkirk last Saturday and Motherwell bode well for the future. From right midfield he is showing, according to his manager, "tremendous application and enthusiasm."

Right now, with injuries ruling the roost, things aren't all that bright.

But if United come out of it all with the bonus of, for instance, Clark and Page proving themselves first team material, then the situation won't all have been bad.

With Paul Hegarty injured again, responsibility for the centre of United defence will fall on the broad shoulders of John Clark. The prospect doesn't seem to worry John, seen at Tannadice getting a helping hand from teammate Ian Redford.

Nothing is certain

It's half-time in the 44-game Premier League season—22 games played, with the exception of Hamilton Accies and Rangers, who have one outstanding.

Celtic have streaked ahead in the title race with 36 points, but I am not alone in believing, with the number of games to go, that they are anything but a certainty.

Take Dundee United manager Jim McLean, for instance.

United, despite a frightening injury list and the loss of players like Richard Gough, Davie Dodds and Billy Kirk-

By THE SPORTS EDITOR

wood, are tailing Celtic relentlessly and are currently five points behind them.

"But," says the United manager, "if we get the same number of points again in the second half of the season I honestly believe we would win the league."

He goes on, "I do not think other clubs, Celtic in particular, even though I appreciate they are without Davie Provan and Tommy Burns, can go further through the season and not be picking up injuries.

"Aberdeen and ourselves have already had the bulk of the serious injuries—Aberdeen early on, us now.

"The bad run has ended for Aberdeen, I hope it soon ends for us, then we can continue to push forward in the league."

Up the road, manager Jocky Scott reflects, "The early part of the season was good. We did well. In the middle part of the 'first half' we developed inconsistency and now we are going through a period where things keep going wrong, where we are making too many mistakes.

"Although it would be easy to put it down to injuries to our influential players, you can't dwell on a fact like that.

"What has happened in the past few weeks has made it harder for us to get into a European place. But, having said that, we just need to get into a run of 10 games without defeat and that would bring us right back into contention.

"And let me remind you that we did this last year and the year before—and in the period of the season still to come."

United injury worries ease

By STEVE BRUCE ||||||||

Dundee United boss Jim McLean was relaxed and confident yesterday as he talked of the task confronting his side in the UEFA Cup return with Hajduk Split—a mood due at least in part to a considerable easing in his injury worries.

United trained at Tannadice prior to departing for Yugoslavia and defenders John Clark and John Holt both participated thus quashing fears over their availability.

And the news of key doubts, Paul Sturrock (tendon), Eamonn Bannon (hip) and Maurice Malpas (thigh) was also better.

"Were I a betting man," revealed the manager, "I'd bet on one of them being fit, one possibly making it and the other being out."

Who falls into which category however is being kept secret meantime.

All three are under the care of physios Andy Dickson and Jim Joyce, who within hours of arriving in Split had turned a hotel bedroom into a treatment room, aided by various machines taken with them from Scotland.

Optimism was the key note of Jim McLean's remarks as he surveyed the match to be played in the magnificent 55,000 capacity Poljud Stadium, drawing on Saturday's 0-0 draw with Aberdeen as evidence of what his side are capable of.

"Are Hajduk a better side than Aberdeen? No way," he said.

"And name a Premier League side who would give us a 2-0 start and beat us?

"We fully deserved the point on Saturday against a Dons side containing seven full internationals.

"And were circumstances to necessitate it I would confidently field the 10 players remaining from that game again.

"Hajduk will be better in the return than they were at Tannadice but as long as we don't set out to defend our advantage we'll be okay.

"It's in our own hands—we can toss it away by losing 3-0 or tuck away till March, a place in the quarter-finals."

Youngster Brian Welsh was called into the party yesterday in place of injured midfielder Gordon McLeod bringing to four, the compliment of teenagers in a 21-strong pool, 11 of whom are aged under 23.

Hajduk are hoping to have midfield maestro Zoran Vulic fit to face the Tangerines.

He missed the first leg through suspension and sustained an injury a week ago in an Olympic trial which forced him out of the weekend defeat by Sloboda Tuzla.

Referee is one of Europe's top whistler's Jan Keiser of Holland.

● While United are in Yugoslavia, Gordon Mcleod and ineligible striker Iain Ferguson will be receiving treatment for injuries from Dundee physio Eric Ferguson.

Iain sustained ankle and shoulders knocks against Aberdeen.

Billy Thomson shows the kind of form that has won him seven caps.

Cup hopes in safe hands

In 450 minutes of European football this season, Billy Thomson has conceeded only two goals, which tends to suggest Hajduk Split face a formidable task in trying to oust Dundee United from the UEFA Cup.

The Tannadice keeper has been in magnificent form as evidenced by that statistic and a tally of 19 shut-outs from 32 matches.

"It's always nice to keep a clean sheet," says Billy. "It gives myself and, just as important, the defence confidence.

"I feel the team has done magnificently this season bearing in mind the injury problems we've had to overcome, particularly at the back."

Billy is approaching tomorrow's match in a happy frame of mind.

"You have to be optimistic about going through," he says. "If we approach the return in a positive way then I don't forsee any problems.

"I don't think Hajduk are as good as Lens, whom we put out in the first-round. Having said that, though, they cannot be underestimated.

"The Yugoslavs looked a competent side at Tannadice and the last thing we want to do is let them start well.

"It's an identical situation to that which confronted us against Vardar Skopje last year.

Hopefully we can again get an early goal to ease the pressure," added the 28-year-old keeper.

Thomson's fine displays have started a campaign for his restoration to the national side, and the player does not hide the fact he desperately wants to add to his tally of seven full caps.

"The fact United are doing so well compensates for being out of the international scene, but I'd be lying if I said missing two World Cups didn't hurt," he said.

"I would dearly love to get back into the Scotland team, but all I can do is keeping playing well and hope Mr Roxburgh picks me."

Hard afternoon ahead

BY STEVE BRUCE IN YUGOSLAVIA

Dundee United this afternoon bid to secure a place in the latter stages of a European competition for the fourth time in their history.

In the magnificent Poljud Stadium, they seek to capitalise on a 2-0 first-leg lead and send Hajduk Split tumbling out of the U.E.F.A. Cup.

The Tannadice men, however, will set about their task minus the services of three vastly-experienced players—Paul Hegarty, Paul Sturrock and Maurice Malpas—each of them either a current or past internationalist.

Sitting in the team's comfortable hotel yesterday afternoon, the Adriatic sea lapping against a breakwater just feet away, manager Jim McLean talked frankly about the injury situation which has hogged his thoughts since the weekend and the selection of a side to do the job.

World Cup man Eamonn Bannon—sidelined since injuring a hip against Hajduk a fortnight ago—is fit and plays.

"We intend fielding him in the middle of the attack, a role in which he did exceptionally well against Craiova in the last round," commented the manager.

"However, fellow casualty Maurice Malpas is a definite non-starter and the best striker Paul Sturrock can hope for, is a place on the bench."

The United boss revealed that, because of the nature of the task confronting his side, he would have dearly loved to have Malpas, Bannon and Sturrock all fit, in that order of preference.

A morning training session at the match venue brought further worry when mid-fielder Jim McInally—who scored in the first leg—reported a groin problem.

"To lose McInally on top of the others would be a ridiculous blow, but the problem is slight and it looks like things will settle down allowing him to play," said the Tannadice supremo.

Jim still hasn't settled on the line-up. Providing McInally is able to play, he'll partner Ian Redford and Jimmy Page in midfield with the front three comprising Milne, Gallacher and Bannon.

Dave Narey and comeback John Holt are certainties in defence, leaving a choice of two from John Clark, Dave Beaumont and Gary McGinnis for the right-back and centre-half roles.

In the normal course of events, Clark will be the obvious choice to partner Narey, however, ankle injuries have interfered with his training over the last ten days and that is worrying the manager.

If Jim McLean is a little concerned over his choice of defenders he has absolutely no doubts over the side's ability to march into the quarter-final draw.

Only twice in the club's history have they surrendered a two-goal advantage in Europe and those painful experiences in Rome and Nis were touched upon yesterday.

"I would be ludicrous for us to be anything but confident in this position," he declared.

"The only thing we must guard against is sitting back and handing Hajduk the initiative.

"To do so would be fatal," he continued. It happened against Roma and Radnicki although, in the latter instance, the referee had a lot to do with what occurred."

Moving onto the subject of whistlers he continued, "Getting a good referee in Europe is vital for there is a greater chance of outside influence affecting them in European competition than in a domestic games."

Not that Tangerines worry too much on that score for today's official, Jan Keiser of Holland, is one of the most-experienced and highly-respected on the continent.

As far as those outside influences are concerned, only 25-30,000 people are expected to attend an arena which holds around twice that number and the stand and terracings are situated well away from the pitch.

Hadjuk will be boosted by the return of 25-year-old former internationalist Zoran Vulic in mid-field.

Vulic is available again having served five match Euro bans by U.E.F.A. following an ordering-off against Waregem during last season's competition.

Coach Sergije Kresic indicated yesterday he would be restoring Stipe Andrijasevic, who also missed the first leg through suspension, to the side

● **The match will be shown live on B.B.C. 2, starting at 3.30.**

but there are suggestions that Jerko Tipuric will play the first 45 minutes with Andrijasevic kept on the bench.

Morale is reportedly low in the Hadjuk camp after four successive defeats and there is talk of squabbles between players.

In broken English coach Kresic commented, "The backing of our supporters has fanatical approach from the players which this occasion demands, could tip the balance in our favour."

It promises to be a hard afternoon for the Tannadice men but so often in the past they've snatched a vital away goal to ease the pressure and, even without Paul Sturrock, are capable of doing so again.

The U.E.F.A. Cup quarter-final draw on January 24 awaits.

United's attack force—Ralph Milne, Kevin Gallacher and Eamonn Bannon.

Boasting a 2-0 lead from the first leg, and with recent experience of defending these kinds of advantages in Europe, McLean made his expectations very clear — it was time to claim a quarter-final place.

Workmanlike effort sees United through

HAJDUK SPLIT 0, DUNDEE UNITED 0 (aggregate 0-2).

Dundee United fought their way into the quarter-finals of the UEFA Cup with a brave display in the Poljud Stadium, Split, yesterday.

The Tannadice men survived several anxious moments in this third-round return before securing a fourth visit to the latter stages of a European competition in five years.

Manager Jim Mclean said afterwards, "Technically, it was a magnificent performance. There were a couple of near things, but you expect that away from home in Europe.

"With several top players out, we had to rely heavily on the experience of such as Bannon, Narey and Thomson but I cannot praise highly enough the effort of everyone."

Narey was superb but so, too, were young lions Dave Beaumont and Gary McGinnis.

No such joy, however, for Hajduk and their coach Sergij Kresic in particular.

Kresic's job was reported to be under threat if his side failed to win this match and judging by the crowd's reaction at time-up, he won't last long.

The home boss was pelted with various objects as he left the dug-out and disgruntled fans lit fires on the terracings.

Four times in the first 25 minutes Hajduk created excellent openings—then squandered each. Chief sinner was international striker Milos Bursac, who missed three of them.

With seven minutes on the clock he was found virtually unmarked at the back post by a swerving Asanovic corner but headed over.

Moments later, winger Deveric capped a fine run down the left with a square pass

STEVE BRUCE reports from Yugoslavia

but Bursac blazed the ball over the bar. Then, when a Celic shot was deflected into the striker's path and he had only Thomson to beat, he headed straight into the United keeper's arms.

Teammate Jeromilov was equally guilty of generosity in front of goal when, from 16 yards out, he glanced a header well wide when picked out, unmarked, by Vulic.

United, forced into their own half for much of the first period, had to wait 22 minutes for their first shot at goal.

McInally's 20-yarder was gathered easily on his line by Pralija but, six minutes from the break, the 30,000 crowd was silenced with a couple of near things.

Centre-half John Clark was in the thick of the action. First he tested Pralija with a 25-yard free-kick which the keeper scrambled round a post, then he got on the end of a Ralph Milne corner kick, only to head over when well placed to do better.

United were seen to better effect as an attacking force after the interval yet needed some stout defending, a degree of good fortune and the assistance of more poor finishing to keep the score-sheet blank.

On three occasions during the second period, Hajduk came desperately close to forcing a breakthrough.

Had they done so in 59 minutes, thanks would have been due to referee Jan Keiser who, throughout, refused to halt play when a United man was hurt.

In this instance, John Clark was clearly toiling with an ankle knock on the far side of the park yet the Dutch whistler refused to allow treatment.

Minus their big centre-half, the Tannadice men lined-up to face an Asanovic corner. Jeromilov stole in on the end of the cross but Gary McGinnis stood his ground at the post and blocked the effort.

Twice in a matter of minutes the increasingly frustrated Slav's were denied, first by the brilliance of Thomson, then by the woodwork.

Andrijasevic couldn't believe it when the keeper launched himself to the left to fingertip his powerful 20-yarder onto the crossbar.

And the Tangerines were lucky to escape when Deveric drifted past McGinnis and beat Thomson only to see his shot come back off the inside of a post.

On the break, however, United gave

Hajduk one or two anxious moments, most notably when Gallacher only just failed to connect with a Holt cross and Narey had a Milne centre taken off his toes.

With the end drawing close, Thomson, under pressure from Jeromilov, failed to punch away a long through ball from

Peruzovic. Fortunately, Narey was lying handy to clear the danger.

After the match, the bitterly disappointed crowd showed the sporting side of their nature with warm applause for the United party, carrying out their now traditional warm down.

A worrying moment for United as Gary McGinnis goes down injured. He was able to resume after treatment.

Hajduk—Pralija; Miljus, Setinov, Andrijasevic, Vulic, Celic, Jerolimov, Peruzovic, Bursac, Asanovic, Deveric. Subs—Varvodic, Drazic, Jarni, Mise, Tipuric.

United—Thomson; McGinnis, Holt, McInally, Clark, Narey, Beaumont, Milne, Bannon, Gallacher, Redford. Subs—Page, Bowman, Coyne, Sulley, McKinlay.

Referee—J. Keiser (Netherlands).

United's win reserves five places in Europe

By THE SPORTS EDITOR

Dundee United didn't only qualify for the quarter-finals of the U.E.F.A. Cup and become Britain's only surviving European representatives by beating Hajduk Split 2-0 on aggregate after Wednesday's third round tie, they also ensured Scotland's continuing five-club representation in Continental competitions.

Had they, like Rangers, failed to get into the next round, Scotland's tally in Europe in two seasons' time would have been four clubs on the basis of points won for success, or perhaps more accurately, lost through failure.

So it wasn't only a blow for the club that was struck in Yugoslavia, it was a blow for the country.

It is worth recording, too, United's record over the last seven Euro campaigns—quarter-final, third round, third round, semi-final, quarter-final, quarter-final. Few can equal that.

Yesterday manager Jim McLean wasn't basking in glory after the goalless draw in Split.

He was too busy planning for the next game—against Clydebank away tomorrow—on the basis that "we have lost vital league points after mid-week European games in the past. We have got to get our feet back on the ground, and quickly."

He did take time out, though, to look back—and forward.

Among the points he made:

★ At last we have a bit of time on our side before the next round in Europe (home and away March 4 and 18, draw on January 24). I am looking forward to having our international players back alongside the younger ones who have come through. We will need our class players back next time.

★ We have plenty of good professionals here but we are looking for two more really class players. When I say "really class" it means if they became available, Celtic, Rangers and some of the big English clubs might get them before we got there, but that won't stop our search.

★ Europe is part and parcel of our club. It fires the supporters that there are. The support is spoiled. They are even allowed to use their season tickets for Europe. It doesn't happen elsewhere. Without Europe people would say we are ham-and-eggers. We aren't.

> "We have lost vital league points after mid-week European games in the past. We have got to get our feet back on the ground, and quickly."

★ We expect to lose money in Europe or break even at best, though we might do all right this time with TV fees coming into it. But we all need Europe, it gets the adrenalin flowing. I hate to think what we would be like without it. No matter who we play we should make money at the quarter final stage.

★ I'd like the weakest team in the quarter final, whoever they are. I'd like to get to the semis—and get the weakest again. I'd also like short travel and the second leg at home!

★ We have had a season far and away better than I expected. Yesterday we had only three of the Premier League-winning team on the park. All credit to coaches Gordon Wallace, Doug Houston, Steve Murray and our scouts—and to the players.

★ The blood is pulsing through the veins of this club—yet it looked like we had been drained

when Davie Dodds, Richard Gough, Wattie Smith, yes and Alex. Taylor, too, among others, left for other places. Then we have had this horrendous run of injuries. To put it another way, it proves that the loss of a few bricks doesn't mean the building has to fall down.

★ No one man could carry this club now. It was a great club to come to with its atmosphere and potential, but now it is far too big to be run by one man, too big compared to before, to when I came here almost exactly 15 years ago.

★ If I walked out on this club now, it would definitely not fall apart. If anyone doesn't believe that let them look back at the blows we have suffered since Davie Dodds announced he was leaving—yet here we are in the quarter-finals in Europe and second top of the league. If the foundations hadn't been solid we would have struggled.

★ Actually, the next two or three years could be the dodgy period. We haven't been getting a sufficient number of youngsters through of the Dave Narey, Andy Gray, John Holt, Ray Stewart quality. We have exciting youngsters on the way again, though—while appreciating that there are no guarantees how they will turn out.

★ Our result was important for Scottish football, yes, but we are selfish and say it was firstly important for Dundee United ... then Scottish football.

★ I will be very, very pleased, as long as I am here, to be part of keeping Dundee United around the top. That does not mean we EXPECT to win trophies. We HOPE to win them, but have no divine right. We are the corner shop competing with the super stores, as our real supporters realise. People say I am pessimistic. That is not being pessimistic, it is being realistic!

With victory over Hajduk Split, United were left flying the flag for Scottish, and British, football. But little did anyone know about what was to come next...

Holt in mystery injury scare

It was a relieved—and mystified—manager Jim McLean, player John Holt and medical staff at Tannadice yesterday (reports THE SPORTS EDITOR).

The player had to be taken from the plane to the team bus at Glasgow Airport in a wheelchair on Wednesday night, feeling sick and dizzy with the pain from an ankle which had mysteriously developed severe swelling.

"It was a real scare—but happily has turned out to be only a scare," said manager McLean yesterday, while Holt's comment after seeing a specialist who gave the all-clear was, "I don't know what happened, but I am glad it seems to have gone."

He has, of course, just returned after an ankle injury, but this was the other ankle and it is being put down to a possible circulation problem. He may even be available for the Clydebank game tomorrow.

The manager is trying a new approach for this one after a European tie.

The players have been told to stay away until Saturday!

"As long as they do a bit of walking and the like they will be all right," said the manager, "but it wouldn't surprise me if most of them come in."

Gary McGinnis took plenty of praise for his performance on Wednesday. His manager commented, "When he has to face a winger he is good. He is getting stronger now, though he still has a bit to go."

Gary suffered not one, but two severed medial ligament injuries. One has been known to end footballers' careers, which is the measure of his bravery and determination.

Lack of success fuels Hajduk crisis

By STEVE BRUCE

Hajduk Split, ousted from the U.E.F.A. Cup by United, are a club in crisis.

They lie seventh in the Yugoslav First Division, which enters its winter shutdown this weekend, and the fans are none too happy, as evidenced by the near-riot which occurred at the end of Wednesday's game.

Although 30,000 watched that U.E.F.A. Cup third-round match, the average gate is down to 15,000, which isn't sufficient to keep the club in a healthy financial position.

Hajduk, Yugoslavia's longest-established team, employ 72 people just to maintain their magnificent 55,000-capacity Poljud Stadium and need an annual income of around £1,000,000 to stay in the black.

The root of Hajduk's problems lies in their proud history.

Nine times champions and domestic cup winners on seven occasions, the fans have come to expect success—a feeling heightened by a proud record in Europe.

However, it is two years since the club last secured a trophy and you have to look back to 1979 to find their last title triumph.

Then, to cap it all, during this summer, star players Zoran and Zlatko Vujovic and Blaz Sliskovic were transferred to French clubs.

"Things have gone from bad to worse as far as the supporters are concerned," explained a leading Yugoslav sports journalist.

"They gave the club one last chance, against Dundee United, hence the larger crowd but the reaction at the end of the game showed just how serious the situation is."

Coach Sergije Kresic, who took charge only nine months ago, is reputedly set for the chop, with suggestions that his predecessor, Tomislav Iviv, would return.

However Iviv, in Split this week for the United game, made it clear he has no wish to return to the coaching side of things after an unsuccessful spell at Anderlecht in Belgium.

Brilliance v Barcelona

Success against Hajduk Split meant United should have almost three months to concentrate on domestic matters before returning to thoughts of Europe — but the result of the quarter-final draw changes all that.

Once again, Jim McLean's wishes are ignored — but few among the United support are complaining this time. Rather than facing the weakest side left in the draw, as McLean had hoped, the draw on January 24 pairs United with one of the world's biggest clubs, FC Barcelona.

Led by English manager Terry Venables, and with household names Gary Lineker and Mark Hughes newly signed to lead their attack, it is a tie that immediately becomes the talk of British football and sparks pandemonium in Dundee as fans scramble to ensure they secure precious tickets.

Finally, United can rely on a bumper pay day for their European exploits — but they do all they can to reward their most loyal fans.

The club announce a voucher scheme, with McLean declaring: "The most important factor is that the regular Dundee United supporter is safeguarded."

The coverage also breaks out of The Courier's sports pages, with the news teams helping to tell one of the biggest stories in the city for years.

An international match between England and Spain takes on extra significance for United fans, as they see Gary Lineker score four goals against his adopted country. Ominous stuff.

United's players also seem to respond to the excitement, embarking on a remarkable run of victories in January and February that reignites their league challenge and sends them into the fourth round of the Scottish Cup.

Time, then, for McLean to try to bring everyone back to terra firma by insisting ahead of the first leg at Tannadice: "It is not the biggest game that we have been involved in — it is one of the bigger games."

He adds: "Title winning day at Dens (in 1983) was a bigger game. Manchester United (UEFA Cup in 1984) was a bigger game. Roma (European Cup semi-final in 1984) was a bigger game. Cup finals are big games."

Did he really mean it?

Only he will know, but McLean's calmness amid the pressure cooker atmosphere helps United to a first-leg victory in a "Tannadice fiesta" witnessed by over 21,000 fans.

Perhaps inevitably, United's domestic form dips and they can only draw against Clydebank and Dundee in the league before scraping a replay against Forfar in the Scottish Cup four days before Barca Part II in the Camp Nou.

Is McLean fazed? Not a bit of it.

The massed ranks of media can hardly believe how the manager of a club the size of United can be so at home on such a grand stage, prompting one to describe him as "stunningly brilliant".

Hours before the match kicks off, McLean declares: "If we play to our form ... there is no way we will go out."

He is proved right...

Barcelona will be United's biggest earner

By The Sports Editor

Barcelona.... The very name conjures up visions of a football club steeped in tradition, and rolling in money.

Six million pounds bought two English League players alone—Gary Lineker and Mark Hughes—last summer. Hughes, of course, having played for Manchester United against Dundee United in the same competition two years ago and scoring the first goal in the second game.

And as the England and Wales internationalists were wrested from two of Britain's richest and greatest clubs, Everton and Manchester United, the true extent of the Spanish club's size becomes evident.

Their manager is also English—Terry Venables, capped at every level by England, but never quite a player in the Bobby Charlton, Bobby Moore category at full international level, though then, as now, a deep thinker on the game.

Last season he could have had the Costa del Sol as a present he was so popular. This season? Mutterings that his team isn't attack-minded enough despite the massive expenditure on Lineker and Hughes are growing.

Now, Barcelona have been drawn to face Dundee United, Britain's only surviving European representatives, in the quarter final of the U.E.F.A. Cup at Tannadice on March 4 and the breathtaking Nou Camp Stadium on March 18.

The United players, directors and staff heard the draw in their team bus on the way back from the Hibs game on Saturday.

Gary Lineker and Mark Hughes in action.

The players had earlier been told by manager Jim McLean, in the dressing room after the Hibs game, not to comment on the draw, no matter who the opposition turned out to be.

They abided by this ruling yesterday, refusing politely numerous Press requests for comment.

Presumably, the manager, (also unavailable yesterday, but having said on Saturday night that he was delighted with the draw though he had wanted the away leg first and hoping that history would repeat itself) believes that, with so many weeks to go to the games, there are more important immediate issues to concern everyone—such as winning Scottish Cup ties and keeping going with their very real challenge for the Premier League title.

Distractions such as too much talk about the U.E.F.A. Cup tie could knock the club off course in these other directions.

At the least the tie is a tremendous event for everyone connected with the club to look forward to.

The reaction of director Doug Smith, who played in the first-ever United Euro tie against Barcelona in October and November, 1966, was, "From the point of view of drawing power it is probably the best tie we could have had.

"When we played them it was our first time in Europe and we didn't know what to expect. Now, we have one of the most experienced Euro teams of them all and I believe we are capable of beating anyone on our game."

Just to refresh your memory—United played away first those 21 years ago, winning 2-1 with Hainey and Seeman (penalty) goals. In the second leg they won 2-0 through Mitchell and Hainey...and among the crowd on the terracing was Dundee player Jim McLean, now, of course, in charge at Tannadice.

It was called the Fairs Cup then and they went out 3-1 on aggregate to Juventus in the next round, though winning the second leg at home 1-0 via a Dossing goal.

United's team for the first leg against Barcelona—Davie, Miller, Briggs, Neilson, Smith, Wing, Seeman, Hainey, Mitchell, Gillespie, Persson. For the second leg it was—Davie, Miller, Briggs, Neilson, Smith, Wing, Seeman, Gillespie, Mitchell, Hainey, Persson.

As a final point, United have always claimed they have only made real money out of two European ties—those against Roma and Manchester United. They will assuredly make a considerable amount out of this one.

There's talk already of £100,000. When you consider television coverage, trackside advertising and a guaranteed full house at Tannadice, that might not be too far off the mark.

No British club will ever be a Barcelona in financial terms, but if United then win through to the semi-final, they will certainly have found Europe at last paying off in a big way and their already high standing in the game in Continental eyes enhanced even further.

Will his wishes be granted?

Dundee United manager Jim McLean has three wishes he would like granted at the U.E.F.A. Cup quarter-final draw being made in Cologne tonight (reports STEVE BRUCE).

The Tannadice boss wants—1 United paired with the weakest side remaining in the competition; 2 The first leg away from home; 3 A draw requiring the minimum amount of travel.

While a pairing with Barcelona or Inter Milan would be financially lucrative, McLean is happy to leave meeting either until the semi-final stage.

Drawing old foes Borussia Munchengladbach, Gothenburg—who like the Germans are in the middle of their winter shutdown, Guimares of Portugal, or Austria's Svarovski Tyrol would likely suit United.

The Tannadice club, as is the norm, will not be represented at this evenings draw.

The remaining UEFA Cup combatants are—Dundee United, Inter-Milan, Barcelona, Torino, Borussia Munchengladbach, Gothenberg, Guimares and Svarovski Tyrol.

U.E.F.A. Cup
DUNDEE UNITED v. BARCELONA (Spain).

Borussia Moenchengladbach (West Germany) v. Vitoria Guimaraes (Portugal).

Torino (Italy) v. Swarovski Tyrol (Austria).

Gothenburg (Sweden) v. Internazionale Milan (Italy).

Cup-Winners' Cup
Real Zaragoza (Spain) v. Vitosha Sofia (Bulgaria).

Malmo (Sweden) v. Ajax Amsterdam (Netherlands).

Bordeaux (France) v. Torpedo Moscow (Soviet Union).

Lokomotiv Leipzig (East Germany) v. Sion (Switzerland).

European Cup
Bayern Munich (West Germany) v. Anderlecht (Belgium).

Dynamo Kiev (Soviet Union) v. Besiktas Istanbul (Turkey).

Red Star Belgrade (Yugoslavia) v. Real Madrid (Spain).

Porto (Portugal) v. Broendbyernes (Denmark).

Ties to be played on March 4 and March 18.

Hegarty comeback could be delayed

By STEVE BRUCE

Dundee United aim to step up their championship challenge at Douglas Park tonight.

Victory over relegation-threatened Hamilton—a feat they have already achieved twice this season—would move the Tannadice men to within one point of second-top Rangers and within three of leaders Celtic, with a game in hand over the latter.

Watching them attempt to increase the pressure on the Old Firm duo will be a representative of U.E.F.A. Cup opponents Barcelona.

The Spanish giants are sending a spy to run the rule over United, despite the fact their trip to Tannadice for the first-leg is five weeks away.

United add skipper Paul Hegarty, Chris Sulley and Gordon McLeod to the 13 involved in the 2-0 defeat of Hibs.

Hegarty's planned return to first team duty, however, is in jeopardy because of a calf muscle injury.

Midfielder Eamonn Bannon is also doubtful with a thigh knock and a decision on both will be made this morning.

United's last visit to Douglas Park, on September 20, resulted in a 5-1 win with Hegarty (2), Paul Sturrock and Iain Ferguson (2) the men on target.

Two months later, they followed up with a 3-0 victory at Tannadice—Ferguson and Sturrock again getting on the score-sheet, along with John Clark.

Manager Jim McLean rates the five-goal performance as his side's best of the season so far and is looking for them to complete a hat-trick of wins over Accies.

Hamilton, yesterday returned from a three-day break in Blackpool and their line-up is unlikely to vary much from that which gained a morale boosting victory over St Mirren at the weekend.

United from—Thomson, Kirkwood, Malpas, McInally, Clark, Narey, Ferguson, Gallacher, Bannon, Sturrock, Redford, Beaumont, Kinnaird, McLeod, Hegarty, Sulley.

Added to the United squad which was at Easter Road are Paul Hegarty, Chris Sulley and Gordon McLeod.

Ticket rush on ice for now

By THE SPORTS EDITOR

The switchboard at Tannadice has been red hot with calls and anyone with even the vaguest connection with Dundee United is already being inundated with requests.

The target is tickets for the home leg of the UEFA Cup quarter final against Barcelona on March 4 (the second leg is a fortnight later).

Right now, though, there are no tickets and no information on when they will be on sale, how much they will cost, or anything else.

The United board will meet this week to thrash out the details in relation to a game that is undoubtedly an attraction to rival the best ever seen in Dundee, but which is still five weeks away . . . and with other vital Premier League and Scottish Cup games between now and then.

I believe the system adopted for the sale of tickets will, largely, be a voucher one, with attendance at more than the odd game the qualification.

But all will be revealed once the directors have finalised their plans. All manager—and director—Jim McLean would say yesterday was, "The most important factor is that the regular Dundee United supporter is safeguarded."

He was equally reticent over discussing the tie itself, bearing out in the process the comment I made yesterday on his trying to have everyone at Tannadice concentrate on one game at a time, especially as these games could, if won, mean United pushing ahead in the Scottish Cup and increasing their challenge for the Premier League title.

"Our players could have been excused if their minds had strayed to the European Cup draw during Saturday's game with Hibs," he said, "but they stuck to their task and won two valuable points.

"The attitude of concentrating on the game in hand is vital and I sincerely hope we can continue to do this.

"I must emphasise that we are not being awkward. I will say what has to be said at the appropriate times.

"The players will be told to act normally in the sense that the next game, no matter who we are playing against, is the most important—especially after the way they set themselves up in the league with the Hibs result on Saturday.

"As the season progresses every game becomes more important with the most vital one right now being the away league game against Hamilton on Wednesday night.

"Then it will be the turn of the home cup tie with Airdrie on Saturday.

"We simply do not have room to let our thoughts stray from the tasks in hand as they come up."

What United will plan is a visit or two to watch Barcelona.

But, strangely enough, there might not be the urgency in this there would be had the opposition been relatively unknown.

Barcelona are so well documented, their players so well known, their television coverage so regular that it would be difficult for them to change much.

"We will watch them," said manager McLean, "exactly as we watch any other team. We will have no more than a normal dossier on them."

So now it is on to the Hamilton game tomorrow night with Paul Hegarty still doubtful with his calf injury, but also still progressing, Eamonn Bannon suffering from a thigh knock and young Billy McKinlay a bruised ankle.

"The return of John Clark on Saturday gave us a boost, the return of Paul Hegrty would give us an even bigger boost—and he is very close to that," said the manager.

He admits to being "just as delighted" with the choice of three United youngsters for the Scotland under-18 team to play Wales at Tannadice on February 3.

"The present is important for a club, but so is the future—and young players are our future," he said, announcing the threesome as Alan Preston, Scott Kopel and Paddy Connelly.

Voucher plan for regulars

Dundee United yesterday announced plans to give Tannadice regulars a discount on tickets prices for the glamour U.E.F.A. Cup quarter-final clash with Barcelona on March 4 (writes STEVE BRUCE).

Vouchers are to be issued at each of the next three home matches, against Airdrie, Falkirk and Motherwell and fans posessing all three vouchers will be entitled to purchase a ticket for the Euro tie at a reduced rate.

United stressed, however, the discount will only be given to holders of all three vouchers.

No vouchers will be issued at the away end of the ground or the stand.

Prices for the clash with the Spanish giants are expected to be revealed this weekend.

Meanwhile, the players who faced Barcelona in United colours 20 years ago are being asked to contact Tannadice secretary Anne Diamond.

The men involved are to be invited to watch the home leg as guests of the club.

United's line-up in the matches that achieved the 4-1 win on aggregate over the Spanish aces was—Sandy Davie; Tommy Millar, Jimmy Briggs; Tommy Neilson, Doug Smith, Lennart Wing; Finn Seemann, Dennis Gillespie, Ian Mitchell, Billy Hainey, Orjan Persson.

Dundee United were suddenly at the centre of a football circus — and everyone wanted to be involved.

Securing a big pay day while ensuring the most loyal fans did not miss out became a key focus at Tannadice.

United reveal prices for European glamour tie

Dundee United yesterday announced a massive rise in prices for their UEFA Cup quarter-final clash with Barcelona on March 4 but at the same time, revealed a large discount for regular Tannadice attenders (reports STEVE BRUCE).

Any supporter possessing the special vouchers, which are to be issued at each of United's next three home matches, will be able to purchase a ground ticket for the glamour Euro tie for only £4—a saving of £6.

Non-voucher holders, however, will have to pay £20 for a stand ticket and £10 for entry into the ground . . . that is four times the normal admission price to a domestic match.

United feel they have come up with a square deal for loyal fans and there is no doubt that £4 is a bargain price for the clash with the Spanish giants.

By way of comparison, two years ago, the cost of entry to the European Cup tie with Roma was £10 (stand), £5 (ground) and that same season, north-east neighbours Aberdeen charged up to £8.50 for a Cup Winners Cup semi-final against Porto, without any discount for regular fans.

There will be no additional reduction in prices for Barcelona's visit for O.A.P.'s and juveniles but by way of compensation, the club are to allow youngsters and pensioners to enter the ground for the Premier League fixture with Mothmier League fixture with Motherwell on February 14, free of charge.

Immediately after that match and on Monday 16, tickets for the UEFA Cup tie will be on sale to voucher holders. The selling of tickets at full price will commence the following day.

The first of the three vouchers are to be issued at this afternoon's Scottish Cup tie with Airdrie but only at turnstiles permitting entry into the areas of Tannadice reserved for home supporters and the main stand and those gates will close at 3.30 p.m.

That should ensure a large turnout, which could have a marked affect on the attendance at Dens where Dundee's match with East Fife kick's off at 2 p.m.

Barcelona tickets go on sale tonight

Dundee United's loyal supporters are again to be rewarded in the sale of tickets from tonight for the eagerly-awaited U.E.F.A. Cup quarter-final first leg clash against Barcelona at Tannadice on March 4.

The fans who received discount vouchers for attending recent home games will be given the added priority of buying the previous briefs for covered areas of the ground for the match against Terry Venables' team.

Ground tickets to holders of all three vouchers, distributed to fans who attended the matches against Airdrie (cup) and Falkirk (league), together with today's league match against Motherwell, can be purchased from tonight at the discounted price of £4 each.

At 5 p.m., after the ground has been emptied of spectators, voucher-holders are invited to re-enter and buy tickets from the canteen at the corner of the ground from where they want to watch the match.

The exception is for tickets on sale at the uncovered away (east) end's canteen. Tickets for sale there will be for the covered (west) or 'shed' end.

Tickets for the two pitch-side enclosures, at the largely-covered stand side and the covered north side, will also be on sale tonight from the Dundee United Supporters Club offices in Tannadice Street in addition to the nearest canteens.

Voucher-holders who are unable to queue tonight will be given the chance of buying the tickets again on Monday from the stand canteen.

All unsold tickets for non-voucher holders for all parts of the stadium, at full prices of £10 for the ground and £20 for the stand, will go on sale at the stand canteen from Tuesday.

Another important game on the horizon for Dundee United is next Saturday's Scottish Cup fourth round tie at Brechin.

The capacity of Glebe Park has been reduced to 3200 for the match and entry will be by ticket only. The briefs allocated to Tannadice will go on sale at the ticket office from Wednesday.

A United worst—McLean

Back in 1974, Dundee United were hosts to Airdrie in the Scottish Cup. Attendance was just under 6000 (**reports THE SPORTS EDITOR**).

The two met again at Tannadice in the League Cup eight years ago—attendance 5750.

United themselves reckon the hard core home support these days to be around 6000.

So all the figures point to the fact that of the 9169 people (receipts £15,846) who watched United and Airdrie draw 1-1 in their third round Scottish Cup tie at Tannadice on Saturday, some 2000—allowing an Airdrie travelling support of 1000-plus—had returned, probably after a long absence, to get voucher No. 1 for the U.E.F.A. Cup-tie against Barcelona on March 4.

Without exception, they and the basic 6000 must be hoping for a lot better performance than this on the night—not to mention in Wednesday's replay and every other game to come!

Manager Jim McLean certainly is. His after-match comment was, "In all the time I have been manager here, that is as bad as any United team has played and the most disappointed I have probably ever been by a performance."

He went on, "There is nothing good in the whole game I could talk about from our point of view. Airdrie battled well, but that is exactly what we expected."

After briefly mentioning the difficulty of trying to play skilful football on a hard, bouncy surface, he commented, "But there is still something far wrong in a performance like that from a team still in a European competition.

"Airdrie came out of the game with all the credit."

Before the kick-off, former world-class referee Bobby Davidson, now an Airdrie director, said to me—"See you at the replay."

After it, Ian MacMillan, one of the greatest ex-Airdrie players, later to become the "wee Prime Minister" in a great Rangers' team, said, "United are class, but we did talk on the bus on the way up of a draw and we did deserve it."

Former Dundee stalwart John McCormack, now the Airdrie skipper, chipped in with, "We're in the promotion race and wanted a test against a top Premier League team. We aren't surprised we did so well. We can battle a bit you know."

Last season, Kilmarnock drew 0-0 with United before losing 1-0 at home. Now Airdrie have proved, for the umpteenth time in football history, just how true the cliche is that "the cup is a great leveller."

The actual game? Scrappy, the ball treated like a hot potato, little flowing football on display.

Airdrie kept grafting away to equalise a Gallacher strike in 43 minutes, when his header rocketed off defender Lindsay to completely wrong-foot 'keeper Martin.

Otherwise, Martin was magnificent, which couldn't be said of Billy Thomson in the 58th minute. He made one of his very, very few mistakes this season when he had the ball in his hands, but lost it when challenged by Lawrie.

It broke to McCabe, who lashed it past Malpas on the goal line.

United protested that Thomson had been fouled, but the well-positioned referee awarded a goal.

The defence, though stretched at times, didn't do much wrong otherwise, but up front the various permutations of Gallacher, Ferguson and Sturrock (who should have finished the game in 55 minutes but was too deliberate with hi shot, which Martin cleared wit his feet) were as uncertain ar ineffective as they were pos tive and dangerous against Hi last week.

The midfield was so bu battling with the lively Aird midfield, that they seldom l the room or time to control game.

Substitutions were Wa and McKinnon for Hughes Lindsay for Airdrie; Beaur for McKinlay for United.

Lineker hands out warning

By THE SPORTS EDITOR

Dundee United coach Gordon Wallace ran the rule over Barcelona in their Spanish League game with Real Madrid on Saturday night, which Barcelona won 3-2, thanks to a Gary Lineker hat-trick, in front of a 115,000 crowd.

It means Barcelona are now three points clear of Real at the top of the Spanish First Division.

When the United coach files his report for manager Jim McLean and his technical staff to study, it will add to an increasing dossier being built up on the Spaniards by United.

A compilation video of three of Barcelona's games is already in United's possession and a further video of a full game will soon be handed over by a friend of the club.

● On the ticket situation regarding the home game . . . those who hold three vouchers will have the Saturday night after the Motherwell fixture and the Monday following it to pick up their tickets in exchange for their vouchers.

Any tickets left after this go on general sale from the Tuesday.

What price a match against one of the world's biggest clubs, and one whose talismanic English striker was the World Cup's top scorer just months earlier? Well, in 1987 that price was the grand sum of £10 (or £20 for the posh seats) — and United still faced accusations of cashing in!

Fly to Barcelona with Dundee United

DUNDEE UNITED play Barcelona in the U.E.F.A. Cup fourth round second leg match on Wednesday, March 18, in the fabulous 120,000-capacity Nou Camp stadium in the Spanish city.

And two lucky "Courier" readers will be flying out to Spain with the team to see the match—absolutely FREE!

In conjunction with VG Food-stores, United's sponsors, we're offering two seats on the team's aircraft, three night's accommodation with breakfast and evening meal and, of course, tickets for the match.

The winners will join the official party at Tannadice for the trip to Glasgow Airport on Monday, March 16.

The party will fly direct to Barcelona and return to Dundee on March 19.

This competition is limited to those aged 16 and over.

All you have to do to enter is find in the wordsquare the following places where United have played in Europe:

Stockholm, Manchester, Dublin, Neuchatel, Lens, Split, Eindhoven, Bremen.

Once you have found them—and remember, they can be written up, down, backwards, forwards or diagonally—draw a line round them with a pen and send your entries to Dundee United Competition, "The Courier," Bank Street, Dundee, DD1 9HU.

The competition closes first post on Saturday, February 28. The winners will be the senders of the first two correct entries opened after that date.

S	T	O	C	H	O	L	T	E	D	A	J	M	N
D	U	N	R	D	E	I	U	I	N	I	A	E	W
E	S	T	E	B	L	P	G	E	M	W	U	I	A
I	P	J	T	P	S	T	M	B	D	C	T	N	G
N	L	A	S	N	C	E	S	N	H	O	B	D	T
D	T	W	E	A	R	W	D	A	S	T	T	H	A
H	P	B	H	B	S	I	T	I	A	L	D	O	B
V	T	I	C	A	Y	E	F	W	M	J	U	V	T
E	O	T	N	I	L	B	U	D	O	I	G	E	H
N	E	P	A	I	R	E	F	E	U	F	N	N	G
T	L	U	M	O	F	R	N	T	S	B	F	T	A
M	L	O	H	K	C	O	T	S	T	E	L	R	F
A	N	T	M	I	O	R	B	W	K	S	W	N	T
F	W	M	B	A	O	R	N	T	S	I	E	L	I

NAME ....

ADDRESS ....

.... Postcode ....

Employees of D. C. Thomson & Co., Ltd., and their immediat relatives cannot enter this competition.

No cash alternative will be offered.

Barcelona tie will be on TV

Following yesterday's near sell-out of tickets for the glamour visit of Barcelona next month, Dundee United last night confirmed that the match will be televised—but not necessarily live.

Club chairman George Fox said there would definitely be highlights of the game shown in Scotland and England, but he made it clear that no decision would be made on live coverage in Scotland until the board has met to discuss the matter.

He added, however, that the Tannadice leg will be shown live around Barcelona, with only around 250 Spanish supporters expected to make the trip to Scotland.

Almost 17,000 tickets were available for sale to United supporters.

The ground capacity is 22,000, but under U.E.F.A. conditions 5% of that must be left vacant to comply with their safety regulations. The club has several thousand season-ticket holders.

The club offices opened 15 minutes early yesterday, at 8.30 a.m., and remained open over an hour later than usual, until 6 p.m., to accommodate supporters.

When they closed last night, under 1000 tickets were still to be sold—only a handful of those for the stand, despite the £20 price tag on tickets for that part of the stadium.

By the time the box office opened, a queue stretched from the ground to Arklay Street—headed by three intrepid souls determined not to miss out on one of local football's great occasions.

Brian Deans, Andy Keenan and Donald Cameron arrived at Tannadice at 11.30 p.m. on Monday armed with sleeping-bags in a bid to fight off the cold.

The reaction of the fans to the tie looks to have vindicated

Mr Fox

United's decision to charge £10 a head for ground tickets and £20 for the stand.

The decision had met with some criticism, despite the introduction of vouchers for those attending the last three home games which reduced the price to £4.

There was no limit to the number of tickets each individual could purchase and the demand was highlighted by some supporters buying as much as £100 worth at a time.

This is going to be a hectic week for the office at Tannadice.

As well as the anticipated last-minute rush for the remaining tickets for the U.E.F.A. Cup tie, today tickets also went on sale for Saturday's Scottish Cup tie with Brechin with demand again expected to outstrip supply—particularly since United have been allocated only 2600 tickets for tiny Glebe Park.

Narey is on a busy hat-trick

In the space of five days, beginning on Saturday, Dundee United captain Dave Narey has three of the biggest engagements of his life.

First, at Pittodrie in four days' time, he will be the linchpin as Dundee United strive to maintain their very real challenge for the Scottish Premier League title.

In another four days he will captain the last British team left in European competition against one of the world's biggest clubs, Spanish cracks and current league leaders Barcelona.

In the first game he will probably face his former team-mate Davie Dodds, in the second, England's goal-scoring sensation Gary Lineker.

But being "Big Dave" he will take that in his stride—which can't be said for the engagement in between.

That is his testimonial dinner in Dundee's Angus Hotel on Sunday.

Before principal speakers Andy Cameron, Archie McPherson, Bob Valentine, Craig Brown and United manager Jim McLean have their say, chairman Vic Herd will introduce Dave—and I can tell you the few words he has to deliver at this point will have caused him more worry than all the great strikers he has faced in over 600 games for United put together.

Not that he doesn't appreciate the praise that has been heaped on him as a player over the years—he is the most capped Tannadice star ever—but he is, without doubt, one of the most private of the thousands of players I have known.

He isn't unsociable, but is his own man with his own way of life. His manager has described him as the model professional—and he should know!

By THE SPORTS EDITOR

He trains as hard for a Forfarshire Cup tie as he does for a game against Brazil in the World Cup—and he has played in both.

This season, his long-time partnership with Paul Hegarty, at the centre of United's defence, has been broken with both having suffered injuries after years of never missing a game.

But on his return he took the new situation in his stride and, yet again, one immaculate performance has followed another. I once described him as a "Rolls Royce of a player". I have never had reason to change that opinion.

"I never, ever want to be put in the situation of saying who is the best player I have ever had, because there have been many, but Dave Narey automatically goes into the top group," said manager Jim McLean yesterday.

"I have always said and still say that he is one of the Scottish players who could play for Brazil and not look out of place.

"If he has a fault it is that he doesn't stamp the authority he has on games. He seems always to play within himself. If you run him against the slowest player on the staff he will beat him by a yard. Run him against the fastest and he will again beat him by a yard.

"In other words he does everything necessary, whereas if he really pushed himself he would beat the slower man by ten yards."

On Sunday night, however, Dave really will have to push himself.

Tickets are still on sale for the testimonial dinner, but are going fast and an assembled company of 400 is expected.

With excitement building, The Courier sought the views of Barcelona's "forgotten man" Steve Archibald. He revealed Scottish sides were rarely covered in Spanish media.

However, the Spaniards would soon know all about the likes of Dave "Rolls Royce" Narey.

The forgotten man of Barcelona

Former Scotland striker Steve Archibald could have been playing a vital role in Rangers' revival this season had Ibrox player-manager Graeme Souness succeeded in a bid to end his continental exile.

Instead, Steve will remain Barcelona's forgotten man when Terry Venables' side lines up to face Dundee United in the first leg of the U.E.F.A. Cup fourth round tie at Tannadice on Wednesday week.

In fact, the ex-Aberdeen star will not even be in the stand to watch the match. He'll be sitting at home in Spain watching on television.

Archibald, when I spoke to him at England's team headquarters in Madrid for this week's friendly international against Spain, revealed "Rangers were among several clubs who have made offers for me this season.

"I'd have been delighted to talk

terms with them. What they have done for Scottish football has been remarkable.

"But the deal never got off the ground. Terry Venables has refused to let me go."

Since the Spanish league leaders signed Gary Lineker and Mark Hughes last summer, Archibald has been forced to take a back seat. The rule which limits the number of foreign players to two per team has left him as the odd man out, and he admits the prospects of a recall are not good.

"It's no secret that I've tried to find another club, and offers have also come from England and Belgium, but the manager has ruled that out.

"It's not the ideal situation, but there's nothing I can do. The decision has been made and I can't change that."

Barcelona's coup in signing the English and Welsh duo has inevitably led to them stealing Archibald's thunder. He'd been a big hit with the Catalan club and is still popular among their legions of fanatical fans.

However, he is philosophical about the spotlight's recent change in direction.

By A SPECIAL CORRESPONDENT

He goes on, "I had the thunder when we were winning the league and getting to the European Cup final. Now it is Gary and Mark's turn.

"The ironic thing is that they were bought partly because I was injured a lot last season and the club didn't want to take any risks. But now I'm as good as new and can't get into the team.

"Mark, in particular, has experienced early problems in settling down here.

"It's hard enough fitting in at a new club, but 10 times more difficult when you are playing in another country.

"However, when you pay £5 million for two new players, you have to play them."

Meanwhile, Archibald's main difficulty is staying match-fit.

"Although I'm still a member of the senior squad during training sessions, I'm not playing any matches and I can't even travel with the team to watch them play.

"We have a reserve side in Barcelona, Athletic, which plays in the Spanish second division, and I played a couple of matches for them earlier this season to keep my fitness topped up.

"But the club quickly put a stop to that. They considered it too dangerous. When a foreign player plays at that level, opponents do a bit more to try to stop him and things become just too physical."

Steve has been keeping in close touch with the football scene in Scotland and warns that the Barcelona players will have done plenty of homework on their Dundee United opponents, although David Narey and company will be an unknown quantity as far as the Spanish fans are concerned.

He says, "Despite their good record in European competitions during the last few years, little is known about them here.

"The media in Spain tend to concentrate heavily on English clubs when they cover football in Britain. The Scottish sides are given little publicity."

Trying to strengthen pool

By THE SPORTS EDITOR

The average attendance at the three games which qualified Dundee United fans for vouchers towards the purchase of tickets for the home U.E.F.A. Cup-tie against Barcelona on March 4 was 9305, some 3000 up on what might have been expected from visits by Airdrie, Falkirk and Hamilton in my estimation.

This has delighted United manager Jim McLean, who obviously hopes gates of that level will continue "the crowd created a great atmosphere for all three games."

He is also disappointed, however, "that, though we won two of the games and drew the other we did not send them away happy with our performances."

He went on, "The visiting teams made it awkward for us, but that is to be expected.

"What we did not do was achieve the standard of play of which we are capable and, therefore, I am disappointed for the supporters."

Having said that, he then admitted to an even bigger disappointment.

"I feel that people will think that, because things are going well in the sense of a winning run, we are not needing to buy.

"In fact, the past few weeks was when we needed quality players added to the strength, but we found it impossible to get them.

"We are trying again and again to build an even stronger pool of players but haven't so far been successful.

"The search will go on both to help the players we have here already and to show our supporters how intent we are on maintaining and improving standards.

"But we are being knocked back by Scottish clubs, among others—and that,

Injury victims Ian Redford, Billy Thomson and Iain Ferguson.

believe it or not, has a good side in that it proves there is ambition to improve by many clubs up here.

"What I am looking for isn't players who will be useful to us in the short term, although I don't dismiss them out of hand. "The real search is for players who will serve this club well over a period of years—and they are difficult to find, as more than us are finding out."

Turning to the more immediate situation, the manager commented that just when it seemed they had "turned the corner" with injuries, they were now hit by a run of illness and further injury.

Ian Redford, for instance, suffered a knee gash on Saturday which required five stitches; Billy Thomson has a shoulder knock which caused him to pull out of the Scotland get-together prior to the Eire game, and Iain Ferguson a groin strain.

Thomson and Ferguson should be ready for Saturday and the cup-tie against Brechin City, however.

Paul Hegarty is making "no progress at all and it looks as if he has no chance now of playing against Hearts reserves at Tynecastle on Wednesday afternoon."

Paul Sturrock is fit and could have played on Saturday, "but until he gets the 'spark' back in his play, younger players are being given their opportunity and Paul Kinnaird and Billy McKinlay have shown up well," said the manager.

● Tickets for the home game against Barcelona, price £10 and £20, go on general sale today at Tannadice (9 a.m.-6 p.m.) and daily until sold out there, and at VG Foodstores in Byron Street, Fintry Road, St Boswell's Terrace and Claypotts Road, Dundee.

Tomorrow tickets for the Scottish Cup-tie at Brechin on Saturday are on sale at Tannadice.

Hegarty may miss home leg

Time is running out for Paul Hegarty as far as at least the home leg of the U.E.F.A. Cup tie against Barcelona is concerned (**reports The Sports Editor**).

In the past 26 games he has started only one—and had to be substituted in that.

Yesterday, he started ball work again following achilles tendon trouble. Today his reaction will be judged, "but if he doesn't get a game and a bit in, he will not be starting against Barcelona," said manager Jim McLean yesterday.

It was hoped that game would be against more or less anyone this week, but so far there is no fixture available.

Billy Thomson took a thigh knock against Brechin City but should be fit in a day or so.

Young flu victims Main, Welsh, Preston and Bishop are expected to be back in training today.

Thinking it through, manager Jim McLean was speaking no less than the truth yesterday when he said, "This is the best season we have had as far as I am concerned considering what we have had to put up with."

A glance at the team lines for the start of last season and last Saturday proves just how major the change within the club.

McAlpine, Gough, Hegarty, Narey, Malpas, Kirkwood, Beedie, Bannon, Milne, Sturrock, Dodds became, against Brechin City, Thomson, Kirkwood, Malpas, McInally, Clark, Narey, Ferguson, Gallacher, Holt, Kinnaird, Redford.

Three "survivors"—Kirkwood, Malpas and Narey, and Kirkwood has been away to Hibs and back again.

Yet United are still chasing the Premier League title, the Scottish Cup and U.E.F.A. Cup, have played eight games since New Year and have won seven and drawn one.

What the manager emphasises is that he is considering what has happened up to now, not predicting what is going to happen, but he did have this to

say on the broad issue of the future:

"At the end of this season, the way things are going and unless there is a vast change in some players form we will be fielding the youngest team we have ever had.

"It is not my intention, just because someone is older to play him. I will be looking closely at what exactly they are contributing and assessing them on that."

United have had less than praise for recent performances against cup and league opponents, but the manager points out that what they are now faced with is their reputation going before them and teams packing in defence—something any team can find difficult to play against.

I believe, however, that this is probably the biggest compliment that can be paid the club.

I recall the days when United beating teams like Airdrie, Motherwell, Falkirk, Hibs and the like would have earned inches deep headlines.

Now, because they are acknowledged as being one of Scotland's top four and top class European contenders, the headlines are reserved for opponents like these putting up a good show against them.

Ex-stars will be at United's big game

FIVE OF the players, or six if you include Tannadice director Doug Smith, who took part in Dundee United's famous Fairs Cup triumph over Barcelona 21 years ago, are to attend Wednesday night's U.E.F.A. Cup re-match as guests of the club (reports Steve Bruce).

The five, Jimmy Briggs, Dennis Gillespie, Tommy Millar, Ian Mitchell and Billy Hainey, will be joined by Smith, ex-manager Jerry Kerr, then trainer Andy Dickson and former team-mate Jim Moore, who although on the playing staff at that time wasn't involved in the Euro tie.

The party will dine together before taking in the quarter-final, first-leg which kicks off at 8 p.m.

Messrs Briggs, Gillespie, Mitchell, Kerr, Moore, Dickson and Smith all live in Dundee while Millar will travel from Edinburgh, Hainey from Renfrew.

Missing will be keeper Sandy Davie who lives in New Zealand, Tommy Neilson—last heard of in South Africa, Orjan Persson and Lennart Wing now residing in Scandinavia, and Finn Seeman who died in 1985.

Venables' spy hard at work

WHEN DUNDEE UNITED play Aberdeen at Pittodrie tomorrow, one man in the stand will be watching every move they make.

He is Enrique Orizaola and his task is to prepare reports on future opponents for Barcelona.

By THE SPORTS EDITOR

That report on United will be waiting for Barcelona manager Terry Venables and his assistant Alan Harris when they arrive at their pre-match headquarters on Monday, as will Senor Orizaola, ready to clarify any points which might be in doubt.

Barcelona are making no mistakes with their pre-match comments.

The latest from manager Venables is to the effect that United are "a very difficult team with a lot of good players.

"It will be difficult for us in both games."

No one can accuse him of pre-match under-rating of the opposition!

Meanwhile, wading through television and radio interviewers, camera men and assorted technicians, not to mention a larger than usual quota of Press and radio men, was a hazardous occupation en route to speak to manager Jim McLean yesterday.

While he—and everyone at Tannadice—is trying to keep the Barcelona game in the background until the visit to Aberdeen on Premier League business is out of the way tomorrow, the media representatives are pouring in (seven different television companies alone in the past few days, including two from Spain) to talk to the people who matter within the last British club left in Europe.

The McLean concern is, "That while we don't want to be inhospitable, while we want to

Jimmy Page . . . . fit again.

co-operate, the blunt fact is that I haven't been able to get involved in the training this week as much as I should have been.

"It is wonderful that the club is receiving this publicity, but after TV-am interview tomorrow morning, that is it as far as morning talks with anyone go. I'll be at training.

"It really has been extremely difficult for everyone at the club this week, but I must say the players have coped remarkably well.

"Frankly, we would like this sort of thing every week because it is an indication that you are a successful club. But if we had that, we would be programming it better than has been the case this week."

Then, turning to tomorrow's game—"I am glad it is Aberdeen we are facing. They, like us, are in the league title race and it will be difficult—exactly what we need to concentrate the players' minds on the job in hand.

"Actually, we have to win the next two games, hoping that there are no injuries, especially from the first.

"As far as we are concerned, last night's results—Aberdeen beaten, Hearts drawing—were great. Rangers and Celtic will welcome them, too."

On the injury front, the major problem is still Paul Hegarty.

It is hoped that Joe McLeod, on loan to Dumbarton for a month, will be fit to play for them on Saturday after treatment for an ankle knock; Jimmy Page is fit again and will be considered for a weekend game, while Gordon McLeod is doubtful after having had a toe nail removed.

No live cover in Scotland

While the football world's eyes turned to Tannadice, the club agonised over how to handle the attention. Would accepting live TV money be unfair to fans who had paid to be at the match? It's a question still being debated today.

Dundee United's U.E.F.A. Cup quarter-final first leg clash with Barcelona at Tannadice next Wednesday evening, will not be televised live in Scotland **(writes STEVE BRUCE).**

The decision was taken by the club's directors at a specially-convened board meeting yesterday.

United took the view that in fairness to those fans who had paid up to £20 for a ticket for the game, they could not agree to the action being relayed live.

Chairman George Fox commented, "After supporters had queued to buy tickets for the game, it would not have been right to show it live on TV."

It's a decision which will cost the Tannadice outfit around £30,000 in lost TV fees, but they clearly believe a principal is involved.

The match, which will be seen live in Spain, is to kick-off at 8 p.m.

It seems certain that recorded highlights will be shown by Scottish Television but anyone wishing to witness the full 90 minutes can still do so. A small number of tickets, under one thousand, are available for purchase.

As expected, club-captain Paul Hegarty is to miss the clash with the Spanish giants.

City neighbours Dundee had come to United's aid in offering to meet them in a friendly on Thursday to accommodate Hegarty's comeback bid.

However, the veteran defender isn't yet ready for an outing and is therefore out of the Euro reckoning.

Over the course of the next few days, manager Jim McLean will set aside time in which to study six video tapes featuring Barcelona.

Of more immediate concern to him at the moment though, is Saturday's important league meeting with Aberdeen.

On the injury front, midfielder-cum-striker Jimmy Page was yesterday consulting a specialist about his back problem.

49

Paul Hegarty.

Paul to play in reserve game

UNITED SKIPPER Paul Hegarty, for whom season 86-87 has turned into an injury nightmare, will play in the reserves against Rangers at Tannadice, kick-off 2 p.m.

Hegarty, whose problems began the last time United visited Pittodrie four-and-a-half months ago, managed a 45-minute run in a friendly with Dundee on Thursday afternoon and is hoping to last the distance today.

However, even if he comes through without reaction, it seems improbable he would be fielded against Barcelona on Wednesday night, bearing in mind his lengthy absence from first-team football.

Pittodrie pointer to European places, says United boss

EUROPEAN PLACES as well as Premier League points will be at stake for the Dundee United players at Pittodrie this afternoon (**reports STEVE BRUCE**).

Concious of the danger of the U.E.F.A. Cup clash with Barcelona intruding on his men's thoughts today, manager Jim McLean had handed them an additional incentive for the meeting with Aberdeen.

"This will be a difficult match for us both because of the opposition and the fact that the Barcelona game is so close," he admitted.

"However players must realise some can play themselves into the team for Wednesday night with a good performance at Pittodrie. Others could play themselves out."

One spot definitely up for grabs is at right-back. Recent incumbent Billy Kirkwood is ineligible for the Euro tie and, as he is also unavailable this afternoon through suspension, McLean is afforded the opportunity to find a replacement.

Included in a 14-strong pool for the trip north are John Holt and Gary McGinnis. It looks like a straight choice between this pair for the number two shirt and the more experienced Holt, who played in midfield against Brechin last Saturday, could get the nod.

Also listed in the squad are Eamonn Bannon, rested for the Scottish Cup tie, and Paul Sturrock, a second-half substitute at Glebe Park.

With the Euro quarter-final just days away, it will be a surprise if both do not feature at some stage to prime them for Barcelona's visit.

A run of 14 games, with only one defeat, has strengthened United's championship challenge and moved them into the Scottish Cup quarter-finals

Holt   **McGinnis**

but McLean feels there is still room for improvement in their play.

The Tannadice side are chasing victory at Pittodrie to keep the pressure on Celtic and Rangers. Aberdeen need a win to breathe fresh life into their title challenge after slipping at Paisley in midweek.

Of the last seven meetings between the sides in the Granite City, four have gone the Dons' way, three United's. A draw

between these well-matched north-east rivals is overdue and could well come this afternoon.

United from-Thomson, Malpas, McInally, Clark, Narey, Ferguson, Gallacher, Bannon, Kinnaird, Redford, Sturrock, McGinnis, Holt, Bowman.

Ian Porterfield is taking no chances of a repeat of Wednesday night's defeat against St Mirren, naming a strong 17-man pool for this afternoon's match.

John Hewitt, the Dons transfer-listed striker, is one of the 17, recalled to the squad after an absence of three weeks.

That doesn't mean, however, that the Dons now want to hold on to Hewitt. If a decent offer for him comes in, he'll be on his way.

Brian Irvine is also back after two games with the reserves following an injury.

"We don't have a reserve game, so we've put them all in the squad."

After Wednesday's fiasco, Porterfield acknowledges that two points are a must for Aberdeen today.

"We try to win every game, no matter where we play, and we'll be trying to win tomorrow."

Aberdeen—from Leighton, McKimmie, Robertson, Stark, McLeish, W. Miller, J. Miller, Bett, Dodds, Grant, Weir, Wright, McQueen, Porteous, Irvine, Hewitt.

From left—Eddie Thompson, Brian Petrie, Alistair Hastie and Jim McInally.

"Courier" winners of Barcelona trip

TWO LIFE-LONG Dundee United fans were both delighted yesterday to receive news that they had become the lucky winners of a free trip to Barcelona to watch their favourite team compete in the return leg of the forthcoming U.E.F.A. Cup tie.

The competition, organised by "The Courier" and United's sponsors, V.G. Food-stores, was entered by thousands of United fans from all over Tayside and Fife because on offer were two seats on the team's aircraft, three nights' accommodation with bed, breakfast and evening meal and tickets for the match itself.

The two winners, Brian Petrie (31), Portree Avenue, Broughty Ferry, and Alistair Hastie (27), Cambridge Street, Dundee, received telephone calls yesterday from V.G.

In the afternoon at V.G.'s premises in Blackness Road they were presented with their tickets by United midfielder Jim McInally and V.G. divisional director Eddie Thompson.

"I've really got to thank my mother for winning the ticket because she entered the competition for me. I think the trip to Barcelona will be a great experience," said Brian.

Alistair, equally delighted, said, "I'm really looking forward to the match and I hope we come away with a result."

The winners will join the official party at Tannadice for the trip to Glasgow Airport on Monday, March 16.

Has The Courier ever handed out a better prize? While most of us had to settle for a night in front of the telly, two local men won trips to Barcelona. Meanwhile, Barca fever meant references to the match could be found throughout the paper — even on the advertising pages.

Quietly confident McLean says, "We can most certainly do it."

By The Sports Editor

LOOKING AT his most relaxed as he conducted a larger-than-usual Press conference in the Tannadice boardroom yesterday, manager Jim McLean quietly interjected, "We can most certainly do it," into discussion on the Barcelona U.E.F.A. Cup quarter-final tomorrow night.

It wasn't said boastfully and there was no enlargement, but I have seldom heard him so positive.

He admitted that he has, in his mind, roughly the line-up which will start the game—and it was pretty obvious from the thread running through all his comments that it won't differ much from Saturday's winning team against Aberdeen.

The worrying injury referred to over the weekend was to Eamonn Bannon, who was "clattered" by Jim Bett on the touchline late in the game when United were playing possession football.

It looked serious and the same view was taken by the Tannadice staff.

But Bannon did full training yesterday which means it was probably a muscle spasm or trapped nerve, both of which can clear as quickly as they come.

Jim McInally, thigh and ankle knocks, turned out to be the most worrying of Saturday's "casualties", but, though he didn't train—he and Jimmy Page were the only absentees—he will likely be fit in time.

What of skipper Paul Hegarty, who has been out with an achilles tendon strain and who has only played parts of two first-team games in the last 26?

He had a hush-hush try-out last Thursday in a "bounce" game against Dundee and played a full game for United reserves against Rangers reserves on Saturday.

Result? He is fit again and even if he isn't there all the time, I expect to see him among the five substitutes allowed and going on as and when required.

"He is definitely now in my thoughts for the tie," said manager McLean.

"Rangers' reserves were a great test for him and he was directly facing Colin West, a big, strong player, good in the air.

"The stretching he had to do in the air and on the ground to compete with him was exactly what he needed after an achilles tendon injury.

"Actually, the other players were raving about his display after an uncertain start."

There is no doubt in anyone's mind that a fit-again Hegarty would give everyone a tremendous boost—and if you are cynical and say, "not John Clark who

COUNTDOWN TO TOMORROW'S BIG MATCH AT TANNADICE

has been in his place," let me make the point that it might not be John Clark who comes off if there has to be a substitution!

"I have 22 players to choose from and, if we stay clear of injury, my toughest job might be working out exactly who will be the five substitutes," the manager continued.

Hegarty is an important factor in United's set-pieces and there is definitely a sharper edge to these situations when he is playing, so look out for him being on the bench and being on the field at some point. One "possible" on the bench, and I stress he is no more than a possible, is Alan Main, recently signed from Elgin City and even more recently the victim of a broken finger injury.

He and Scott Thomson are deputies to first team 'keeper Billy Thomson and both have, in turn, proved themselves extremely able.

It would be a real rise into the big time for Main should he be a sub.

Those who are still wondering about the Hegarty-Clark situation might be interested to know the manager says, "John Clark had his best 45 minutes in any Premier League game for us on Saturday, so it is a nice headache for me to sort out."

The one criticism of Clark against Aberdeen is that he had his name taken for arguing first half and had to tread warily after that, losing his authority in the tackle in the process.

My passing thought on that is to wonder—yet again—why players get involved in arguments with referees they can never win.

Looking at that sensational 4-0 defeat at home suffered by Barcelona at the weekend, manager McLean's comment was, "I was happy to hear that .. it might just make them that bit more jittery in defence and, if it does, we must exploit that."

Had the United players thoughts strayed since the draw was made?

"Definitely, but I don't think they can have strayed that far considering the results we have had!

"They began to look really sharp in training on Thursday last, which is great considering we are already coming up for our 50th game of the season."

Any special plans?

"Gordon Wallace and I will talk to the players as always.

"I will do about 90 per cent. of the talking because I will be concentrating on how we play. Gordon will tell them what he saw when he watched Barcelona.

"We won't be doing man-marking even though we know people like Lineker are good players. We play a different system and will continue to play it.

"It might be different in the away leg. We had Billy Kirkwood marking Bryan Robson against Manchester United. We might try something similar again—we might . . .

Actually United have played the approach to the tie very low key—deliberately.

The manager hasn't specially watched them, Gordon Wallace has—once. There has been no contact with, for instance Jock Wallace, now managing Seville.

The idea—rightly, I believe—is that United have to do their own thing, not be over-influenced by the opposition.

Finally, manager McLean commented, ""We have no complaints about how ready we are. Results have been great recently for us. The injury situation is the best we have had all season.

"At the end of the day there will be no excuses at all."

If the media descending on Dundee expected to find a club and a manager overawed by the scale of the task ahead of them, they soon had to revise their thoughts. United went into the match on the back of six straight league victories and were into the quarter-finals of the Scottish Cup. When McLean said United could beat Barca, he meant it.

Clinical view of Spanish strike force

THE MARK HUGHES/Gary Lineker obsession which seems to have gripped some commentators would have you believing that if these two emerge alone on the park against Dundee United Barcelona will still win (writes The Sports Editor).

It would be stupid to ignore their talents, but there is a lot more to the game than that.

And, fortunately, United goalkeeper Billy Thomson prefers to take more a clinical than a hysterical viewpoint, especially over Lineker and Hughes.

"Of course I respect them," he said.

"They have proved themselves in extremely fierce competition and clubs like Barcelona don't shell out a lot of money on duds.

"Having said that, it would be stupid to worry about them.

"If you do that and make them the main focus of your attention, you can bet someone else will sneak in and give you trouble.

"I will be making no special study of the Lineker or Hughes approach to things. I will be assessing them as I assess all opponents.

"But making hard and fast decisions on how to cope with them would be wrong.

"I have seen Hughes when he played for Manchester United against Dundee United and Hamish McAlpine was in goal.

"I haven't seen Lineker other than on television.

"I'm looking forward to the contest against Barcelona as a team, not specifically against any individual players.

"I joined Dundee United to play in big games, to pit my ability against top players.

"I certainly haven't been disappointed either in domestic competitions or in Europe."

● When is a Spaniard not a Spaniard? That may sound like a riddle, but the answer is a very serious one indeed if you come from the Iberian Peninsula, and particularly when you play for the national football team

(writes A Special Correspondent).

Barcelona goalkeeper Andoni Zubizarreta is a one in point.

He is currently Spain's international goalkeeper, and by asking him that question you might very well spark off a political debate.

The fact is, he doesn't consider himself to be totally Spanish. Evidence of that fact can be seen by looking at his socks when he turns out for the national side.

I did just that when he faced England in the Bernabeu Stadium in Madrid last month.

While all his team-mates wore the Spanish colours of red and yellow on the turn-overs of their socks, Zubizarreta's hose displayed a plain red band.

The explanation goes back to the days of his predecessor in the Spanish goalkeeper's jersey—Luis Arconada.

His international career was dogged with death threats by the Basque separatist group ETA.

Arconada is himself a Basque. His tormentors accuse him of representing their political opponents and take every opportunity of emphasising their accusation.

When Northern Ireland beat Spain in the 1982 World Cup finals, Gerry Armstrong's goal which provided the Irish winner came as a result of an Arconada mistake. The whole Spanish nation were suspicious. They accused him of succumbing to intimidation.

The prospect of suffering similar treatment obviously doesn't appeal to Zubizarreta.

That's why, when he plays for the national side, he refuses to wear their colours on his socks.

He is also loathe to speak publicly about his appearances in internationals. Some say that silence is the result of fear.

There will be no such apprehension tomorrow, however. Zubizarreta is regarded in Spain as potentially one of the world's great keepers.

● HERE IS A LOOK AT THE TWO MEN WHO ARE THE LAST LINE IN DEFENCE FOR THEIR SIDES—GOALKEEPERS BILLY THOMSON AND ANDONI ZUBIZARETTA.

Pamela gets in first for interview with 'El Tel'

A DUNDEE GIRL has "scooped" the huge Press corps that will be covering Wednesday night's big game between Dundee United and Barcelona at Tannadice by getting probably the only person-to-person interview with the manager of the Spanish giants, Terry Venables.

Pamela Wares (17), a member of one of the commentary teams that regularly cover United and Dundee F.C. games for hospital radio, will conduct her interview with "El Tel" tomorrow night, following a chance letter she sent a few weeks ago.

Pamela was working on a game with colleague John Spence just after the draw for the U.E.F.A. Cup-tie was made. She "jokingly" suggested that she could fix up an interview with Terry.

"I decided to write him a letter to see if he would be willing, but I didn't honestly expect a reply," she said.

"However, a couple of weeks later he wrote back personally saying that he would be delighted to talk to us.

"It was quite a shock, but it says something about Terry that he is willing to take time out from his busy schedule to give us an interview."

Pamela and John will meet Terry after he puts the Barcelona players through their paces at Tannadice tomorrow night. The interview will later be broadcast on hospital radio throughout Dundee.

"John and I are writing up a whole host of questions to ask him," added Pamela.

"We believe that we are the only people who are getting a face-to-face interview with him, and we're both really looking forward to it."

● Picture shows Pamela with the letter from Spain.

Barcelona arrive in St Andrews

Dundee United's U.E.F.A. Cup opponents Barcelona arrived at their hotel in St Andrews last night at roughly the same time as Dundee were advancing to the Scottish Cup quarter-finals with a 2-0 win over Meadowbank Thistle at Dens Park.

In last night's other fourth round second replay, Raith Rovers ended the hopes of Highland League Peterhead at Gayfield, Arbroath, winning 3-0. (See Pages 12 and 13.)

● Our picture shows Gary Lineker with some female admirers at the Old Course Hotel and Country Club.

On the eve of the biggest match Tannadice had ever seen, United relented and allowed live TV.

There was also time to remember the Class of '66 and ask the question: Could United maintain their 100% record against the Catalans…?

Man who makes Barcelona tick

AN EARLY goal tomorrow would be a great tonic for United (writes a Special Correspondent).

An equally effective insurance policy, however, could be a solid, bone-jarring tackle on midfield man Carrasco.

He's the man who makes Terry Venables' side tick, but he's also known to be a "bit shy" when he knows there's a strong opponent facing him.

A spy in the Barcelona camp told me this week, "Let Carrasco play and he'll be a thorn in your side.

"But I've never seen him make a tackle in his life. One good early challenge could be enough to make him hide for the rest of the match."

Rangers defender Terry Butcher had a good opportunity to watch Carrasco at close quarters recently when they were opponents in England's 4-2 victory over Spain in Madrid.

Terry says, "He had a tendency to wander from one side of the field to the other, so it was difficult for anyone to pin him down and do a proper marking job on him.

"One minute he would be hovering in a seemingly harmless midfield position, the next he was behind our defence, getting on the end of a cross."

Terry Venables about to meet the Press.

Weary senors make a late appearance

IT WAS a travel-weary Barcelona party which booked into their luxury St Andrews hotel two hours late last night (reports The Sports Editor).

Manager Terry Venables said they had trained in Barcelona in the morning but would have a quiet day today until having a work-out under the Tannadice lights this evening.

The party comprises 16 players and, though he said he wasn't yet sure of his line-up and didn't plan on sweeping changes after the 4-0 week-end defeat, he must be close to a decision as 16 is a team plus five substitutes as is common in Europe.

"We have Maratella, Victor and Caldere available again," he said, claiming that the bad result was now behind them and the only thing they were interested in was the game against Dundee United.

He anticipated a "great atmosphere" at Tannadice and a "very difficult" game.

I queried if, as an acknowledged golf fanatic, he was planning a round over the world's greatest course.

"Possible, distinctly possible," he said with a smile before departing for a delayed dinner.

No win situation for United

Dundee United have sensationally about-turned on their decision to have no live television of their U.E.F.A. Cup quarter-final game against Barcelona at Tannadice.

The game will now be seen live all over Scotland.

"Announcing this yesterday, manager Jim McLean said, "'It was a long hard discussion and a very difficult decision to make.

"We were swayed by criticism that the unemployed, old age pensioners and particularly people in hospital wouldn't be able to see the game."

Grampian Outside Broadcast cameras will be on the scene and the vital fact to tell your wife is that Coronation Street will start at 7.15 p.m.!

This is to allow the match report to start at 7.45 p.m., 15 minutes ahead of the kick-off.

Actually United were in a no-win situation from the time the game was announced.

If they hadn't made it all ticket, it would have been impossible to contain the crowds. When they did, there was talk of over-charging.

They were criticised for no television. Now they'll be criticised for allowing it.

My tuppence worth is that they have been extremely logical all the way along the line.

Someone will always feel left out on occasions like this. Fewer than normal have been.

The comparison that matters will be made at Tannadice tonight

IF FINANCIAL power, stadium facilities and fame meant anything on the football field, then Dundee United would hardly need to bother turning up at Tannadice tonight to face Barcelona in the first leg of their U.E.F.A. Cup quarter-final tie (**writes the Sports Editor**).

In terms of facilities and finance there is no comparison between the clubs. While United aren't poor, their "riches" constitute but a few weeks' spending money for Barcelona.

Where the scenario changes is when the referee blows his whistle to start the game.

Then, the permutations of 22 to 26 men kicking a round ball while being presided over by a ref and two Linesmen takes over—and on this stage, the oblong between touchlines and bye-lines—I firmly believe United are at least the equals of their Spanish opponents.

In fact, the only thing United have to fear in the tie is themselves, not Barcelona.

The Spaniards have been hyped up, even by some Scottish commentators, as virtually invincible.

Rubbish, as their 4-0 conquerors at the week-end, Sporting Gijon (now, how many people have heard of THEM?) might well say.

They are good, very good.

They have international players in their ranks. They have a manager-coach of the highest calibre. They are experienced in Europe.

But isn't that exactly the description you could also apply to Dundee United? Of course it is.

We Scots are far too self-effacing—well, the Scots in this area at any rate.

Aberdeen fans never believed it possible for Aberdeen to win a European honour... until they did.

Dundee United fans are treading the same path. Oh they are going in numbers tonight, but they don't **BELIEVE. I** mean really believe they have a team capable of coping with the best.

Let's get this straight. There are no better defenders anywhere than Dave Narey and Maurice Malpas.

There are no better creators than Paul Sturrock and Eamonn Bannon—and if there is a blink of a goal chance don't bet against Kevin Gallacher or Iain Ferguson, or one of the creators, taking it.

In saying this, I do not ignore other good players in the United ranks.

What I am pointing out is that for every player the Spaniards can nominate as worth talking about, United can match him.

Do I except Gary Lineker and Mark Hughes? No. No-one can ignore Lineker's scoring talents in particular, but when he netted his recent four against

OUR FOOTBALL TEAM PREVIEW TONIGHT'S BIG EUROPEAN TIE AT TANNADICE

Spain, the Spanish defence couldn't exactly be called blameless—and Barcelona were well represented there!

He has scored in many games.

He has also NOT scored in many games.

Hughes is extremely physical. But United have had a look at him when he faced them as a Manchester United player. They won't be overawed.

And that is the key word looming over the entire tie.

United must not be overawed. It has happened in the past in certain games. There is absolutely no need for it to happen again.

I add one thing which makes me even more optimistic.

There have been United teams in the past which didn't, perhaps, react the right way when things were going against them. That is no longer the case. The number of times the current team has been on the receiving end early and come storming back for victory is impressive.

So what do I predict?

O.K., then, you have twisted my arm... 2-1 United at Tannadice, 2-2 over there. If I'm wrong, write your criticism on ten pound notes and send them to me!

Even when Jim McLean got home yesterday his work was far from over (**reports Steve Bruce**).

The United boss settled down in front of his television set to

watch a video recording of Barcelona's 4-0 weekend defeat by Gijon.

United have had at their disposal, ample video evidence of Terry Venables' side in action.

In fact on the team bus to and from Aberdeen last Saturday, a recording of Barcelona's recent match with Real Madrid was played.

It appears, however, the players do not set great store by the information that can be gleaned from such sources. The United boss offered them the use of any of the six video recordings he had in his possession and only Paul Hegarty took advantage.

Amongst the McLean collection is a film of Barcelona's 1985-86 European Cup clash with Gothenburg, supplied by Liverpool manager Kenny Dalglish.

Coincidentally, the referee of that match in the Nou Camp Stadium was Italian Paulo Casarin, the man in charge at Tannadice tonight.

This is Casarin's second trip to Scotland this season. He handled the U.E.F.A. Cup clash between Rangers and Borussia Munchengladbach back in November, and was heavily criticised for letting the Germans away with some crude fouls.

FLASHBACK... Ian Mitchell and Finn Seemann celebrate Billy Hainey's goal against Barcelona in their Fairs Cup match at Tannadice in 1966.

Night of nights at Tannadice
Mitchell and Hainey goals do the trick

By TOMMY GALLACHER

DUNDEE UNITED 2, BARCELONA 0.
(Aggregate 4-1)

Dundee United, Fairs Cup shockers supreme, have done it again!

On a bitterly cold, gale-swept night at Tannadice last night they completed the double over the holders, Barcelona, to knock them out of the competition.

It was never a good game — the conditions were all against it — but United could do what the Spaniards seemed unable to do — put the ball in the net.

This was the vital difference between the teams.

Barcelona played some delightful man-to-man football but, faced by a dour-tackling defence, they lacked the finishing punch, and seldom looked dangerous.

The only real shot which troubled Sandy Davie came from right-back Benitez — a shot from 35 yards, which the keeper touched round the post.

The golden goals which saw United through came one in each half.

Ian Mitchell, United's chance-snapper-in-chief, put the Tannadice side ahead after only 17 minutes, and at a time when United were nervy and struggling.

He took the ball from Orjan Persson and swept it past Sadurni with the aplomb of a veteran.

This goal settled United but, playing as they did, with a strong breeze behind them, the Tannadice men never really settled to play as we know they can do.

The defence was as solid as a rock, but too often the full-backs and wing-halves overkicked the forward line.

One ahead at half-time, and with the Spaniards playing a lot of skilful, fluent football, United could have been in trouble in the second period.

What a goal!

But four minutes after the restart Billy Hainey put the issue beyond doubt with a great goal from fully 30 yards out on the right touchline, which flashed past Sadurni into the far corner of the net.

A tremendous goal at the right time, and from then on United never looked back. They took all the Spaniards had to offer and,

coming out from defence, the Tannadice attackers were always more dangerous than their rivals.

Great team work

As in Barcelona, long before the end United, long playing well within themselves, were completely on top, although Barcelona never gave up.

A great victory for United, and once again one inspired by great teamwork.

Jimmy Briggs, who passed a late fitness test, was an inspiring captain in a defence which had no weaknesses. Doug Smith and Tommy Neilson were on a par with the left-back.

Orjan Persson again had a good game, and Dennis Gillespie worked like a beaver.

But when this game is recalled perhaps it will be scorers Mitchell and Hainey who will be remembered most — and Hainey in particular for that tremendous goal which finished the game.

Queer decisions

I thought United should have had a penalty in the first half when Jimmy Briggs was blatantly pushed off the ball, and I saw nothing wrong with Dennis Gillespie's first half goal which was chalked off, supposedly for offside.

But all these things can be forgiven when the result is right in the end.

Now United look forward to Saturday's draw and, having accounted so confidently for Barcelona, they can have no fears about who they get in the third round.

Attendance — 28,000.

"Fergie" ready for action

By **THE SPORTS EDITOR**

IT COULD well be that the man savouring most the hope of playing in tonight's game will be United striker Iain Ferguson.

After a great start to his career with Dundee came a move to Rangers—and, eventually, disillusionment as he slipped out of the first team reckoning and into the reserves.

A brief return to Dundee preceded a move £145,000 transfer and now, if chosen, he will get, almost unbelievably, only his third game in Europe and his first in a United jersey.

"My main feeling is how great it is to be back in action," Iain told me.

"I am not accepting I'll be in the team, but if I am it will be what I hoped for—a first team place and playing in Europe."

There is, in the Ferguson approach to the game, a certain similarity to Gary Lineker.

Both are goal scorers rather than creators, both only need a sniff of a chance and they'll try their luck at scoring.

But in no way will Iain allow comparison.

"I am just making my way back into the game after a year in Rangers reserves," he said, "and I have managed to get a few goals.

"But he is knocking them in everywhere—internationals, league games, cup ties.

"I always believe I can score in every game, but I do not rate myself in his class. It simply isn't logical."

And how does Iain rate United's chances.

"If we approach the game in the right manner, there is no reason why we can't do it."

Terry Venables is besieged by reporters after the Press conference.

Venables will leave selection late

BARCELONA'S PRE-MATCH plans are straightforward—a quiet day yesterday, when most players went shopping or sight-seeing, followed by the training session at Tannadice last night.

Today, a quiet morning, with a walk included, a rest in the afternoon and, somewhere along the line a discussion with the players on the way the game is to be approached.

It is likely at this point that the players will be told the team, but the Venables hint was that it will not be announced officially to others, including United, until just before the game.

"All I can say is that everyone who travelled is available for selection. We have no injuries," he commented.

Would Saturday's result alter his thinking on the line-up?

"Wait and see."

Moratalla, Victor and Caldere are available again after injury and suspension. Will they be in the original line-up?

"They will be considered along with the others."

More persistent questioning—from all sides this time—on the effect last week's defeat would have were answered finally with, "What has happened is gone and is not important.

"We are now thinking about Wednesday and after Wednesday we will know what kind of team we are and what we are made of.

"I actually know quite a lot about the Scottish Premier League sides.

"Dundee United are strong in most areas of the park and they have, of course, several players of international standard.

"Their young players, too, are looking good."

"European competition is good for them and they have been in European competitions for a long time. I believe it will be two great games between us and we are looking forward to them."

When the point was made that a visiting team in Europe often plays for a draw, the Venables answer was, "I think that would be very dangerous.

"I fully realise the importance of an away goal and we will be trying to get just that."

One theory expressed by some United fans is that, following comments by such as Gary Lineker that he hoped it wouldn't be too cold, the current raw, wet weather might be to United's advantage.

The manager's answer to that one, "I have been pleasantly surprised at the weather—and don't forget that many Spanish League games are played in very cold conditions.

"No, I don't see any problem for us with the weather."

The list of players who have travelled is, in alphabetical order: Caldere, Carrasco, Esteban, Fradera, Gerardo, Hughes, Lineker, Manolo, Migueli, Moratalla, Pedraza, Roberto, Urbano, Urruti, Victor and Zubizarreta.

That divides neatly into five defenders, five midfield players, four forwards and two goalkeepers. Keeper Urruti's full name is Urruticoechea, but if Barcelona and he are happy to accept the abbreviated version—as they are—I'm delighted!

Postscript—One regret . . . I wish some British managers who complain of Press harassment had been there yesterday. That really WAS Press harassment.

Spanish spotlight is turned on Archibald

By **THE SPORTS EDITOR**

HARD THOUGH Barcelona manager Terry Venables tried to concentrate on tonight's game at a Press conference in the golf centre of St Andrews Old Course Hotel yesterday, he failed.

And it was all down to the coterie of Spanish journalists present, one of whom said to me later, "This is even more important than the game against Dundee United."

The issue?

A story in the Spanish papers yesterday morning that Barcelona were to re-register Steve Archibald as one of their two permitted foreign players in place of Mark Hughes, who has been singularly unsuccessful as a scorer since signing for the club for £2m. from Manchester United last year.

If this happened, of course, Hughes, at 23, would be unlikely to accept demotion and transfer talk would explode.

At one point, despite the excellent efforts of Press officer Ricardo Maxenchs, near-confusion reigned as the questions had to be asked in Spanish, translated into English, then the Venables replies had to be given in English and translated back into Spanish.

And some of the questions weren't that, they were statements which took a couple of minutes to deliver, even in lightning-fast Spanish!

In the heat of television lights, with microphones, television cameras and photographers' cameras in almost non-stop action, the visiting journalists were tripping over their tongues trying again and again to get more out of the manager than oft-repeated statements like, "Why does this sort of thing always seem to appear when we are away from home?"

"If there's a Press Council back in Spain I'll be reporting this story to them."

"I haven't said anything at all on this subject to anyone, yet it has obviously come from someone in the know."

"If you think something written in Barcelona won't affect us here . . . well, it will."

> **❝** This is even more important than the game against Dundee United. **❞**

What he never did was categorically deny that there was anything in the story.

When the main conference finished I and one other Scottish journalists stayed behind to witness Phase Two of the situation.

Trying to get to British radio and television appointments already made, manager Venables was pinned against a wall by most of the Spanish Press Corps and again and again asked to clarify the situation.

He started the conference smiling, answered politely all other questions put to him, but it was patently obvious that he got more and more annoyed with the persistence of the pressure over the Archibald-Hughes story.

Even his ready smile was more than a little strained come the end of the proceedings!

Why I detail this is because I believe it is indicative of the state of mind of the people surrounding Barcelona right now.

The Archibald-Hughes angle is only part of the story, a story built on mounting dissatisfaction with the way the team is playing this season, culminating in that humiliating 4-0 defeat at home at the weekend.

The manager insisted that after another defeat earlier in the season they set off on a run of good results—but that wasn't greeted with any great enthusiasm by the Spanish Press posse.

This is not good on the eve of a European tie—for Barcelona. But it is doing Dundee United no harm!

If the manager cannot stop the tide of comment and pressure reaching his players, what will be the effect on them be in the game?

In between the Archibald-Hughes questions, there were actually comments made which referred to the game.

When I queried him whether or not he had personally seen United, the reply was, "No, but don't read anything into that. We have a procedure in which my assistant Alan Harris and scout Enrique Orizaola watch future opponents.

"They have done that with Dundee United and I also have video recordings of United in actual games.

"These I will be studying thoroughly this afternoon. The reports I will study thoroughly again and I will then discuss with Alan any points which I feel are important or need clarifying."

Big night ahead for lucky Scott

A group of envious primary six schoolboys from Gowriehill School, Dundee, will have all their attention focused on the smallest of the 26 people who will take the field at Tannadice tonight for Dundee United's glamour U.E.F.A. tie with Barcelona.

Because 10-year-old Scott Mitchell, of Strathaird Place, is the United fan who will get the closest look at the multi-millionaires of Barcelona when he turns out as the Tangerines' mascot for the big occasion.

The luck of the draw saw Scott's name pulled out of the hat as the lad who will shake hands with both captains and the referee come kick-off time —and he is already thrilled to bits at the prospect.

To make sure he will not be too overawed tonight, "The Courier" took Scott to Tannadice last night to have a close look at the famous opposition as they went through their training paces.

His father, Charles, also made the trip and was equally impressed with what he saw.

The youngster, a Dundee United fanatic who goes to most home matches, admitted it was quite a thrill to see the famous faces of the opposition so close up.

"I was able to recognise Gary Lineker right away," he said.

If the Tannadice programme is to be believed, the little fellow may find himself a spot on the United bench since, due to a minor slip-up, the mascot is named as Scott Thomson—one of the two candidates as the club's reserve keeper.

"That doesn't bother him at all, though," said Mr Mitchell. "Scott just can't wait for the match!"

● Scott watching the Spanish side training.

United 21 years on—in more ways than one!

THE DUNDEE UNITED side which beat Barcelona in 1966 had a nostalgic reunion yesterday.

The club organised the get-together, with the players reminiscing over a meal in the Queen's Hotel and then going to Tannadice to see if history could repeat itself.

Barcelona were the holders of the Fairs Cup when United shocked them in 1966 by winning home and away.

In the run-up to last night's U.E.F.A. Cup quarter-final, first leg, many fans have been recalling the night Barcelona went down 2-0 at Tannadice—and in particular, the spectacular goal scored by Billy Hainey.

At yesterday's reunion were former manager Jerry Kerr, trainer Andy Dickson and players Doug Smith, Tommy Millar, Dennis Gillespie, Ian Mitchell, Jimmmy Briggs, Billy Hainey and Jim Moore.

"I can remember both games very well," said Mr Kerr. "When the draw was made we felt we were up against it, but after winning over there, we went into the second leg at Tannadice full of confidence."

The former Tannadice boss admitted that unlike these days of spying missions and dossiers, he had not seen Barcelona play before facing them.

Ian Mitchell, who scored the first goal in the Tannadice match, recalled, "I can remember the fantastic atmosphere that night.

"Dennis Gillespie put me through for the goal. It was one-to-one with the keeper and I managed to slip it past him," said Ian, who now has a business in Broughty Ferry.

Dennis Gillespie said, "I can't actually remember a great deal about either game. It wasn't until I read it in 'The Courier' I realised I had a goal chalked off at Tannadice.

"One thing I can recall, though, is Billy's goal. I was shouting for him to cross the ball when he shot.

"Barcelona's stadium was magnificent even at that time. It even had a chapel."

Bill Hainey took a bit of ribbing yesterday over his goal, with some of his former team-mates joking that he had really been trying a cross!

"It was a real block-buster from at least 40 yards out," he laughed.

Everyone was convinced United could do it again this time over the two legs.

"I can't see why we won't beat them," said Doug Smith, former captain and now a director of the club.

Players from that history-making side who couldn't make it to the get-together were goalkeeper Sandy Davie, who has emigrated to New Zealand, wing-half Tommy Neilson, who now lives in South Africa, Swedes Lennart Wing and Orjan Persson, who returned home after their playing days, and Norwegian Finn Seemann, who died tragically in a car crash several years ago.

Decision made on Hegarty, but McLean keeping quiet

By STEVE BRUCE

UNITED MANAGER Jim McLean has taken the big decision over whether or not club captain Paul Hegarty will line up against Barcelona tonight, but isn't revealing the outcome.

Holding court in his Tannadice office yesterday afternoon, he looked relaxed and talked freely about the task confronting his side, but refused to answer the big question—will Hegarty play from the start?

"I have decided, but do not want to reveal it to Barcelona," was the manager's response.

"Hegarty is a vital and influential player for us, but on the minus side he has managed only 20 minutes first-team football against Motherwell and half-an-hour against Dundee, since being injured back on October 11."

The United boss also made it clear that even if Hegarty is restored to the side, it is odds against John Clark being the player who makes way for him.

That being the case, it could be that if Hegarty returns, Clark will switch to right-back, the role taken by John Holt at Pittodrie last Saturday.

Or is it possible the Tannadice tactician is contemplating a three-man central defence?

Even the players don't know. The selection will only be revealed to them during the usual pre-match team talk, held shortly before kick-off.

That said, the involvement of specific players in the practising of special moves at training yesterday morning will have given them a good indication as to who is and who isn't playing tonight.

Officially, United's starting eleven will come from—W. Thomson, Holt, Malpas, McInally, Clark, Narey, Ferguson, Gallacher, Bannon, Redford, Sturrock, Hegarty, Kinnaird, McGinnis.

However, it seems certain the team will be drawn from the first twelve named in that list.

The three players left out from the original group will occupy places on the bench where they'll be joined by either Alan Main or Scott Thomson and one of Bowman, Beaumont, Sulley, G. McLeod or McKinlay.

Midfielder Jim McInally is certain to play despite the knock he sustained against Aberdeen. "McInally will definitely make it, you'd need a ball and chain to keep him out," quipped the United boss.

Humour in fact reared its welcome head on various occasions during yesterday's press conference, with the media even being praised by the manager for the manner in which they'd conducted their quest for interviews, while still allowing United to prepare for the tie.

And on hearing of the business involving Archibald and Hughes, McLean laughed, "I'll have to ask Terry Venables if he's freeing Hughes, because I'd take him. The only problem is we couldn't afford his wages and mine!"

Not that the manager is taking tonight's match lightly.

"Any victory would be a good result, although we'd preferably want to win without conceding a goal," he stated.

"This is a tie which will definitely require two very good performances to take us through, but you can expect no lesser demand at this stage in the competition," he continued, citing previous Euro ties with Standard Liege and Borussia Munchengladbach as evidence of his side's ability to produce the goods over two legs.

"We cannot afford to have any passengers at all, and while everyone has rightly been talking about Lineker, Hughes and to a lesser extent Carasco, I'm hoping they'll be talking about Gallacher, Ferguson, Sturrock, Bannon and Clark, after the match."

He also played down the importance of his own part in this evening's proceedings.

"I don't think people realise how easy these type of games are for managers," he claimed.

"If players can't perform in front of a full house and in the atmosphere that generates, for the money they are playing for, and when they are representing Scotland, then there is no magic wand Jim McLean can wave."

Star strikers stay cool

JUST HALF an hour in the thin sunshine of a brisk St Andrews morning was enough to convince Barcelona's £5 million strike force of Gary Lineker and Mark Hughes that it was not as warm as they thought it was.

Alone of the Barcelona squad staying at the Old Course Golf and Country Club, they had passed on the shopping trip to Dundee and settled instead for a stroll on the famous links.

Within minutes the pair had donned tartan golfing caps and were posing for pictures at the famous Swilcan Bridge.

But in spite of saying how much they were enjoying the weather at the start of their jaunt, they were soon complaining of the cold.

A little exercise was called for and what better than a chance to swing a club at the home of golf.

The pair were persuaded to tackle one of the course's fearsome bunkers and set to willingly.

If their shooting is as good as their shots from the sand, then United's defence has little to fear.

Former Dundee United players (standing, from left)—Doug Smith, Andy Dickson, Jimmy Briggs, Jimmy Moore, Dennis Gillespie, Billy Hainey and Tommy Millar; seated—Ian Mitchell and Jerry Kerr.

Compared to the chaotic scenes involving Terry Venables and the Spanish press pack, United's preparations were serene.
Not for the last time in this campaign, McLean seemed to thrive on the pressure — even insisting his job was "easy".

● Mark Hughes (left) and Gary Lineker try on some suitable headgear in the golf shop at their St Andrews hotel. United will be hoping it's the only "hat-trick" the pair manage on their visit to Scotland.

Kevin Gallacher's looping shot that produced United's goal.

United are half-way there after a class performance

DUNDEE UTD 1, BARCELONA 0

THERE ARE no prizes for winning the first leg of a two-legged tie, but Dundee United's performance in the first leg of their U.E.F.A. Cup quarter-final last night was excellent, and proof that they are a quality side by any standards (writes The Sports Editor).

For the next fortnight every football fan in Scotland will be asking, "Is it enough?"

There is no reason why it shouldn't be, although at times Barcelona looked ominously efficient, without having the final thrust that should have

come from the British spearhead of Mark Hughes and Gary Lineker.

To be honest, I have seldom been so disappointed in strikers of their reputation, and who jointly cost £5,000,000. How Lineker, for instance, missed one particular chance from "whites of the eyes" distance, I'm sure even he will never know.

I expected and got a truly class performance, yet again, from David Narey, but what about John Clark?

People were worried about him coping on the grounds of inexperience. I can't remember him putting a foot wrong.

The United defence was

immaculate, Jim McInally—bidding to qualify for the tag of United's best-ever buy—and Ian Redford non-stop as they beavered away in midfield, with Eamonn Bannon looking a bit more like himself than of late.

Iain Ferguson took a lot of physical "stick" up front and Paul Sturrock and Kevin Gallacher were constant threats to the visiting defenders.

It is a pity for United that the dream start of Gallacher's goal within two minutes wasn't built on in the sense of goals, but even an unbiased neutral would be inclined to think they might have had at least one, maybe two penalties.

I was most impressed in the

Barcelona line-up by Victor and Caldere, with Migueli a steady mid-defender.

It is 21 years since United created one of football's biggest ever shocks by beating these same opponents twice in the Fairs Cup, the forerunner to the U.E.F.A. Cup.

To this day people on Tayside remember that, and, if they were there, talk about it with understandable pride.

Twenty years from now, the people who were there can talk—again with pride—about last night at Tannadice. And if they have survived to talk about both, they are indeed privileged!

THE SPORTS EDITOR and STEVE BRUCE report on the big match

Gallacher goal shocks Barcelona

FERGUSON NEARLY opened up the visiting defence in the first minute when a great pass from a free kick sent Sturrock through.

He fed Gallacher, but the youngster was forced wide and a throw-in resulted.

And from that throw by Holt, sensation, as United opened the scoring with exactly one minute and 50 seconds gone.

Gallacher accepted a pass from Sturrock on the right and, in an instant had wheeled and sent a dipping shot high over Zubizaretta and into the net.

It was his first goal in Europe and his eighth in nine games for United.

The United fans were still roaring and singing five minutes later, but suddenly went quiet when Caldere ran on to a great through pass to hammer in a shot which Thomson did well to turn round his right hand post.

With Sturrock back at his best spearheading the attack, it was mostly Gallacher who wriggled past two defenders in the 10th minute to chip the ball beyond the far post and only just out of the reach of Gallacher.

Barcelona were over the early shock by now though, and edged through to force two corners in quick succession, the second well cleared by Narey after Thomson had to punch the first clear under pressure.

Then followed two more United attacks. First Bannon took a long clearance from Thomson in his stride, moved inside two defenders and had a crack from 25 yards which wasn't all that far wide.

Then Sturrock popped up on the left and crossed for Bannon to head just past the post again.

It wasn't all United as Caldere proved with another snap shot,

but the flowing moves were coming from the home team, with Redford and McInally giving excellent backing to the efforts of Sturrock, Bannon and Gallacher.

Lineker and Hughes were switching constantly in an attempt to "lose" Clark and Narey, so far without success.

Jim McLean was worried about Barcelona free kicks, and when Narey handled on the edge of the box, the crowd went quiet. . . then let out a roar of relief when Carrasco hooked his kick high over the bar from 22 yards.

Redford was really turning it on in midfield, and when he sent Sturrock away with a 40-yard pass, the wee fellow was hammered to the ground by Gerardo on the edge of the box.

Unfortunately for United Redford's kick didn't match the pass and was easily headed clear by Migueli.

It was more a slogging battle at this stage than a football

classic, proved by the fact that Gallacher cropped up at left back to stop Victor, then Victor repaid the compliment by stopping Gallacher in the right back spot.

As the interval approached, a sudden shock for United. Carrasco created an opening and crossed from the right. Hughes back-heeled and Lineker missed a close-in chance he would normally have tapped in.

At the same time his half-hit shot was awkward and Thomson did well to save.

The nerves were showing at the back with Barcelona. Under pressure, Gerardo panicked and gave away a corner, again cleared rather easily, then Gallacher crossed for the keeper to beat Ferguson to the ball—but only just.

The talk throughout the interval was still of that miss by Lineker. He doesn't let many of those get away!

Sturrock set United off again within a minute with a marvellous left wing run, but his

cutback from the bye-line went just behind Ferguson.

A long throw from Thomson to Malpas caught out the Spaniards, and when the full back "fed" Sturrock, his cross from the left wing was missed by inches by Gallacher.

Then Gallacher repaid the compliment in the 52nd minute with a great cross from the right, and though Sturrock got to the ball, it bounced off his boot and past the post.

United lived dangerously a minute later. Redford fouled Hughes right on the edge of the box, but luckily for United Roberto's shot was driven into the wall and cleared.

A "was it a penalty" incident had the crowd roaring again a minute later. Yet again, Sturrock began the move. He raced in from the left and flicked to Bannon.

As he tried a flick-through pass, the ball seemed to hit Roberto on the hand, but the ref, who was beginning to needle the

crowd with some of his decisions, said "no."

In the next couple of minutes, first Sturrock, then Gallacher were sent crashing by Barcelona tackles.

In 72 minutes came the game's first substitution. Gallacher, who had run his legs off down the right and left, went off for Kinnaird.

United had lost a bit of their rhythm, but, with the battling McInally constantly urging them on, they were still very much in the game.

In 75 minutes came the warning that they couldn't ease up for a minute, however.

Roberto was allowed to advance from deep and keep going, and his shot unleashed from outside the box wasn't far away.

As United again pressed forward in 78 minutes, Ferguson got himself booked. He went down inside the box and the ref decided he was guilty of ungentlemanly conduct in that he "dived" inside the box.

Legs were tiring as the closing minutes approached, but, typically, Eamonn Bannon was still running and running. When he raced off down the left and delivered a perfect cross Ferguson was sandwiched on the six yard line by two defenders, and his complaints brought him another talking to by the ref.

A first class game ended with a Bannon shot which had Zubizaretta stretching and the crowd applauding both teams off the park

Attendance—21,322.

Dundee United—Thomson; Holt, Malpas, McInally, Clark, Narey, Ferguson, Gallacher, Bannon, Sturrock, Redford. Substitutes—McGinnis, Kinnaird, Bowman, Hegarty, S. Thomson.

Barcelona—Zubizaretta; Gerardo, Migueli, Manolo, Victor, Moratalla, Carrasco, Lineker, Hughes, Roberto, Caldere. Substitutes—Fradera, Gonzalez, Urbano, Pedraza, Esteban.

Referee—Paulo Casarin (Italy).

Paul Sturrock goes flying as he tries to break through.

Jim McLean praises his heroes

UNITED BOSS boss Jim McLean said afterwards, "I really can't complain at all, the players' effort was tremendous (writes Steve Bruce).

"We've had better results in Europe, but we can still do it. Sometimes in European football 1-0 can be better than 2-0.

"We will cause them problems over there as long as we show the same self-belief and don't lose important players to injuries."

The Tannadice manager mentioned three players in particular. He described Jim McInally's contribution as "magnificent," said Sturrock was "utterly outstanding" and

suggested that John Clark more than any other deserved the highest praise.

Italian referee Paulo Casarin, however, was not the target of praise from McLean.

"I'm disappointed at the standard of refereeing considering that we are in the quarter-final stage of the tournament," he said.

"We had two hand balls in their box, but after we scored I felt any doubt and every decision went their way."

The manager also revealed his reasons for leaving club captain Paul Hegarty out of the starting line-up.

"There was no way we could leave Clark out, he had only once played right-back for us and considering the length of his absence from first team football we simply couldn't play Hegarty," he commented.

It also emerged late last night that goal hero Kevin Gallacher had been withdrawn suffering from an ankle injury.

Terry Venables was far from unhappy at the outcome. "To lose to a fluke goal in a place like this is not too bad," he said.

The Barcelona boss also confirmed that Francisco Carrasco will miss the return through suspension following his booking last night.

"Fiesta" ... "Conquistadors" ... "Olé"

No Spanish cliché was off limits as The Courier reported United's remarkable first-leg victory.

While fans across the city, and across Scotland, celebrated United's win, a busy night-time operation swung into action to ensure the newspaper fully reflected the scale of the Tangerines' achievement.

United's goal hero, Kevin Gallacher, propels another shot towards the Spaniards' goal.

Mascot Scott Mitchell looks on as the captains, United's David Narey and Barcelona's Victor, shake hands just before the kick-off.

A Tannadice fiesta

It was fiesta time for home fans at Tannadice last night when Dundee United gave the senors of Barcelona a lesson in chance-snapping to take a 1-0 lead to Spain in two weeks time.

The Tangerines got off to a dream start in the first leg U.E.F.A. Cup quarter-final tie.

The whole city was shaken to its foundations at 8.02—only two minutes after kick-off—when a simultaneous roar from 22,000 throats greeted the goal that gave United hope of advancing to the semis.

A first time cross-cum-shot from Kevin Gallacher on the right left the keeper stranded as the ball dropped just under the bar at the far post to a chorus of Spanish sighs.

The much-vaunted strike force of Lineker and Hughes was hardly seen, although the former had the miss of the match about five minutes from half-time. In the clear only yards out with Thomson to beat, he side-footed a weak shot straight at the grateful keeper who scrambled it over the bar.

And that was the Spaniards' best—and just about only—real chance.

In a clean and sporting game, dominated by the raiding of Paul Sturrock up front and the defending of John Clark at the heart of defence, each side had a strong penalty claim turned down in the second half.

The general feeling of most United supporters was reflected in the contented smiles and conversations seen and heard as they trooped down Hilltown to the city centre, waving scarves in triumph.

As far as the home faithful were concerned the odds were on a favourable overall result after the return leg in Barcelona.

According to Geoff Fitzpatrick, 31 Ballantrae Place, Douglas, a one-each draw is on the cards there.

"If United play as well as they did then I reckon we will be through," he said delightedly.

Gary Henderson, 176 Balunie Drive, also predicted United's forward march into the semi-finals, forecasting a 2-1 win for the Dundee side.

The late decision to have the match televised live seemed to convince most fans without a precious ticket that home was the best place to view the game.

During the match itself the city centre was almost deserted—certainly no-man's land—and pubs throughout the city admitted business was slow until full time.

The Royal Hotel, which had invested in £11,000 worth of satellite TV equipment only to see the United board have a change of heart regarding TV coverage, tuned into the local broadcast rather than the Eurovision link.

However, staff at the hotel said the new equipment was a long-term investment, allowing the hotel to pick up games and other events from all across Europe during the future.

Gabriels in Meadowside showed the match live on a big screen to attract fans.

They're top dogs

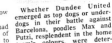

Whether Dundee United emerged as top dogs or underdogs in their battle against Barcelona, poodles Max and Putzi, resplendent in the home team's colours, were determined to view the action from kick-off to final whistle.

And if the atmosphere in front of the TV could not quite match that on the terracing, at least they could take comfort from the fact that their master, his daughter and son-in-law were seeing it all first-hand at Tannadice.

Max lives at the Tullo household at 16 Lynnewood Place, Dundee, while Putzi stays with Mrs Stevie Ewart across the street at Number 9.

Said Mrs Isabel Tullo, "My husband, Larry, daughter Margaret and her husband Fraser are all United fans, and Margaret knitted the dogs' United scarves as a Christmas present, begging me to make sure they wore them on all important occasions. Obviously, tonight qualifies as one of those.

"Larry, with Margaret and Fraser, who now live in Tillicoultry, are all going to the match, but the dogs will just have to be happy to watch TV."

Tayside Region convener Mr John McAllion and Dundee Lord Provost Mr Tom Mitchell sent a "good luck" letter to Dundee United before last night's match.

Gary Lineker can only look on as Eamonn Bannon heads clear.

All action as Paul Sturrock fires in a shot.

Tangerine conquistadors set to invade Barcelona

Dundee United's U.E.F.A. Cup heroes travel to Barcelona in just under two weeks time, taking with them two major advantages—a one goal lead and, in European terms, what will amount to a huge travelling support.

Wednesday night's overshadowing of the millionaire senors by the Tangerines has, it seems, fuelled the fervour of a large proportion of the Tannadice faithful.

At least 3000 fans are expected to make the trip for the second leg, and indications are that that number could continue to rise.

"The phones haven't stopped ringing all morning," was the stock reply from a cross-section of Dundee travel agents yesterday as they struggled to cope with a flood of requests for air tickets, coach seats and accommodation in Spain.

Many had begun taking bookings and organising charter trips for the return match long before

Wednesday night's initial encounter between the two teams.

Now, with the scent of victory in the air, Jim McLean's men can look forward to some added vocal support when they step out on to the turf of the Neu Camp stadium on March 18.

"I don't think there will be any problems getting tickets over there," said Colin Ramsay, of Ramsay World Travel.

"It's not that big a game for the Spaniards and I don't think there's any question of a capacity crowd.

"That means that the two or three thousand United fans who are going will be all the more noticeable."

The Tangerine invasion has begun already, with a vanguard of fans preparing to leave for Barcelona within the next few days.

GORDON WILSON

Commons congrats

Scottish M.Ps. were quick off the touchline yesterday to congratulate Dundee United on their "magnificent victory" over Barcelona, writes Our Man at Westminster.

A Commons motion, sponsored by M.P.s, including Dundee's Ernie Ross and Gordon Wilson and North Tayside's Bill Walker, met with a rush of signatures.

The motion made a special point of noting the "exemplary behaviour" of the fans throughout the game.

And it wished the team every success in the second leg of the U.E.F.A. Cup.

ERNIE ROSS

Crowd great help, says McLean

ELEVEN HOURS after the final whistle blew in the U.E.F.A. Cup tie between Dundee United and Barcelona at Tannadice (with United winning 1-0 in case you've been on a desert island and have just returned!) United manager Jim McLean was back at his desk preparing to conduct a Press conference.

I said earlier in the week that I had seldom seen him so relaxed. I repeat that. He obviously not only enjoyed—naturally—the display of his team, he enjoyed the fact that 22,000 inside the ground and millions on television had seen an outstanding football match based on the skills of the game.

As he talked . . . and talked . . . and talked . . . he roamed over the game, the past, the future, just about everything connected with the club and didn't finish until over an hour later, with the assembled journalists, by mutual consent, having enjoyed every minute of the "talk-in."

I condense his comments:

Injuries—"Looks like we are well off. Kevin Gallacher took an ankle knock, Dave Narey twisted an ankle and had ice put on it. They'll be O K. Jimmy Page is the only other injury, but he should be all right for consideration at the weekend.

You didn't lose an away goal—"It was very, very important not to. We do well in away games, so it is definitely good that we can go there without the worry of having conceded a goal at Tannadice.

"We are very, very confident playing away from home. This is a different team from the other teams we have had,

❝ As for you McInally, just be your usual magnificent self. **❞**

they play differently, but I see no reason why we can't do it, especially if Paul Sturrock plays like he did last night and with Eamonn Bannon fresher again.

"It was some result when you consider we were playing our 49th game of the season—46 plus three Forfarshire Cup ties."

You have a game against Clydebank on Saturday. Not quite on the scale of Barcelona!—"There's no way the same team will play in that one, and that is a disgrace because of the way they played last night.

"But we must always be looking to freshen up things and after that magnificent atmosphere from that wonderful crowd who really got behind the team we face a different set of circumstances.

"One of the players who may be there on Saturday is our new signing from Dumbarton, left back Harry Curran.

"Getting back to the crowd, we've built it from about 2500 to 6000 or 7000, but 6000 to 7000 here on Saturday after last night . . .

"I'm not getting at anyone, just stating facts.

"You know, it wasn't bonuses or Jim McLean or anybody who made them play like they did last night, it was that

crowd. These are easy games for me and Gordon Wallace. Motivation will, however, be very difficult on Saturday.

"That's why there will be changes, though none of last night's team will be dropped in the sense of being out because of the way they played."

Billy Thomson played well—"Do you realise that in the 46 competitive games he has had 26 shut-outs—and that, at 29, he is into the best ten years of his career because I expect him to go on for at least as long as Hamish McAlpine did.?

"That speaks for his form, and when you think that, also, 50% of the back four have not been available for long periods, you realise what kind of record that is.

"It is a tremendous tribute to Gary McGinnis, Dave Beaumont and John Clark and Thomson, Dave Narey and Maurice Malpas who, because of their experience, have carried the brunt of the pressure.

"What makes me even more proud is that not one of last night's back four cost a penny—John Holt, John Clark,

Two of United's heroes from Wednesday night—goalscorer Kevin Gallacher (left), and the night's midfield maestro, Jim McInally.

Dave Narey and Maurice Malpas all came up through the ranks here. Scotland could play a back four of Ray Stewart, Richard Gough, Dave Narey and Maurice Malpas . . . all groomed by Dundee United, all of whom cost us nothing.

"To us, Narey is the most important one of all. A great reader of play."

You are still involved in the race for three trophies, Premier League, Scottish Cup and U.E.F.A. Cup. How do you react to that?—"I want to be involved as long as we can. I am desperately keen to win anything and everything we can. It is no use players saying, 'that one gives us the best chance.' I want them to be involved in the lot for the whole of the season.

"And I honestly believe we can achieve it as long as the players are hungry.

"I am not saying we are the best team in Europe, but we are involved in a lot of things. However, it is as soon as we start concentrating on one trophy that we will end up with nothing.

"We have to concentrate, as we have been doing, on one game at a time."

Which one do you most want to win?—"If we win any one of the three I will be really pleased, but there is no doubt the league title shows what you are really made of."

You seemed to know a lot about Barcelona—"They were the easiest team to spy on. I had a video of their 4-0 defeat also two other videos. They are easy to check up on . . . and cheap!

"On last night's showing we definitely didn't give them much chance. Our team was magnificent, playing old-fashioned Scottish football.

"The orders to Billy Thomson, for instance, were not to throw out the ball,

but to hit it as far up the field as possible and put them under pressure.

"It will be harder over there with the size of the pitch.

"Jim McInally likes the smaller pitches, but then players like Paul Sturrock and Kevin Gallacher like them big, so maybe it will even itself out.

"You know, we were an exceptional side last night. It was one of the best performances we have ever turned on, I'm only disappointed the score was only 1-0. We deserved 2-0 at least. All right, they had the best chance through Lineker, but as far as control of the game is concerned we deserved more than 1-0."

Jim McInally was Man of the Match—"Yes. He has been outstanding

for us all season. He'd be my player of the year. I know we have Narey and Malpas, but we accept them as being exceptional. "It's amazing seeing his performances when you consider that, at the start of the season, I was thinking on challenging him on sprints and stamina, well almost!

"I played him out of sympathy in his first game. We were on the bus to Hamilton, he was sitting on his own we were wondering who to put in midfield. He was bought to play full back, but when I asked him about midfield he just said 'O K.'

"From that day he has never looked back. He has been invaluable—and he only cost about £80,000 to £85,000. I tried for him before Celtic sold him to Nottingham Forest but failed with a £40,000 bid.

"Actually I thought he was 24 when we bought him. He was 22. His career is only beginning. I can't remember him having a mediocre game.

"Mind you, while I'm talking about him as a good buy, I have had my bad ones as well!

"They kid me on about him being my favourite. It might be connected with the fact that at team talks I'm inclined to say, 'as for you McInally, just be your usual magnificent self' which is unusual for me!"

John Clark had a great game—"He

❝ I was disappointed at people like Gough and Dodds moving. I felt they owed it to their team-mates to help keep us going. **❞**

had his best first half against Aberdeen and a great game last night. With his shooting power and great long passing he could be a personality like Hamish was."

It has turned out to be a magnificent season—"It was said at the start that the bubble had burst. It certainly hasn't. This has already been as good as any of the seasons I have been here.

"I was disappointed at people like Gough and Dodds moving. I felt they owed it to their team-mates to help keep us going, but they went and we are having a great season.

Then on more general terms . . .

"I could have been sacked by now if I had taken the Rangers job. I couldn't have done it the way Graeme Souness does it—and that's no criticism of him.

"I believe in a youth policy and that would have taken twice as long as it used to.

"Our directors don't get the praise they should. They have been magnificent in allowing us to keep the players we have kept, turning down £600,000 for Sturrock, £250,000 for Hegarty ten years ago, £400,000 for Malpas and so on.

"We are £950,000 up on transfers. And we look at 100 youngsters a week—25 of them on 'S' forms played before the big game last night."

And then it was over. I wish I'd taped it, it was that interesting.

Paul Sturrock.

Paul's on top of the world

PROBABLY THE most delighted United player yesterday was Paul Sturrock.

For the second game in succession it was vintage stuff from this truly class performer—against Aberdeen on Saturday, Barcelona four days later.

"The World Cup and niggling injuries have meant a miserable spell for me," he said. "It was great in the last two games to be feeling at my best."

"I have a toe injury which never goes away. I added to that a thigh problem and a general feeling of being 'down'.

"Now I have changed my lifestyle—a lot of rest, a no red meat diet, jacuzzis. That and the fact the injuries have cleared and I feel great.

"I'm enjoying working in from the left, too. It was a decision taken by the boss and it certainly suits me.

"I enjoyed every minute of last night and can't wait for the return. We have nothing to fear."

How the men involved saw the big game

THE HEROES of 12 hours earlier trooped into Tannadice yesterday—some to train, some to receive treatment, some just to talk over one of the great games in the history of Scottish football.

Man of the Match Jim McInally, "All along I have just wanted to enjoy this one. It's what you join clubs for—to be involved in games of this size.

"And I did enjoy it—every minute."

His award as Man of the Match, a crystal tankard and

By THE SPORTS EDITOR

glasses, "will be treasured" even though "I didn't think I was the winner—in fact you don't think about awards when you are out there, just about giving the lot."

He said he had to thank manager McLean for any success he was having.

"He could have put me straight into the team because he had spent money on me, but instead he waited and introduced me when he thought I was fit enough and ready to play.

"That day we won 5-1 at Hamilton and I was off to a great start in the team and with the fans."

Jim has lost over a stone since joining United and feels "fitter than I have ever been."

He is now a midfield player—of real quality, too—but earlier in his career was always looked on as a full back. Did he enjoy the change?

"Definitely the way things are going, but I honestly had never thought of myself as a midfield player.

"In fact, I played there a couple of times for Dundee and twice for Coventry. Down there I was really struggling, so I never thought I could develop in midfield."

And the second leg? "The pressure is all on them. If we can keep them out for a spell the fans will be on their backs. That should be good for us."

The question for goalscorer Kevin Gallacher was simple—Terry Venables says they were beaten by a fluke goal. Was it a fluke?

"It was not a cross, it was a shot," was the reply. "And it was a shot for goal.

"If I didn't try the same thing in training moves with Paul Sturrock coming in from the far side I might say it was questionable. But I had a real winder at it and it went on target. That was my intention.

"Call it a fluke that it actually went in if you like, but the fact that it counted is what matters."

That's eight goals in nine games since the youngster switched to striking more through the middle.

On that he says, "I was struggling a bit on the wing, then I had a break.

"Maybe I was suffering a bit from a car accident early in the season, but whatever it was I wasn't as sharp as I should have been.

"The break did me good and though I never expected to score as many goals in so few games, I am delighted it is happening."

And the outcome of the tie?

"If we play the way we played last night we definitely have a good chance."

The problem about being David Narey is that you seldom get Man of the Match because your standard is always so high it begins not to be noticeable!

On Wednesday night he was at his immaculate best—but the talk was of his partner, young John Clark.

Typically, Narey was as full of praise for the youngster as anyone.

"He had a great game. First class. And it must have done him a lot of good to be pitched against two players of the calibre of Lineker and Hughes and come out absolutely on top."

And the skipper himself? "I really enjoyed it. What an atmosphere. It was a big night in every way and though I'd have liked one more goal it was an excellent result against a really good team."

My personal postscript to all this is that, having seen European games since these tournaments first started, I rate this one right up there in the top echelon.

It had a quality of skill and attacking intent that mean few, if any, dull moments. Something that cannot often be said about Euro ties.

Hegarty returns to starting line-up as Clark is rested

By Steve Bruce

CLUB CAPTAIN Paul Hegarty returns to Dundee United's starting line-up for the visit of Clydebank.

Hegarty, who has played just 66 minutes of first-team football since sustaining a groin injury at Pittodrie last October, resumes this afternoon and it's almost certain the man to make way for him will be midweek Euro-hero John Clark.

Manager Jim McLean, who was warm in his praise of Clark's performance against Barcelona, admitted, 'It is ludicrous to leave John Clark out after he has produced his best displays yet in our last two games.

"However, we must get Hegarty back to first-team fitness as soon as possible bearing in mind the programme of matches that confronts us, and for that reason he will play against Clydebank."

The United boss considered switching Clark to right-back

Long-term injury victim Paul Hegarty is back in the first team, while John Clark is rested.

and the possibility of tackling Bankies with three central defenders, but as he wants to freshen up the side without making major tactical adjustments, decided against these alternatives.

Further changes to the U.E.F.A. Cup line-up are on the cards with recent signing Harry Curran possibly making his debut. The former Dumbarton left-back is set for at least a sub's spot today.

Mr McLean is looking to stimulate as much competition for first-team places as possible as the season heads for its climax, with United involved in the hunt for three trophies.

"No way can we tackle the busy programme confronting us with just 11 players. We need to have everyone champing at the bit, eager to play."

The Tannadice manager, however, is adamant that his planned team changes are in no way an indication of United taking Bankies lightly.

"This game is just as vital to us as the one against Barcelona was," he said.

United made ground on both Celtic and Rangers in the championship chase last Saturday when they defeated Aberdeen and will be looking to maintain their push against the relegation-threatened Kilbowie side from whom they've already taken seven points this term.

Bottom-of-the-table Bankies, though going well in the cup with a quarter-final tie against Dundee coming up, face a battle to stay in the top flight after collecting only eight points from their last 22 matches.

To make matters worse, they've been hit by a flu bug making both Mike Conroy and Jamie Fairlie doubtful. Amidst fears that the problem might spread, Clydebank are taking a squad of 17 players to Tayside, including youth international Sean Sweeney.

Secretary Ian Steedman accepts his men are up against it today. "We have never taken even a single point off United at Tannadice and this week, of all weeks, no-one wants to be going there for not only did they beat Barcelona, they also had that good win over Aberdeen," he commented.

United from—Thomson, Holt, Malpas, McInally, Hegarty, Narey, Clark, Redford, Bannon, Sturrock, Gallacher, Ferguson, Kinnaird, Curran, Bowman, G.McLeod.

● United's reserve fixture with Aberdeen, due to be played this afternoon, has been called off because of pitch conditions at Pittodrie.

Barcelona unrest rumbles on

THE REPERCUSSIONS of that amazing St Andrews Press conference six days ago, which saw Barcelona manager Terry Venables and the Spanish media at loggerheads, are still rumbling on (**reports the Sports Editor**).

While Barcelona were in Scotland for the game against Dundee United, a story was "leaked" to a Spanish newspaper saying Barcelona wanted to re-register Scot Steve Archibald as their other foreign player alongside Gary Lineker because Mark Hughes wasn't scoring goals.

Archibald went out of favour when Barcelona signed Lineker and Hughes for £5 million because Spanish teams are only allowed to have two foreigners in the first team.

Now, manager Venables has, in effect,

told his directors (they are supposed to be the source of the "leak") to stay out of team matters and is reported to be threatening to resign if they don't.

Maybe that is what they want, because word is they have lined up Everton's Howard Kendall as Venables' replacement, while my information is that, had he been a little bit longer in the managerial game, they would have considered an approach to Rangers boss Graeme Souness!

Whatever happens, it isn't doing Dundee United any harm in advance of the second leg of the UEFA Cup quarter final.

● If Hughes is on his way, Alex Ferguson could make him his first major signing for Manchester United, the club he left to go to Spain.

Dropped point provides a timely warning for United

LAST WEDNESDAY Dundee United's players strode proudly off the field after a magnificent 1-0 UEFA Cup first leg victory over the giants of Barcelona.

Sixty-seven hours later their departure for the dressing room was a muted affair to a chorus of booing after a 1-1 Premier League draw with lowly Clydebank.

However, this was mild compared to the reception the Barcelona players got yesterday after losing 2-0 away to Real Zaragoza—their third defeat in a week.

Let's look for reasons for United's performance on Saturday.

There was a bitterly cold, gale-force south-east wind blowing . . . but it was blowing for and against both teams.

There were changes from Wednesday night's team—Paul Hegarty in after injury, Harry Curran making his debut at left back.

But, though Hegarty took time to settle and Curran was substituted for Redford late on—after an impressive debut let it be noted, and only for tactical reasons—there's no excuse there.

So it boils down to the fact United gave their worst display of the season, after one of their best.

And it posts clearly the warning that EVERY game is a big

game and be there gales or storms or heat or cold or an attendance of 21,322 (Wednesday) or 5541 (Saturday) you have to cope if you want success.

It looked great for United early on with Paul Sturrock in scintillating form.

But from the moment Dave Narey blundered with a short pass back ("His first mistake since 1972," was the Press box crack) United increasingly struggled.

The ball was taken on by Stuart Gordon, who rounded

By THE SPORTS EDITOR

Thomson and popped it into the empty net.

That was in 10 minutes. It took United until five minutes from the interval to equalise, when Hegarty headed home a Sturrock free kick.

There the scoring ended, and though Hegarty should have netted late on when a deliberate left foot shot went wide, Bankies can point to several chances they scored.

The 1-1 draw was the first point the visitors have taken off United in the Premier League at Tannadice.

I exclude Jim McInally and Maurice Malpas from criticism.

Sturrock's early burst gives him pass marks, too.

In the case of Iain Ferguson, you can't argue against his 14 Premier League goals in 27 games, but only two have come in the past nine.

With his style he has to keep on scoring to hold the critics at bay—and he isn't doing that right now.

Afterwards, manager Jim McLean said, "The players let everyone down today. There was a small crowd, a fierce wind, but it is mind over matter and the players should have pushed themselves through it all.

"It's always difficult in a wind like that and Narey made it doubly difficult, but there are really no excuses.

"We got the credit on Wednesday. Now we deserve all the stick we get.

"The only plusses are Curran for his display and Hegarty coming through fit."

Bankies manager Sam Henderson applauded what United had done against Barcelona, "but we emphasised to the lads not to be too respectful."

He went on, "We weathered the early storm and hit back. Getting that goal made all the difference and, though we are blowing hot and cold with our form, it sets us up nicely for the Cup tie against Dundee at home on Saturday."

Last chance for £1 flight to Barcelona!

THE TRAVELLING support is building up for Dundee United's visit to Barcelona on UEFA Cup business next week, but there are still places to be found—or even won! **(writes THE SPORTS EDITOR).**

For instance, in conjunction with a travel firm, Dundee United Supporters' Club are running a charter flight which goes out on the day of the game and back immediately after it—price £155.

There are still around 30 seats available on the plane and, when they eventually take off, three people will be there for £1.

This is because the club has been operating a draw at £1 a ticket for a seat on the plane. Two draws have already been won, there will be one other before the flight departs.

Paul Hegarty (No. 11) celebrates his return to the first team by scoring United's goal.

Back to earth with a bump for United as they can only draw at home to relegation-threatened Clydebank. After such a fine run of victories in league and cups, it was perhaps the first sign that the hectic fixture schedule was starting to take its toll. They would go another six league matches without recording a win.

Change of role for Clark in United's defensive set-up

DUNDEE UNITED manager Jim McLean is still wrestling with the situation of playing three men looked on by many as central defenders in his back four (reports THE SPORTS EDITOR).

He carefully pointed out for starters that it was a mistake to say he was playing three centre-halves, a tactic which some have said he is adopting.

"The truth is that John Clark wanted to play at right back before he was moved to centre-half," he said.

"Now he has been there for a couple of games.

"We had to have Paul Hegarty fit for a run-in which is full of important games and this has now been achieved.

"His timing was off in the early stages of the Clydebank game, but I rated him as having a great game against Dundee in the derby.

"Hegarty is not at the stage of his career where we could move him to right back, so Clark is there getting the chance to fill the role which Richard Gough used to play.

"He feels more involved in the position than he does at centre-half.

"I know this may seem unfair on John Holt, who played so well against Aberdeen and Barcelona, but it is what is happening."

At the same time, I wouldn't yet write off Holt's chances of appearing in Barcelona.

Billy Kirkwood is another contender for the right back position, of course, but that problem—a happy one for the manager—isn't likely to arise until after the Barcelona game because Kirkwood is ineligible for Europe.

Fears that Ian Redford's hamstring injury was serious have receded slightly—he was taken off at half-time against Dundee as a precaution after injuring himself early on.

But there is still doubt over full recovery in time for the cup tie against Forfar Athletic this week-end, and, in fact, about the Euro tie next week.

"He is our real worry," said the manager.

Kevin Gallacher and Paul Sturrock suffered knocks in the derby, but, along with groin injury victim Gary McGinnis, should train today and tomorrow.

Jimmy Page is causing concern. He definitely won't be considered for Barcelona because of a back injury which is proving difficult to diagnose.

● In the magnificent Nou Camp Stadium, Barcelona, on Wednesday night, Dundee United embark on one of the greatest adventures of even their long-running European football experience when they face the multi-millionaires of what is reputedly the biggest club in the world. They are already 1-0 up in their UEFA Cup quarter-final tie after a Tannadice thriller last week, but it is only "half-time" and the real test lies ahead. Flying out with United and in close contact with them throughout their trip will be the "Courier" SPORTS EDITOR.

Optimistic trip for Peter

There is nothing like hope, as they say—and Dundee United supporter Peter Mackie made no attempt to hide his unbridled optimism for the future when he not only booked a ticket for the forthcoming Barcelona game but took out a 10-year passport to boot.

Nothing unusual in that, one might think. But Peter, of Marryat Terrace, Dundee, will next week be celebrating his 90th birthday.

Peter is the honoured companion of five other United supporters who set off in high spirits last night for the long trip to Barcelona, congregating first in the Plough Bar, Strathmartine Road, where Peter drew admiring glances from youngsters of a mere 70 years or so.

He has come in for some good-natured ribbing already from his fellow-travellers—especially about the 10-year passport—but the group are delighted to have Peter with them for what is bound to be a memorable week.

Peter will be accompanied by George Davie, Andy Scott, Gary Foulis, Andy Hendry and Andy's dad Joe, all of whom will be spending a few days sunbathing in Lloret Del Mar before travelling to Barcelona for the big game.

Said George, "It'll be great to have Peter with us—he's just as keen as anyone on seeing the game, and he doesn't see his age as a barrier at all.

"I'm sure he'll fit in fine everywhere we go."

He added, "We'll take a few days on the beach before going to Barcelona itself.

"I don't know what the Spaniards will be like at all. We're hoping for a good welcome, but we've followed United about Europe and know that some places—Rome, for example—can be less than friendly.

"One thing is certain—United will have a great support. We make it about 600, in all, going across for the game, which will be the largest travelling support in Europe the team's ever had."

Peter explained that he was treating the trip as a holiday to make up for one that fell through last year, with the added bonus of the United game.

"I don't see any problems at all," he said. "I'm told I'm quite good for my age—most people put me at 70 rather than 90—and I'm looking forward to a bit of sunbathing."

On the game itself, Peter was equally optimistic.

"It'll be a 1-0 win for someone, no doubt about that," he said. "But, no matter which, United will go through."

The group set off by bus at two o'clock this morning for Gatwick. They will be flying to Lloret at four this afternoon, arriving at tea-time.

And there is a hectic journey in store next Friday on the group's return for Andy Hendry, who has a rather important appointment hours after landing in London.

The plane touches down at Gatwick at 9 p.m. on Friday and Andy will hardly have time to adjust to the rain before he is on a bus to Dundee, arriving at 8 a.m., and then driving furiously through to Perth—where at 10 in the morning, tired, tanned and, hopefully, triumphant, he steps forward as best man at his friend Grant Martin's wedding!

Big game live on TV

Viewers will be able to follow United's quest for U.E.F.A. Cup glory when B.B.C. Scotland provides live coverage of the second leg of the quarter-final tie from 8 p.m. The match will be on B.B.C. 1, with the nine o'clock news being accommodated on B.B.C. 2. The game will also be covered live on "Sportsound" on B.B.C. Radio Scotland from 7.30 p.m.

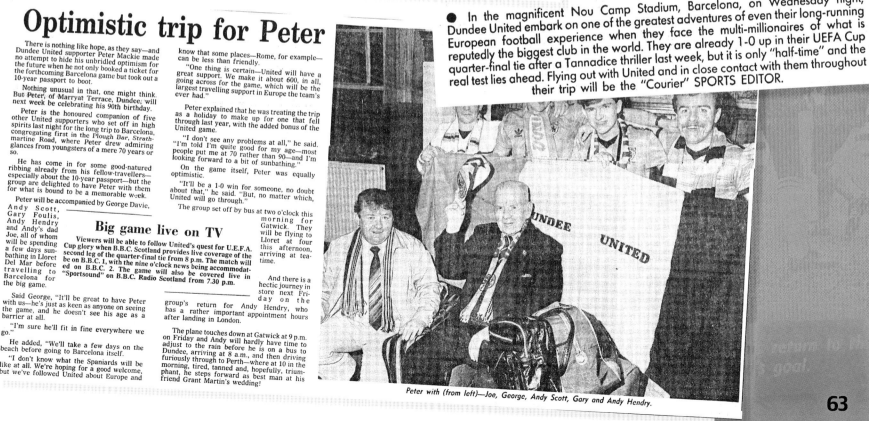

Peter with (from left)—Joe, George, Andy Scott, Gary and Andy Hendry.

Still nothing stirring on the Tannadice transfer front

By the Sports Editor

EIGHTEEN DAYS to the deadline and still nothing stirring on the transfer front for Dundee United.

"It is the same as ever—with one difference," said manager Jim McLean yesterday.

"This time we have had more money, but that certainly has not made the search any easier.

"Mind you, we are on the lookout for the player everyone wants, and who is in very short supply—the physically big striker of top quality who can lead the attack and get goals.

"We have Kevin Gallacher, Paul Sturrock, Iain Ferguson and Paul Kinnaird, but we could really do with that big one.

"Even clubs like Rangers are still looking. That doesn't make it any easier, but we won't give up."

Tomorrow it is Forfar Athletic at Tannadice in the Scottish Cup, with United doing exactly the same build-up as they did for Barcelona.

"We train our way and it would be foolish to change for any game," said manager Jim McLean, emphasising that there was absolutely no question of underestimating Forfar.

Looking ahead briefly to Barcelona on Wednesday he said a party of 18 players "as usual" would be travelling.

Not in the party will be the ineligible Billy Kirkwood and Harry Curran.

The problem being pondered by the manager is which of his young keepers will understudy first choice Billy Thomson.

Both Scott Thomson and Alan Main have proved they are excellent performers, but one will be left behind.

At their age, though, that won't be the end of the world!

Injury victim from the local derby, Ian Redford, did light training yesterday, but it is too early to discuss his prospects for tomorrow or next week. A decision will be nearer when he starts sprinting.

The others injured are Gary McGinnis, Jimmy Page, Brian Welsh and John Bishop.

The good and bad news about failure to fix a reserve game this weekend is that there is no risk of injury, but players like Billy Kirkwood will miss match practice.

● The 10,500 programmes printed for the Dundee United-Barcelona game last week were sold out. Tomorrow before and during the cuptie against Forfar at Tannadice a further print of 3000 programmes will be on sale.

● Got your ticket for the Rangers game a week tomorrow? They are on sale at the ground and other outlets and are going steadily, but many people are so intent on the Barcelona game that they may have forgotten the equally important league encounter with the Ibrox club at Tannadice!

Drama behind the drama at Tannadice

THERE WAS drama behind the drama at Tannadice on Saturday (writes The Sports Editor).

Yesterday, manager Henry Hall disclosed that John Clark, the central figure in the late, late penalty award, had only gone back to work on Friday from a bout of flu.

On Saturday morning he did half an hour's training—"some session," joked Henry, "I told him that's about what we get from him on match days . . . half an hour."

The manager's over-all feelings after the tension, the excitement, the despair?

He took over from Doug Houston in the close season and, despite Forfar having beaten St Mirren 5-1 in the Skol Cup earlier in the season, he says, "To think we could get a result like that at Tannadice—almost get a better result, in fact—means my career in the game has reached new heights, as it has for all our players.

"Now we have them at Station Park. It doesn't matter what I think, what is vital is that my players now believe they can go through."

Then there is Stewart Kennedy, at 37 giving a performance of superb quality.

He had his own personal timekeeper sitting in the stand, his attractive wife Elaine.

"Second half I was so busy I had only time for occasional glances to check how long I had to go," he says. "When I thought there was only five minutes left, there was actually 15.

"Then I got the signal that it was time up. I'm shouting 'nearly there, keep it going,' when Dave Narey humped the ball forward, Paul Sturrock crossed, Kevin Gallacher headed and the referee gave a penalty.

"Iain Ferguson really thrashed the ball to my right."

Finally, United manager Jim McLean, making no bones about it—"As far as I am concerned Forfar came out of the game with all the credit.

"We didn't take time to make our passes. The only time we did first half we scored."

● The replay is on Tuesday, March 24, and will be all-ticket.

"Courier" competition winners Alistair Hastie (left) and Brian Petrie with Dundee United players Eamonn Bannon and Paul Hegarty before setting off to fly to Barcelona with the team for tomorrow night's U.E.F.A. Cup tie second leg. For more on the build-up to the match see Page 11.

United squad to be named this morning

IT'S GOING to be nail-biting time for Dundee United this morning.

In the hour or so between the players reporting and leaving for Glasgow for their flight to Barcelona, manager Jim McLean has to decide on his pool—with worries centred on the fitness of key men Paul Sturrock (calf muscle) and Eamonn Bannon (bruised ribs).

There is also a slight worry over a Dave Narey ankle knock, but meantime it is believed he should be all right.

"I definitely won't finalise the party until tomorrow," said manager McLean yesterday. "It could be a case of everyone who is left, with the exception of Jimmy Page, who is definitely unavailable because of his back injury."

● One piece of good news has come the way of 19-year-old 'keeper Alan Main, signed from Elgin City earlier in the season.

He travels as deputy to Billy Thomson.

Main has not long returned from a broken finger injury and is fully fit again. The manager rates his Highland League experience as equipping him well for his step-up.

He did, of course, play in the Forfarshire Cup final against Montrose.

● On Saturday night a still none too convincing Barcelona beat Real Betis 2-0 in a Spanish League game to end a run of three defeats and a draw.

Scorers in 61 and 81 minutes were Esteban, a substitute at Tannadice, and Roberto, who played in the first leg.

Still missing from the line-up were Mark Hughes and Caldere. Hughes has a knee injury, but is rated "70% cent certain to play." Caldere hasn't played since the first leg at Tannadice, when he was undoubtedly one of the Barcelona stars.

"No contest" turned out a TV thriller

By THE SPORTS EDITOR

While United's league challenge was beginning to falter, they also stuttered in the Scottish Cup — salvaging a replay against Forfar.

There were better fortunes for the winners of that Courier trip to Barcelona.

SPECULATION BEFORE Saturday's Scottish Cup quarter final between Dundee United and Forfar at Tannadice centred on the question "Why has B.B.C. television chosen this game?"

The tie of the quarter-finals was expected to be Hearts v. Motherwell (the Beeb lost the toss for screening that one).

Then there was Clydebank v. Dundee with promise of a close encounter of the interesting kind and Raith Rovers v. St Mirren, with the possibility of a shock result.

United and Forfar? No contest. The Premier League club chasing honours on three fronts—league, Scottish Cup and UEFA Cup—the Sky Blues lower middle of the First Division.

In the event, the B.B.C. team were "delighted we came here" at the end and everyone present had an afternoon of unforgettable drama, with an ending which would have been considered too far-fetched had you suggested it for a boys adventure book.

We didn't know it at the time,

but the most vital happenings were actually two injuries.

Bobby Cormack needed on-field treatment in 62 minutes (with Paul Hegarty being booked for the challenge) and Eamonn Bannon got the same five minutes later after colliding with keeper Stewart Kennedy.

Referee Jim Duncan of Gorebridge decided on a couple of minutes added to play to compensate for the hold-ups.

Exactly 12 seconds into that period United mounted a desperate attack with the ball finally headed powerfully by Kevin Gallacher. As it raged towards goal Forfar's John Clark was in the way—and it hit his arm.

Without even a moment's hesitation, referee Duncan raced forward pointing to the penalty spot.

Significantly, the Forfar players made no real protest and manager Henry Hall commented, "There is no way we will complain about it."

As Iain Ferguson, showing remarkable "cool," lashed the ball home from the spot at the

Arklay Street end, a colleague tells me there were grown men on the terracing behind the goal —it was the well-populated Forfar end—with tears in their eyes.

Having been brought up supporting a small club which so often seemed to suffer ill-fortune when competing with one of the top outfits, I know how they felt!

On the day, Forfar, who consistently delight me with their ability in major cup ties and for whom I confess to having a soft spot because of this, were truly a team.

They didn't have the sheer

class of Maurice Malpas or Dave Narey, the skills of Paul Sturrock or Eamonn Bannon (second half).

But they had teamwork, discipline, an effective "counter-punching" technique which posed considerable threat to United time and again.

And they had men like Bobby Cormack, voted the games's Mr Superfit by the Press. He must have covered 10 times the road and the miles to Dundee and he wasn't alone in his industry.

If I single out Stewart Kennedy, Rab Morris, Phil Smith and Ian McPhee to put alongside him it is only because I give

them five stars out of five . . .the rest getting 4.9999.

I don't know exactly what it is that got to United—apart from Forfar, I mean. Thoughts of the Barcelona tie intruding? Under par performances by key players—I exclude the magnificent Malpas, the excellent Dave Narey and Billy Thomson? The sheer weight of 49 games in league, Scottish and European Cup ties—every one vital?

Maybe it is a combination of all of those factors, but they certainly were not at their free-flowing best, which, I must repeat, takes no credit at all away from Forfar.

For most of the first half, United leant heavily on the Sky Blues goal and when they scored in 43 minutes it was deserved on the count of their pressure and because it fell to their best player.

Kirkwood, Gallacher and Bannon combined to open a route to goal and Malpas was into it in a flash to rap the ball past Kennedy.

Then United made what I consider one of their most vital mistakes of the season. They seemed to give a collective sign

of relief and relax just when they should have been winning the ball and keeping it away from Forfar.

Within a minute they paid the penalty (if that's not too unbearable a word for Forfar readers).

Narey, Hegarty and Malpas got into an almighty fankle on the edge of the box after a Hamill throw-in and the ball bobbed around aimlessly before John Clark stepped in to rap it past Thomson.

United still seemed to be suffering a hangover from that when Forfar made it 2-1 in 54 minutes.

When Cormack raced down the right and crossed the United defenders unanimously claimed offside against Macdonald. Without waiting he smashed the ball home—and found the referee agreeing he wasn't offside.

From then on the tension became almost unbearable—until that unbelievable moment beyond the normal 90!

Cormack was booked for a foul on Malpas, John Clark went on for Kirkwood for United and Mark Bennett for Craig Brewster for Forfar. Crowd 7985, receipts £12,769.

Off to Spain with United

FRESH FROM that Scottish Cup thriller at Tannadice, the SPORTS EDITOR joins Dundee United this morning to head off for Barcelona and the U.E.F.A. Cup quarter-final second leg in the Nou Camp Stadium on Wednesday night.

Saturday's result must go down as disappointing for United—yet the same score over there would see them through to the semi-final of the European tournament as they lead 1-0 from the first leg at Tannadice.

It is all to play for, and "The Courier" will give you day-by-day news and the day's most comprehensive report on Thursday morning.

Gallacher, Sturrock and Redford appeal for a penalty as Clark (right), who was adjudged to have handled, desperately tries to clear the ball.

Ferguson about to lash home the penalty with Ray Lorimer and Mark Bennett ready to pounce on any mistake.

Holt is set for move to Forfar

INTO THE now-it-can-be-told category comes the story of why John Holt has not played as first choice in the games since the Barcelona tie, in which he was right back.

John, aged 30 and 14 years at Tannadice since signing as an "S" form player, is likely to join Forfar as a player and assistant to Henry Hall when the current run of games ends for United.

The fee is reported to be about £15,000.

And why does that stop him playing?

John is at the age where a player has to consider whether to continue full-time (he has two years of his contract to go) or look further ahead.

I understand he will be working outwith the game as well as playing and coaching at Forfar, thus securing his future.

But the worries of such a vital decision are adjudged to have been too much for him to combine with playing in what have been—and is tonight night—absolutely vital games.

I understand the United approach is that they don't really want to lose him in view of other player losses this season, but that it would be unfair to stand in his way of the opportunity that has been presented.

Minister sends good luck message

Mr John MacKay, the Minister for Education, Agriculture and Fisheries at the Scottish Office, whose responsibilities include sport in Scotland, yesterday sent a good luck message to United.

Here we go, Here we go, Here we go . . . Paul Sturrock, Paul Hegarty, John Clark and Eamonn Bannon boarding their plane at Glasgow Airport.

The story of how John Holt almost turned his back on the chance of European glory to join Forfar has entered United folklore.

Thankfully, the "stunningly brilliant" McLean helped to persuade him otherwise.

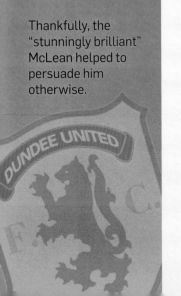

Injury doubts linger but McLean sees United approach as the key

"I DO NOT want us to think we are 1-0 up. This is an entirely new ball game and if we approach it as such and play to our form—instead of the way we play against Rangers at Ibrox and anyone at Hampden—there is no way we will go out."

The confident words of Dundee United manager Jim McLean, even though he will be wrestling with a team selection problem well into the latter hours of this morning at least.

The problem is Eamonn Bannon's rib injury and the formation of the back four and midfield.

First, that injury. Bruised ribs are notoriously difficult to clear.

"Eamonn was making Gordon Wallace look like a buzz bomb," was the joky McLean comment after a training session yesterday in which Bannon was involved but running at nothing like top pace.

He added, "I don't think he will make it, but we will be pushing him in a training session tomorrow to see if he can do everything necessary.

"Actually, his absence isn't as desperate as it might have been at one time as we can push Redford to the left, where he is better."

Paul Sturrock didn't take too much part either, but that was more a precaution against him pulling a muscle because of the tenderness in his calf than anything else.

Dave Narey, worry No. 3 when we came out here, looked his normal self and if the ankle knock he got against Forfar is bothering him, you'd never know.

With Bannon available, we would be talking of a midfield involving him alongside Ian Redford and Jim McInally, behind a strike force of Kevin Gallacher, Iain Ferguson and Paul Sturrock.

It is if he isn't available that the permutations start.

Manager McLean seemed to rule out Gordon McLeod (19) on the grounds of youth and inexperience meantime, but brought into play the names of Dave Bowman and John Holt.

Holt, because of another issue (see elsewhere on the page) might not be considered though I wouldn't rule him out altogether, so Bowman seems a reasonable bet to get close.

I have deliberately left out the

The Sports Editor previews tonight's big European tie in Barcelona

the view that Mark Hughes, seemingly certain to return for Barcelona, might be able to 'rough up' Paul Hegarty, recently returned from injury.

The manager didn't agree and made the point that United's European fortunes had in many ways been built on the Hegarty-Narey partnership in central defence.

Which indicates, again with John Holt in mind, but slightly second favourite, that John Clark could be in the right back slot.

I'll take a guess, then at a line-up possibly starting 4-4-2 then becoming—Thomson; Clark, Hegarty, Narey, Malpas; McInally, Redford, Bannon; Gallacher, Ferguson, Sturrock.

The McLean hint was of a 15 minutes 4-4-2, then a switch to 4-3-3 to counter and attack Barcelona's 4-4-2, which is more of a 4-3-1-2 . . . which shows you have to be a mathematician as well as a student of football to understand the game today.

A vital factor in the game will be the attacking of the Barcelona full backs by Gallacher and Sturrock (and Bannon if fit), a tactic that had

back four formation in front of keeper Billy Thomson until now, because that is the manager's other problem.

One interviewer expressed

the Spanish team rocking at Tannadice.

"We have no chance of not losing a goal if we try to defend for 90 minutes," said the manager, "so we must again be looking to score."

In a final summing up, the manager made it clear that the emphasis would be on how United will play, not on worrying about Barcelona.

"In training this morning they built moves better than they have done for ages," he remarked.

"We have told them to relax and express themselves and they have certainly done that up to now.

"Every player in Scotland—even more especially in England right now because of their ban—would love to be where the Dundee United players will be tomorrow night.

"And don't make the mistake of thinking that is me saying 'all we are happy about is being here.'

"We want them to enjoy themselves, yes, but we also expect them to do exactly the same as they did in Dundee and win by playing to their full potnential."

Jim is bearing up well under pressure from media masses

THE SINGLE most striking feature as Dundee United prepare for tonight's second leg of the U.E.F.A. Cup quarter-final against Barcelona in the wonderful Nou Camp Stadium is the approach of manager Jim McLean.

Few dispute he is "Mr United."

I have seen him in all his moods—angry, worried, communicative, quiet.

I have also—despite the image he tries to create himself—seen him happy. But I have never seen him so relaxed, so ready to crack a joke as he has been here.

I do not predict the future, merely say that under the greatest media pressure I have ever seen imposed on a club manager from Britain he has been, to quote one veteran observer of the scene, "stunningly brilliant."

I counted over a score of radio and television interviews on and around the Nou Camp pitch yesterday morning before and after a strenuous training work-out. He took them all in his stride—then got down to the really important business of dealing with the football writers!

He was a mixture of the serious and the humorous, ranging over every aspect of the game.

Why was he so relaxed?

"I learned many things when I was with Scotland as Jock Stein's assistant, not least that there was more than the 'goldfish bowl' of the club alone.

"I thought at one time the only thing that mattered was working with the players, but I now realise we sold ourselves short as a club, that dealing with the media was important, too.

"There have been cameras and lights and people sticking microphones under my nose today.

"But it is part of life at this level of football, and because I am proud to be competing at this stage of a European tournament I accept it."

Stadium very impressive

THE 120,000-CAPACITY Nou Camp is something else. A batch of trophies on show numbering hundreds—and that's only some of the club's awards; a battery of floodlights spread not on pylons but all round the stadium; a miniature chapel on the way from the dressing-rooms where players go before a game; 60 yards along a tunnel and up steps before emerging "out of the ground" and on to the pitch.

Once there tiers of seats rear high into the sky and create a superb bowl.

The pitch? In excellent shape, much better than most in Scotland, and measuring six yards wider and five yards longer than Tannadice.

Abrupt end to conference

AFTER A Press conference at which he looked totally bored, Barcelona manager Terry Venables last night abruptly rose and left following a question about a demonstration on behalf of deposed star Berndt Schuster in the city earlier.

Had he any comment to make on it? "I know nothing about it," he rapped back.

Maybe it was just a coincidence that this more or less ended the conference!

The pressure on Venables is immense—mostly from the Spanish Press, but combined with constant mutterings from the fans who seem completely disillusioned with the man they lionised only a year ago.

But our interest is in tonight and, summarised, his view of the game is that it isn't when a goal comes but that it comes that matters to the Spanish.

He appealed for patience if it didn't come early, to which my reaction is 'fat chance' the way he is being treated here.

"We are confident, but not over-confident," he said. If it runs to penalties he will decide on the night who takes them, obviously remembering how Barcelona lost out to Steau Bucharest in the last Euro shoot-out.

He is still not definitely committed on Mark Hughes' return after a knee injury, but it looks like he will be there, as will Manolo and Caldere, other injury doubts.

He is very conscious of the pressure on Hughes, making the point that if he had scored eight instead of four goals it would be all right, but that the fans, seeing the £2 million outlay on him expected more.

"I shouldn't think he is unaffected by the criticism, but he is determined to do well and wants to play tomorrow," he said.

What he claims to know nothing about is talk that Hughes will be returning to Manchester United.

Hughes himself says he wants to play out his eight-year contract with Barcelona, but that Manchester United is the only English club he would want to play for.

Venables won't be announcing a team until today but has a pool of 17. It is likely there won't be many changes from Tannadice, with the exception of Carrasco, now suspended.

Gary Lineker, cornered by mostly Spanish radio men after training, refused to talk about tonight's result or whether he would score.

On Dundee United he said Paul Sturrock had impressed him first game but he hadn't been surprised at that because he knew him as a good player.

"What did surprise me was that he worked off the left so much," he said.

United keeper Billy Thomson (right) uses a bit of nifty footwork to keep the ball away from striker Iain Ferguson during a training session in Barcelona yesterday.

United shatter mighty senors of Barcelona

Mark Hughes takes the ball up to Paul Hegarty as John Clark looks on.

BARCELONA 1, DUNDEE UTD 2 (agg. 1-3)

SCOTS MEN and women all over the world will be celebrating today, no matter their club loyalties because here, in the stunning Nou Camp Stadium, a side which by comparison with the multi millionares of Barcelona is home spun, completed a job they started so magnificently in a thriller back home in Dundee two weeks ago.

The magnitude of United's achievement is possibly best illustrated by remembering that while they play on occasions in front of crowds of under 6000, Barcelona are worried just now because their gates are falling below 80,000.

It was a David v. Goliath job as soon as the draw was made but the David again didn't just beat the odds but totally shattered them.

When the morning news broke that Eamonn Bannon wouldn't be playing because of a serious rib injury which happened in the cup tie with Forfar Athletic (who if results were all that counted are a better team than Barcelona!), there were long faces among the travelling fans of United supporters.

But now, oh how much Eamonn must regret that he missed such a stirring, such a thrilling, such a historic game.

I have to admit that I thought after Barcelona scored that they were in the driving seat.

But this United defence, which has been so magnificent so often, fought and battled and worked and refused to give in to the prodding of Victor or any of the thrusts by Barcelona.

They tamed the £5 million strike force of Gary Lineker and Mark Hughes, they took everything that Victor could inspire against them in their stride.

Then, in the most amazing last three minutes of any of the thousands of matches I have seen, they got their reward.

It came via the heads of John Clark and Iain Ferguson, it came via radar-like crosses from Ian Redford and Paul Sturrock.

It will never be forgotten by every Scot present in the stadium or by millions watching on television.

THE SPORTS EDITOR reports on the big match in Barcelona

Twenty-one years ago United beat Barcelona home and away. Then they were Europe's great unknowns. But that achievement laid the foundation for, truly, a reputation which has grown and grown and reached new heights last night. I refuse point blank to talk about any weakness in the United team.

They did the defensive job they had to do. They did the midfield job they had to do. And, in the end, they did the attacking job they had to do.

You cannot ask for more and if, during the minute by minute development of the game there were moments of worry, moments of drama in which United were on the receiving end, it would be churlish to reiterate them in such a moment of triumph.

Having said that, if there are better defenders in the world than David Narey and Maurice Malpas, more skilful, thoughtful attackers when it matters than Paul Sturrock, then they genuinely must be priceless.

I, frankly, do not rate any of the 73 games United had played in Europe before this one as a greater achievement because the opposition was arguably the world's biggest club.

And to think that the Tannadice men lost such experienced European players as Richard Gough and Davie Dodds before this season started and that top Euro scorer Ralph Milne went recently!

This puts even more clearly into perspective this amazing and wonderful achievement.

As I finish this report, darkness has fallen on the Nou Camp Stadium. Only when the lights went out did the cheering, chanting United fans who got their wish of a return to the pitch in their now famous warm down, wend their way into the streets of this huge Spanish city.

No doubt they will already be starting the celebrations which should go on in those of Tangerine persuasion in and around Dundee until at least the next round—the draw for which takes place tomorrow.

Venables tips United

AFTERWARDS, AN obviously delighted Jim McLean said, "Paul Sturrock tore them apart in both legs.

"Perhaps I did think of replacing tired legs in the second half but who could I possibly have taken off?

"It is our greatest achievement in Europe."

Terry Venables, under even greater pressure after this defeat than he has been up to now—and that's been pretty heavy—summed up by saying, "United could go on and win the U.E.F.A., considering the opposition."

The Spanish club's supporters called for the heads of Venables and Welsh international striker Mark Hughes after the 2-1 defeat by the Scots.

Venables said, "I am not prepared to talk about my future or the Mark Hughes situation at this stage.

"We have just suffered a huge disappointment and the most important thing is to try to lift the players for our remaining league games."

Old adversaries Borussia through

UNITED'S OPPONENTS in the the semi-finals could come from either West Germany, Sweden or Austria.

Old adversaries Borussia Moenchengladbach, from West Germany, strolled through at the expense of Portuguese side Vitoria Guimaraes, winning 5-2 on aggregate.

United lost 2-0 to the West Germans in the first leg of their U.E.F.A. Cup clash in season 1981/82, then beat Borussia 5-0 at Tannadice in the return leg.

Gothenburg, from Sweden, last night put out the highly-rated Inter Milan, going through on the away goals rule.

The dark horses of the tournament, Swarovski Tyrol, of Austria, put out another Italian outfit, Torino, by 2-1.

Last night's results in European cup competitions

U.E.F.A. CUP.
Quarter-final, second leg.

Barcelona 1, Dundee United 2 (aggregate 1-3).

Inter Milan 1, Gothenburg (Sweden) 1 (agg. 1-1. Gothenburg qualify on away goals rule).

Vitoria Guimaraes (Portugal) 2, Borussia Moenchengladbach (W. Germany) 2 (agg. 2-5).

Swarovski Tyrol (Austria) 2, Torino (Italy) 1 (agg. 2-1).

CHAMPIONS' CUP.

Real Madrid 2, Red Star (Yugo.) 0 (agg. 4-4. Real win on away goals rule).

Dynamo Kiev (Soviet Union) 2, Besiktas Istanbul (Turkey) 0 (agg. 7-0).

Broendbyernes (Denmark) 1, Porto (Portugal) 1 (agg. 1-2).

Anderlecht (Belgium) 2, Bayern Munich (W. Germany) 2 (agg. 2-7).

CUP-WINNERS' CUP.

Torpedo Moscow (Soviet Union) 3, Bordeaux (France) 2 (agg. 3-3. Bordeaux win on away goals rule).

Ajax Amsterdam (Netherlands) 3, Malmo (Sweden) 1 (agg. 3-2).

Sion (Switzerland) 0, Lokomotiv Leipzig (E. Germany) 0 (agg. 0-2).

Vitosha Sofia (Bulgaria) 0, Real Zaragoza (Spain) 2 (agg. 0-4).

Late one-two from Clark and Ferguson

IT WAS a disappointing crowd in the huge stadium which looked to contain only about half its 120,000 capacity.

In the second minute came the first moment of danger on the park when Marcos moved down the left and was tripped by Holt.

The United defence quickly cleared the free kicks but only three minutes later the home side got through the United defence after a build-up by skipper Victor.

Lineker was put in possession 12 yards out but his shot was brilliantly saved low left by Thomson.

It was Clark, Hegarty (even though he was wearing the No. 9 shirt), Narey and Malpas at the back with Holt, McInally and Redford in midfield.

Victor was prodding on Barcelona as he did at Tannadice and when he sent Lineker wide down the right the striker should have done better than pass straight to Hegarty.

After a solid start United began to look a bit ragged as the home side piled on the pressure.

Gallacher and Malpas cleared anywhere in quick succession then Clark hit Marcos with a heavy tackle and was lucky to escape a booking.

In 18 minutes came a real scare.

Gerardo raced down the right and crossed. Roberto had slipped through unnoticed and headed over the bar.

It was getting nerve-wracking for the United fans dotted here and there round the vast stadium but they did get a moment of relief when the ball eventually reached Sturrock. His cross, however, was too weak to do any damage.

In 28 minutes, though, he did better when Redford sent him away.

He forced a corner—United's first—and though nothing came of it, it must have been a relief to the United men at the back.

It got better a couple of minutes later. Ferguson was on the verge of breaking through when Moratalla pulled him down 25 yards out. Redford tapped the free kick to the side but Ferguson's shot raged just over the bar.

We were back at the other end for a corner a couple of minutes later. It was gathered easily by Thomson.

The tension was tremendous and when Ferguson again burst through he was halted by his own mistake in fouling Migueli.

John Holt was battling well in midfield along with Redford and McInally and though they weren't getting the build up quite right, their defensive abilities were being tested and so far, at any rate, found adequate.

Then a real moment of hope for United.

A piece of brilliant ball control by Malpas on the left sent Sturrock off. His cross was well nigh perfect and Gallacher got a touch on it. Not enough of one though as Zubizarreta went down to clear.

Thomson's anticipation in goal was proving a tremendous asset. Twice he was out several yards to gather what could have been dangerous crosses.

But even he had to admit defeat as the interval approached.

When Migueli sent Roberto away, Clark cleared desperately for a corner which proved disastrous for United.

It was headed on and the lurking Caldere smashed in a tremendous shot from 20 yards. Thomson seemed to be in line but the ball took a deflection and rocketed into the net.

Any time is a bad time to lose a goal but five minutes from the interval comes into the category of the worst!

The patience Barcelona decided they needed had paid off and as they flowed in on Thomson again, Narey downed Hughes in the box and there were loud appeals for a penalty.

We nearly had an even bigger sensation in the first minute of the second half. Holt and Gallacher combined well on the right and the winger sent over a great cross.

Ferguson couldn't quite reach it but when the ball broke off a defender Sturrock hit a tremendous shot which struck Gerardo and went wide.

Then, after a couple of dangerous-looking thrusts by Barcelona, Sturrock sent in a great through pass which Zubizarreta just beat Gallacher to.

He quietly turned and tapped the ball back to Thomson while surrounded by four Barcelona players. Some nerve!

Gallacher was obviously looked on as a particularly dangerous United player—he was being sent crashing every time he looked to be posing a threat.

The thrusts weren't bot! ering Thomson because of the cover provided by the magnificent defensive abilities of the men at the back and in midfield but there was a cutting edge was proved when Roberto broke through to shoot just past the post.

Sturrock kept testing the Barcelona right defence when the opportunity arose but he was well policed when he did get in a cross and the defensive cover was solid.

Rojo went on for the limping Marcos as United got back in the game but Redford's cross was only glanced with his head by Ferguson as the ball slipped past the post.

Rojo's name cropped up again in the 75th minute.

He was in the clear in the United box but should have done better than chip the ball over the bar.

This really was a wonderful United rearguard action as Barcelona strove to get the one more that would have seen them through.

But the whole thing blew up in their faces in the 86th minute. It was the magnificent Malpas who stepped in at this point.

He set off deep on the left and worked his way right until he was 35 yards from goal.

When he turned the ball back to McInally the midfield man found Sturrock on the left.

As he went to go past Gerardo he was sent crashing.

The referee, who had been ignoring many of the fouls against United's attackers, this time gave a free kick.

It was taken left-footed by Redford and typically the cross was deadly in its accuracy.

John Clark, who had been having a tough time at the back, rose and rocketed the ball into the net with his head.

It was a sensational turn of events, completely stunning the Barcelona crowd and raising roars from the United followers scattered round the stadium.

And worse was to follow . . for the home crowd I mean! With a minute to go and Barcelona suddenly looking a lot less than adequate, Redford moved infield then switched a pass to Sturrock on the left.

Showing all the coolness born of experience, he strolled in and chipped the ball into the goalmouth.

High above everyone rose the blond head of Iain Ferguson and United were definitely and emphatically in the semi-final of the U.E.F.A. Cup.

As I telephone in this story the lights are dimming in the Nou Camp Stadium. The place where the lights went out for Barcelona.

Barcelona—Zubizarreta; Gerardo, Migueli, Manolo, Victor, Moratalla, Calvere, Lineker, Hughes, Roberto, Marcos. Subs—Fradera, Urruti, Urbano, Rojo, Clos.

Dundee United—Thomson; Holt, Malpas, McInally, Clark, Narey, Ferguson, Gallacher, Hegarty, Sturrock, Redford. Subs—Bowman, Kinnaird, Beaumont, Main, McLeod.

Referee: Karl Heinz Tritschler, West Germany.

Ferguson determined to get Hughes back

ALEX. FERGUSON, manager of Manchester United, accompanied by director Bobby Charlton, confirmed on arrival in Barcelona yesterday that he is here to start talks with manager Terry Venables over the future of striker Mark Hughes, who joined the Spanish club from United (**reports THE SPORTS EDITOR**).

He indicated he was disappointed Hughes had gone in the first place and expressed determination to get him back, despite Hughes's statement on Tuesday that he wanted to play out his Barcelona contract and Venables evading the issue altogether.

Obviously, there will be a lot of hard bargaining before the siuation is resolved—not least on the question of Hughes' terms.

OLE—MAGNIFICENT UNITED TAME THE SPANISH GIANTS

MAGNIFICENT DUNDEE UNITED achieved the near-impossible last night, defeating the mighty multi-million £ Barcelona in front of their home crowd and turning in one of the greatest ever performances by a Scottish club in European football.

It was a result that no-one but the most ardent fans dared hope for, a result that silenced the masses in the huge arena of the Nou Camp stadium and a result that will send shock waves throughout Europe.

Right from the kick-off the Tannadice men played out of their socks in a frantic bid to press home their slender one-goal advantage from the first leg.

Not even the disappointment of conceding a first half goal to the Spaniards could dampen the undercurrent of enthusiasm that ran throughout the team and the small but vociferous *armada* of fans who yelled themselves hoarse as footballing history unfolded before them.

If Drake singed the King of Spain's beard then it was McLean who shaved it off.

Right from the re-start his Tangerine terrors dogged an unhappy Barcelona side whose millionaire reputation let them down badly on the night.

The tactics worked a dream. The grumblings of a massive home support were slowly overcome by a resounding, repetitive chorus of 'You'll never walk

alone' as United turned on the screws.

Minutes later the real celebrations began. A Redford cross, a Clark header and Barcelona were left with a mountain to climb.

They didn't even get started. Sturrock and Ferguson between them drove home the final nail with a last minute goal that left Terry Venables' men looking like a ten a penny Sunday side.

By the time the glittering Nou Camp stadium had vanished from TV screens, Dundee had already become the city of jubilation.

From the ritziest bar to the darkest front room in the city, fans sang, danced and hauled each other into the action replays.

Young and old, man and women, United and Dundee supporters alike, all let fly with one voice, their inhibitions—and drinks—forgotten for the moment.

And many celebrations were still going on well into the night. Grinned one merry fan, Paul Blackley of Ardler, "We're not going home until United get home themselves. It's going to be quite a night..."

All over the town, the message was the same—the city's most glorious footballing night of recent years, if not of all time.

Dignitaries were queuing up to register their delight.

Said Dundee East M.P. Gordon Wilson, stranded in London and having to listen to a crackling radio commentary, "I'm immensely proud of the team.

"It seems that Barcelona have now made the Dundee discovery."

Tayside Region convener John McAllion was ecstatic.

"Absolutely brilliant—a tremendous result," was his verdict.

"I have always thought Dundee United are the best ambassadors Tayside could wish for."

Mr John MacKay, Scotland's Minister for Sport, added his praise for United's performance.

"Well done, Dundee United," he said. "A marvellous result and a very well deserved win.

"I hope you have a good draw in the semi-finals and I'm sure everyone in Scotland would like to see Jim McLean and his team winning through to the final."

Back in Dundee, Alistair Derrick, of Park Avenue, said, "It was a tremendous night.

"It's great for the town, great for Scotland and great for British football in general."

Added William Kay, of Hilltown, "To think that the team from Tannadice can do this—it's unbelievable. But that

stadium didn't frighten them one bit, did it?"

"It was a magic night; one of the best British performances ever, apart from in the European finals," said Dave Lawrie, Ancrum Drive.

"They were up against it, certainly—but the £5 million boys never got a look-in.

"I think what triumphed, in the end, was the pure Scottish fighting character. When we're up against it, we'll fight till we drop."

One of the most telling comments came from a Dundee F.C. fan, of all people.

Said Jim Kenny, of Forth Crescent, "It was great to see United go through, I've got to admit it. There were real blood and guts on show there."

Jim and his friends had been watching the game on the large screen in Gabriels bar, which erupted in a wash of delight at the first goal and reached fever pitch with the late bonus.

And there was a carbon copy reaction up the road in Alan Bannerman's Phoenix Bar, which was giving away free beer with every United goal.

"At half time I thought I would be sending the beer back," grinned mine host, "but we've been drunk dry of the stuff."

"We've been packed to the doors tonight, and everybody, United and Dundee fans alike, are absolutely thrilled."

Picture from B.B.C. Television.

Picture from B.B.C. Television.

A night of celebration for United fans in Barcelona

In photos: The UEFA Cup run

4

5

6

1: United's squad at the start of the 1986/87 season.

2: Bright spark Maurice Malpas (seated) gives Paul Hegarty, Dave Narey and Paul Sturrock a lesson in computing.

3: Maurice Malpas, Ralph Milne, Eamonn Bannon, Billy Thomson and Paul Hegarty return from Romania.

4: Paul Sturrock goes close in the second leg against RC Lens.

5: Ian Redford scores against Universitatea Craiova.

6: Eamonn Bannon puts the boot in against Craiova.

1: Jim McInally opens the scoring in the first leg against Hajduk Split.

2: The players pose before heading to Yugoslavia for the second leg against Hajduk Split.

3: United powerhouse John Clark competes for a high ball against Hajduk.

4: The young mascot looks overawed as Dave Narey and Barcelona captain Victor toss the coin at Tannadice.

5: Eamonn Bannon smashes a shot on goal against Barca.

5

6

7

8

1: Kevin Gallacher races down the wing against Barcelona.

2: Eamonn Bannon clears in the box with Mark Hughes and Gary Lineker threatening.

3: A Bannon piledriver.

4: Jim McInally rushes to congratulate Kevin Gallacher on his early goal.

5: That magical moment Gallacher's shot (or was it a cross...?) floats towards Zubizaretta's net.

6: Mark Hughes gets a grip of United keeper Billy Thomson.

7: Paul Sturrock battles hard.

8: United players mob Gallacher after his goal.

1: Ian Redford has a shot at goal in the first leg against Borussia Moenchengladbach.

2: The Germans threaten the United goal.

3: Jim McInally takes charge in midfield.

4: The Germans clearly believe 0-0 with a home tie to come should be enough to see them into the final.

5: Maurice Malpas thinks United have scored.

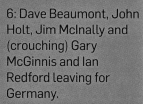

6: Dave Beaumont, John Holt, Jim McInally and (crouching) Gary McGinnis and Ian Redford leaving for Germany.

7: Jim McLean signs autographs before setting off.

8: A young fan bids United farewell.

9: John Holt with son John and daughter Sarah.

10: Jim McInally and John Clark surrounded by adoring fans.

1: The squad setting off for Gothenburg.

2: Paul Hegarty is wished good luck from wife Linda and son Christopher.

3: Iain Ferguson and Jim McInally get stretching.

4: Fitness work for Joe McLeod, Dave Bowman and Maurice Malpas.

5: The ball-boys for the UEFA Cup final look forward to playing their part in history.

6: Some of the backroom staff at Tannadice who did so much to help in United's famous season.

7: The two Pauls, Hegarty and Sturrock, work on flexibility.

8: The United squad loosen the muscles on the eve of the final.

9: The effort to get the pitch in its best shape for a worldwide audience.

1: The United players look pensive after their narrow first-leg defeat in Gothenburg.

2: John Clark drives forward in the second leg at Tannadice.

3: Iain Ferguson gets stuck in after a scuffle in the box.

4: United press on goal.

5: Jim McInally hopes to pick up scraps from the Gothenburg keeper.

6: Ian Redford tries to direct a shot on target.

7: An acrobatic effort from Kevin Gallacher.

8: Dave Narey leads the United players on a lap of honour at full-time.

9: The Gothenburg players raise the famous trophy.

10: Sportsmanship from Lennart Nilsson and Paul Hegarty.

11: Kevin Gallacher thinks of what might have been.

12: Paul Hegarty reflects on the bitter disappointment of defeat.

The favourites fall

United's band of travelling supporters have not even made it back from Spain before semi-final fever erupts.

The draw pitches the Tangerines against Borussia Moenchengladbach — two-time UEFA Cup winners and a team who have knocked out Rangers on their way to the 1987 semi-finals.

Buoyed by the stunning success against Barcelona, and with a victory over Borussia in 1981 still fresh in the mind, Jim McLean is again willing to talk up his side's chances against the tournament favourites.

"This is the most attractive team we could have drawn and there is also added stimulus in the fact that our result against them in 1981 really put Dundee United on the map", he says.

The manager later adds: "Borussia are definitely beatable, and all our men must ask of themselves is a repeat performance of the way they played in both legs of the quarter-final against Barcelona."

United have also advanced in the Scottish Cup, and face a mouth-watering semi-final against city neighbours Dundee only three days after the first leg against Borussia.

However, the hectic schedule has started to impact on United's league form and a match away to St Mirren sees McLean resting some of his key men in a clear sign that he is now focusing on cup glory.

As he puts it: "The only teams we've beaten recently are Barcelona and Forfar (so) it's ridiculous I've not made changes before."

The Courier hails the excitement of "double semi-final week" by declaring it "...a tremendous week in the football history of the city, probably unparalleled..."

Remarkably, with only a day to go until Tannadice stages a major European semi-final, there are still thousands of tickets available — prompting a spirited rebuke from The Courier's sports editor to readers who are passing up the chance to "be in one of the biggest sporting occasions in the history of the city."

At just short of 16,000, the crowd is indeed significantly down on the 21,322 who packed into Tannadice to see United beat Barcelona, and a frustrating 0-0 draw leaves many wondering if the dream is over.

The Germans seem to believe so, with high-fives and celebrations at full-time suggesting they think the home leg will be a formality.

However, United soon have their own reasons to celebrate as they lift themselves to beat Dundee in what The Courier sports editor declares "the greatest semi-final it has been my privilege to see in a lifetime of sports writing."

As the Tangerines then switch their focus on trying to win their other semi-final, an extraordinary row breaks out over live TV coverage from Germany.

With the UEFA Cup adventure winning friends across the country, SFA secretary Ernie Walker steps up to try to protect fans from what he sees as over-exposure to United's efforts, insisting: " Dundee United have been on television far too often lately."

It's all too much for United's much-respected chairman George Fox, who responds: "I wasted six years of my life over a dictator in Germany and I am not going to waste any more time over a dictator in Scotland."

 Mr Fox wins his battle. And so do Dundee United...

Draw sees Borussia return to Tannadice

By STEVE BRUCE

THE U.E.F.A. CUP semi-final draw, made in Geneva yesterday, paired Dundee United with old foes and trophy favourites Borussia Moenchengladbach.

The first-leg will be at Tannadice on April 8, the return in the 35,000-capacity Bokelberg Stadium on April 22.

It's a draw which will revive happy memories for all connected with United.

The clubs met in this competition back in season 81-82 when the Tangerines overturned a 2-0 first leg deficit in stunning fashion, blasting five past the Germans without reply at Tannadice.

"This is the most attractive team we could have drawn and there is also added stimulus in the fact that our result against them in 1981 really put Dundee United on the map," commented manager Jim McLean.

"People started to take notice of us after we beat Borussia 5-0 and it would be nice if we could do the same again," he added with a smile.

The Tannadice boss however won't be banking on a repeat performance to take United through to their first ever Euro final for he believes that nowadays the nature of European football is such that sides need to produce their best form over both legs to succeed.

"At this stage in the competition you can sometimes win these ties away from home," he claimed.

A crowd of only 15,330 witnessed the home leg last time, but a sell-out is certain for this re-match.

Borussia have quite a U.E.F.A. Cup pedigree, having won the trophy twice and reaching the final on three other occassions.

They made the last four of this season's competition by beating, Partisan Belgrade (1-0 at home, 3-1 away), Feyenoord (5-1, 2-0), Rangers (1-1, 0-0) and Vitoria Guimares (3-0, 2-2).

The clash with Rangers was a stormy affair with Davie Cooper and Stuart Munro both being sent off in Germany.

On the domestic front, the five times Bundesliga champions, twice German Cup winners, currently lie mid-table and have off-field worries to contend with.

Coach Jupp Heynckes is reportedly set to leave them at the end of the season, to take charge of Bayern Munich and star striker Uwe Rahn is being linked with PSV Eindhoven.

They also have problems on the European disciplinary front. Right-back Bernd Krauss misses the visit to Tannadice, through suspension and six other players already have one yellow card against their names in the competition which means,

a booking in the semi-final, first-leg would rule the men involved out of the return.

This is probably the hardest draw United could have had but after disposing of Barcelona in such style and bearing in mind their vast experience in continental competition, the Tangerines have an outstanding chance of reaching the final.

● United are already drawing up plans to watch Borussia, who play Werder Bremen away tomorrow.

On March 28, they entertain Bochum VFL and on April 4, travel to face Eintracht Frankfurt.

Tannadice coach Gordon Wallace will be dispatched on a spying mission to one of these matches.

First-hand help from Wattie

UNITED ARE to receive help from former assistant manager Walter Smith in plotting the Germans' downfall.

Walter, now No. 2 at Ibrox, is to pass on the dossier Rangers assembled on Borussia, who beat them in the third round of the competition.

The file contains personal notes on the German players as well as videos of Borussia in action.

"I don't believe Dundee United have anything to fear. We still consider we should have beaten them," said Walter.

Walter Smith.

Same prices for 'semi' tickets

TICKET PRICES for the home leg of the U.E.F.A. Cup semi-final were yesterday announced by United.

The Tannadice club are to charge £20 for a stand seat and £10 for a place on the terracing—the same prices as were in force for the quarter-final with Barcelona.

Due to the fact that United have, after today, only one home League match before the Ger-

mans visit Tannadice on April 8, the voucher system which drastically reduced the cost of admission to the Barcelona game for regular attenders, isn't being repeated.

However, fans buying Borussia tickets will find two stubs attached to their purchase and these will allow holders free entry into the home matches with Hamilton (April 11) and Hibs (May 2).

See the return game free

THERE WILL be an opportunity for two lucky readers to see the return game free.

A competition, run in conjunction with VG, will appear in "The Courier" soon.

An announcement of the starting date for the competition will be made within the next few days.

Strong at the back, says Bob

ONE MAN man with an up to date knowledge of Borussia is Dundee referee Bob Valentine who took charge of the second leg of their quarter-final tie with Vitoria Guimares, in Portugal, on Wednesday night.

"They are a typical German side," says the Tayside whistler.

"Borussia are particularly strong at the back and the defence could deal with high balls all day but they definitely didn't look too good when players ran at them."

Bob was particularly impressed by striker Uwe Rahn and midfield playmaker Gunter Bruns, coincidentally, the only surviving members of the Munchengladbach squad who lost to United in the U.E.F.A. Cup in 1981.

"I refereed Bayern Munich two rounds ago and would rate

them more highly than Borussia, although it is difficult to judge a side on the evidence of 90 minutes, particularly away from home in Europe," concludes Bob.

Bob Valentine.

United's next opponents had won the UEFA Cup twice, and knocked out Rangers in the third round.

The draws

U.E.F.A. CUP, SEMI-FINALS.
Gothenburg (Sweden) v. Swarovski Tirol (Austria).
Dundee Utd. (Scotland) v. Borussia Moenchengladbach (West Germany).

CUP-WINNERS' CUP.
Real Zaragosa (Spain) v. Ajax Amsterdam (Netherlands).
Bordeaux (France) v. Lokomotiv Leipzig (East Germany).

EUROPEAN CUP.
Bayern Munich (West Germany) v. Real Madrid (Spain).
Porto (Portugal) v. Dynamo Kiev (Soviet Union).

In the final of the UEFA Cup, played in two legs on a home-and-away basis, the winner of the semi-final match between Bothenburg and Swarovski Tirol will be at home in the first leg on May 6, and the winner of Dundee United-Borussia Moenchengladbach will be at home in the second leg on May 20.

The final of the Cup-Winners' Cup will be played in Athens on May 13, and the final of the European Cup in Vienna on May 27.

Now it's the turn of the Germans!

STILL DRUNK on the atmosphere of Barcelona's Nou Camp Stadium, and buzzing about the news of their team's U.E.F.A. Cup semi-final draw against Borussia Moenchengladbach, the mass "diplomatic corps" of Dundee United fans returned by coach to their home city yesterday afternoon.

In North Lindsay Street 92 fans poured off two coaches—although passers-by might have been forgiven for thinking they had changed allegiance during their visit to see United's historic quarter-final victory.

They soon explained that the reason most of them were swathed in red and blue and carrying huge Catalan flags was that they and the home fans had got on like a house on fire.

"All the Barcelona fans were really friendly, even after the game," said Keith Hogan, who had much of his journey home to Inverness still in front of him. "They were very keen to swop scarves, badges and flags and most congratulated us on the result."

Keith, who travels to see United wherever they play, described the last 10 minutes of the game as "unbelievable."

"When John Clark scored it was absolutely brilliant—we were dancing around like mad-

men—and Fergie's goal was the icing on the cake!"

Paul Phillips, of Lochee, is confined to a wheelchair but that did not stop him travelling to Barcelona.

"I actually saw the game from way up in the high stands," he said. "The Nou Camp is enormous, like an airport, but there are lots of ramps and there were no problems."

Ian Horne and Norman Burns, of Lochee, were rushing home to see if their huge Scotland flag had been seen by the TV cameras.

"My wife videoed the game," or at least, she'd better have," said Norman. "It was a fantastic trip—great city, great stadium and brilliant match.

"I used up part of my holidays to go but I'll be trying to make sure I can get to Germany for the semi-final."

And what about United's prospects for the match against Moenchengladbach? "After that? No problem!" was the general opinion.

Yesterday's draw provided another glamour tie for the Tangerine Terrors. Borussia despatched Rangers and Feyenoord from the tournament and, with 17 goals, are joint highest scorers so far.

Announcement of the plum tie—first leg at Tannadice on April 8, with the return in Germany on April 22—brought a flurry of activity among travel agents in Dundee, who are anticipating a rush for bookings from fans.

Within five minutes of the announcement of the draw A.T. Mays had already started arrangements.

"Our head office is arranging a charter flight and some buses," said a spokeswoman. "We are expecting a large response after the Barcelona success, and particularly if United do well in the home tie."

Watson's Tours see the German opposition as a bonus for the fans.

"I would think that, as far as getting fans there by coach, Germany is better than Sweden and Austria," said a spokesman. "Gothenburg would have been expensive, not just for distance but because of the cost of living."

The United support could also be swollen on the away leg by British soldiers serving in Germany and Holland. Several bases in both countries lie within easy reach of the German club.

Mr Colin Ramsay, of Ramsay World Travel, Dundee, said he

had been "absolutely swamped" with fans inquiring about trips to Germany.

"The response has been fantastic and we'll certainly be laying on a few trips for the match," he said.

Within hours of the draw being announced he had already laid on a special flight to Dusseldorf.

"We've got 80 seats on that but we've already taken about 40 names of folk who're interested," he added.

Also on the cards are a number of specially arranged coach trips, leaving direct from Dundee.

Dundee District Council's tourism department will be holding a meeting next week to draw up a strategy which will best reflect the city in the eyes of the expected influx of German supporters on April 8.

Tourism officer Toni McPherson said German language information on accommodation formation and Dundee's attractions would be available in the tourist office in the Nethergate Centre.

She expected the city's hotels would also be gearing themselves up for the invasion which could number as high as a couple of thousand.

The jubilant fans on arrival in Dundee.

Billy Kirkwood

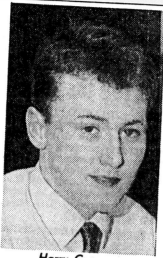
Harry Curran

Chris Sulley

Differing fortunes of United's full-backs

Tickets for semi-finals on sale now

WHAT DIFFERENCE can a few days make?

Quite a lot if you happen to be a Dundee United full-back!

Consider the cases of Billy Kirkwood, Harry Curran and Chris Sulley.

Kirkwood, a vital component in the United side that fared so well in Europe during the early eighties, was ineligible for the U.E.F.A. Cup quarter-final tie with Barcelona after returning to Tannadice from Hibs.

However, having rejoined United before January 15 he is available for the semi-final with Borussia.

By STEVE BRUCE

Left-back Curran, though, cannot harbour dreams of Euro glory for even if the Tangerines reach the final he won't be involved.

The unlucky youngster signed from Dumbarton on February 18, three days the wrong side of U.E.F.A.'s deadline for final eligibility.

Then there is the situation involving Chris Sulley, currently on loan to English Second Division side Blackburn Rovers.

He isn't scheduled to return north until April 5 and as Scottish Cup rules demand a player should be with his club for 14 days before a tie, the Englishman will not be available for the semi-final tie with Dundee.

The problems concerning Sulley and Curran aren't too serious for United, providing Maurice Malpas remains fit and healthy but with such a congested programme confronting his club and the additional risk of injury that brings, manager Jim McLean would have preferred to have all his first-team squad to call upon.

A FULL-SCALE rush is anticipated at Tannadice today as tickets for the semi-finals of the U.E.F.A. Cup and Scottish Cup go on sale.

Because Dundee United are expecting so many people, the two lots of tickets will be sold at different parts of the ground.

Those seeking briefs for the U.E.F.A. Cup tie with Borussia Moenchengladbach should go to the staff canteen.

Stand tickets for that match are priced at £20 and ground tickets at £10.

While no voucher system to reduce prices for the Borussia match is operating, as was the case for the quarter-final with Barcelona, those who buy tickets for that match will receive vouchers for free entry to the subsequent home matches against Hamilton Accies and Hibs.

Supporters looking for stand tickets for the Scottish Cup derby match with Dundee, at Tynecastle, can buy them from the club office priced £7 for the main stand and £5 for the south stand.

Entry to the terracing will be £3 cash at Tynecastle turnstiles on the day of the match.

Lothian police have contacted United to advise them that supporters arriving by car will be allocated parking facilities at Chesser Avenue, approximately one mile west of Hearts' ground.

Tickets for both occasions can also be bought from the usual out-lets, various V.G. foodstores and Dundee United Social Club.

Opening hours for ticket sales at Tannadice this week are—Wednesday—9 a.m.-5 p.m.; Thursday 9 a.m.-8 p.m.; Friday—9 a.m.-8 p.m.; Saturday—9 a.m.-12 noon.

'Spies' to watch Borussia

DUNDEE UNITED manager Jim McLean and coach Gordon Wallace are flying to Germany next week to watch U.E.F.A. Cup semi-final opponents Borussia Moenchengladbach in action(reports Steve Bruce).

The Tannadice duo will take in Tuesday evening's German Cup semi-fnal between Hamburg and Borussia.

Meanwhile, McLean plans to play out-of-touch international Eamonn Bannon in the reserves in the hope he can recapture his form in time for the exciting programme which lies ahead for United.

Bannon would have taken part in last night's second string cup tie against Motherwell but was ruled out after his rib injury flared-up again.

The World Cup player is actually one of 12 United men on the causalty list.

The Tannadice injury list reads—Billy Thomson (ankle), Maurice Malpas (thigh), Eamonn Bannon (ribs), Paddy Connelly (glandular fever), Gerry Brennan (dislocated elbow), Billy McKinlay (back), Alan Preston (side strain), Steve Bremner (side strain), Bruce Deas (knee), Jimmy Page (back), Kenny Macdonald (ankle) and Raymond McKinnon (ankle).

Malpas, however, is expected to be fit to face Dundee at Tannadice tomorrow.

Borussia tie is the chance of a lifetime, says Jim McLean

"I AM not underestimating Borussia Moenchengladbach in any way, but this is the chance of a lifetime for our players which they should not throw away."

Manager Jim McLean, back at Tannadice yesterday after watching Borussia losing in the German Cup semi-final (and Scotland being beaten in Belgium), emphasised that the

vital game was tomorrow's Premier League fixture against St Mirren at Love Street, but was willing to look back at the performance of next week's UEFA Cup semi-final opponents.

He continued, "The players must realise they have a great chance.

"Borussia are definitely beatable, and all our men must ask of themselves is a repeat performance of the way they played in both legs of the quarter-final against Barcelona.

"I also appeal yet again for patience from our supporters.

"Borussia love to frustrate the opposition and are magnificent on the break.

"In fact they base their game on frustrating the other team and here is where our supporters must be as patient as our team.

"The fact they have 'grown up' with us in Europe and know about the tactics of visiting teams will help."

What United must also be hoping for is that referee Marcel van Langenhove (Belgium) is a strong official.

It is an well-known fact in the game that Borussia are extremely physical on occasions.

If the ref keeps blowing up for fouls and doing nothing in the way of name taking, he will be falling into the trap of interrupting the rhythm of United's play, while doing nothing to stop the Germans achieving their objective of doing just that.

Looking back at Borussia's earlier elimination of Rangers from the UEFA Cup, manager McLean said, "Over the two games Rangers should have progressed to the next round.

"Borussia definitely are not a better team than Rangers.

"Over 180 minutes we must not fall into the trap of handing them a goal.

"We must attack, pressure them, play in their half of the park—but avoid being stupid at the back ourselves.

"I can't repeat too often that we must have patience and in that, must be joined by our supporters.

"Borussia pass back to the keeper, play the ball sideways along the back, try to suck the opposition into moving too far forward, then hit on the break.

"But our players have been in Europe many times.

"They know what to do. They dictated the game against Barcelona home and away. They deserve every credit for that— and they can do it again."

Then, finally, obviously thinking back to the 5-0 thrashing of Borussia at Tannadice six years ago—and the poor United display against Roma, he said, "I wouldn't want to go back there. Borussia won't relish coming back here."

Then it was on to tomorrow's game against St Mirren, important because no one at Tannadice is yet in the mood to concede that the Premier League championship is decided.

Amazingly, keeper Billy Thomson, out of plaster after his ankle injury only on Wednesday, actually believes he might make the Love Street game— but he is more or less alone in that, despite the fact others are pretty sure he will be available for Wednesday against Borussia.

Most worrying injury is that to young Jimmy Page.

It is a mystery problem involving his back, which stiffens up and goes into a spasm if he plays.

So seriously are the club treating it that he will be sent to a specialist in London to try to solve the problem.

It looks like he will be out for what remains of the season, a cruel blow to the lad with so much to be played for.

Only other "casualties" are Gordon McLeod, with a heavy cold, and Gary McGinnis with a strained thigh.

Of course, this was not the first time Dundee United and Borussia had met in the UEFA Cup.

With the memory of that glorious 5-0 Tannadice victory over the Germans in 1981 still fresh in the mind, McLean had no reservations in declaring this a tie his men could — and should — win.

Proud to be of service!

DUNDEE UNITED could have done without seven players being involved in Scotland's mid-week trip to Belgium in view of their double semi-final programme next week following tomorrow's league fixture with St Mirren.

That is the generally-held view of those who follow United, but there is one important exception to the opinion— manager Jim McLean!

When I mentioned the thought to him, his reply was, "Every player who signs for this club must want to play for Scotland.

"I will never, ever criticise selction of my players for their country.

"Football is not about taking all the time. There are times you have to give and I was proud we gave so many to Scotland.

"The benefits are actually considerable.

"The players get the adrena-lin flowing, it gives them confidence to be involved at that level and that far outweighs any inconvenience.

"I know we have the most important week of the season so far coming up, but we have had important weeks ahead before and do not consider the Scotland call-ups anything but an honour."

All United's Scotland men have returned without the complication of injuries, but the manager emphasised this was not what prompted his remarks.

● Before the game against Belgium fans from that country were asking the manager for his autograph and expressing their compliments over the Barcelona results.

It was only the tip of the iceberg.

Literally hundreds of letters of praise have arrived at Tannadice since the games against the Spanish giants to add to as many telephone calls of congratulation.

85

Poor league results prompt McLean to swing the axe today

THE COLLAPSE of Dundee United's championship challenge has prompted manager Jim McLean to swing the axe for this afternoon's meeting with St Mirren at Love Street (reports STEVE BRUCE).

With the U.E.F.A. Cup semi-final against Borussia a matter of days away and the Scottish Cup semi against Dundee due next Saturday, the Tannadice boss plans to ring the changes after seeing his side go without a Premier League win since February 28.

He declared, "When you look at the number of points we've dropped and consider that the only teams we've beaten recently are Barcelona and Forfar, its ridiculous I've not made changes before.

"Obviously it was easy to stand by players after Barcelona but in view of our league results, changes are long overdue.

"I have examined the recent contributions of certain players and, based on that, some will be dropped, others rested, to freshen them up for the two semis.

"And make no mistake, people will be playing for places in the side for both ties, at Paisley."

United may be without international defender Dave Narey who has a leg strain and is rated "very doubtful."

With the exception of Billy Thomson, Gary McGinnis and Gordon McLeod, the Tangerines entire first-team pool will be reporting.

Thomson and McGinnis are still on the injured list although McLean hopes to have both

Dave Narey . . . doubtful.

available to face Borussia, while McLeod is suffering from a heavy cold.

"It's unfortunate for Gordon that he's sidelined as I had definitely intended playing him against St Mirren," commented the manager.

Saints, themselves just seven days away from a Scottish Cup semi clash with Hearts, have a doubt over centre-half Peter Godfrey who is afflicted by the same ailment as McLeod and faces a late check.

Better news though of Paul Chalmers and Brian Gallagher. Chalmers is available again after injury while Gallagher makes his comeback in the reserves following a two months' absence because of a fractured leg.

Assistant boss Jimmy Bone commented, "Both clubs have a big week ahead of them and the possibility of this meeting being a Scottish Cup final dress rehearsal adds to the occasion."

United have won all three of their previous games with Saints this season and the completion of a clean sweep today would be a nice boost for them prior to switching attention to cup matters.

Jim McLean sees Borussia beaten

DUNDEE UNITED manager Jim McLean and coach Gordon Wallace last night saw U.E.F.A. Cup semi-final opponents Borussia Moenchengladbach beaten 1-0 by SV Hamburg in the German Cup semi-final at Hamburg.

The winning goal came in the final minute of the game when striker Kastl scored.

"The only teams we've beaten recently are Barcelona and Forfar".

It's a line we're unlikely to ever hear again from a United manager but it perfectly summed up the Tangerines' differing fortunes by this stage of the season.

With the league campaign all but over, attention turned to making the most of double semi-final week.

United match: hopes for fair play on—and off—the field

DUNDEE UNITED manager Jim McLean would no doubt want to be as confident as local community officials about Wednesday night's eagerly awaited U.E.F.A. Cup semi-final first-leg tie against Borussia Moenchengladbach at Tannadice Park.

Big matches at Tannadice and Dens bring congestion and sometimes mayhem to the streets and pavements outside.

The area's regional councillor Mr Mervyn Rolfe has experience of the problem, having risked his own safety to shepherd drunken spectators away from his constituents' homes and on to the grounds without disturbing the peace.

Mr Rolfe said yesterday, "I don't anticipate a lot of problems with it, but I and others will be watching what happens very closely, just in case anything goes wrong.

"Most of the problems in the past have involved Scottish League or cup matches where large numbers of out-of-town supporters have arrived on convoys of buses.

"The fans have drunk alcohol on board and have wanted to relieve themselves as soon as they have reached the football grounds, without searching for toilets.

"We have identified a number of ways to try to stop this practice, with the help of the police. The situation has improved and we want the trend to continue," Mr Rolfe added.

Wednesday's match has been made an all-ticket affair with the 22,000 briefs ranging from £10 each for the terracing, to £20 each for the stand.

It is understood that early sales of tickets have been low, but with Jim McLean announcing at the weekend that the match will definitely not be screened live on television, the Tannadice ticket office is likely to become busier over the next three days.

A small contingent of German spectators are being expected to cheer on their team, but numbers are thought unlikely to exceed 500.

Tayside Police suggest that to lessen inconvenience to local residents, spectators should arrive early and fans are advised to share vehicles to minimise congestion.

Gussie Park will be available for parking for those who arrive early and drivers who park elsewhere are urged to leave corners, bus stops, access to premises and double yellow lines clear.

One-night stay for Borussia

By STEVE BRUCE

DUNDEE UNITED's U.E.F.A. Cup semi-final opponents Borussia Moenchengladbach, will fly into Scotland less than 28 hours before Wednesday night's first leg and do not intend training at Tannadice prior to the game.

The Bundesliga side are scheduled to arrive in Edinburgh at 4 p.m. on Tuesday and will depart for West Germany immediately after the match.

Meanwhile, United have transferred left-back Chris Sulley to Blackburn Rovers for a small fee.

Sulley, who joined the Tangerines from Bournemouth last summer, has spent the past month on loan to the English Second Division outfit and in fact played in their Full Members' Cup winning side at Wembley last weekend.

In view of the 2 p.m. kick-off imposed on next Saturday's Scottish Cup semi-final with Dundee at Tynecastle, United are considering spending Friday evening in Edinburgh.

Double time for Dundee

It's double semi-final time for the city of Dundee this week.

First comes Dundee United's eagerly awaited U.E.F.A. Cup clash with Borussia Moenchengladbach . . . what an attraction after that stunning tie against Barcelona!

Then it is on to what some may consider an even bigger tie—Dundee v. United in the Scottish Cup semi-final, with the city guaranteed one team in the final against Hearts or St Mirren.

It is a tremendous week in the football history of the city, probably unparalleled . . . and "The Courier," as always, will be recording every move along the way, giving you the best coverage of all.

Keeper worry in 'double semi week'

By THE SPORTS EDITOR

KEEPER BILLY THOMSON, with an ankle injury, has emerged as Dundee United's big worry as they head into "double semi week" with Borussia Moenchengladbach first in the U.E.F.A. Cup at Tannadice on Wednesday.

Said manager Jim McLean yesterday, "It really is touch and go with Thomson. He is not making the progress we had hoped for."

There is better news of central defender Dave Narey, whose problem is a leg injury.

"He was in again this morning getting treatment and has improved a wee bit," said the manager.

Now, of course, there is the added complication of Billy Kirkwood's serious ear injury and the multiple bumps and bruises suffered at Love Street on Saturday, though, other than Kirkwood, the manager reports that none of them appear at this stage to be serious.

Kirkwood was not available for the earlier rounds, but now he is.

One who will not make it is injured Gary McGinnis, while Jim McInally and Paul Sturrock are expected to be ready along with young Gordon McLeod, who might have played at Love Street, but had a heavy cold.

Though the manager will have a better idea of the exact extent of the problems today, he makes it clear that the real decisions on availability won't be made until Wednesday.

One definite decision that has been reached is that there will be no live televising of the Tannadice game.

Said the manager, "Under no circumstances will there be live television.

"Live television is definitely killing people coming to games.

"Anyone thinking there might be a change of mind is wrong. There is absolutely no chance of that.

"What we are seeking is the atmosphere we had against Barcelona in the last round—and to have that we must have a big crowd in the ground. That is absolutely vital."

Wondering, after the Love Street game, over the exact nature of United's injury list and the possible Wednesday line-up was Wolf Werner, Borussia's assistant coach, who, next season will become their top coach when current boss Jupp Heynckes goes to Bayern Munich.

While he tried to elicit as much information as possible about United, he was cagey about his own team.

He did, however, express disappointment over the fact that they had lost 4-0 to Eintracht Frankfurt while he was watching United.

"Not a happy result for us," he said, with a shake of the head, while, back home, Heynckes was "absolutely disgusted" with the team's performance, especially in the second half and bemoaning the fact a display like that would be suicidal against United.

After considerable insistence that he could not really understand or speak English, it transpired coach Werner could do both competently.

As the conversation developed, it became clear that the two main injury worries for the Germans are midfielder Dirk Bakalorz (23), in his first season with Borussia, and Uwe Rahn, possibly the club's top player, 25 next month and a survivor of the first meeting between the clubs.

Werner politely said he had been impressed with United against St Mirren though the gale-force wind had been the real winner.

"We respect particularly the United defence," he said, then again expressed his interest in whether or not key men in that defence, Dave Narey and Billy Thomson "and the very good McInally" and "the excellent Paul Sturrock" would be out against his side.

Borussia will arrive in their St Andrews hotel some time tomorrow afternoon and hope to train at Tannadice tomorrow night.

The estimate of the number of fans likely to be travelling with Borussia varies from 200 to 500.

● Tickets for the game have been selling steadily up to now. This week will tell the tale of how many will be there to see the action. A European Cup semi final deserves a full house. It will be interesting to see how near it United get.

Will it be a European baptism for young stand-in keeper Alan Main or will experienced semi? Picture shows club physio Jim Joyce giving Billy treatment while young Alan looks on.

McLean needs all the fans to play a part in this one

By the Sports Editor

AS WE move into Dundee United's double semi-final week, ticket sales for the first big game against Borussia Moenchengladbach in the U.E.F.A. Cup semi-final (first leg) (kick-off 8 p.m. to allow people to travel from any distance) are picking up.

But not enough to have even manager Jim McLean predicting a full house. His view is that the gate will be "from 12,000 to 15,000" which is up to 7000 short of capacity.

Just in case you are holding back, let's get a couple of facts straight—

(1) There will be no live television, so, if you aren't there you won't be in on one of the biggest sporting occasions in the history of the city;

(2) There will be no paying at the gate. This is what is nowadays called a category "A" game, as are all at European semi-final level, which means they must be all-ticket—and all ticket means just that!

With the Tannadice office open until 7 p.m. tonight and 5 p.m. tomorrow night—and tickets available in the Supporters' Club after that—the opportunity is certainly there to buy the necessary ticket or tickets.

Emphasising again and again how much he and the players would like a full house, manager McLean said, "The players got the credit for the result against Barcelona, but, believe me, the supporters deserve as much appreciation. It was the atmosphere they created which did so much to lift the team.

"Look at Paisley on Saturday. Just over 2000 people there and you could see the effect on our players. They started coasting when they should have been getting on with winning a game in which they were in front.

"We do not have enough Richard Goughs, Andy Grays, Jim McInallys, whose pride in performance and enthusiasm means they don't need a crowd to lift them.

"We need a full house here to enhance our chance of upsetting the frustration type of game Borussia will undoubtedly play. The proper atmosphere can make players play 50 per cent. better ... even 100 per cent. sometimes!

"Barcelona were a team who believed they could beat us by playing their normal game.

"Borussia are a team that will be attempting to stop us from playing, plus playing a possession and frustration game themselves.

"The crowd must be patient, must be behind us all the way.

"They must allow us to pass the ball about, to keep possession. Borussia will at times have 11 players in their own half, but they 'break' magnificently and that's we will have to be constantly aware of.

"No one can run about for 90 minutes chasing the game. We proved again how difficult it is to play against the type of team Borussia are this very morning when the reserves played their style and gave the opposition plenty of headaches.

"We always have this type of game, just before a European tie like the one on Wednesday, just to remind our players how important patience is.

"Borussia are beatable—and I am not underestimating them when I say that. The relationship between our supporters and players has built up over the years in Europe and will be needed probably more than ever on Wednesday.

"I am an admirer of German football and of the Dutch football of a few years ago. The Germans are winners. It will not be easy."

The manager then disclosed that he now had four videos of Borussia in action, including one from Germany which had been forwarded by a Larkhall Rangers' supporter!

It shows that, in the manager's opinion, Rangers were unlucky to go out of the U.E.F.A. Cup to Borussia.

He ended—"The players must realise that it is the last 30 weeks' effort that has put them in the position they are in this week, with two semi-finals. It is a magnificent achievement and we must now improve on that."

Borussia arrive about teatime today and have so far not asked for training facilities at Tannadice.

Where are the absent thousands?

SURELY YOU Tayside, Fife, Perth, Angus (and points north, south, east and west) football fans are going to prove Jim McLean wrong tomorrow night (writes THE SPORTS EDITOR).

He is talking in terms of a 12-15,000 crowd for a U.E.F.A. Cup semi-final. That's around one-third short of capacity.

I appreciate football is a costly exercise, especially with another semi, Dundee v. United, in Edinburgh on Saturday, but surely two-thirds capacity is pitching it a bit short?

Manchester isn't exactly a booming area, and Manchester City are fighting what seems to be an unsuccessful battle against relegation from the English First Division, yet, recently, I was at a game at Maine Road and there was a 23,000 crowd.

The opposition was Newcastle, in just about as bad a state as Man. City, but the crowd was enough to fill Tannadice and have a couple of thousand left over.

Can it be possible that 23,000 turn out in England to watch a non-event, and significantly less show up in Scotland for a European semi-final involving a German club and the last remaining British team in Continental competition?

Surely not.

● If tomorrow night's crowd were to reach 18,750 that would mean United's 37 home ties in Europe would have been watched by exactly 500,000.

No decision yet on who plays

"TEAM CHOICE is going to be difficult. One or two crowd favourites might well be left out because there are 14 players in my thoughts."

Dundee United manager Jim McLean summing up his approach with the U.E.F.A. Cup semi-final against Borussia Moenchengladbach edging steadily closer.

On goalkeeper Billy Thomson, the main casualty, the news is slightly better than it was on Sunday (reports THE SPORTS EDITOR).

"We will be going right up to Wednesday before we make a decision on his fitness," said the manager yesterday.

"Yesterday he had not shown progress, but today there has been a wee bit—and we still have 48 hours to go.

"Having said that he is still very, very doubtful. It is going to be really close.

"We have another semi-final on Saturday, don't forget, and we wouldn't want to force him into the first one and have him completely unfit for the second."

Gary McGinnis won't be available and the manager describes this as "unfortunate."

"He played for us in the reserves to help us out and pulled a muscle which was only strained before," he said. "He has been involved in every European game up to now."

Surprisingly, Billy Kirkwood, 11 stitches in an ear injury after Saturday's game against St Mirren, will be available.

The manager described the likely absence of Borussia's injured Uwe Rahn as "to our advantage."

Sixth meeting with Scots

BORUSSIA FACE Scottish opposition for the sixth time when they play United. They have won three of their five home games, drawn one and lost one, while away they have won one, drawn one and lost three.

They have scored 17 goals, conceded 25, with a disastrous Cup Winners' Cup defeat against Rangers back in 1960 of 11-0 on aggregate contributing to that minus figure. United also contributed, of course, with that 5-0 victory at Tannadice six years ago.

Jupp Heynckes.

The Borussia "old boys"

SOME OF the "greats" who have worn the Borussia colours (the official strip is all-white jerseys, shorts and stockings) are Berti Vogts, Gunter Netzer and Herbert Wimmer.

Top striker in the top years was Jupp Heynckes, now the club coach but who will join Bayern next season, when Wolf Werner will take over his present post.

More recent big names to play for Borussia are Rainer Bonhof and Uli Stielicke.

COUNTDOWN TO TOMORROW'S BIG MATCH AT TANNADICE

Slow rise—and quick fall

BORUSSIA WERE founded in 1900, but it took a long time for them to make their mark in German football—60 years to be exact, when they won the West German Cup. It wasn't exactly the start of greatness. Next season they went out of the Cup Winners' Cup 11-0 to Rangers in the first round.

Five times Bundesliga champions

BORUSSIA WON the Bundesliga title in 1970, retained it the next year and won it again in 1975, 1976 and 1977.They play in the Bokelberg Stadium, Moenchengladbach.

Routes to last four

THE FOLLOWING is the route both clubs have taken to the semi-final:

UNITED—First round: v. Lens—lost 1-0 away, won 2-0 home; **second round:** v. Universita Craiova—won 3-0 home, lost 1-0 away; **third round:** v. Hajduk Split—won 2-0 home, drew 0-0 away; **quarter-final:** v. Barcelona—won 1-0 home, won 2-1 away.

Scorers: John Clark (3), Ian Redford (2), Ralph Milne, Tommy Coyne, Jim McInally, Kevin Gallacher, Iain Ferguson. Aggregate 10-3.

BORUSSIA—First round: v. Partisan Belgrade— won 1-0 home, won 3-1 away; **second round:** v. Feyenoord—won 5-1 home, won 2-0 away; **third round:** v. Rangers—drew 1-1 away, drew 0-0 home (won on away goal); **quarter-final:** v. Vitoria Guimares—won 3-0 home, drew 2-2 away.

Scorers: Rahn (4), Drehsen (3), Krauss (2), Brandts, Lienen, Bruns, Thiele, Criens, Bazalorz, plus two own goals. Aggregate 17-5.

Another potential best-seller?

THE PROGRAMME for tomorrow night's game is edited by Peter Rundo and includes fascinating reading and statistics in its 46 pages.

There had to be a reprint of the Barcelona programme, and I wouldn't be surprised if the same thing happened again.

United's record in figures

AN EXACT breakdown of Dundee United's European ventures shows that they have played 8 games in the European Cup, won 5, drawn 1, lost 2, with 14 goals for and 5 against.

In the Cup Winners' Cup (which they got into as losing finalists in 1974) their record is played 4, won 1, drawn 1, lost 2, for 3, against 3.

In the U.E.F.A. Cup the tally is played 62, won 27, drawn 17, lost 18, for 94, against 60.

Pictured on their arrival at St Andrews are (from left)—Gunter Thiele, Thomas Eichin, Andreas Brandts and Michael Frontzeck.

Borussia most dangerous opponents to date

By The Sports Editor

DUNDEE UNITED tonight head into their 75th game in European competition—eight in the European Cup, four in the Cup Winners' Cup and 62 in the UEFA Cup to date.

There have been tough ones in the past—Standard Liege, Roma, Juventus, Sparta Prague, Bohemians Prague, Borussia Moenchengladbach themselves, Manchester United and a host of others maybe not so well known, but dangerous opponents nevertheless.

Yet I doubt if at any time the opposition has been more dangerous than Borussia.

I say this not because of the German club's current form, which isn't all that impressive, but because of what happened in the immediate past—United's two stirring victories over Barcelona.

In most people's eyes, Barcelona are possibly the world's biggest club. Those looking from the outside predicted they would brush United aside in the quarter- finals. In fact, in both legs United proved the superior team in every way.

So, suddenly, from being unfancied, they are everyone's idea of the outstanding team in the competition—everyone but the bookies that is, who fancy Borussia to take the Cup.

If they approach the tie with the same dedication and effort, plus the considerable skill with which they demolished the Spaniards, I haven't the slightest doubt that a place in the final will be theirs.

Should even one person on the staff dwell rather on what has gone before that place is in jeopardy.

The greatest plus on United's side, apart from the ability of their players and the knowledge and skill of manager and assistant Jim McLean and Gordon Wallace, is those 74 games to date.

With that experience behind them, I believe they really have reached the stage where they can isolate each game and concentrate on it to the exclusion of all other matters.

For that reason, I therefore take them to win at home and do no less than draw away.

You want a score prediction? O.K. then—at home 2-0, away 1-1.

Thomson confident he'll be there

By STEVE BRUCE

DUNDEE UNITED have received a massive boost as they prepare to face Borussia Moenchengladbach in the UEFA Cup semi-final first-leg at Tannadice tonight.

Former Scotland keeper Billy Thomson who, at the weekend appeared likely to miss the tie, now seems set to face the Germans.

Manager Jim McLean revealed yesterday, "Billy is very confident of playing and our medical people also believe he'll make it."

Thomson (29) has been out of action since damaging ankle ligaments during the warm up for the Premier League match with Rangers on March 21.

A week ago, he was still in plaster but, having trained yesterday, appears set to return, albeit with the ankle strapped.

"Up until Sunday I was still experiencing a bit of pain but our physios Jim Joyce and Andy Dickson spent some time manipulating the ankle and by Monday morning the difference was unbelievable," said the player.

"I've no doubts over my fitness," he continued. "I did a bit of goalkeeping training this morning, dealing with crosses, &c., without reaction and I feel 100% fit."

McLean commented, "Although it will be a blow for young Alan Main who has done well for us since coming into the side, from the team's point of view it would be great to have Billy back.

"He has been outstanding for us and is as responsible as anyone for what we've achieved in Europe."

Thomson, has in fact conceeded only three goals in eight UEFA Cup matches this season.

Given that the big keeper's fitness is indeed confirmed this morning, United find themselves in the best position injuries wise that they've been in for a Euro tie during the current campaign.

"In previous rounds we've had to play without important players, so what a boost to have almost everyone available," commented the manager.

McLean has listed 15 players for this evening's encounter and will add a further name—probably that of Billy Kirkwood—today.

Kirkwood, who was ineligible for the quarter-final tie with Barcelona after rejoining the club in early January, had 11 stitches inserted in a bad ear injury at Paisley but will make the squad providing he satisfies the Tannadice boss of his "physical and mental" fitness.

No team yet from the Tangerines with Jim McLean still pondering his selection.

"The 12 players involved over the two legs against Barcelona are obviously uppermost in my mind," he revealed, "but I'm honestly not certain they are all playing well enough to go out on this platform, although perhaps they've been saving themselves for Borussia.

"I'm also thinking about Dave Bowman but whatever happens, two men we cannot leave out are Paul Hegarty and John Clark.

"Hegarty is our top scorer in Europe while Clark has netted three UEFA Cup goals this season and, at this level, set-pieces are extremely important as was demonstrated against Barcelona."

The United manager remains convinced his side are perfectly capable of disposing of Borussia and securing their first European final appearance but yesterday sounded a warning note.

"It's important we aren't stupid in our desperation to win," he said, "We must realise we have two games in which to do it.

"I still feel Borussia are beatable but they'll be a tougher opponent than Barcelona. Like ourselves, they are confident about playing away from home and we must be careful not to allow them to score at Tannadice.

"We will try to get as many goals as we can in this home leg but at the same time musn't be stupid at the back," he continued.

"Barcelona tried to play us and found to their cost that they'd have been better off attempting to stop us.

"Borussia, however, will try to frustrate, therefore we must be accurate when we have the ball and play passes to open them out.

"I want the players to express themselves, to enjoy the occasion and if we play to our potential then Borussia will require two very good performances to beat us."

McLean knows the eyes of Scotland and Britain are on Dundee United but claims he doesn't feel under any greater pressure than normal.

"Semi-finals are notoriously nervous situations but I don't feel under any more pressure," he commented, adding with a smile, "Mind you, our record in semis is somewhat better than it is in finals."

There is an air of confidence about Tannadice as the hours tick away towards kick-off time.

In Paul Sturrock, Paul Hegarty, Eamonn Bannon and company, United possess men with vast experience of European football—players who have been the course and can now see themselves passing the winning post in first place this time around.

When these sides met at Tannadice in this competition five-and-a-half-years ago, United crashed in five goals in a never-to-be-forgotten night.

It seems unlikely they'll repeat that feat tonight but a victory to set them firmly on course for the final definitely looks on the cards.

United from-Thomson, Main, Holt, Malpas, McInally, Clark, Narey, Ferguson, Gallacher, Hegarty, Narey, Redford, Bannon, Bowman, Beaumont and A. N. Other.

Around 15,000 crowd expected

A CROWD OF about 15,000 is expected at Tannadice tonight.

Following manager Jim McLean's confirmation that the game would not be televised live, ticket's were yesterday reported to be selling "very steadily".

The home section of Sandeman Street enclosure is sold out.

United's office will remain open until 5 p.m. today with tickets on sale at the Supporters' Social Club thereafter.

● United go into this evening's match carrying with them the best wishes of Scotland and having received much in the way of assistance from several Premier League rivals.

Rangers, beaten in an earlier round of the U.E.F.A. Cup by Borussia, have supplied United with all the information they have on the Germans.

Celtic have lent them the services of ace masseur Jim Steele, and when the Tannadice washing machine broke down yesterday, Dundee stepped in to help with their laundry.

United's office will remain open until 5 p.m. today with tickets on sale at the Supporters' Social Club thereafter.

OUR FOOTBALL TEAM PREVIEW TONIGHT'S BIG EUROPEAN TIE AT TANNADICE

Injured Uwe Rahn not with German party

THE BORUSSIA PARTY arrived in Scotland last night with coach Jupp Heynckes bemoaning the absence of injured star Uwe Rahn (**reports STEVE BRUCE**).

"Rahn is the best player in West German football and anyone who has seen us play would realise how important he is to us and how much he will be missed," said Heynckes who will take charge of Bayern Munich at the end of this season.

Included in a 16-strong squad of players are Swedish international Kai-Erich Herlovsen and midfield man Dirk Bakalorz, both of whom were reported to be suffering from injuries.

Heynckes said, "The best teams in Europe have been competing in this tournament and any side which makes the semi-finals has to be respected and we know we will be in for a difficult match in Dundee.

"The fact that we lost here in 1981 has no relevance to this tie as we now have an entirely different team and come to Scotland in totally different circumstances."

The Germans arrived at their St Andrews hotel two hours behind schedule after their flight from Dusseldorf was first delayed, then redirected from Edinburgh to Glasgow because of the weather.

The Borussia line-up will come from—Thorstvedt, Kamps, Frontzeck, Herlovsen, Dreben, Borowka, Bruns, Thiele, Brandts, Criens, Winkholdt, Hochstatter, Bakalorz, Lienen, Jung, Eichen.

United left on a knife's edge for the return leg

DUNDEE UNITED 0, BORUSSIA MOENCHENGLADBACH 0

ON A COLD, wet night dragged from the edge of winter into spring, Dundee United struggled for most of the game against a team which is immortalised in Tannadice history as having been beaten 5-0 on a glory night six years ago (reports THE SPORTS EDITOR).

In this semi-final (first leg) of the UEFA Cup, that score was never on.

United, so smooth, so effective against mighty Barcelona in the last round were disjointed, only building up the rhythm which normally characterises their play in Europe well into the second half.

If they had been a goal or two down at half-time, it would not have been a shock for the watching and worrying crowd.

When they got themselves together a bit better second half, it was mostly because of the efforts of Redford and McInally, especially the former and the fast substitute Kevin Gallacher added an edge to the attack.

And there will always be an argument that they scored with minutes to go, when, for the second time in the game, Ferguson lashed the ball into the net but was adjudged offside.

How the linesman and ref worked that out as the ball came off a German defender is a mystery.

Mind you, the fact remains that it is only half-time and that United have not conceded an away goal to the Germans.

To write them off would be crazy, even though it is disappointing that they are on such a knife-edge for the return in two weeks' time.

That will be a game for strong nerves and a display by United more in keeping with their normal Euro form.

This was a Borussia belying their recent form, yet playing exactly as United boss Jim McLean had predicted...keeping it tight at the back and breaking rapidly and dangerously at every opportunity.

On a night when United looked suspect when the Germans attacked, even though, in the end, Billy Thomson didn't have all that much to do, the best players emerged after the interval in the driving Ian Redford and Jim McInally.

Paul Hegarty looked as though he had never been out for that three months and Iain Ferguson, who might have had two goals, deserves credit for being there again and again, even though the ball didn't always reach him.

I suspect that his sharpness will have been well noted by Borussia and, if his luck is in at all, he could be the one to get a vital counter in the second leg.

The German defenders battled well, but my eye was taken mostly by Hochstatter and Criens. Both will have to be well-watched next time round.

An indecisive night for United maybe ... but what a game that second leg is going to be!

Ferguson 'goals' could have tied it up

The rain had stopped, but there were only 70 people in the uncovered Arklay Street end at kick-off, though it grew to half full by the interval.

As predicted by manager Jim McLean, it was going to be a night for patience.

This became obvious when, for the first seven minutes, the ball barely left midfield—until Ferguson burst through on to a Redford head-down and his shot was gathered by Kamps.

The manager also warned of the Germans' speed on the break and they proved this with a burst which earned a corner, taken by Bruns and cleared by Narey.

For United, it was Clark, Hegarty, Narey and Malpas at the back, with Holt joining McInally and Bannon in the midfield and Redford up with Sturrock and Ferguson.

The sparring stopped in the 13th minute when a Clark free kick was headed on by Hegarty and Ferguson. It dropped to Redford who left-footed the ball high over the bar.

Then it was Borussia's turn—and the nerves showed in the United ranks.

After a Narey foul on Drehsen 20 yards out, Criens back-heeled the ball to Bruns, whose shot was scrambled clear.

It was twice Hegarty to the rescue in the next minute. First clearing for a corner from Criens, then blasting the ball away off the line from a Bruns cross badly fumbled by Thomson and hammered in by Hochstatter.

United were strangely hesitant and the Germans were playing smooth football, working off the back in quick bursts.

McInally forced United back into the game with a couple of battling runs from midfield, and when Redford got another header down into the penalty area, Narey lost narrowly in a race for the ball with Kamps.

Narey was in the news again in 29 minutes. Drehsen threw in a reckless tackle, which downed the United skipper, clutching his leg.

Drehsen's name immediately went in the book and that was him out of the second leg as he was one of the Borussia players booked earlier in the competition.

In 34 minutes, another moment of worry for a still edgy looking United. Thomson raced off his line to tackle Lienen 20 yards out. The ball broke to Hochstatter who lobbed for the empty goal.

Luckily for United, his aim was off and the ball bounced past the left-hand post.

This was followed by another less-than-impressive piece of United defending. No one shouted and Holt, obviously not sure who was behind him, lashed away a hasty clearance which fortunately didn't drop right for Lienen.

In 40 minutes, with the crowd getting restive and United looking strangely disjointed, Hochstatter was allowed a free run at Thomson. His 20-yard shot was well held by the keeper.

Holt had gone to right back with Clark as main striker and Redford back in midfield, but it still didn't stop the Germans being ahead on points at half time.

Half time reflections were that this was either one of United's poorest performances in Europe or the Germans were playing "out of their skins."

Whatever, it was fair to say that, at the least, United were fortunate not to be behind.

Clark was off and Gallacher on at the start of the second half. It was Sturrock who caused the first stir, with a twist and turn which saw him past two defenders on the right and a cross which Ferguson headed past the far post.

That was only the start of the drama.

As United at last built up a wave of attacks, Bannon weaved into the box on the left and crossed.

The ball was cleared, but only to Ferguson, who lashed a great shot from 15 yards into the net.

As the stadium erupted, roars of applause changed to anger as the ref said "no goal," indicating offside against Sturrock.

The Germans were under the collar and fouls on Malpas and Gallacher proved they weren't about to surrender easily.

But their danger on the break became evident again when, after Winkhold had been warned for time-wasting over a throw-in, the ball broke badly for McInally and Frontzeck's corner was scrambled clear by Gallacher.

United had built up some momentum, though, and twice Sturrock corners caused the German defence problems.

Third time he had the keeper desperately fisting clear then, as the ball was lobbed back into the penalty area, Kramps smashed Hegarty to the ground coming out to clear again.

He was lucky to escape without even a finger-wagging from the referee.

The smoothness was still absent from United play and they had a scare in the 64th minute when Hochstatter set off on a run in which he beat Narey then set Criens free.

Thomson raced off his goal-line to clear for a corner.

It was a Sturrock corner at the other end a minute later, from the right this time. It dropped for Bannon after Drehsen headed on and his shot raged past the post.

That danger on the break by Borussia was evident again in 69 minutes.

The dangerous Criens raced off from the halfway line pursued by Malpas. The full back inched closer and got in a tackle 15 yards out which put the tall German just enough off balance to spoil his shooting chance.

Redford, battling hard in midfield, got United back into the game with a perfect pass to Ferguson who lashed in a great shot after dummying to pass.

Kamps was perfectly placed to save.

Back went Borussia and a tremendous shot from Bruns flashed just past the post.

It was a hard slogging event now. The heavy pitch was taking its toll but United were lasting the pace better—and it looked like their persistence had paid off with minutes to go.

First, in the 83rd minute, Gallacher got on the end of a Bannon cross. His left foot shot didn't have any great power, but Kamps had still to throw himself to his left to palm the ball away.

More pressure followed and then came the nearest thing of the night.

Gallacher made room for Ferguson to get in a piledriver of a shot which raged into the net.

Again the crowd rose in adulation—again their roars of applause turned to roars of anger as again the "goal" was chalked off for offside.

It got even more tense in the dying minutes.

As United powered forward again and again, Holt went crashing inside the box, brought down by Hochstatter. Despite agonised "penalty" appeals from every United player and almost everyone in the crowd, the ref again said "no."

And the drama wasn't over.

As the ref looked at his watch, a clearance dropped perfectly for Redford, hovering on the edge of the box.

He steadied and calmly drove in a great shot ... which, sadly for United, clipped the outside of the post.

A dramatic ending to a game that had built up to a nail-biting finish.

Attendance—15,789.

Dundee United—Thomson; Holt, Malpas, McInally, Clark, Narey, Ferguson, Bannon, Hegarty, Sturrock, Redford. Substitutes—Bowman, Gallacher, Beaumont, Kirkwood, Main.

Borussia Moenchengladbach—Kamps; Winkhold, Fontzeck, Herlovsen, Drehsen, Borowka, Bruns, Hochstatter, Lienen, Bakalorz, Criens. Substitutes—Jung, Brandts, Thiele, Eichem, Thorstvedt.

Referee—M. van Langenhove (Belgium).

We can still do it, says Jim McLean

UNITED MANAGER Jim McLean told STEVE BRUCE afterwards, "Borussia are now in the driving seat, but we can still do it.

"Over the piece, a draw was probably a fair result," he continued.

"I thought we were lucky to go in level at half time and unfortunate not to score after it.

"The Germans' technique was magnificent, and in the first half we stood back and admired it.

"Fortunately our second half performance was a lot better, and I thought we had a certain penalty turned down in the final minutes when John Holt was clearly pushed inside the area.

"I'm disappointed, but we are by no means out of it.

"Nil-nil is a better score line than 1-1 and we can definitely still go through if we play as we can in Germany."

United keeper Billy Thomson rises high to punch clear.

Now United have a mountain to climb in Germany

One of the many disappointments on the night for United as Iain Ferguson shoots home, only for the effort to be disallowed. For more pictures and report, see Pages 14 and 15.

DUNDEE UNITED will need to reproduce their heroic performance against Barcelona in West Germany in two weeks' time to claim a place in their first European final.

After a disappointing 0-0 draw against Borussia Moenchengladbach in their U.E.F.A. Cup semi-final first leg at Tannadice before a crowd of 15,789 last night, the Tangerines face an uphill struggle to overcome a tough German side in a fortnight's time.

Twice in the second-half United had goals disallowed for borderline offside decisions, but they failed to scale the heights they reached against Barcelona in the quarter-final.

However, manager Jim McLean says his team can still do it.

Martyn's mighty clanger

B.B.C. NEWSCASTER Martyn Lewis made the boob of the season yesterday on the lunchtime national news.

During an item previewing last night's game he referred to the fact that the tie would be played at 'TANNADICHI.'

A few moments later, presumably after bells at the B.B.C. switchboard had been set jangling by irate callers from north of the border, Martyn apologised and smilingly acknowledged that he had got it wrong—Tannadice it was at the second attempt.

Cafe Allemagne for most of the day

POPULAR DUNDEE pub Cafe American in Union Street resembled a German bierkeller yesterday when a hundred Borussia Moenchengladbach fans descended upon it for refreshment before the match.

Extra bar staff had to be brought in to cope with the thirsty supporters and free food was laid on for them.

Some were waiting outside tor the doors to open in the morning and by the time they left at tea-time the management had nothing but praise for them.

"They've been enjoying themselves having a drink and a song but they've been really well behaved," said manager Luis Perez.

"On a Wednesday I'd usually be serving here myself but I've had to get two girls in to help behind the bar."

Also there was manageress of McGonagall's bar June Koshiba who said, "We've had some of the supporters in our pub and they've all been saying how much they like Scotland and been well behaved."

Karl-Keinz Pechtloff and some friends drove from Moenchengladbach and arrived in Dundee at 8 a.m. yesterday.

"I love Scotland and Dundee," said Karl Heinz. "We have always got on very well with Scottish fans. They like to enjoy themselves like us and do not look for trouble."

The Germans were bedecked not only in their team's green and white but also in United favours.

United also had fans travelling in for the match. Mixing with the Germans was Alan Johnston from Aberdeen, but a life-long Tangerines fan.

His friend Iain Rowe, who also travelled from Aberdeen, said, "I'm a Celtic supporter but not tonight. United are representing the whole of Scotland."

● Picture shows some Borussia fans warming up for the match at the Cafe Americain.

For the first time, United's indifferent league form continued into their European game.

A 0-0 draw must have left many feeling the dream was over.

However, the fans continued to win friends with their welcoming attitude — and, thanks to a BBC newsreader, they even had a new name for their home ground.

"Tannadichi", or "Tannadeechee", is often used to this day.

Thanks Mr Lewis!

From left at the presentation—Mr E. Thompson (divisional director with Watson and Philip), Mr Speed, Mr Cosgrove, and Dundee United's David Narey.

Friends win contest

Mr John Speed, of Shamrock Street, Dundee, explained yesterday that he had worked alongside Mr Bert Cosgrove, of Ancrum Gardens, at Tayside House until Mr Cosgrove retired last year.

The pair had kept in touch, though, and met up last Friday, when they discovered they had entered the competition separately.

"The last thing I said to Bert was 'I'll see you on the plane,' but I never really expected it to happen," said Mr Speed.

"In fact, when they told me on the phone who the other winner was, I thought at first the whole thing must be a hoax."

Mr Cosgrove, who describes himself as a "fanatical" United supporter, agreed it was a remarkable coincidence.

"But it's nice having someone you know going with you," he added.

"If they want it enough they will be in the final," says Jim

IT WAS the day after the semi-final before and two days before the semi-final after, as Dundee United manager Jim McLean settled down at Tannadice yesterday to look back at the U.E.F.A. Cup first leg semi against Borussia Moenchengladbach and forward to the Scottish Cup semi against Dundee at Tynecastle tomorrow.

First came the look forward—the Tynecastle local derby.

"This is what it is all about

now. It is all down to how much they want to win and how much they want the Scottish Cup.

"If they want it enough and are determined enough to go out and get it, they will be in the final."

Then it was back to an opinion he has expressed before—that Dundee cannot really support two teams, as evidence the 15,000 attendance at the European semi-final. "If that game had been at, say Ibrox, it would have been 40,000 tickets away at least.

"While I'm on the subject, Rangers are the ones who have progressed this season. They are the best team in Scotland. Aberdeen, Celtic and us have dropped back.

"Mind you, Celtic have more of Scotland's best players than the rest, but because of the way they play—attacking—and the way we play—sitting back—it's Rangers who have made the most progress.

There was little time for United to pick over missed opportunities in the first leg against Borussia.

Just three days later they lined up for a Scottish Cup semi-final against city rivals Dundee.

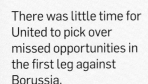

"Now, if we could get a blend between Celtic and us . . . !"

The injury report doesn't look like being serious after Wednesday night.

Paul Sturrock took a knock on the toe that has bothered him on and off all season; Maurice Malpas took a calf muscle knock and Dave Narey had a "crick in the neck," but all should be fit for tomorrow.

United's "key" four—Billy Thomson, Dave Narey, Maurice Malpas and Jim McInally.

United, like Dundee, will spend tonight in Edinburgh.

Then it was on to the look back, with the aid of a miniature football pitch and plastic magnetic discs representing players.

People might think it was the introduction of Kevin Gallacher for John Clark at half-time that caused the change in the game and United taking over. Not so, claimed the manager.

Most vital had been the switching of John Holt further forward—and here the reasons forward—and here the reasons were illustrated by means of the discs.

Hegarty, counting right now, but that could change very quickly.

"I cannot see where both can go in the team," said the manager, adding that the gap left by Richard Gough had not yet been filled although Dave Beaumont had played competently there for a spell.

Were there other reasons for United's poor first half?

"Possibly there was a reason for feeling nervy. After all that is the first time Borussia have failed to score away from home in Europe this season.

"In the end of the day, 0-0 is better than 2-0, because then

"I know I'm right, they know I'm right when I blame the back four first half for the bother we were in. We defended too far back. Second half we got forward and caused them problems."

The game had also confirmed it was a straight contest between John Clark and Paul Hegarty for mid-defence, with experience, in the shape of

you would go out to defend the lead—and that could be very dangerous.

"Actually I feel more relaxed and confident as the manager now that I know what is needed and if we get it we are O.K."

He then re-emphasised the contribution of four key players to this season's success so far—Billy Thomson, Dave Narey, Maurice Malpas and Jim McInally.

"They have been the key men, but Ian Redford and Iain Ferguson have also made terrific contributions in different directions, while Paul Hegarty isn't mentioned because he has been injured and Kevin Gallacher has done well for a 20-year-old."

Borussia?

"The way they played is the right way to play. Their passing technique, control and movement is exceptional, yet they did not overlook marking our best players.

"Uwe Rahn was missing, but he is more important in their home game anyway."

Then, after a reflective pause—"Nothing is lost for us yet except the Premier League.

"Last week after the St Mirren defeat and at half-time, I was blazing with the players. They were coasting second half thinking about the two semi's and lost the last genuine chance they had of the league.

"Now the key is ambition. It isn't about Dundee United, it isn't about Jim McLean, it's about the ambition of the players to win things."

Narey has faith in his team producing right result

Dave Narey.

WHEN PAUL HEGARTY was injured earlier this season, his long-time centre-back partner Dave Narey took over as captain of Dundee United (writes The Sports Editor).

Hegarty is now once again a regular in the side, but still doesn't have the captaincy.

Narey has retained the job because manager Jim McLean felt that, "When Paul returned after a long spell out it was better that he concentrate on his game rather than cope with the added responsibility.

"Paul is still club captain, with Dave team captain—and he has responded magnificently to the added responsibility."

So I tossed a coin and it was to the team captain I went for his views on today's local derby confrontation at Scottish Cup semi-final level.

"It's definitely different because it's a semi. We don't meet one another in a lot of them in the Scottish Cup," Dave began.

"It means that if you do something special it won't just be remembered in the city until the next game, but until the next semi-final . . . and that could be a long time.

"A local hero could definitely come out of this one.

"Mind you, make a mistake and it will live with you for a long time, too!

"It also means the supporters of the winners can talk about it that much longer,

which doesn't make it all that good for the people who support the losers!

"Semi-finals are notorious for being tense affairs. I suppose it's because everyone connected with a club realises they are only one game away from the final.

"Personally I don't suffer from nerves. I enjoy big occasions like this and if most of the players do the same it could be one to remember.

"Dundee have hit a good run and their confidence is high because of their results, which will make it harder for us.

"We have beaten them on many occasions in my time at Tannadice, but every game is different and we will be taking nothing for granted.

"The players of Dundee and United meet regularly at functions in the city and around, but that will be forgotten today.

"We both want to win the cup, and I believe it will be a great game.

"It will certainly be different from the European tie on Wednesday. There one of the most vital things is not to lose a goal at home.

"This time that doesn't apply . . . though, naturally, neither of us will want to lose a goal, while scoring plenty.

"After Wednesday the right result on Saturday would make it a great week for us, and I believe we can get it."

STEVE BRUCE PREVIEWS TODAY'S BIG MATCH AT TYNECASTLE

Which team has the stuff that Hampden dreams are made of?

THERE WAS a genuine air of confidence in both camps yesterday as Dundee and United wound-up their preparations for this afternoon's Scottish Cup semi-final at Tynecastle.

With all the players they wanted available for selection, managers Jocky Scott and Jim McLean have settled on their respective line-ups, but neither will go public until shortly before kick-off time. Both took large squads to Edinburgh yesterday.

2 o'clock kick-off

Fans are reminded the kick-off at Tynecastle today is 2 o'clock.

The bookies make United firm favourites to secure an interest in events at Hampden on May 16. However, Dundee are convinced they can defy the odds and make the final for the first time in 23 years.

"This is the most important match we have played since 1984, when we lost in the semi to Aberdeen," commented the Dundee manager.

"To reach the final and win the cup would give the whole club and our support a big lift, and the players need no more incentive than the knowledge they are only 90 minutes away from Hampden.

"They are relaxed and, stemming from recent results against United, very confident of winning."

"This has all the makings of a good game," he continued, "and although personally I don't fore-

see a lot of goals being scored, I know that when goals are there to be got, we have men capable of getting them."

United boss Jim McLean, however, is adamant that if his men play as they are capable of doing, and match the Dark Blues' appetite, they will win.

"Dundee are quite rightly talking about their improved results against us this season, but back in November when they won 3-0 we were without Narey, Hegarty, Gallacher and Sturrock," he said.

"No disrespect to Dundee, but when we have everyone available, as we do at present, and our best players play to form, there can only be one winner.

"It was clear a few weeks ago that of the three competitions we were involved in, this one offered us the best chance of success. "Now comes the crunch when the players have to do the business."

"There's nothing tactical or magical I can do, it's all about how much they want to reach Hampden.

"We have the better players and if we want a place in the final enough, and get a share of the breaks, we'll win."

United are facing their 56th competitive match of the season, just days after a hard 90 minutes on a rain sodden pitch against Borussia, but McLean rejected suggestions that his side might feel the effects of their exertions.

"There can be no excuses over tiredness," he said. "I've heard all this talk about how much the heavy pitch must have taken out of us in midweek, but I'd point out that it was only a strip down the middle of the park that was really muddy on Wednesday night and that Jim McInally was the only man who

played the entire 90 minutes in that area."

Cards are being kept close to the chest by both managers as regards team news.

With Vince Mennie having recovered from his rib problem, only Graham Harvey and Alan Lawrence are unavailable for Dundee, while United injury victims Paul Sturrock and Maurice Malpas trained yesterday and were passed fit.

The major question mark concerning Dundee's line-up is whether or not Jocky Scott will utilise the system of three central defenders which proved so effective against Clydebank in the quarter-final.

Changes from Wednesday night are likely to be kept to a minimum by United, but Edinburgh men Billy Kirkwood and Dave Bowman could be involved.

Reserve keeper Scott Thomson was included in the Tannadice travelling party yesterday as cover for namesake Billy after Alan Main was laid low by a chest infection.

Around 12,000 fans are expected to follow the teams to Edinburgh. Had common sense prevailed and a Dundee venue been chosen to host the tie, it is certain a larger crowd would have been attracted.

Should a replay be required to settle the issue, it will go on at either Dens or Tannadice on Wednesday, the venue to be settled by the tossing of a coin.

Records point to Dundee

TODAY'S TIE is the sixth meeting between the Dundee clubs in the competition and, if past clashes are anything to go by, expect a scoring draw this afternoon, with Dundee favourites for the replay.

The Scottish Cup derby record reads—

1927-28: Second round—Dundee United 3, Dundee 3 (Dundee won replay 1-0).

1928-29: Third round—Dundee 1, Dundee United 1 (United won replay 1-0).

1950-51: First round—Dundee 2, Dundee United 2 (Dundee won replay 1-0).

1955-56: Fifth round—Dundee United 2, Dundee 2 (Dundee won replay 3-0).

1979-80: Third round—Dundee United 5, Dundee 1.

Dundee from—Geddes, McGeachie, Forsyth, Smith, Glennie, Duffy, McKinlay, Rafferty, Mennie, Shannon, Angus, Brown, Campbell, Coyne, Jack, Wright.

United from—B. Thomson, Holt, Malpas, McInally, Clark, Gallacher, Narey, Ferguson, Bannon, Hegarty, Sturrock, Redford, Bowman, Beaumont, Kirkwood, S. Thomson.

Page consults back specialist

UNITED MIDFIELDER Jimmy Page is to consult a specialist in London on Tuesday about the back problem which has sidelined him recently.

...u would go out to de...ed—and that could...angerous.

"Actually I feel more...d confident as the...ow that I know what...nd if we get at we ar...

"He then re-empha...contribution of four key...to this season's success...Billy Thomson, Dave...Maurice Malpas a...McInally.

"They have been the...but Ian Redford and Ia...son have also made...contributions in differe...tions, while Paul Hega...mentioned because he...injured and Kevin Gall...done well for a 20-yea...

Borussia?

"The way they play...right way to play. Thei...technique, control a...ment is exceptional, ye...not overlook marking...players.

"Uwe Rahn was mi...he is more important...home game anyway."

Then, after a r...pause—"Nothing is lo...yet except the Premie...

"Last week afte...

Left—Dundee players Rab Shannon, Tosh McKinlay, Jim Smith, Stewart Forsyth and Tommy Coyne reckon they're going to polish off more than their boots today. Right—a high-stepping United squad, led by Paul Hegarty, appear to be practising a victory salute as Gordon Wallace (far right) puts them through their training paces.

What a pity the S.F.A. robbed Dundee city of this classic

BECAUSE OF the arrogance of the Scottish Football Association, some 8000 Taysiders on Saturday missed the greatest semi-final it has been my privilege to see in a lifetime of sports writing.

Forced to travel the 130-mile round-trip to Tynecastle for the game, only 13,913 attended.

There would assuredly have been over 20,000 had the venue been either Dens Park or Tannadice.

And if you only saw this Scottish Cup event on television, I feel doubly sorry for you because the 23 minutes of highlights shown some seven hours after the end were like the trailer for a great film—showing just enough to make you

BY THE SPORTS EDITOR

want to see it all, but not enough to encompass the whole drama.

From the magnificent start to the nail-biting finish there was not a moment you could take your eyes off the play.

There was skill, there was power, there was courage, there were great goals and great goalkeeping and there was no lack of the physical challenge which makes the tag "a man's game" absolutely accurate.

It is a privilege to be in a city where there are two teams who can provide this sort of classic encounter—and how I wish more people appreciated this fact.

There is no doubt that, in the final analysis, Dundee United deserved their 3-2 victory. There is no yardstick in football, other than goals, by which results are achieved and it is

fitting that it was by the minimum possible gap that this particular one was decided.

First half, Dundee were spurred on by human dynamos in the shape of Rab Shannon and Stuart Rafferty, backed by a solid defence and with Tommy Coyne, Keith Wright and Ross Jack running at the United defence at every opportunity.

The normally cool Tannadice men were never allowed to find their rhythm, to control the game.

It was therefore correct that, though Ian Ferguson calmly blasted home a tremendous opener for United on the half-hour after a great run by right back John Holt, Dundee should hit back to go in at half-time 2-1 up.

Paul Hegarty, No. 5, heads the winner past Bobby Geddes.

The first fell to Tommy Coyne. Thomson blocked a Rafferty shot, but Coyne was on hand to crack home the rebound.

Then Wright ignored United appeals for fouls as Paul Hegarty, Jim McInally and Ian Redford all hit the deck, and rose perfectly to head home Coyne's great cross via Jack's back.

But if Hampden on Cup final day was a gleam in Dundee's eye this early, it was soon extinguished by a team which has, in the past, but no longer after this season, been inclined to wilt when the heat was really on.

All the class of Paul Sturrock suddenly surfaced, Eamonn

Bannon produced the marvellous runs which pull defences apart, Jim McInally and Ian Redford were on full throttle, Ferguson on a hair trigger with his shooting and the defence pulled itself together.

And Dave Bowman, in his part-defensive, part-attacking role on the right began to show the form, defensively and creatively that made him such a favourite at Tynecastle not so long ago.

The sum total was that, hard though Dundee tried, they lost the initiative.

In 54 minutes, McInally chipped the ball over an offside trap, Bowman unselfishly tapped it aside to Ferguson when he might have scored and the ball was swept home.

In 64 minutes Sturrock was fouled by Duffy, took the free kick on the right himself and as Hegarty and Redford both went for the ball unmarked, the centre-half headed home the winner to bring to a high point a season which, for him, at one time was being ruined by injury.

Two truly great saves by Thomson from equally great bending free kicks by John Brown—one at the right hand post, one at the left—in 78 and 87 minutes saw the game into a searing and fitting climax.

I believe there are those in the Dundee camp who blame keeper Bobby Geddes for United's winner.

I disagree. My question is—how could not one, but two

United players get a free header as the ball came over from a free kick . . . and to the fan who chased me to blame Geddes I'll add what I said then, "but for him you wouldn't have been in the semi-final."

Jim Duffy was excellent throughout, but most of Dundee's other heroes were on show first half.

Shannon, Rafferty—I feel a nasty knock took the edge off his play—Wright and Brown, all still trying to the end, deserve most praise.

For United, Thomson underlined his claims to a Scotland place while, overall, performances improved the further the

game went, with Sturrock, in particular, yet again the thorn in Dundee's side.

Iain Ferguson has been stung by recent criticism of a falling off in United's goal standard. Here he gave the perfect answer with two beauties to make it 26 for the season . . . so far!

Referee George Smith? He kept losing control of the game and if United's Dave Narey cannot be excused for nearly getting himself sent off for almost refusing to go back upfield to have his name taken for dissent, even this normally unflappable individual must be allowed annoyance at a succession of weird decisions which affected both teams.

In all there were five bookings—Wright, Jack and Duffy of Dundee, Narey and Redford of United.

Surely now a Scotland cap for Thomson

BILLY THOMSON can surely no longer be ignored by Scotland boss Andy Roxburgh.

Thomson's Tynecastle performance proved once and for all that he is truly international class and that a Scotland recall is long overdue.

The United keeper broke Dundee heart's with three quality first-half stops in quick succession and two quite brilliant saves in the closing minutes of Saturday's semi-final.

Save one—He somehow turned a powerful Rab Shannon shot around the post after it had taken a wicked deflection off his own foot.

Save two—From the resultant corner he blocked a Keith Wright header on the goal-line after having his view obscured by another Dundee player.

Save three—Seconds later he fingertipped away a Ross Jack effort which had struck Jim McInally's boot and was spinning into the net.

Save four—A John Brown 25-yard free-kick, curled over United's wall, looked a goal all the way until the big keeper dived to his right to push the ball away.

Save five—Another Brown free-kick, from the same distance, had equaliser written all over it, but again Thomson came

By Steve Bruce

to United's rescue, throwing himself to his left to somehow keep the ball out.

A magnificent performance and all the more remarkable when you consider that a mere seven days ago, the player was still experiencing pain from an ankle ligament injury and looking doubtful for the UEFA Cup-tie with Borussia.

"It is absolutely fantastic to reach the Scottish Cup final at last," said Billy yesterday.

"I've never won a medal in senior football and after losing

in four semis it is great to finally get to Hampden.

"I've felt all along that we could win the trophy this year and while it did not matter who we met in the final, I am pleased for my old club that they've made it.

"Although Dundee pinned us back for a spell on Saturday, I think over the piece, we deserved to win, but what a great game it was."

On the subject of those super saves, the modest Tangerines hero expressed pleasure at keeping the scoresheet blank with his hat-trick of stops, but—not surprisingly—confessed to drawing even greater satisfaction from his twice denying Dundee an equaliser.

"John Brown is a great striker of the ball and you never really know where he'll hit it," he said.

"I saw his first free-kick a little late, but had the second one in my sights all the way."

Billy Thomson, despite being on his way down, reaches up to touch the ball past the post as Tommy Coyne waits to pounce.

Old values in evidence

By THE SPORTS EDITOR

AS A "survivor" of the days when you could stand on the terracing in safety, even while expressing opinions on the play, then head homeward sure in the knowledge that you weren't liable to be mugged—at best!—I landed in a pleasant time-warp on Saturday.

I deliberately chose to be among the fans at Tynecastle for the Dundee-Dundee United Scottish Cup semi-final and found the banter as good as it used to be and not even a hint of violence.

Going to the game and returning, I passed bus after bus with scarves featuring Tangerine and Dark Blue hanging out of the same windows.

Before the game I saw groups of fans of both clubs walking towards Tynecastle together. After it I saw them meet up again.

I am not naive enough to believe there are no troublemakers in Dundee—there are and always have been people to whom "aggro" is a cult.

But there is now no shadow of doubt that the supporters of both city clubs deserve as much praise for their off-the-field conduct as the teams do for their on-the-field thriller on Saturday.

Dundee is promoting the slogan "City of Discovery" just now.

As far as football is concerned, if we have discovered the old values—or re-discovered them—then that is a flyer of a start.

Extension to contract keeps Jim McLean at Tannadice until 1992

DUNDEE UNITED boss Jim McLean has committed himself to the Tannadice club until 1992.

The United manager's contract was due to expire at the end of next season but chairman George Fox yesterday announced a four year extension to the agreement.

"I've been negotiating for several months with Mr McLean, whose present contract ends in June 1988, and I'm delighted to say he has agreed to it being extended until June 30, 1992," revealed Mr Fox.

This new deal—providing it runs its full course—will see Jim McLean (48) pass the 20-year mark as manager of United. He joined the club in December 1971.

"I'm delighted to stay on," he commented yesterday.

"There isn't another club I'd rather be with and I'm only too happy to serve them as long as I can."

"I've demanded loyalty of players and others around me and hope I've been loyal in return," he continued.

"Finance obviously comes into such a decision but there are more important things to me than money.

"For example, I cannot think of anywhere I'd be happier living in than Dundee."

By Steve Bruce

This news will delight United fans who have seen McLean transform their club from an unsuccessful provincial outfit into one of the most respected names in European football.

In 15 years at Tannadice he has led the Tangerines to one Premier League title and two League Cups. In addition, they have also reached three Scottish Cup and two League Cup finals.

And in the next few weeks United could complete a dream Scottish and U.E.F.A. Cup double.

A meeting with St Mirren at Hampden on May 16 is already secured and next week in Germany, they will attempt to reach a European final for the first time in their history.

McLean's achievements at Tannadice haven't gone unnoticed in other quarters.

Over the years he has turned down numerous offers, most notably in November 1983 when Rangers wanted him to succeed John Greig as manager.

Now he is set to lead United into the 1990's and, according to George Fox, the former Dundee coach has a job for life with the club.

"I don't know how he'll feel when his contract expires in 1992 but if I'm still here then, I'd want him to stay on. In fact I would like Mr McLean to remain with us in some capacity until pensionable age," quipped the clearly delighted chairman.

Following the announcement of his new contract, Jim McLean is pictured with club director Dr H. Leadbitter (left) and club chairman George Fox.

United triumphed in a fiercely fought semi-final — one that brought out the best in both clubs and their fans.

How many fans took up the managers' invitation to support their rivals is not so clear.

Request to home fans to "lend" support

By THE SPORTS EDITOR

ARE YOU a Dundee fan willing to go to games at Tannadice and give United your support when you can't get to Dark Blues' away games?

Are you a United fan willing to go to games at Dens and support Dundee when your team is away and you can't follow them?

If the answer is "yes" either way, managers Jocky Scott and Jim McLean would be delighted to welcome you.

Both yesterday agreed on that point—and the basis is the marvellous advertisement for the city the supporters of both clubs were before, during and after the Scottish Cup semi-final at Tynecastle on Saturday.

First—making it strictly alphabetical order!—Jim McLean.

"The clubs at coaching and management level are closer than they have ever been in my time.

"I would now like supporters, who can't afford to travel to away games, or cannot attend them for any other reason, to strengthen the other club by going to their home games.

"One thousand, or even 500, doing this would be a great thing not only for the clubs but for the city.

"I still honestly believe it would be better if there was only one team in the city but, the only way we can both get better as things are at present, is by having more people coming through the gates with one set of supporters helping the other team.

"If a person simply cannot afford to travel it might be possible to pay £2.50—or £1.50 if you are a pensioner—to see the 'other' team at home. It would be a great gesture from both sets of supporters.

"We must encourage that feeling of Saturday. The game was competitive, it was exciting, with the only pity that there had to be a loser, but the supporters of both clubs definitely deserve nothing other than the highest praise."

Over to manager Scott.

"Even though there might have been a bigger crowd at Dens or Tannadice, the atmosphere those who were at Tynecastle generated was great.

"It would really be tremendous if the support from both sides could help boost the numbers at the other ground when their favourites were away. . . . while still, of course, supporting their 'own' team.

"I am sure there are Dundee fans who go to Tannadice when United are playing in Europe and get behind them and I am equally sure there are occasions at Dens when United followers who cannot travel support us.

"I have known the football scene in Dundee for a good spell now and in recent years fans haven't seen a sign of trouble.

"Obviously people have been taken out of the ground for minor offences, but I have never, for instance, seen trouble which has caused supporters to spill out on to the track or anything like that even though some of the games between the clubs have been fiercely competitive."

Having agreed on this subject, the managers then both commented on other aspects of the support on Saturday.

This time, manager Scott first. "What was heartening for me was that as we came home we passed a large number of supporters' buses, full of fans who must have been as disappointed as us, yet they cheered us.

"It really is such a pity that we didn't do it for them. The way they got behind us was tremendous.

"The experience of Dundee United in big games had a lot to do with the result. We now have a bit more experience and want to be back."

Over to manager McLean—"We have a magnificent band of 6000 or 7000 supporters who are loyal to Dundee United, who back us all the way.

"All credit to them because there has certainly been a large drain on their pockets recently.

"Having said that I'd love to see their numbers increase by 50%—and, with the evidence of Saturday and other games behind us now, I see no reason whatever why women and children should not attend games at Dens or Tannadice.

"In passing, let me add that it is full credit to the wives of the hard core of supporters for being understanding in the recent run of expense they have had.

"Let me finally pay tribute to three people in particular from Dundee.

"Manager Jocky Scott and his assistant Drew Jarvie came into our dressing room after the game and congratulated us. I know what it is like to lose at this stage of a cup competition and thought that gesture was magnificent.

"Then there was John Brown.

"He is a competitor all right, but, at the end, he shook hands with every one of our players before leaving the park.

"I am not criticising anyone else, just drawing attention to something which does him tremendous credit."

850 United fans for Germany

DUNDEE UNITED will have 850 supporters travelling to cheer them on in Moenchengladbach next week for the second leg of the U.E.F.A. Cup semi-final against Borussia.

Originally, 650 places had been allocated, but the interest

By The Sports Editor

in Dundee was such that 200 more places were applied for and received.

The system for distributing the tickets is that those travelling will have to have a voucher, issued at Tannadice, to exchange for a ticket in Germany—so, if you are going, an early call at the ground is advised.

But Borussia is next week.

First there is the matter of a major game against Celtic, challenging Rangers at the top of the Premier League, at Parkhead on Saturday—and while it may seem more important for the Glasgow club, it is no less so for United.

They are locked in a battle for third top spot with Hearts and Aberdeen and, having taken only four points from the last six games, will be anxious not to drop any more.

There are games in hand, but they aren't points!

Meantime, manager Jim McLean promises he will be making changes ("freshening up the team considerably" is his own phrase) after the disappointment of the 0-0 draw with bottom club Hamilton Accies on Tuesday night.

United have now played 60 games this season, including three Forfarshire Cup ties, and

if they continue to be successful could reach 70—with, ahead of them, six in the league, one in the Scottish Cup final and three in the U.E.F.A. Cup.

"I am hopeful we will reach the 70 mark," is the McLean comment.

The problem now is keeping everyone fresh, judging training properly.

"You lose a week with a Continental game and we are in another spell of Saturday-Wednesday-Saturday games," said the manager.

"Getting the balance right is difficult."

Yesterday, there was no training for the first team men who have played most games this season.

They had a golf, lunch and jacuzzi break at St Andrews.

Jim McInally is "a bit doubt-ful" for the Celtic game, Dave Narey and Billy Thomson also took knocks but should be available.

Gary McGinnis is fit again after injury, Jimmy Page has been seen by a London specialist over his back injury and the result is awaited and Alan Main has had blood tests as a chest infection is taking longer to clear than expected.

Hamilton are now due to visit Tannadice on April 29, with an outstanding game against Hearts dependent on the outcome of the U.E.F.A. Cup second leg next week.

Reserve fixtures planned—v. Clydebank, Tannadice, April 25; v. Dundee, Tannadice, April 30; v. St Mirren, Love Street, May 4.

On Monday, April 27, there is also an away Under-18 Youth Cup semi-final tie against Celtic.

NOW THE S.F.A. BANS LIVE TV FOR UNITED

"They will have been six times live on television. We do not feel this is good for the club or for Scottish football."

THE SCOTTISH FOOTBALL Association, in the particular shape of its secretary Mr Ernie Walker, is heading for another head-on clash with the football public of Tayside in particular and Scotland in general.

Following the controversial decision to have last week's Dundee-Dundee United semi-final played in Edinburgh, the issue this time is next week's UEFA Cup semi-

By The Sports Editor

final (second leg) in Germany between Borussia Moenchengladbach and Dundee United.

Mr Walker insists that the game will not be televised, Scottish Television and Grampian Television are equally adamant that it will be.

The Walker argument is that "Dundee United have been on television far too often lately."

The story began, according to TV sources,

when the game was "put on offer" in the usual way of European games for Eurovision.

Scottish Television—in conjunction with Grampian TV—said they wanted the whole game live and this was agreed. This happened on Tuesday.

Yesterday the TV companies started re-organising their schedules and completed this after a few hours.

During a conversation on another matter later in the day with Mr Walker, claim the TV people, it was mentioned as "a matter of courtesy" that the United game would be going out 'live'. He refused to agree.

Mr Walker said yesterday that the decision was taken by the television sub-committee of the S.F.A. and Scottish League.

He went on to claim that the position was that the West German F.A. asked the S.F.A. yesterday if they were looking for live

"I wasted six years of my life over a dictator in Germany and I am not going to waste any more time over a dict-a-t-o-r in Scotland."

coverage as they had had no application from either the B.B.C. or Scottish Television.

The television companies, in turn, say it wasn't until yesterday morning that they had received their approval.

Mr Walker said yesterday, "United have

been live already in both Barcelona games and did not have the first Borussia game on television other than highlights.

"If, as we all hope, they go through to play both legs of the final it will assuredly be shown live.

"And they are due to appear in the next few weeks in the Scottish Cup final.

"They will have been six times live on television. We do not feel this is good for the club or for Scottish football."

He then detailed the games which will be on TV within the next month—the European Cup final live; the Cup Winners Cup final live; Scotland v. England live; England v. Scotland schoolboys live; the Scottish Junior Cup final live and, possibly, the Scotland v. Brazil game.

Additionally, of course, there is the two-legged UEFA Cup final, also likely to be live.

Asked what would happen if the television authorities defied any "ban" on showing the UEFA semi-final involving United he re-

marked that this would be "a petulant move."

The S.F.A. are so determined that the game will not be shown that, should the TV people continue with their defiance, they will contact the West German FA and ask them to tell Borussia Moenchengladbach to refuse to allow television cameras to be present at the game.

Last night the reaction of Dundee United chairman George Fox to the situation was brief and very much to the point.

He said, "I wasted six years of my life over a dictator in Germany and I am not going to waste any more time over a dictator in Scotland.

"Mr Walker should remember that he is a servant of football clubs of all descriptions in Scotland and not the master.

"If he wants to put this to the test he should call a special council meeting and either agree with their decision or resign."

Mr Fox was a volunteer at the start of the second world war and served throughout it.

United battle on as Borussia take a well timed break

IN THEIR latest outing on Tuesday night, Borussia Moenchengladbach beat Bayern Leverkusen, who are fourth in the German Bundesliga, 2-0 with goals by Thiele and Herlovsen.

That is the last game Borussia will play before meeting Dundee United in next week's U.E.F.A. Cup semi-final second leg—a gap of eight days.

In the meantime, United, who were in a Scottish Cup semi-final three days after their first leg tie, played Tuesday night (against Hamilton) as well, and face Celtic in what is sure to be a highly competitive game tomorrow.

The German games due this weekend were put back mostly because of the pending international against Italy, but as only a couple of Borussia

players, at most, will be involved, it is the perfect break for the club side before the United game—and is yet another example of Continental nations putting international

By the Sports Editor

competitions before domestic outings.

Yesterday, manager Jim McLean, commenting on the gap between games for the German opposition, said, "They have a professional set-up over there where local situations are organised so that they are helpful to European causes at club and international level.

"By contrast, take our idiotic situation last week where we were playing a European tie, a semi-final at that, three days before a Scottish Cup semi-final.

"I would hope that the people who organise things here would, possibility that a team or teams from Scotland could be competing in the later stages of European competitions.

With the Celtic game in the offing, not to mention the Borussia encounter, United have injury worries over two key men—Dave Narey (knee) and Jim McInally (ankle).

Both are "a bit doubtful" for Saturday at least.

● I repeat a warning which I gave yesterday—if you do not have a voucher which entitles you to a ticket for the game in Moenchengladbach, it is no use going to Germany.

Tickets will only be issued by the German club to people who can produce a voucher issued at Tannadice.

Just as United were becoming more comfortable with the idea, SFA chief Ernie Walker decided it was time to "protect football from the ravages of live television" and so moved to prevent coverage of the second leg in Germany.

It was too much even for United's gentlemanly chairman George Fox, who put Walker in his place in the most memorable way.

DECISION TODAY ON UNITED PLEA FOR LIVE CUP TV

TODAY LOOKS like being D for "decision" day on whether next week's eagerly awaited Borussia Moenchengladbach-Dundee United UEFA Cup semi-final second-leg tie will be screened live on television in Scotland.

There was a barrage of protests yesterday against the Scottish Football Association's controversial move to deprive home fans of live coverage of the top European encounter.

With the scoreline from the first leg at Tannadice nine days ago at 0-0, and interest in the return leg in Germany at fever pitch, the S.F.A. stepped in to blow the whistle on Scottish Television's live coverage bid.

United's twin-legged victory over Barcelona in the quarter-finals was screened live on television in Scotland and with a series of further games in the weeks ahead also being broadcast in full—at least one of them, the Scottish Cup final, involving the Tannadice side—the S.F.A. ruled that enough was enough.

Dundee United chairman Mr George Fox responded immediately, "We will appeal. I think the decision is deplorable and our letter should arrive at the S.F.A.'s office in Glasgow on Friday morning."

United's fans were in uproar as were football followers the length and breadth of the land, incensed at the S.F.A.'s decision.

It came only weeks after Scottish football's administrators ignored a similar public outcry by refusing appeals to play last week's Scottish Cup semi-final between Dundee

United and Dundee in the city, insisting the match be played at neutral Tynecastle Park, Edinburgh, instead.

The man at the receiving end of most of the criticism was S.F.A. secretary Mr Ernie Walker who, as in the earlier controversy, was accused of acting like an arrogant dictator.

Feeling he had become a fall-guy over the two issues, Mr Walker retorted, "I am only the S.F.A.'s spokesman in these matters. I didn't take the decisions.

"It's a bit like blaming the town clerk if your rates are too high. He wouldn't have taken that decision, but he's seen to be responsible for it."

Considering the number of games to be screened live in the weeks ahead, and what the S.F.A. believe to be the detrimental effect live coverage can have on football attendances, Mr Walker stated, "The association has attempted to protect football from the ravages of live television.

"The football authority will control how much of the game is seen on television, not television companies."

Mr David Will, S.F.A. president and chairman of Brechin City, said everyone wished Dundee United well in their bid to win the UEFA Cup, but he believed banning live television coverage from Germany was necessary "for the good of our own football."

He rejected suggestions there was a vendetta against Dundee's two senior teams, saying their involvement in the two recent controversies was "a complete coincidence."

A solicitor, Mr Will said there was an agreement between all members of the Union of European Football Associations, which their national television companies were expected to comply with, governing such matters.

In general, a football association had the right to ask a foreign football association to instruct a television company in the latter country not to broad-

cast a game to the former association's country.

The S.F.A. would, Mr Will said, be contacting the German football association to activate the UEFA agreement.

Scottish Television has a contract with the S.F.A. allowing it to broadcast up to 40 minutes of highlights of a European tie.

It was when it contacted the S.F.A. on Wednesday indicating

it wanted to make a special case out of next week's match, bearing in mind there were no corresponding domestic fixtures scheduled for the same time, that the S.F.A. decided to get tough.

On Monday of this week the television sub-committee of the S.F.A. and the Scottish League decided unanimously there should be no additions to the then-envisaged series of matches to be screened live, and the S.F.A. told the television company there could be no change.

Messrs Walker and Will said the appeal would be considered

Politically united on this issue. From left—Mr Ross, Mr McAllion, Mr Mitchell, Mr Wilson.

by the sub-committee whenever the letter arrived. The sub-committee, comprising the president, vice-president and treasurer of both association and league, would discuss the issue over the telephone owing to the geographical distance between them.

Both officials were confident the sub-committee should be able to reach a decision some time during the day, if Dundee United's letter arrived by first post. Mr Walker stressed he did not have a vote on the sub-committee, but only announced its decisions.

Even if the sub-committee endorses its first decision, there still appears a definite prospect the game will be screened live.

STV controller of sport, Mr Russell Galbraith said, yesterday, "We have paid the German TV station ZDF a substantial sum to receive live coverage of the match.

"We have an agreement with them and, as far as we are concerned, we will be screening the game live in Scotland.

"The S.F.A. are referring to an agreement involving international football authorities have. There is no such agreement involving television companies as well.

Grampian TV would also screen the match in an agreement with Scottish Television.

Speaking from ZDF headquarters in Mainz, Germany, yesterday, Rosemary Von Oertzen said, "We have received a request from Scottish Television for coverage of the game and we will be sending the pictures out live."

A lot at stake at Parkhead for UEFA pool players

ON THE face of it, today's Celtic-Dundee United clash is of greater importance to the home side than the visitors.

Trailing Premier League leaders Rangers by two points and several goals, Celtic cannot afford to slip-up this afternoon if they are to retain their title.

United on the other hand— while still requiring a top four finish to be assured of European football next season—are no longer concerned with the championship issue.

However, Tangerines' manager Jim McLean is placing great emphasis on his side's display, if not the result, at Parkhead.

With the UEFA Cup semi-final second leg against Borussia Moenchengladbach a matter of days away, the United boss is still looking for what he terms "consistency of performance" and because of that, plans line-up changes.

"The second-half displays against Dundee and Borussia apart, I've not been satisfied with our performances in recent weeks," he commented.

"I will definitely be making changes and those who come into the side will have plenty to play for.

"At stake will be places in the team for Wednesday night and the chance to put pressure on for a Scottish Cup final spot," he continued.

"More than half the side that takes the field at Parkhead will be under pressure to either grab or confirm a first-team place but, whatever changes I make, we shouldn't be weakened for not one of the players listed in our squad would consider himself anything other than first-team material."

Not all of those regulars marked absent this afternoon will have been axed, however, for the manager also intends resting a couple of players with Germany in mind.

Today's line-up will come from—W.Thomson, S.Thomson, Holt, Malpas, McInally, Hegarty, Narey, Ferguson, Bowman, Bannon, Sturrock, Redford, Gallacher, Kirkwood, Beaumont, Clark and G.McLeod.

Those 17, plus Gary McGinnis, will comprise the travelling party for Moenchengladbach.

Scott Thomson is named back-up keeper in place of chest infection victim Alan Main.

Celtic are well aware of the danger posed by United, whatever the make-up of their side.

The Tangerines' 3-0 win at Parkhead on October 26, 1985, was Celtic's last league reversal on home soil and Davie Hay knows that 18-month unbeaten run simply has to be extended if his men are to have any hope of overhauling Rangers.

They need victory and by as big a margin as possible although Hay was yesterday playing down the latter aspect.

"Winning the match is the priority. Beyond that, the number of goals scored would be a bonus," he said.

Hay adds Anton Rogan, Tommy Burns and Mark McGhee to his squad.

Celtic from—Bonner, Grant, McGrain, Aitken, McGugan, Whyte, McClair, McStay, Johnston, MacLeod, McInally, Shepherd, Archdeacon, Rogan, Burns, McGhee.

By Steve Bruce

Scott Thomson.

Tommy Burns.

Places available on United's charter

FOLLOWING SEVERAL late call-offs, a small number of places are available on Dundee United's official charter to Germany for next week's clash with Borussia.

The cost of the four-day trip is £245.50.

Anyone interested should contact club secretary Ann Diamond at Tannadice Park between 9 a.m-1 p.m. today.

Supporters who have bought vouchers for the U.E.F.A. Cup tie are reminded they must exchange them for match tickets. This can be done by contacting Peter Rundo at the Ambassador Hotel in Moenchengladbach on Wednesday afternoon.

Injured Malpas and Holt doubtful but will travel

Incredibly, the second leg in Germany would be United's 65th competitive match of the season. Offered a rest the preceding weekend against Celtic, his top men refused.

AT ONE time on Saturday, the Dundee United challenge for a UEFA Cup final place seemed to have floundered four days early because players were falling injured all over Parkhead.

When the dust cleared yesterday, however, what was left was Maurice Malpas, "very doubtful, although he will travel," and John Holt, who "should be O K, but is a wee bit doubtful," according to manager Jim McLean.

Malpas has half a dozen stitches in a foot injury; Holt a leg injury. In Holt's case the fact he went off immediately he felt a recurrence of the bother in the second half, might mean the difference between him being available against Borussia Moenchengladbach or not.

Malpas's knock, when he went to shoot and his foot was blocked by an opponent, is more serious.

Paul Sturrock and Ian Redford, who didn't play on Saturday, "Sturrock because he needed a break in view of the number of games we have had

By the Sports Editor

lately," and Redford, "because we need him fresh for Wednesday" according to the manager, trained yesterday.

After detailing the injury and availability situation, the manager went on to pay tribute to Billy Kirkwood's performance against Celtic.

"He truly proved his worth to Dundee United," he commented.

"He played midfield, right-back and left-back because of our injuries.

"Typically, John Holt wanted to go back out second half to give his knock a try-out. It was obvious he might have to come off and Kirkwood, who had already been in midfield and right back, immediately volunteered to switch to left-back if that happened."

All of which—though the manager won't enter into any speculation—indicates that the Kirkwood versatility and experience will be fully used on Wednesday night.

There will no training in Germany tomorrow because of arrival time over there. However, the players will go for a long walk to loosen up after the flight.

By the way, before Saturday's game, manager McLean gave his players the opportunity of a rest, particularly midfield dynamo Jim McInally. All refused.

From Germany the news is that Borussia's spirits are high because word is that Uwe Rahn, the top scorer who missed the first leg with a hip injury suffered when playing for Germany, is available this time..

And it hasn't exactly been hectic for their players lately. They have had no game since last Tuesday, with only Frontzeck appearing—and that as a substitute—in the goalless international between West Germany and Italy on Saturday.

Out of the Borussia line-up is the excellent midfield player Dirk Bakarloz, due a hernia operation tomorrow.

Overall, the Germans are reported as "confident they are over the worst part".

Maybe . . . or maybe not!

United's travelling party of players, with team selection unlikely until Wednesday—W. Thomson, S. Thomson; Holt, Malpas, McInally, Hegarty, Narey, Ferguson, Bowman, Bannon, Sturrock, Redford, Gallacher, Kirkwood, Beaumont, Clark, G. McLeod, McGinnis.

An ideal "warm-up" for Euro tie

"I SHOULD HAVE known better," said an irate Dundee United supporter on the telephone yesterday. "I've seen United take a point or points at the death again and again this season—yet I was stupid enough to leave Parkhead a few minutes early and miss their equaliser."

He wasn't alone. Thousands of the Celtic faithful in the 30,798 crowd were streaming out of the ground calculating their chances of the Premier League title when John Clark "did a Barcelona" with a late, late goal—in the last minute this time—to make the final score 1-1.

In the process, he probably made certain the league title goes to Rangers, eased United worries about dropping behind Hearts and Aberdeen for a European spot next season and confirmed my callers comments about his team's ability to come back.

"Not long before the goal, there was another head flick and I couldn't get to it. This time Paul got it dead right from Dave Bowman's throw-in and I went through a gap between two defenders to score," was Clark's own description yesterday.

It was a game where Celtic, at the start obviously determined to keep the pressure on Rangers, went from being a determined outfit, through uncertainty to disarray.

Mind you, United's magnificent defence, even minus the injured Maurice Malpas from the 20th minute and Holt later and reading variously along the back Holt or Kirkwood or Hegarty, Clark, Narey, Malpas or Holt or Kirkwood had a lot to do with that.

Brian McClair, almost inevitably, got the home team's goal in 68 minutes when Billy Thomson hesitated

By THE SPORTS EDITOR

coming out for a flick on by Maurice Johnston but, overall, the deadly duo were kept out of scoring range.

Then, when the ball was won, Bannon, McInally, Bowman, Kirkwood and not least the battling young Gordon McLeod, quickly transferred the pressure on to Celtic.

The Celtic defence isn't all it should be. Frequently United strikers Iain Ferguson and Kevin Gallacher came within an ace of punishing them— and they were in almost total confusion as Clark surged through for the equaliser.

A repeat of this result would be perfect in Moenchengladbach on Wednesday night and the game, those injuries excepted, was an ideal "warm-up" for the UEFA tie.

It wasn't a perfect United display by any means, but the grit and determination which has been so evident this season was again on show against a team which, once they get in front, usually destroy the opposition.

I rated John Clark, apart from his goal, outstanding and blending perfectly with the masterful Dave Narey.

Kevin Gallacher had a quiet game but he and Iain Ferguson took a lot of physical "stick" and kept on trying.

Thomson, his mistake for the goal apart, was in top form.

Mathematically, Celtic can still win the title, but weakness in mid-defence and lack of a partner for Paul McStay in midfield and for Mo Johnstone and Brian McClair up front, looks like being very, very costly.

"We had two points and threw one away even though we'd been warned by the previous long throw," said manager Dave Hay at the end.

"It was a bad goal for us and has done a fair bit of damage to our chances.

"Obviously Rangers are favourites now. We'll just have to keep plugging away."

Maurice Malpas, John Holt and Billy Kirkwood.

Injured United star will still be kicking every ball

THE LAST time Dundee United played Borussia Moenchengladbach in Germany, Paul Sturrock missed the game because of a broken wrist.

This time, the Borussia bogy has struck again with the absence of another international, Maurice Malpas.

Injured as he attempted a shot for goal against Celtic on Saturday—he caught a defender's studs above boot level—six stitches were inserted, with United announcing that it was only two to leave their German opponents in the dark about the serious nature of the injury.

"He believed and I believed on Sunday that he would be making the trip," said manager Jim McLean on our arrival in Moenchengladbach on a warm, windy Easter Monday with almost everything closed down for the holiday.

"This morning he turned up at the ground and the injury had worsened. It is worst in the ankle joint itself and is badly swollen.

"The club doctor immediately said he could not travel—other than in a wheelchair, which would have given

BY THE SPORTS EDITOR

our opponents a last minute boost when we announced on the eve of the game that he would not be fit.

"It is better they know now and that we get on with alternative plans."

Maurice himself told me, "This is the biggest disappountment of the season. There is no way I could have been 100 per cent fit in time.

"I'm not even fit enough to travel in this condition.

"All I can do meantime is rest the foot until the swelling goes down and I can have massage.

"The disappointment is doubled because I love playing in Europe.

"I'm the world's worst spectator, but I'll watch the game on television. . . even though I'll kick every ball and probably injure myself again!

"Honestly, it's a proper sickener, especially after Barcelona.

"That said, I still believe we have a great chance of reaching the final.

"My priority now is to be fit for the first leg of the final (May 6, second leg May 20) and the Scottish Cup final (May 16)."

Now in the party is Joe McLeod, here for the experience of a European trip.

No choice but to put his feet up—Maurice Malpas at home last night with his wife Maria and son Darren.

A strong United line-up for five-a-sides? Pictured before setting out for Germany yesterday are—back: Dave Beaumont, John Holt, Jim McInally; front: Gary McGinnis and Ian Redford.

Billy Kirkwood (centre) looks set to play a key role tomorrow alongside Eamonn Bannon and Paul Hegarty.

Plenty of options available but United give little away

By the Sports Editor in Moenchengladbach

FIRST THING manager Jim McLean announced after we settled in Moenchengladbach following a perfect flight and the quickest burst through airport formalities (at Dusseldorf) I can ever remember was the good news—that John Holt should recover from knee bruising in time for tomorrow night.

Then it was into the Maurice Malpas injury (see Page 9) and all its ramifications and team selection complications.

Had any Borussia "spy" been listening he would have had to go back with alternative names for every position, but, wading through the possibilities I'll say this . . .

Had Malpas been here, the line-up would have been Holt, Hegarty, Narey, Malpas at the back; Kirkwood, McInally, Bannon, Redford in the middle and Sturrock and Ferguson up front, with, of course, Billy Thomson in goal.

Now? I expect it to be close to Kirkwood, Hegarty, Narey, Holt at the back; Bowman, McInally, Bannon, Redford in the middle and the same two up front, with, again, Thomson in goal.

But I could be wrong because the manager detailed the many and various permutations he could produce and the one he finally decides on is, as things stand at the moment, unlikely to be named until match day—and late on match day at that.

What . . . no John Clark?

"The Paul Hegarty-John Clark situation is a real teaser, especially with Clark scoring that goal at Parkhead on Saturday," said the manager.

"But, even there, would he have scored if Hegarty hadn't been there to flick the ball on with his head?"

He made the point that he had said previously it had come down to a Clark or Hegarty situation rather than Clark and Hegarty.

"It has never really worked with both of them in the team."

He then said his philosophy was to go for experience in the middle of a defence with inexperience in the wide positions, rather than the other way round.

"It's like I would rather have an experienced goalkeeper and an inexperienced centre-half than the reverse," he explained.

So it looks like Hegarty, although I say an equal certainty is Clark on the bench because of his scoring knack, though Hegarty's ability in this direction must not be discounted either.

One who will be in is Billy Kirkwood.

He doesn't have it easy from a section of the Tannadice crowd, but those who play and manage rate him highly.

"He will definitely be playing somewhere," was the categorical statement from the manager.

"It was always my intention, before injury problems, to consider him for this game because his record in Europe speaks for itself.

"I believe it is down to how players handle situations and Kirkwood handles them well.

"He would have played midfield if they had played Rahn there and man marked him. What we will do now, I'll decide later.

"He is a great man marker. Remember he did the job against Bryan Robson of Manchester United and did it really well. I know Robson scored one, but it was from a set piece.

"It was good that he got the game against Celtic and had to switch around so much, though the reason for the switches, all the injuries, wasn't so good!"

I suspect Kevin Gallacher will be another of the substitutes. He is young, he has, I am certain, a great career ahead, but it is felt that right now his form isn't at its peak.

Having said that, he is just the kind of player to get on and play so well that you wonder why there was any doubt in your mind about him.

Dave Bowman, operating wide and deep on the right, did

> **❝** No matter what I do it could be that, if things don't work out, I'll be wondering why I didn't do something else **❞**

himself no harm in the semi-final against Dundee.

That will certainly be considered, allowing his tackling and distributive properties, as one of the possibilities.

As I say, decisions are going to be difficult and will be taken late.

"And no matter what I do it could be that, if things don't work out, I'll be wondering why I didn't do something else," the manager summed up.

COUNTDOWN TO TOMORROW'S BIG MATCH IN GERMANY

As if going to Germany without a lead to protect was not hard enough, United suffered the loss of Scotland star Maurice Malpas to injury.

But, once again, United set off with an air of quiet confidence.

A very confident Sturrock likely to revert to old role

PAUL STURROCK hasn't had it easy this season, with injury dogging him almost throughout **(writes the SPORTS EDITOR)**.

But the sparkle was back when we spoke in Germany last night.

"Go on, ask me for a forecast," he said. So I did—and it is "1-0 for us or 1-1".

What is unlikely is that Sturrock will play mostly wide on the left, as he has been doing a lot lately, especially on that unforgettable night in Barcelona.

The Spanish giants went out and played a normal game against United, so Sturrock was faced with no special plan to stop him and, outstanding performer that he is, he took full advantage, especially late on.

Borussia won't "neglect" him in the same fashion.

With typical German thoroughness they have assessed his performance rating, his importance to United in an attacking sense and my news from the Borussia camp is that he will be man marked with cover defender added if he plays on the left.

Said my informant, "We respect many of the United players, but some even more, and Sturrock can be terribly dangerous with his twisting and turning and creating space for himself and others.

"He will most certainly be watched very, very closely."

Which is not unexpected within the United camp . . . so they will counter by playing Sturrock more through the centre, probably alongside Iain Ferguson, in more of his old striking role.

And to say the lad is confident is putting it mildly!

It's in the bag . . . a confident Dave Bowman puts his luggage on the team bus.

Kirkwood is the key to United's line-up mystery

I WARNED yesterday that the permutations in the absence of Maurice Malpas were such that predicting a Dundee United team for tonight's UEFA Cup semi-final second leg against Borussia Moenchengladbach in the Bokelburg Stadium—with the score at 0-0 and all to play for—was fraught with danger.

And so it has come to pass, because manager Jim McLean's comments yesterday about the difficulty of playing Paul Hegarty and John Clark in the team at the same time have

turned to comments calculated to make you think they will, in fact, both be lining up at the start.

The real key to it is Billy Kirkwood.

The manager wants him in midfield in a marking role—"he and Jim McInally could look after three Germans there"—and it is now easy to see Clark at right back in order to make this possible.

Part of the reason for all the mystery and conjecture is so that Borussia don't know the United line-up until as late as possible.

There were few clues to anything in a hectic practice match yesterday morning—except that Paul Sturrock played through the middle and was in great form; that Iain Ferguson took penalties against Ian Redford in goal, who said "I don't fancy this much," as shots whistled past him, adding, "but fortunately I keeping diving the right way—

the opposite to where the ball is going!"

The consensus vote is now that the line-up will be—W. Thomson; Clark, Hegarty, Narey, Holt; Kirkwood, McInally, Bannon, Redford; Ferguson, Sturrock.

The manager, though, couldn't help "keeping the pot boiling" over all the speculation by saying, "But Scott Thomson was brilliant in goal this morning.

"If we don't ruin them, he and

Alan Main are certainties to make it.

"And what about Kevin Gallacher's goal-scoring? But can anyone guarantee his form just now?"

All very deliberately confusing, so why don't you have a few bets among yourselves as to the actual starting line-up?

I'll put my money on that one five paragraphs back, but knowing Jim McLean's habit of springing late surprises will keep the stake low!

Billy Kirkwood

Scotland watching Tannadice men tonight

MR JOHN MACKAY, M.P., Minister for Education, Agriculture and Fisheries at the Scottish Office, whose responsibilities include sport, sent a "good luck" message to Dundee United yesterday.

Mr Mackay said: "Dundee United are carrying Scotland's footballing hopes with them in their crucial second leg tie in the UEFA Cup semi-final.

"I know that they will be well supported by their fans, who

have a proud record for sporting conduct on these occasions.

"The team showed their brilliance in defeating Barcelona. I wish them another good game and a result to take them forward to the final."

"We are good enough," says McLean

Jim McLean

"THERE ARE no excuses at all. We gained great confidence from the Barcelona result. It was tremendously significant winning over there in particular.

"We are good enough, we could not be going into the game better prepared.

"In football things can have a snowball effect—and our particular snowball is running the right way since Barcelona."

Dundee United manager Jim McLean summing up things from United's viewpoint on the eve of tonight's semi-final.

He went on, "We like playing away from home. It suits our style.

"There are stories they will play four up against our back four. What is much more likely is two up and one playing off them.

"I am not worried about them. It is how we play that counts. They aren't going to give us anything, obviously, but we are good enough to get the right result.

"People talk about the problems they will cause us. Paul Sturrock, for instance, will

definitely cause them problems.

"It was a blow losing Maurice Malpas. They are supposed to have Uwe Rahn back after his groin injury when he played for Germany against Israel.

"It is better for them that he is available for this leg rather than the first.

"It would have been better for us to have had Malpas this time and him have missed Tannadice.

"But things don't always happen the way you want in football, so we will just get on with the job in hand.

"We still have enough left to do the job. They definitely are not unbeatable. Rahn is an excellent player, but how fit is he? When I saw him he wasn't all that fit and had a poor game. I hope he is as fit this time!

"The absence of the suspended Drehsen is a good thing for us. He is good in the air and dangerous at set pieces.

"Some of our teams in the past have had more ability, but this one has more grit—and grit is going to be vital.

"I'd like to see us get a goal.

I don't think they will fight back too well. If we get a goal we should be OK.

"They will try and suck us in and hit us on the break. I'll be looking for us to play in their half of the park, defend if necessary well out of our penalty area.

"We have to win the midfield battle. They are good at set pieces, control and crossing the ball. We must allow them as few opportunities as possible to do any of these things.

"In the end, though, it is all down to how we play."

Narey in confident mood

UNITED TEAM captain Dave Narey pondered the question for a moment, then said, from the depth of experience gained in over 70 European ties, "Borussia are as good a team as I have played against.

"They know the business, are technically excellent and keep possession well."

Then, "But we know a thing or two as well and certainly aren't worried by what is ahead of us."

Dave feels that "possibly because it is a semi-final there is more tension involved."

But he quickly added, "However, going across and beating Barcelona on their own ground should make everyone feel nothing is impossible, because nothing is bigger than that.

"And I believe Saturday's result against Celtic was great for us.

"People will say the pressure was all on them, that we could go out and just play, but it isn't as simple as that.

"Celtic at Parkhead and trying to stay in with a shout of the title is as difficult a game as you will have to face.

"I thought we played some excellent stuff, especially first half, and to come away with a point was a wonderful boost with a European tie ahead.

"The loss of Maurice (Malpas) is a blow, but we have overcome injuries before—a lot of them this season—and won through, so there is no depression."

Rahn, Krauss to return

BERND KRAUSS, the 22-times-capped Austrian internationalist who missed the first leg because of suspension, will be in the Borussia line-up tonight.

But you could almost hear the sigh of relief in the town when it was announced that Uwe Rahn is

fit again and that Hans George Criens, whom rumour had it was also injured, is available.

He is the big lad who gave United's defenders many a scary moment at Tannadice.

Missing will be Hans Georg Drehsen, suspended after being booked in the first leg, and

Dirk Bakalorz, in hospital for a hernia operation.

There is expected to be a capacity gate of 34,000, with receipts from this, television and advertising bringing in around £350,000.

Here in his capacity as S.F.A. security chief on the invitation of United is Mr David McLaren.

He has obtained 300 extra vouchers for any United fans who might turn up without one, which can be exchanged for a ticket.

Neither he nor the German police anticipate any trouble, but there will be a big police presence.

What isn't known is how many British servicemen, stationed all around the area, will be at the game.

Central role suits Sturrock

PAUL STURROCK is delighted at the thought he will be playing through the centre rather than on the wing.

"It means I'll have a marker," he told me, "and that suits me.

"With a marker it is a one against one situation, which gives me the opportunity to turn my man, to create trouble.

"Possibly the worst thing that could happen is for them to score early. Then they would sit back and we would have to chase the game, stretch out.

"Scotland had to do that against Belgium recently and from doing all right, things fell apart because if you push forward there must be space at the back which can be exploited by the opposition."

The score at the moment—0-0, of course—favours United in Paul's opinion because it means the Germans have to set their stall out to score at some point, yet cannot afford to attack too much.

"That suits our style of play," he said.

Second chance for final place

UNITED HAVE now played 65 UEFA Cup ties. Their away record is won nine, drawn 10, lost 13. Their total number of games in Europe is 77.

This is their second semi-final. The other was against Roma in the European Cup on April 25, 1984, when they took a 2-0 lead into the away game and lost 3-0.

Paul Sturrock

Jim is praying for some rain

THERE WAS a flash of lightning and a few drops of rain as Dundee United manager Jim McLean finished talking about tonight's tie against Borussia.

He opened the curtains in our hotel, looked out and said, "Great. Pray for a night's rain—or even for playing in rain."

This is because his firm belief is that when his players see a bad pitch they don't fancy playing on it.

A grassy, wet pitch is ideal.

And a walk over the Borussia ground early in the day proved it to be heavily grassed "if they leave it like that we'll have a job seeing Paul Sturrock," the manager cracked, adding, "it's certainly in much better nick than the surfaces back home at this stage of the season."

The grass was cut later but the United party had to come off and train on a practice pitch as the groundsman told an official to inform them that running about when the grass was long would prevent him making a proper cut.

There were no complaints as the manager had quietly paced out the yardage and found it corresponded so much to the Barcelona pitch "that I was tempted to think on Paul Sturrock playing wide again."

He recalled Barcelona watering the pitch heavily—much to his and the players' delight—and hoped Borussia would do the same, or that April showers would be heavy and prolonged, as they could be if the cloud closes in much more in the next 24 hours.

103

Brilliant United reach the final and make history

The English connection means the win over Barcelona is the one most remembered in the UK.

But those who really knew European football ranked this as United's finest moment.

Inspired by the graceful Ian Redford, they were in the final!

BORUSSIA 0, DUNDEE UNITED 2 (agg. 0-2)

IT IS difficult to try to remain calm enough to write objectively as every Scot here in the Bokelberg Stadium tonight has either started celebrating or is preparing to do so—and not stop for quite some time.

Dundee United have created history by becoming the first Scottish club to reach the U.E.F.A. Cup final, and will now meet Gothenburg of Sweden in that two-leg final on May 6 and 20, the first leg being played in Gothenburg.

Their place in the final was secured with a second successive win on foreign soil—remember Barcelona—through goals by master striker Iain Ferguson and my outstanding player of the night, Ian Redford.

I have to dwell first on the Errol lad's contribution.

He played in midfield, and at the back, and as a wide player, and as a striker. He was back, he was forward. It was a piston-like performance seldom equalled by what used to be called a wing-half.

But he was only one of 11 major heroes, who were added to late on when John Clark and Kevin Gallacher came off the bench to take part.

As I write, the United fans to my right, who kept up a non-stop barrage of sound throughout and were rewarded with a trip to their corner on the final whistle by the entire United company, are still dancing and cheering and singing while their heroes go through a warm-down.

If it had been me, I'd have been flat on my back in a hot bath long ago, but they are doing—would you believe—laps and sprints.

I always felt, as I said some time ago, that United would win through, even though I rated this opposition more highly than Barcelona.

United must be proud of their performance. It must even be acknowledged to be good by their master critic, manager Jim McLean, who agonised over his team selection all week, then came up with the perfect line-up.

Borussia had beaten Rangers in round three, they had never lost at home in Europe, they are highly rated everywhere the game is played.

But despite the crowd being mostly—and loudly—against them, despite tremendous pressure from the Germans, inspired by the return of Uwe Rahn, even though he didn't look at his peak to me, United took all that could be thrown at them, and then twice struck magnificently.

It seems only hours ago Paul Sturrock was saying "0-0 is perfect for us. They'll have to think about scoring and are bound to give us a chance or two."

How right.

THE SPORTS EDITOR reports on United's triumph

This fellow Ferguson is deadly. He was hovering throughout the first half, two or three times looking as though he might make the break.

Just on the interval he struck like a cobra to head United into the lead. Just as late in the second half Redford almost casually made it two.

Unfortunately Ferguson will now miss the first leg of the final against Gothenburg, the away leg, because of the booking he picked up last night.

You cannot dismiss the Germans lightly. They surged forward again and again, inspired by Fontzeck and Bruns, and with Criens giving United many a moment of anxiety.

But the night belonged, without doubt, to United. Would I be right in giving the back four of Kirkwood, Hegarty, Narey and Holt five stars and indicating that others deserve fewer?

I don't think so, because it was a night when you could not differentiate between performances.

The back four were indeed magnificent, and Redford absolutely inspired, but didn't Ferguson make the vital break, didn't Bowman and McInally battle for that midfield, didn't Bannon make run after tireless run and Sturrock consistently wriggle his way deep into the German defence?

And, at the back, Billy Thomson was in the form that has earned him most people's award as Scotland's keeper of the year.

United qualified for their first ever European final in front of 30,000 people in the stadium and millions watching on television all over Europe.

Iain Ferguson (right) scores Dundee United's first goal.

Brilliant United in Euro Final

⚽

See Pages 9, 14 and 15

Paul Hegarty shows how he feels at last night's result.

Now for Gothenburg

DUNDEE UNITED'S opponents in the final of the UEFA Cup next month are Gothenburg.

The Swedes last night put out Austrian side Swarovski Tyrol, winning 5-1 on aggregate.

Gothenburg won the second leg of their semi-final 1-0 at home.

Having won 4-1 away from home a fortnight ago, there was little doubt they would be United's opponents.

Michael Andersson scored the Swedes' goal in 72 minutes.

Gothenburg won the UEFA Cup in 1982, beating Hamburg home and away for a 4-2 aggregate win.

Two goals in the opening 11 minutes swept Porto to an unexpected 2-1 away win over Dynamo Kiev last night, the 4-2 aggregate win taking them into their first European Cup final, against Bayern Munich in Vienna on May 27.

The West German champions and league leaders survived the scorching cauldron of Real Madrid in their semi-final second-leg tie, winning 1-0 last night but going through 4-2 on aggregate.

It was a magnificent rearguard action by the Bavarians after having captain and sweeper Klaus Augenthaler sent off in the 29th minute, two minutes after Carlos Santillana had scored the Spaniards' solitary goal.

Celso, with a low deflected free-kick, and Fernando Gomes, with an unmarked header from a corner, were the marksmen for the Portuguese champions as they took full advantage of their Soviet opponents' fatigue to secure a well-deserved victory and spark street celebrations at home.

Though Alexei Mikhailichenko fired in a 12th minute reply, his low shot through a

European results

U.E.F.A. CUP
Semi-final, second leg
Borussia Moenchengladbach 0, Dundee United 2. Aggregate 0-2.
Gothenburg 1, Swarovski Tyrol (Austria) 0. Agg. 5-1.
Final—First leg on May 6 (Gothenburg), return leg on May 20 (Tannadice).

EUROPEAN CUP
Semi-final, second leg
Dynamo Kiev (Soviet Union) 1, Porto (Portugal) 2. Agg. 2-4.
Real Madrid 1, Bayern Munich 0. Agg. 3-4.

CUP WINNERS' CUP
Semi-final, second leg
Ajax Amsterdam 3, Real Zaragoza 0. Agg. 6-2.
Lokomotiv Leipzig 0, Bordeaux 1. Agg. 1-1. After extra time Lokomotiv won 6-5 on penalties.

crowded penalty area bouncing in off a post, Dynamo Kiev were never able to raise their game to the heights they achieved last year when their accomplished teamwork was the envy of Europe.

Mihailichenko hit the bar with a spectacular overhead kick and had three dangerous headers without reward as the Soviet champions, badly missing the driving force of Andrei Bal, who was suspended after being sent off in the first leg, went in desperate search of goals.

But Porto, including five of the team beaten by Juventus in the 1984 European Cup Winners' Cup final, defended in depth to become the first Portuguese team to reach the Champions' Cup final since Benfica in 1968.

Ajax Amsterdam, coached by Johan Cruyff, revived memories of the early 1970's when they dominated the Champions' Cup for three years as they marched confidently into the Cup Winners' Cup final with a 3-0 win over Spain's Real Zaragoza.

Goals by John Van Schip, Rob Witschge and Frank Rijkaard wrapped up a 6-2 aggregate win and a trip to Athens where they will meet Lokomotiv Leipzig in the final on May 13.

The East Germans squeezed through 6-5 on penalties following a 1-1 draw on aggregate. Bordeaux, trailing 1-0 from the first leg, had levelled the scores with a Zlatko Vujovic goal in the third minute.

THERE WERE reported to be over 1000 United fans in the ground. It looked more than that at kick-off, but "The Blaydon Races" and such like aren't exactly Scottish songs, so it looked like tangerine favours were being worn by a lot of servicemen as well.

It was John Clark who was the unlucky one after the days of speculation. He was on the bench, with Paul Hegarty alongside Dave Narey.

No rain as United had wished, in fact a glorious day and a rapidly cooling evening as Borussia kicked off.

A Bannon foul on Rahn caused the first worry for United. Hochstatter rolled the ball inside to the unmarked Borowka, but he hurried his shot high and wide.

A Bannon break on to a Sturrock pass looked good, but it was hit too hard and went over the bye-line just before Billy Kirkwood fouled Lienen and earned the wrath of the crowd—soon to be followed by Redford, who downed Rahn.

The game was going to expectations, with the Germans working off the back and accelerating via midfield as they tried to get in on Thomson, and United making sure there was defence in depth but not slow to try to

get Sturrock, going through the middle, in on Kamps—mostly via Redford and Bannon on the left.

It was Bannon who came nearest first, though. Kirkwood threw in, Sturrock turned the ball into Bowman's path and he crossed to the near post, where the keeper just beat Bannon to the ball.

A Frontzeck header from a free was followed by two Borussia corners, the first tipped over by Thomson, the second headed clear by Holt.

In 24 minutes Thomson saved United. A Lienen corner was turned inside to Criens by Herlofsen and the big lad turned on a deutschmark to whip a shot in—but Thomson was perfectly positioned to take the ball.

United were living dangerously, with the ball flashing across their goalmouth too regularly for comfort, as evidence a brilliant cross by Winkhold headed just wide by Thiele.

There was also a referee who was being rather easily persuaded to give free kicks as the Borussia players kept falling as if mortally wounded when tackled.

Strangely, the first booking came not for a tackle but for dissent from Iain Ferguson after offside was given against United.

But when McInally downed Rahn another free was awarded, and ended with a shock for the Germans when Redford made a great break, only to be robbed just inside the box after a 30-yard run.

These crosses by the Germans really were out of the text

Redford hits late clincher

United's goal-scoring heroes—Ian Redford and Iain Ferguson.

book, but Bannon showed he knew a thing or two about getting the ball over, a great left wing cross on the run opening up the German defence. However, it didn't get the reward it might have when Sturrock moved just offside.

It was an absorbing contest, with nervous moments at both ends, not least for United when a flash of Rahn magic sent Hochstatter in for a tremendous drive which whipped just past the post in the 40th minute.

The first United corner came just after—and what an end result there was!

Over it swung from Sturrock, and when the German defence made a mess of clearing the ball, Bannon headed it to the right of goal where Ian Ferguson was lurking, and his diving header squeezed in at the post.

The United section to my right sent their praises up into the night sky, their area a blaze of colour and emotion.

The half time thoughts were that this was Ferguson's 28th goal of the season—and his

second vital one in Europe—and that Borussia had never lost at home in Europe, but a scoring draw, many of which they have been involved in, would be enough for United.

Hochstatter was off and a noted physical player, Krauss, on as the second half started.

Within a couple of minutes, after the magnificent Redford had made a couple of punishing runs, it was Bowman's turn and, as his cross whipped over the Borussia box, Ferguson got in a great down header which looked deserving of a better fate than flashing past the post.

Then Ferguson was just offside when Bannon completely split the German defence from the left.

It was tense, it was tight, it was nerve-racking—and that was off the field!

Down there United seemed coolness personified, even when Krauss got on the end of a Bannon head out which went awry and lashed a shot past the post.

When McInally was adjudged to have handled 22 yards out it looked dangerous, but Bruns whacked the ball well wide.

The Germans were throwing the lot in now . . . it was panzer brigade stuff . . . but that thin tangerine line at the back never wavered.

Gough had gone and Malpas was injured, but the Old Firm of Hegarty and Narey were rock solid between an equally impressive Kirkwood and Holt.

And what about Redford? He was off downfield again in 62 minutes, gliding past a couple of opponents, doing a 1-2 with Sturrock, getting the ball back and sending a shot right across the Borussia goalmouth.

He was at it again minutes later as Narey cleared desperately in an avalanche of attacks.

Suddenly it was Redford v. the 'keeper, and as Kamps moved off his line the left foot flashed, similar to the way it did on that famous occasion when he "chipped" Hamish McAlpine in the Scottish Cup final when with Rangers.

This time though the angle was wrong and the keeper took the ball easily.

When Holt went down with cramp the ref refused to stop play and the German pressure went on again, but Criens sent his shot wide.

Sturrock claimed he didn't hear the whistle in 73 minutes, went on to "score" and was promptly booked for not playing to the whistle.

In 77 minutes the nerves were twanging again for United.

Narey was alleged to have fouled Thiele 22 yards out, Bruns hammered in a shot and McInally, sprinting out of defence, successfully blocked the shot.

The ball was still flashing in from the wings as Borussia poured in everything, and when Thomson could only get a hand to one Krauss cross, Kirkwood had to improvise a desperate belt away.

With 10 minutes to go it was another German substitution, Jung for Winkhold.

And within a minute we had a near international incident.

Thomson was adjudged to have carried the ball too far. Rahn was adjudged to be time-wasting—how stupid can you get?—as he waited to tap the ball to the side, and was booked.

Finally he did roll it to Borowka, and his power drive hit the foot of the post and was belted clear by Bowman.

Next it was a corner and another hold-up as Jim McLean appeared on the touchline waving frantically.

It was a substitution—Clark for scorer Ferguson.

The minutes were ticking away and United, first through Bowman, then Sturrock, charged in on Kamps.

Another substitution with two minutes to go—Gallacher for Sturrock.

To the right the United fans were dancing, roaring, scenting victory as the final seconds disappeared off the watch and the news came through that Gothenburg are through and will meet United in the final.

What a night . . . what d result . . . and what a sensational, fantastic ending as United scored again, and it was absolutely fitting that the scorer was Redford.

Gallacher raced into the box, waited for the tireless Redford to arrive, and rolled the ball to him.

He calmly rounded the keeper and smashed the ball into the net, the game ending on that glorious note.

Borussia Moenchengladbach—Kamp; Winkhold, Frontzeck, Herlofsen, Hochstatter, Borowka, Bruns, Rahn, Thiele, Lienen, Criens. Subs—Jung, Brandts, Krauss, Eichen, Thorstvedt.

Dundee United—Thomson, Holt, Kirkwood, McInally, Hegarty, Narey, Ferguson, Bowman, Bannon, Sturrock, Redford. Subs—Gallacher, Clark, Beaumont, McGinnis, S. Thomson.

Referee—Josa Rosa dos Santos (Portugal).

Mixed emotions

IAIN FERGUSON was suffering deeply mixed emotions after the game.

"I am now out of the first leg of the final because of that booking," he said, "yet I scored the goal that helped get us through.

"It really is a terrible feeling, although as I say at least I know I've helped the lads get there.

"As far as scoring the goal goes I have now had the satisfaction of scoring against Inter Milan (for Rangers), Barcelona and now Borussia, three of the outstanding club sides in the world."

A naturally jubilant Jim McLean was remarkably controlled with his quotes at the end.

"I always thought we could do it," he said.

"It really was a magnificent performance, and even better in that we once again did the job away from home."

The manager added that he was glad that he had done it not only for themselves but for Rangers' sake.

His point there is that he has always felt that it was Rangers who should have been through when they played Borussia and went out on the away goals rule.

Ian Redford, without doubt the man of the match in everyone's eyes, was equally self-effacing.

He expressed his pleasure at the victory, adding quietly, "I simply couldn't believe getting a chance like that late on. It was a wonderful feeling to see that ball go in the net and know we were in the final."

UNITED GO ON EURO

DUNDONIANS CELEBRATED de'iriously last night in the city, in Moenchengladbach and many places between—toasting a remarkable 2-0 victory by Dundee United over Borussia to become the first Scottish side to reach the final of the UEFA Cup.

United will meet Gothenburg in the first leg of the final in Sweden on May 6, and the grand finale will be at Tannadice Park on May 20.

A wave of happy congratulations for the Tangerine team rolled round the rainswept Dundee streets soon after the final whistle and there were immediate celebrations in nearly every pub and club and in hundreds of homes.

A goal by Iain Ferguson late in the first half and one by Ian Redford late in the second half brought United their landmark victory, which firmly establishes the Tangerines as a top European club and will net them a cash fortune.

Among the first to offer their congratulations were United's football neighbours, Dundee F.C.

Mr Graham Thomson, the chairman, said on behalf of his club, "We extend the warmest congratulations to Dundee United and all their players who took part. It is a marvellous night for the city of Dundee."

Manager Jocky Scott said, "It was a very good performance. United did really well and took their chances when they cropped up. It is a tremendous victory, a tremendous result, and I wish them all the best in the final."

Mr John Mackay, Scotland's sports minister, said, "Congratulations! A tremendous result for Dundee United and a real tonic for Scottish football. Everyone in Scotland will be behind you in the final and I know you won't let us down."

Tayside regional convener Mr John McAllion forecast United would now go on to bring the cup home to Dundee.

"It was an absolutely wonderful result," he said. "Barcelona was an outstanding result, but this is even better.

"It is hard to believe they have repeated that feat of winning away.

"I am looking forward to the final and United bringing the cup to the city.

"It will be some night in Dundee!"

Dundee West M.P. Ernie Ross, in London last night voting in a three-line whip at the Commons, was forced to follow the football action on the telephone!

"I think, on this occasion, listening to the match on the phone was probably as exciting as it was watching it on TV," he said.

"This was a fantastic result."

Mr Gordon Wilson M.P., speaking from London, said, "Superb! I had to listen to the game on radio rather than watch it on TV, but I sat on the edge of my seat.

"There will be a warm glow of pride throughout Dundee tonight. I am walking tall at Westminster and look forward to the final."

Dundee United's international defender, Maurice Malpas, who had to be left at home with a foot injury, said he had two weeks to get himself fit and in contention for the final.

Of last night's game he said, "I kicked every ball.

"It was a great result and a good game. I thought we played very well.

"I was a wee bit worried with the German pressure in the second half. If they had scored a goal they might have given us trouble.

"But after half an hour I knew they weren't going to score and it was a matter of playing out the half.

> *❝ I kicked every ball. It was a great result and a good game. I thought we played very well. ❞*

"It's two weeks to the final and I've got that time to try to get myself fit."

One of United's longest-serving players of old, Dennis Gillespie, said he thought United had got the tactics right.

"They played the way I thought they would. I thought they would try to hold out until half-time at nil all, but they got the goal as well, which was great.

"United had put the pressure on the Germans and closed them down.

"It was a tremendous result, great. I've been at the home games so far and will be trying to get to the final as well."

There was mayhem in Dundee pubs last night as fans glued to television screens roared their team on.

Cheap beer and free food were on offer in some places as bars vied for the football custom.

Singing from The Phoenix, Nethergate, could be heard some distance up the road and inside there was wild excitement.

"It's been a fantastic night," said owner Alan Bannerman. To make the stay-at-home

fans feel nearer to the action in Moenchengladbach, German beer was on special offer.

By full-time, 42 cases were gone and Mr Bannerman said, "I've spent the night running out for more cases. Just look at the place. People on their friends' shoulders, the pictures knocked squint on the wall and the whole pub singing 'Here We Go.' What a night!

"The Barcelona night was fantastic but this has been unbelievable. The best night we've had here."

The packed crowd in The Phoenix were shouting for full-time when United broke away and scored the second. "I thought the roof was coming off," said Mr Bannerman. "What's it going to be like for the final?"

In the Rendezvous, Union Street, the United team song was playing over the commentary.

The bar, like many others in the city, was bedecked in tangerine and black decorations.

One place where the victory was particularly cheered was Paul Sturrock's pub, Luggy's in Arbroath Road.

East Fife fan Ian Bissett summed up his feelings in one word, "brilliant." He added that Billy Thomson had a superb game.

Another customer in Luggy's, Jim Horsburgh, said, "It's a fantastic night for all United fans. Sturrock, McInally and John Holt were the men who did the business."

Walter Sturrock said, "I'm like every other United supporter tonight—over the moon and celebrating.

"Billy Thomson and Ian Redford were brilliant but everybody did us proud."

● For some United fans there was a desperate rush to get to the game.

Three buses, for one reason or another, were delayed en route.

Two of these arrived at the stadium just before kick-off but the third got there when the game was well under way.

Mr Peter Rundo, programme editor and the man looking after the ticket allocation, had arranged with Mr David McLaren, S.F.A. security advisor—in Moenchengladbach on the invitation of Dundee United—to hand over tickets to the latecomers.

One woman supporter took ill aboard one of the buses. She recovered but arrangements were made to have her sent home.

United fans were last night celebrating in bars and restaurants but no trouble was reported by German police.

For the heroes there were no hi-jinks. As David Narey said, as he went quietly upstairs to bed in the team hotel, "It just hasn't sunk in yet."

Scorer of the first goal Iain Ferguson in ecstacy.

GLORY TRAIL AGAIN

Fans go wild at the Rendezvous bar in Union Street, Dundee, as United go through.

Proposals to charter 3 ferries

WITHIN MINUTES of victory being sealed, an Edinburgh travel agent was making plans to take United supporters to Sweden.

Mr David Ben-Aryeah, chairman of the Dunedin Travel Group, 6a ·Caledonian Road, phoned "The Courier" to say he was Telexing 20 ferry companies to ask if he could charter one, two or three ferries for Gothenburg.

He said, "I'm asking them for ferry availability direct from Dundee to Gothenburg, leaving on May 5 and returning the next day. We're aiming to keep the prices as low as we can as a tribute to the United supporters."

Dunedin Travel had been responsible for travel for the Edinburgh Lothian branch of the supporters' club from the first leg in Lens, France, last year, then to Barcelona and Moenchengladbach.

He said that United supporters had proved themselves to be "top notch" in all their travel.

"They have been no trouble whatsoever, what a fine bunch of lads and lasses. It's great that their team has repaid them in such an exciting way."

For "fine bunches of lads and lasses" celebrations were interrupted by thoughts of "How do we get to Gothenburg?"

European nights becoming favourites with Redford

I MADE it clear that, in the immediate aftermath of Wednesday's game, I couldn't find a player in the Dundee United line-up deserving of anything other than praise, with IAN REDFORD in my opinion the top man.

I see no reason now to change that decision. He truly was superb.

"I love playing in Europe," he said yesterday. "In the Scottish game you can often be isolated in midfield, the ball can whistle back and forth over you or it can be a hard slog—there are so many people around.

"You get more time against European opposition.

"I feel these last few European games I have been playing really well. I'm certainly enjoying myself and feel my career is peaking.

"When I left Rangers I knew I was coming to an outstanding club. Results have proved that."

And what of his goal?

"Once I got into position I was looking across at Kevin (Gal-

lacher) and thinking, 'If he doesn't pass to me I'll strangle him.'

"Then he did—and suddenly I had the responsibility.

"It seemed an awfully long time before I got it round the 'keeper and could see exactly where I was going to put the ball . . . but what a feeling when it went in!"

Over to KEVIN GALLACHER. "Were you in two minds whether to pass or shoot?" I queried.

"You noticed! I was, but the keeper wasn't leaving a gap so I decided Ian was better placed. What a pass, eh? What a goal, too."

BILLY KIRKWOOD was "feeling great."

"I don't think my switch to Hibs for a spell did me any harm, even though there wasn't any of this kind of excitement.

"What it did was give me a new slant on this club—and I realise more than ever how outstanding it is."

As a personal footnote, I would suggest that, instead of "getting after" Kirkwood as some Tannadice fans do, they should start giving him some encouragement.

I know his manager was warm in praise of full-back partner JOHN HOLT, but must also have been equally impressed by Kirkwood.

He proved here, as he has done on many an "away" field, that he has outstanding aspects to his play which, I am certain, would flourish given encouragement from the terracing.

BILLY THOMSON could not understand how the referee thought he caught the ball and gave a free kick dangerously near goal in the second half.

"I knocked the ball down, I didn't hold it," he said. "That free was my only moment of real worry, though I did get a bit under one cross and couldn't hold it."

PAUL HEGARTY, "I am not particularly superstitious, but Dave (Narey) is team captain,

I'm club captain, and I am very happy to leave it at that!

"I am savouring every minute of all this.

"It wasn't so long ago that I was out of action with my injuries, and lying on the treatment table isn't like being amongst the lads, being involved in the chat and the training and playing."

Skipper DAVE NAREY felt there had been a bit of pressure at times, but he never had any doubts United would win after the first goal went in.

He also paid tribute to his long-time colleague John Holt, who "settled into his game right away".

Less than a year ago I sat in the Tannadice boardroom and was introduced to new signings DAVE BOWMAN and JIM MCINALLY from Coventry.

On Wednesday night they were out there battling with the best of them and doing the German cause no good at all!

"I'll give you a brief summing up," said McInally. "It's magic."

"Definitely," said Bowman, "a dream come true."

You couldn't have wiped the smiles off their faces with sandpaper!

It was a more-like-himself-EAMONN BANNON against Borussia.

"That's good to hear," he said with a smile. "I have been feeling more like myself lately.

"Mind you, I never looked like scoring . . . until I tried that passback to Billy Thomson at our end!

"We hugged each other when it was cleared. To say I was relieved it led to nothing serious was putting it mildly."

PAUL STURROCK—"I told you we'd do it"—had a throughly good time and believed, "we deserved to win, probably by more than we did."

And scorer IAIN FERGUSON—again getting the "killer" goal.

"The keeper made a mess of his clearance and the ball broke to Eamonn Bannon. He got it through to me, I spotted a gap between the 'keeper and his post and headed it straight in there.

"It reminded me a lot of the one I scored against Barcelona."

JOHN CLARK didn't have too long on the park but slotted in from the first touch. "It was good to be part of a win like that."

Finally, to coach GORDON WALLACE.

"I am just beginning to take in what we have done. It is incredible to be in a European final. It has always been a dream of mine, at times it was more like a fantasy. But we are there.

"I remember at the start of the season talking to the manager and both of us feeling this might be a season when we might not achieve quite so much, would have to step back slightly and let the younger players develop.

"That proves you never know in football. It could be the most successful season ever."

Then it was thoughts of his 10-year-old son, also Gordon. "His whole life is football. He loves it. He watched the game on television and, I'm sure, will always remember it.

"It was a truly great night which both of us can enjoy talking about."

Jim McInally and John Clark surrounded by admiring fans.

Kudos for the fans

John Holt, who performed so well on Wednesday night, found himself the centre of attention back at Tannadice yesterday.

As Dundee United's band of heroes defied the odds on the pitch, the Tangerines' fans continued to play their part — earning yet more praise after a fun-filled European trip.

By THE SPORTS EDITOR

THE MAGNIFICENCE of Dundee United's victory over Borussia has been acknowledged the football world over.

But there was another victory on the night—achieved by the estimated 1000-plus fans who travelled to Germany.

There was one arrest of a Briton, but he was an English serviceman. There were seven German arrests.

There was not one arrest of a travelling United supporter.

S.F.A. security officer David McLaren was so impressed by the United performance that there is talk that his emotions got the better of him when United's first goal went in and he roared his appreciation . . . in the presence of the police boss of Moenchengladbach!

Ex-inspector McLaren said it was marvellous to be part of such a great occasion and he didn't mean only the game.

After the game, he went to all the United buses to check everything was all right.

He found parties starting in every one, but not even a sign of trouble.

There is also a report that United fans in one bus showed the attitude which, if it was to spread throughout the game all over the world, would end hooliganism in a stroke.

Supporters starting to create trouble on the bus were reported to have been ejected, complete with luggage, at Carlisle.

109

"The best fans in Europe"

Almost as soon as Ian Redford strokes home the second goal in Moenchengladbach to confirm United's place in the final, the ticket rush begins.

Sweden may be expensive — with talk of £4 pints meaning it might not be the booziest of trips — but fans of the Tangerines vow to do all they can to witness history.

With English hooliganism still casting a shadow, it is difficult to charter North Sea ferries and many supporters are forced to consider English Channel services followed by huge road trips.

Rival clubs also rush to congratulate United, and the presentation of a special cake from Falkirk FC leads Jim McLean to declare: "The whole of Scotland is behind us."

However, other efforts to recognise United's success do not go down so well and the city council's plans to sponsor the second leg to the tune of £10,000 bring accusations that councillors are trying to buy their way to much sought after tickets.

For those fans able to afford a trip to the first leg, The Courier prints an in-depth guide to Gothenburg, "Sweden's capital of sport". The paper also brings readers a series of fascinating behind-the-scenes profiles of key Tannadice figures, including McLean himself, chairman George Fox and club secretary Ann Diamond.

The Courier also manages to secure an interview with Jim McLean's wife, Doris, who gives a unique account of life with one of the game's most complex characters.

As their story dominates headlines across the country, United's players handle the pressure in the best possible way — recording three straight league wins.

With confidence high, there is a carnival spirit for the trip to Gothenburg and The Courier photographer captures the players mixing freely with travelling fans.

The trip also produces one of the most amusing fan stories of the whole campaign, as two Dundee worthies step in to apprehend a bank thief on the streets of Gothenburg.

As The Courier launches an effort to track down the heroes, a Swedish police chief comments: "I had heard United had the best fans in Europe, and this proves it ... It's been a pleasure to have them here."

A narrow defeat in Sweden does little to dampen enthusiasm and as Dundee United enter the busiest week in their history Jim McLean takes time out of his diary to show his softer side.

After a young fan breaks his arm and faces missing attending the Gothenburg game, the manager takes the time to personally organise last-minute VIP tickets.

The youngster comments: "It was very nice indeed for Mr McLean to think about me when he's got so much else to think about."

Four days. Two cup finals. It's a week United fans will never forget...

Views of the architect of all United's success

It was a season that had started with United losing key personnel and the manager downplaying expectations.

Now they were in the UEFA and Scottish cup finals.

For McLean, the achievement ranked alongside the famous league title of 1983.

SO THE team I first reported on from a wooden bench on the touchline at Tannadice when Jim McLean was but a lad is in the final of a major European competition under his management.

There are acquaintances living and others no longer with us who, back in these days, no matter their deep and abiding loyalty, would have fallen about laughing if you had even suggested the possibility.

But it has happened. In the forbidding surroundings of the Bokelberg Stadium on Wednesday night the team that was once in the category of also-rans in Scottish football climbed the final step to the top in European—not just Scottish or British football—by beating Borussia Moenchengladbach 2-0 in the semi-final of the UEFA Cup.

And the architect of the run of success sat yesterday amid a barrage of questions, amid microphones and recorders, television cameras, notebooks and pens, and assembled his thoughts on the whole situation.

It isn't so long ago that Jim McLean would not have stood for all the fuss, but he admits that he has realised of late that "the media" is there and success brings inevitable publicity and all that means.

First it was a broad look at his team, "the men who deserve the praise because it is them who have taken us to two cup finals."

He went on, "Everything they have done has been because they have fought and grafted. That typifies United this season.

"People keep asking me what it means to reach a European Cup final. It isn't about Jim McLean, it's about Dundee United and the players of Dundee United achieving fulfilment.

"I believe the players, this season, have got what they deserve. The rewards are there to be won and they have got this far while putting up with me and the coaching staff.

"It would be murder working with us if they weren't having the success they are having at the moment!

"We have had a succession of exceptional players injured—Paul Hegarty, Dave Narey, Paul Sturrock and now Maurice Malpas, for instance, and there would have been no success without grit and determination.

"It all stems from the introduction of Jim McInally. His 'get in about them' approach, added to his all-round ability, has been a tremendous boost."

Of the game, he said the result was "even better than Barcelona, in that it got us into a final instead of a semi-final."

The season overall had been the most satisfying for him since winning the Premier League.

In fact it was greater than winning the league because that team had been built steadily over previous seasons.

This time, assistant manager Wattie Smith had gone to Rangers, Richard Gough had gone to Spurs, Davie Dodds, Ralph Milne, Hamish McAlpine and Billy Kirkwood had gone—"though Billy coming back at £20,000 or £30,000 profit can't be bad"—and the build-up had been totally different.

"I have spent three most frustrating years since winning the Premier League. In many ways it has been like flogging a dead horse.

"Do you know I was ashamed at the number of buys in the team last night?

"I wouldn't want to be the manager of a team that was all bought. It is greater satisfaction to be manager of a team that is reared. But you have to be realistic.

"Only four players out there didn't cost us money—Kirkwood, Narey, Holt and Sturrock—but, having said that, our income from sales has so far outweighed the cost of buying that we are about £1 million up."

The manager's survey then broadened out into other issues.

On the final being first the away leg—he used to think that was best, but recent results proved his team could do it the other way.

"I now believe the players will be going there to win. I hope

By THE SPORTS EDITOR

trouble is that there aren't enough of them—nothing would have been possible.

"It has been a most physically demanding season for the players and it has been the same for me.

"In the league-winning season we had a basis of nine players. At the moment it is wondering who to play. We have used 25 players this year.

"Injuries have been heavy and in the case of the latest, to Maurice Malpas, it is already looking doubtful if he will be ready for the first leg of the final.

they do. I'd like to spend a quiet hour-and-a-half at Tannadice!"

He added that while he truly believed that while United could have a poor result in a one-off situation "we will play anyone in a two-legged tie. We definitely are difficult to beat in that situation."

On John Holt—"I thought he had a magnificent start and an outstanding performance. Everyone got a lift from him winning tackles, being on the ball, using it."

On the televising of the game—He wouldn't have wanted only the 1000 or so present, much though he appreciated their support, to savour the effort the players put in and the result for United any more than he would have wanted them to miss the Barcelona game.

"I am against too much live television, but cannot accept that a game played in another country should not be live. What harm is that doing?

"I believe millions of people have shared in two great performances from United. I'll tell you I am proud to be British at this time."

On the final—"There are no ham-and-eggers in finals. It will be a rush to see them—probably next Thursday against Hammarby—and we will be looking for video footage on them.

"We have not had an easy way through, but we have made it.

"We need worry about no one now and I know the players know that because of what they have achieved."

Falkirk tomorrow—"There are injuries and I will be freshening up the team.

"Paul Sturrock has a strained abdomen, John Holt is doubtful with an ankle injury and Ian Redford is out through suspension for two games.

"I have already chosen the side. Young players like Gordon McLeod have been held back because of success.

"This club survives only on getting younger players through even though we have bought lately.

"It is an important game. Points have still to be won."

Then it was over and, as he left to join his wife and family, the autograph hunters closed in.

Jim McLean makes a young fan's day by adding his signature to an autograph book.

Rush has started by United supporters to get to Gothenburg

CITY TRAVEL agents were yesterday inundated with calls from jubilant Dundee United fans seeking passage to Sweden for the first leg of the U.E.F.A. Cup final against Gothenburg on May 6.

Thousands of supporters were trying to book passages despite the fact that, because of the limited ticket allocations, many may be disappointed.

The clubs involved will not be getting together until Monday at the earliest to decide the question of allocation to Gothenburg's Ullevi stadium, which has a listed 52,000 capacity.

But meanwhile, in the euphoric atmosphere of Wednesday's no - nonsense victory over Borussia, the fans have been besieging local travel agents to book for trips to Sweden—by land, sea or air, and hang the expense.

However, many will baulk at going by ferry from Dundee, if one operator's fees are anything to go by.

Mr David Ben-Aryeah, of Dunedin Travel, Edinburgh, who handles the transport of United fans from Edinburgh/ Lothians area, immediately got in touch with several ferry companies in an effort to give fans an alternative route to the Gothenburg game.

"I was absolutely appalled by a Telex from one major ferry operator," said David.

"They wanted a quarter of a million pounds to run a ferry from Dundee to Gothenburg and back—that would mean each fan having to pay £400.

"But I won't be giving up— P. & O. have no service available, but I'm still in touch with 17 other operators,

> *Everything is having to be done in a hurry, as the game is only days away.*

including DFDS and North Sea Ferries.

Despite the initial reaction from fans clamouring for travel to Sweden, most city centre travel agents were adopting a wait-and-see policy.

A "Courier" reporter spoke to representatives of four travel agents and between them they have had well over 1000 inquiries.

But the number of genuine travellers could well drop over the weekend as the initial euphoria subsides.

Mr Richard McKenna, of Thomas Cook, City Square, said, "we have had over 80 calls today, and many of those are firm bookings for flights.

"We have seats held with one airline, and at the moment our options are wide open.

"The only trouble is that the only direct flight to Gothenburg is from London.

"Edinburgh is out, but SAS, the Swedish airline, does do flights from Glasgow and Aberdeen to Copenhagen and Oslo.

"We are considering the possibility of a charter flight direct to Gothenburg, but that would depend on several factors—getting the right size of plane and a crew to fly it, plus a firm commitment from clients.

"Such a charter would mean us laying out some £20,000, so we would have to be very sure that everyone making a deposit on such a flight actually turned up.

"Everything is having to be done in a hurry, as the game is only days away."

Travel agents Lunn Poly, of 6 Kirkstyle, took hundreds of phone calls yesterday.

"Things were a bit chaotic," said a spokesman, "but we hope to be able to get everyone sorted out on Monday, once the dust has settled!"

A. T. Mays in Nethergate were also deluged by jubilant United fans.

The situation was the same at Ramsay World Travel,

Defender Paul Hegarty receives a welcome home kiss from wife Linda while son Christopher's attention is elsewhere.

Crichton Street, where a spokesman said the demand was "unbelievable".

Mr Stewart Hughes, of Ramsay World Travel, pointed out that a ferry would require some 3000 passengers and would involve a total sailing time of three days.

"The ferry option was perhaps a bit pie in the sky bruited about by ecstatic fans in the heat of the moment," he said.

At 3.30 p.m. yesterday afternoon the vanguard of returning United supporters arrived by coach at North Lindsay Street "tired, bedraggled but delirious" after their three-day haul to Germany and back.

The only signs remaining on their red-eyed, ashen complexions of their joy the previous night were the broad smiles they wore on their faces as they left the coach.

The bus was organised by travel company Bell Travel, who arranged for three coaches to travel to Germany. The manager of Bell Travel in Dundee, Mr Gordon Easson, said that first thing today he would be making arrangements for coachloads to go to Gothenburg.

If ever there was an award for cutting things a bit fine, then strong candidates would be the bus load of United fans who on Wednesday were stranded on the M25 just outside London after the gearbox of their coach had caught fire. Hasty arrangements were made by operators Mason's of Bo'ness and the supporters managed to reach the Bobelberg Stadium with only five minutes of play gone.

Tayside Regional Council yesterday joined unanimously in offering their wholehearted congratulations to United and officers of the council are to meet officers of Dundee District Council to try to arrange a suitable reception for the club, "win or lose in the final."

The council also unanimously agreed that council convener Mr John McAllion should attend.

United received a Parliamentary accolade yesterday, writes Our Man at Westminster. A Commons motion was tabled by Tayside M.P.s extending the "warm congratulations" of the House to the club on being the first Scottish team to reach the final of the U.E.F.A. Cup.

Even for fans of a team with such European pedigree, there was a realisation that the final might be a once in a lifetime opportunity for United supporters.

Thousands wanted to make it to Gothenburg — but it was not going to be easy.

Gothenburg's proud UEFA Cup record

Who are Gothenburg?

That is one of the many questions being asked in and around Tayside.

The answer is . . . a very good Swedish team who know the route to the final, because they have actually won the U.E.F.A. Cup once before, in season 1981-82.

Then, they beat Hamburg 1-0 in their own Nya Ullevi Stadium and provided the real shock by travelling to Hamburg and winning the second leg 3-0.

So United are well warned and will, most certainly, not be guilty of any under-estimation.

As with United and Paul Hegarty, Dave Narey, Paul Sturrock, Eamonn Bannon, John Holt and the like, there is a core of excellent players, all of whom were in that successful team, still with the Swedish club.

By THE SPORTS EDITOR

Keeper Wernersson, defenders Hysen and Carlsson, midfielders Tord and Holmgren are the men in question.

Actually, Gothenburg have played only one league game this season, against Brage, which they won.

The reason is their season runs from April to October and has only just started.

Their first game of any kind this term was the first leg of the U.E.F.A. Cup semi-final against Swarovski Tyrol, which again they won.

The consistency of the team is shown in the fact that they have been Swedish champions 10 times, dating back to 1908, and including a great run in 1982, 1983, 1984.

They have also won the Cup in 1979, 1982 and 1983.

Their ground record is 52,194, though the new European club regulations have, I understand, restricted this somewhat to around 48,000.

As a final early statistic, Gothenburg were defeated 5-3 by F.C. Twente of Holland in their first season in the U.E.F.A. Cup in 1980.

Since then though they have not lost a single one of 22 subsequent games, going out each time on the away goal rule.

It looks certain that Dundee United manager Jim McLean and chief coach Gordon Wallace will be in Sweden this Thursday watching Gothenburg play Hammerby in a league game.

UNITED FANS SAY 'WE'LL GET THERE'

IT'S THE KIND of chance you get only once in a lifetime. We'll get there if we have to swim..."

These words were just typical of the loyal determination being shown throughout Dundee last night as United fans resigned themselves to the fact that there will be no ferries travelling to Gothenburg for their team's first-ever European final.

The tickets are available—3000 of them in total it is understood—the incentive has never been greater.

The only thing standing between United's faithful and that 90-minute UEFA Cup first leg thriller in Gothenburg on May 6 is a large stretch of water known as the North Sea—and that barrier is proving almost insurmountable.

The fates have combined, say travel agents, to make every single North Sea ferry unavailable for the dates in question. Despite unceasing efforts which began as soon as the last ball was kicked on Wednesday night, the ship which would have solved all travel problems in an instant cannot be had for love nor money.

Unless a ship is found—and the chance is put at about a thousand to one—there remain two options for the fans who have followed United all around Europe.

They can fly, most probably from Glasgow, and most probably on a day return which gives very little time in Gothenburg. Minimum cost of such a flight, at the moment, is about £200.

Or they can travel in the usual way, by coach, and for about £100. The problem is that Gothenburg, while fairly close to Scotland as the crow flies, is three days' road travel away from Dundee.

Such a trip, leaving on the Monday, would mean a week off work. Again, it would allow little time in Gothenburg itself in order to get the coach back to Dundee by Friday—and there's the added "torture factor" of five days spent in a coach watching the motorways of Europe hum by.

There's no doubt the fates have been cruel—especially to those who had been "practically assured" of a three-day ferry trip for about £50, and are now having to choose between a £200 air ticket or an exhaustive haul round the three longest sides of a square.

But the message coming through loud and clear last night was simple. United are worth it . . . every single one of those tickets will be taken.

Said a spokesman for Dundee United Supporters' Club, "We realise the ferry is out of the question now, but there's still tremendous interest.

"I think it's fair to say that we'll all get there, come hell or high water."

He continued, "The ferry news is a

> *Many of them can't afford it, many are struggling to get the time off. But they're all determined to be there.*

bad blow. If we'd had a boat, 3000 tickets would never have been enough.

"But the supporters are willing to go to amazing lengths for this game.

"Many of them can't afford it, many are struggling to get the time off. But they're all determined to be there."

Added one European stalwart, Ronnie Taylor, of Fintry, "It's a long stretch in a bus, undoubtedly. But most of the fans will think nothing of it because they'll be seeing the game—in their eyes, anything's worth it.

"We'll get there if we have to swim."

Ronnie is one of those to have booked with Bell Travel, whose Monday-Friday trip costs £135 all in.

The official supporters' club is booking through Moffat & Williamson, who last night announced they would lay on three coaches—146 places in all—at £90 a seat, the best offer yet. Bookings will be taken from 7 p.m. on Monday at the clubhouse.

It's stressed by all, however, that fans will probably need to book as quickly as possible, and with the full fare at hand—time's too short to allow deposits.

Travel agents are also beginning to realise the need for planes, and are doing their best to charter in time.

Thomas Cook's have 42 places left at £210 each for a day-return flight from Glasgow, and these are up for grabs this morning.

Mr Graham James, director of D.P.& L. Travel, announced late last night that he and Clydebank operator Harry Hynds had secured two planes already, carrying between 90 and 100. Cost is £235 for a Tuesday night stay in Gothenburg (£275 for luxury hotel), and £250 for a stay on the Monday as well (£295).

Mr James was just one of the operators whose efforts to secure a ferry fell at the last moment.

He explained last night, "We tried just about everywhere, and there was just nothing doing. We had one last chance, but it fell through."

Mr David Ban-Aryeah, of Dunedin Travel, Edinburgh, said he had tried dozens of ferry operators but no ferries were available.

One thing's for sure, however—those United fans that do make it can be sure of a warm reception.

"The Courier" spoke last night to Mr Bertil Guslen, a sports journalist with the "Gothenburgpost," who said, "Gothenburg is looking forward to having United, there's no doubt about that.

"We've had experience of Scottish fans in the past, with two games against Aberdeen, and the behaviour has been great."

It was Mr Guslen who said he believed Gothenburg had allocated about 3000 tickets for United fans, although the final figure has to be confirmed by United at the start of next week.

It is expected about 1300 Swedes will be able to come to Tannadice for the final leg on May 20.

UEFA tickets on sale next week?

DUNDEE UNITED have set the price of the tickets for the Tannadice leg of the U.E.F.A. Cup final on May 20 as £20 stand and £10 for the ground (**reports The Sports Editor**).

There will be a determined attempt to get those tickets printed and on sale on Friday or Saturday of next week.

The reason for this is so that the fans making the journey to Gothenburg won't be over there when the tickets go on sale, so if, by chance, there is a hold up, the selling dates will be after the first leg.

An announcement will be made nearer the time regarding details of the sale.

There will be no match vouchers on these tickets.

United's "determined" win— from Gothenburg viewpoint

By the Sports Editor

LOOKING ON while Dundee United beat Falkirk was Gothenburg assistant manager Kjell Petersen.

"I appreciate right away that our UEFA Cup final opponents were without four regular players—the injured Holt, Sturrock and Malpas and suspended Redford," he said, proving he has already started on his homework.

"This was a fight between two teams determined to win for different reasons and United proved they are not prepared to give in in any way.

"We have the same problem with teams who desperately need points and know the difficulties."

When I mentioned that United had made eight formation changes during the game, the assistant manager said, "We know Mr McLean can make many changes if there are injuries, so I was not surprised."

That's United's away form studied.

Next Saturday, Gothenburg manager Gunde Bengtsson will watch them at home against Hibs.

On Thursday, manager Jim McLean hopes to watch Gothenburg play Hammerby, along with chief coach Gordon Wallace.

"I hope they don't do what we had to do today and make all those changes and switches," the United boss cracked, "otherwise I'll be as confused as their man must have been."

Two bookings in Europe mean automatic one-game suspension—as happened to Iain Ferguson when he was yellow-carded against Borussia Moenchengladbach last week.

But Gothenburg have no fewer than eight players on one booking, which means another in the first leg of the final in Gothenburg and they could miss the second leg at Tannadice.

The players with the threat hanging over them are: Wernersson, Rantanen, Mordt, Zetterlund, Petterson, Tommy Holngren, Tord Holngren and Carlsson.

Falkirk toasts United's success

After the match, a delighted United manager invited the Press in to see the magnificent cake presented to United by Falkirk.

On it was a replica United player complete with strip, the United crest and the message, "Congratulations Dundee United F.C. U.E.F.A. Cup finalists."

Enthused manager McLean, "The people of Falkirk and Falkirk F.C. prove the whole of Scotland is behind us.

"I hope and pray we won't let them down and am sure we won't.

"When we were presented with the cake, I said a genuine 'thank you,' then added we were still here to win.

"They in turn presented the cake then went out and tried to beat us.

"That is what the game is about. To me it is worth much more than money.

"The only thing is, I'll have to delay my dieting for another day!"

Council to sponsor Tannadice cup final

A MAJOR agreement for Dundee District Council to sponsor the second leg match at Tannadice on Wednesday, May 20, will be announced in the city today.

Details will be given this forenoon by Lord Provost Tom Mitchell at United's ground.

The sponsorship decision was taken by the district council planning and development sub-committee, meeting in private, which has powers to make such a decision.

Dundee's licensed traders will be granted specially-late licences on the night of the Tannadice UEFA cup final match if they apply in time.

Councillor Charles Farquhar, chairman of the licensing board, yesterday acknowledged the contribution Dundee United had made to football and their home city and promised 1 a.m. licences.

"Under normal circumstances extensions, may be granted until midnight," he said.

"But, in view of these special circumstances and with regard to the achievements of Dundee United, I see it as only right that if anyone wishes an extension and applies, then we will grant and applies, then we will grant to 1 a.m. on the night of the match."

Councillor Farquhar said his move had been taken after consideration of the fact that the match, presentation and all formalities could be concluded as late as 10.30 p.m.

Added to this, similar extensions had been granted during the last World Cup.

Applicants need to apply at least 14 days before May 20, date of the second leg at Tannadice.

See United in Gothenburg or at Hampden—FREE

DUNDEE UNITED are on the crest of a wave, with all the excitement of two cup finals coming up—the UEFA Cup and the Scottish Cup.

And in our latest competitions we are offering a double helping of delight for the fans, absolutely free.

There are wordsquare puzzlers to be solved which could take entrants to either Gothenburg for the first leg of the UEFA

Cup final on May 6 or to Hampden Park on May 16 for the Scottish Cup final against St Mirren.

● Two lucky readers will be flying out with the team to see the match in Sweden.

In conjunction with VG Foodstores, United's sponsors, we are offering two seats on the team's aircraft, three nights' accommodation with breakfast and, of course, tickets for the match.

All you have to do to enter is find the following names in the appropriate wordsquare:

Narey, Hegarty, Malpas, Ferguson, Sturrock, Bannon, McInally, Redford.

Once you have found them draw a line around them with a pen and send your entry to Dundee United Competition (Gothenburg), "The Courier," Bank Street, Dundee DD1 9HU.

Time is short! The competition closes second post this Thursday, April 30. The winners will be the first two correct entries opened after that time.

● For the Scottish Cup final at Hampden there will be six prizes of two stand tickets each. The winners will be taken to Hampden by luxury coach, which will stop at a first class restaurant on the way for lunch.

All you have to do to enter is find the following words hidden in the other wordsquare:

Hampden, Dundee United, Tannadice, Jim McLean, Scottish Cup, St Mirren, luxury coach, free tickets.

Send your entries to Dundee United Competition (Hampden), "The Courier," Bank Street, Dundee, DD1 9HU.

This competition closes first post Saturday, May 9. The winners will be the first six correct entries opened after that time.

Both of these competitions are limited to those aged 16 and over. Employees of D. C. Thomson & Co., Ltd., and their immediate relatives cannot enter. No cash alternative will be offered.

HAMPDEN

I	O	W	S	E	M	Z	G	C	Y	U	Q	K	A
S	D	M	J	I	M	M	C	L	E	A	N	K	N
C	J	E	S	T	E	K	C	I	T	E	E	R	F
O	V	I	T	U	H	L	G	L	S	B	R	R	P
T	X	C	A	I	T	U	B	X	A	F	R	Z	Y
T	W	T	N	R	N	X	V	P	D	L	I	T	F
I	O	M	N	N	D	U	K	Q	N	R	M	S	U
S	P	Y	A	W	Q	R	E	V	E	E	T	L	G
H	Z	C	D	X	V	Y	X	E	O	J	S	H	F
C	B	J	I	A	H	C	F	U	D	N	E	M	Q
U	J	D	C	G	W	O	T	Z	C	N	D	M	C
P	I	F	E	E	A	A	P	S	G	H	U	R	N
K	S	H	R	X	B	C	L	Y	O	K	P	D	Q
N	E	D	P	M	A	H	D	J	A	I	O	L	B

GOTHENBURG

C	B	R	Q	N	O	N	N	A	B	P	A	O	A
Z	A	S	Y	U	V	B	G	H	A	P	P	B	N
E	C	N	T	W	C	F	H	I	S	Z	C	D	M
I	Y	G	M	X	E	Y	E	R	A	N	C	G	R
X	L	Y	X	W	J	G	D	G	E	P	D	K	L	E
I	L	H	N	G	Z	H	A	F	L	J	Z	B	D
J	A	L	K	O	Y	S	R	Z	A	A	D	E	F
K	N	M	N	M	S	T	T	A	M	C	B	F	O
P	I	N	J	I	Q	U	Y	U	V	H	G	F	R
Q	C	O	K	P	R	R	G	S	T	H	Q	R	D
R	M	O	L	J	T	R	E	R	F	J	E	P	N
S	Q	M	N	O	I	O	F	D	E	G	P	H	S
W	A	W	B	N	S	C	U	L	T	F	V	S	K
Z	O	B	M	R	Y	K	C	S	X	X	D	U	V

For those fans who had found a way to get to Sweden, The Courier provided a handy city guide — but perhaps put some off by highlighting the £4 pints! The paper even got together with VG again to offer two tickets on the official club flight.

Gothenburg—Sweden's capital of sport

A WEEK TODAY Dundee United take on IFK Gothenburg in the first leg of the UEFA Cup final.

Here we turn the spotlight on Gothenburg the city—home of Sweden's Angels.

WHETHER YOU spell it Gothenburg or Goteborg or even if you pronounce it "gyerteborge" as the locals do, in any language Gothenburg is Sweden's capital of sport.

And commanding a special place in the hearts and minds of the city's 440,000 inhabitants is IFK Gothenburg the football club.

The fans call them the Angels or the "Blavitts—the Blue-and-Whites" after their blue and white strip.

Gothenburg is Sweden's second city after the capital, Stockholm. Situated at the mouth of the River Gota, it is the country's largest port, which was developed by the Swedish East India Company and grew during Napoleon's continental blockade.

The Gota River, which drains from Lake Vanern and flows south west to the Kattegat, forms part of the Gota Canal which links Sweden's two principal cities.

The relationship between Stockholm and Gothenburg is not dissimilar to that between Edinburgh and Glasgow in some respects.

Stockholm is the capital and administrative centre, while Gothenburg is the industrial centre . . . but with much more besides.

There is a friendly rivalry between the two centres, heightened by the Gothenburgers' unique sense of humour, which is, I am told, not unlike Liverpudlian.

There are other connections with Liverpool. During the 19th Century something like a quarter of Sweden's population sailed from Gothenburg to Liverpool and on to the New world.

By any standards Sweden is a prosperous country. Wages are high—a car worker can earn £1300 a month, for example—and the standard of living is high.

Only about 1% of the eight million population are registered unemployed.

As one Gothenburg jounalist told me, "There is work for anyone who wants it in Sweden. Unemployment is not an issue."

This prosperity is based on an abundance of natural resources, mainly forests, mineral deposits and water power.

Industry is largely based on mining, principally iron, aluminium and copper.

But it is the general engineering industry that provides the basis of Sweden's exports.

Scandinavia's largest company is Volvo, which exports 75% of its production and is based in Gothenburg.

Other leading Scandinavian companies based in the city include SKF, the world's largest manufacturer of ball-bearings; ESAB, the giant welding company; camera manufacturers Hasselblad; offshore companies like Gotaverken Arendal and Consafe; pharmaceutical companies like Molnlycke and Hassle; and also Ericsson's defence and space electronics and Saab Space.

Industry and trade in the Gothenburg region employ about 320,000 people.

With its strategic location, Gothenburg is also Sweden's transport centre. On average one container or

The beautiful main street in downtown Gothenburg.

trailer is loaded or unloaded in the port every minute.

Although Gothenburg is a prosperous industrial town, it nevertheless reflects Scandinavian concern for the environment.

It is probably the cleanest city one could hope to visit and a green belt runs through a large part of the downtown area.

Dotted throughout the city and surrounding areas are numerous parks, nature reserves, gardens, and Liseberg, a spectacular Swedish "Disney-type" theme park.

Pedestrian-only streets, some of them over a kilometre long, enhance Gothenburg's shopping environment.

Prices are steep—£4 for a pint of strong beer and £6 for a double whisky—but at least most Gothenburgers will be able to understand visiting fans, as English is widely spoken.

Eating out can be very expensive—£100 for a good meal for two is not considered unreasonable—but there are also less expensive eateries. Gothenburg is a major sea fishing port, and

the seafood restaurants are recommended.

Incidentally, the Swedish currency is the kronor (Swedish crown). There are roughly ten to the £.

But of course it is sport that concentrates attention on Gothenburg at this time and the city boasts a collection of Scandinavia's best facilities.

Ice hockey, gymnastics, horse shows, ice skating, skiing and of course tennis are all important sports, but in Gothenburg football is king.

The chairman of IFK Gothenburg, Gunnar Larsson, is also the chairman of the city council.

The politics of the city are "social democrat" which is more like old fashioned Labour politics under Harold Wilson rather than David Owen's S.D.P.

IFK Gothenburg have always been identified with the "working classes" and the club's following is known colloquially as "The Movement."

Quite recently there was a raging debate in the city about whether or not hospitality boxes should be built in IFK Gothenburg's Ullevi stadium.

The boxes would have meant more revenue for the club, but would have reduced the crowd capacity.

Larsson opposed the move on the grounds that as many people as possible should be able to get into the stadium to watch football. His stand won popular support, and eventually the idea was dropped.

The tie with Dundee United has generated enormous interest in the city. Fans queued all night for the £20 a time tickets.

The Swedish Press has speculated that the club could easily have sold 150,000 tickets for the game next Wednesday.

As it is, the game should net the club a cool £500,000 and that is without television rights.

In all honesty the average Gothenburger knows as much about Dundee as the average Dundonian did about Gothenburg before he read this.

One thing they do know about us—they did not want to play Dundee United in the UEFA Cup final.

The feeling in Gothenburg was that the Angels would have coped better with German opposition.

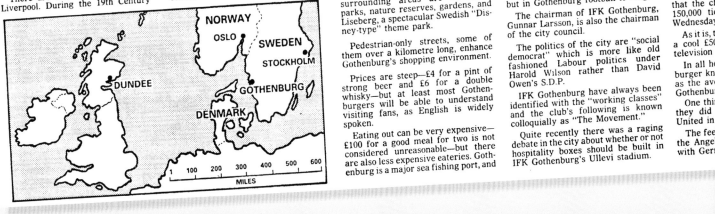

NORWAY
OSLO
SWEDEN
STOCKHOLM
DUNDEE
GOTHENBURG
DENMARK

1 100 200 300 400 500 600
MILES

It's plain sailing for some United fans!

AS WELL as the massed tangerine and black banners in Gothenburg for the Dundee United UEFA Cup game next week, one party of Tayside ambassadors will be travelling under the White Ensign.

The Dundee-based Royal Naval Reserve minesweeper H.M.S. Helmsdale has just been given official clearance to make a 36-hour stop at the Swedish port as part of a training run.

Just in time for the game!

Some 30 R.N.R. officers and ratings will be joining the ship at Victoria Dock, Dundee, this Friday for the start of a week-long exercise which begins with a steam north to Sutherland.

"This will be our second visit to the village of Helmsdale, our affiliated township," said C.O. of Tay Division R.N.R., Commander Mike Dickinson.

"During the course of the subsequent week's training period a visit to the port of Gothenburg has been programmed . . . and very fortunately this coincides with Dundee United's first leg UEFA Cup final game."

The programme of events for H.M.S. Helmsdale will see her

sail to Sutherland under the command of Lieutenant-Commander C. J. B. Jackson, who lives in Cupar, and the ship's company will take part in sporting events, official courtesy calls and community work.

Reservist Wrens will also be travelling to the Highland village for the weekend but they, like Commander Dickinson, will return to Dundee on Monday as the minesweeper heads out across the North Sea.

Although the prospect of being in Gothenburg in time for the game has attracted volunteers for the crew from Tay Division members as far afield as Aberdeen, Perthshire and Fife, work is also in prospect.

Mine counter-measure, gunnery, engineering, seamanship and safety procedures will all be rigorously tested before and after the crew spend time cheering on McLean's lads.

Commanding the ship for the Swedish trip will be Lieutenant Commander Tom Woolley, Inverkeilor, by Arbroath.

Lieutenant Commander Woolley admits he was delighted when Vice-Admiral Sir George Vallings, Flag Officer

Scotland and Northern Ireland, suggested it would be very proper for the Dundee Navy to lend support to the team in its great enterprise.

The ship's crew has a direct connection with Dundee United, because one of three Royal Marine reservists on board is the son of club secretary Mrs Ann Diamond.

H.M.S. Helmsdale, a river class minesweeper operated by H.M.S. Camperdown, will depart Peterhead on Monday, evening and arrive in Gothenburg on Wednesday morning in good time for the match on Wednesday night.

A special Dundee United flag will be flown by the ship and the only disappointed crew members will be the five-man watch who will have to stay aboard.

Their names will be drawn by lots!

Travel agents in Dundee are reeling under the weight of bookings still flooding in for United's trip.

Without a doubt it is the biggest travel event they have ever handled and, so far, there is no sign of demand slacking off.

"It's just incredible," said Colin Ramsay of Ramsay World Travel.

"I have never seen demand like it in my life.

"We have had to tell everybody that it's strictly first come first served and we can't hold seats for them, the demand for our £89 Harwich ferry package is so great.

"We have people paying £390 just for a flight to Gothenburg— no accommodation just the flight.

"You could have a month in Spain for that!"

It's the same story at D. P & L. Travel in Albert Square, where a spokesman described bookings as "Excellent, brilliant, superb!"

So far, D. P. & L. has sold around 250 flights to Sweden.

A. T. Mays are also looking into the possibility of arranging a second Sweden flight for United fans.

"One flight is already full and between our two Dundee offices we have about another 100 names," said a spokesman.

As United fans continued to try to find ways to cross the North Sea, The Courier published an incredibly rare insight into the McLean household.

Voucher holders to have ticket priority

By STEVE BRUCE

DUNDEE UNITED fans who attended the UEFA Cup semi-final with Borussia Moenchengladbach, are to be given priority for the purchase of tickets for the home leg of the final with Gothenburg, at Tannadice, on May 20.

Holders of the voucher, attached to the Borussia tickets, allowing free admission to Saturday's clash with Hibs, will, along with season ticket holders, receive first chance to secure their places at the final.

This Friday, from 9 a.m. until 5 p.m. and Saturday, between 9 a.m.-3 p.m., on presentation of the Hibs' voucher, fans will be able to purchase a ticket for the

final on the basis of one ticket per voucher.

Thereafter, tickets will be made available to the general public with the Tannadice office opening on Sunday from 10 a.m.-4 p.m.

The price of final tickets is £10 (ground) and £20 (stand).

Your chance to see United in Gothenburg or at Hampden— FREE. See competitions on Page 10.

Super-fit Swedes are very good — but not invincible

By the Sports Editor

YOU CAN get a cup final in Europe where one or other team is not of the standard expected.

But the UEFA Cup final between Dundee United and IFK Gothenburg features the two teams who most deserve to be there and are of similar quality.

We all know United's standard. Gothenburg are naturally more of an unknown quantity here—which is why manager Jim McLean and coach Gordon

Wernersson   Frederiksson

Wallace of United will be watching them against Hammarby in Gothenburg tonight. But what is no surprise is that they are in the final.

They have, of course, won the UEFA Cup once before, five years ago, when they defeated Hamburg 1-0 and 3-0 in the two legs.

Like United, they are built on a solid base of certain players who have corner-stoned their efforts over recent years—in fact no fewer than seven of the team which played against Tirol in the recent semi-final of the UEFA Cup were in the cup-winning side back in May 1982.

They are keeper Wernersson and outfield players Hysen, Carlsson, Frederiksson, Tord and Tommy Holmgren and Nilsson.

The games against United could be the last major European events in the magnificent careers of Wernersson and Frederiksson.

Both are due to retire from the active side of the game, but they won't be lost to the club as they are expected to move into the executive side in the financial and public relations spheres.

If they prove to be as good at that as they are on the field it will be a bonus for the club as a whole!

Actually, eight of the current players were in the side which put Aberdeen out of the European Cup last season.

The scores were 0-0 and 2-2, with Gothenburg going through on the basis of away goals counting double.

It is significant—and a pointer to the fact that the Swedish team is superbly conditioned physically—that, after these games, then Aberdeen manager Alex Ferguson put his young players on a special diet, which included a plate of porridge daily, to bring them up to the Scandinavians' standard.

An interesting fact is that, after beating Aberdeen, Gothenburg went on to meet Barcelona—and, having won 3-0 at home and lost 3-0 away, went out 5-4 on penalties.

So they are good, but even though they have gone 22 UEFA Cup games without defeat, they are not invincible.

● The Ullevi Stadium, home of the Angels, as Gothenburg are known, has a 48,000 capacity.

Fans are used to queuing for tickets as the team plays so many big games. For the UEFA Cup final, all the tickets for the home fans were sold out in two hours.

DUNDEE UNITED'S manager Jim McLean, one of the most successful ever in his profession, is at the centre of the European football stage this week as his team prepares to take on IFK Gothenburg in the first leg of the UEFA Cup final. His wife Doris, however, has deliberately kept out of the spotlight.

Here, in an exclusive and extremely rare interview, a "Courier" reporter takes a look—

Inside the very private world of Mrs Jim McLean

Mrs McLean relaxing at home before the most exciting period in United's history.

FOR A CERTAIN type of woman, marriage to a man like Jim McLean could be a career in itself; playing queen to his king, snatching and revelling in a percentage of the praise, and luxuriating in chiffon and champagne.

Doris McLean's light does not come from reflected glory. She is not Jim's spare rib, his alter ego.

She has no sense of being a celebrity, or of being married to one. Quiet-spoken and contained, she prizes her privacy, and pities pop stars for their inability to enjoy the anonymity she craves.

Very much her own person, she enjoys being at home, making their large garden look its best and watching woollens grow on the knitting pins while her husband does whatever it is a manager's gotta do.

She loves the game of football—but in its place, on the pitch, where she is as avid and excitable as anyone else.

This, though, is home; in this large, spotless and airy lounge, its white walls jewelled with gilt-framed landscapes, football is an eight-letter expletive that does not have to be deleted from the conversation—it's just not talked about.

It probably wasn't mentioned either, over 26 years ago, when a young joiner and part-time footballer met a pretty young office girl from Airdrie in very familiar-sounding circumstances . . .

"It was at a local dance hall—the Trocadero," said Mrs McLean, a slim, attractive woman with blonde highlights in her tied-back hair.

"I was working for a clothing firm—we used to be able to buy lovely blouses for only 50p—and Jim was a joiner playing part-time for Hamilton Accies. We started dating right away, and were married a year later."

Although it was the game rather than the woodwork that was to shape Jim's future, he continued to ply his trade on a domestic scale for many years, even building homes for his family.

"He could build houses, but try to get him to do the odd jobs!" she laughed. "Well he just doesn't have the time now. There are too many things going on, even in the close season."

Although she had two brothers, Mrs McLean remained indifferent to football until after her marriage.

Even then, in the early days, at least, there were distractions to contend with.

"I went to the odd game when he was playing, but the boys, Colin (24) and Gary (18) were very young at the time, and always wanted something to eat or drink or to go to the toilet!

"It's really since he became a manager that I've come to love the game."

Perhaps it's because management is where the buck stops, making the joys of victory greater and the pangs of defeat sharper.

> **"** Football is first and foremost. It's his job, and it's our security and what's good for him is good for us. **"**

"Yes, I feel the joys—and the disappointments, but they pass.

"I suppose the worst time was the year the Premier League started. It was either our team, or Dundee F.C., which was going to be relegated.

"I think it went to the very last game of the season. That was a bit worrying, but we stayed in the league."

Mrs McLean brought in a tray heaped with sandwiches and cakes, enough for a football team, but ate sparingly.

She and her husband rarely get the opportunity to relax together, she says without a trace of resentment.

"It's a way of life, and you have to expect that as a manager's wife. Football is first and foremost. It's his job, and it's our security and what's good for him is good for us."

Even when things are very good, there is nothing remotely giddy about the McLeans' response.

Neither of them likes bright lights and big celebrations. "We prefer just to come home."

"Football is a different world, but in company, he is shy."

They do have nights out occasionally, of course, but all too often, "Everyone's eyes turn towards us and you can hear people saying, 'There's Jim McLean!'

> **"** With the European games coming so close together, it seems I've just unpacked one suitcase when I'm packing another. **"**

"I can understand it, but I'm not the sort of person who enjoys being recognised. It hardly helps us relax and enjoy our meal."

A manager's job must at times be a lonely one; the team is a 13-strong group, bound together by interplay, while the manager is a monolith, with few if any buddies at his own level. If Jim feels that sense of isolation, his wife certainly does not.

"Jim may have to be the boss with the players, but I'm just one of the wives," she says happily. "We get on very well together, and enjoy nights out together from time to time."

Holidays abroad, of course, are great equalisers, too. For several years now, the McLeans have headed across the Atlantic, to Los Angeles and Florida.

"I love the climate there, although we did get a bit of rain in Florida. We've seen all the sights—Disneyland, Cape Kennedy—and now we just go for a break.

"Last year, we stayed at a country club. It was ideal, with golf and tennis on the doorstep. Jim loved it."

Lately, though, travelling has proved less relaxing.

"With the European games coming so close together, it seems I've just unpacked one suitcase when I'm packing another," she explained.

"Back home in between times, I have to try to get back into a routine again, catching up on my gardening and keeping the shopping up to date.

"Still, I enjoy travelling, enjoy seeing other countries—and watching the Press corps playing football," she added with a grin that suggested she might just extract some revenge from the spectacle.

She enjoys coming home, too, to a city she has grown to love and regard as her home.

"I love Dundee—the city, and the people—and I love this area—around Broughty Ferry. I'm really glad we've been able to settle here."

While she goes about her normal tasks—selling tickets at Tannadice today and helping count programme money tomorrow—"It helps to keep my mind off the game for a while"—the excitement of the impending visit to Gothenburg is clearly building up inside her.

"I'm really looking forward to it," she says with enthusiasm. "Yes, I've heard it's very expensive, that beer is about £5 a time—but as a teetotaller that won't bother me in the slightest."

And United's performance on Swedish soil?

"I'm quite confident," she says quietly. Does her husband feel the same?

"You'd have to ask him that," she smiles.

Many would say there was no need. They know the man who can coax or bully the best out of his team, and whose body writhes in the confinement of the dugout while his mind is in every different position on the field. Oh yes, they know Jim.

But after more than 25 years of marriage to the man, there is something Mrs McLean knows about him that might surprise them all.

"He is very quiet and shy, especially when meeting people—it's unbelievable."

117

United squad take a well-earned break

DUNDEE UNITED'S first team pool—with two notable exceptions—are enjoying a welcome break before beginning preparations for their bid to lift the UEFA and Scottish Cups.

Immediately after Tuesday night's win over Hamilton Accies, the Tannadice players headed for St Andrews for a spell of relaxation and a few games of golf.

With manager Jim McLean and coach Gordon Wallace flying to Sweden today to spy on Euro opponents Gothenburg, senior men Dave Narey and Paul Hegarty have been left in charge of the party—an indication of the trust the United boss has in his players.

He commented yesterday,

"The lads have built themselves a good reputation which I'm sure they'll keep."

Missing out on the well-earned break, which ends this afternoon, are keeper Billy Thomson and defender Maurice Malpas.

Thomson is suffering from a slight cold and was left behind

By STEVE BRUCE

to prevent his ailment spreading, while Malpas is receiving intensive treatment on the ankle injury which prevented him playing against Borussia in the UEFA semi-final return.

"Maurice is making slow progress but it's too early to say whether or not he'll be available to face Gothenburg in the first-

leg of the final next Wednesday," said McLean.

Club captain Hegarty is also on the casualty list. He returned to Tannadice yesterday for a spell of treatment on the thigh injury he sustained against Accies.

"It hasn't yet been determined whether Paul has strained a muscle or simply taken a knock but although he looks doubtful for Saturday's game with Hibs, he should be okay for Sweden," revealed the manager.

Meanwhile, tickets for the UEFA Cup Final second leg on May 20 go on sale to voucher holders at Tannadice tomorrow.

As usual, season tickets are valid for the European tie.

UEFA spell out position

UEFA YESTERDAY reaffirmed the position regarding entry of the UEFA Cup holders into the following season's competition (reports STEVE BRUCE).

There have been conflicting reports as to the situation which would confront United should they defeat Gothenberg but fail to secure a European place by virtue of league position or winning the Scottish Cup.

A UEFA spokesman confirmed that there is no automatic entry into the following season's competition for the cup winners.

He revealed, however, "Should Dundee United win the UEFA Cup and fail to gain entry into Europe through domestic competition, the S.F.A. could request our organising committee to grant them a place in next season's tournament."

The spokesman indicated that under those circumstances it was "probable" that such a request would be granted.

It is unlikely, though, that United will require to gain admission to Europe by such means for even if they were to lose the Scottish Cup final to St Mirren, they require only three points from their three remaining Premier fixtures to be guaranteed a UEFA Cup spot by virtue of league position.

Live TV coverage

United's UEFA Cup final battle against IFK Gothenburg will be shown live on television in Scotland, it was confirmed yesterday.

The B.B.C. have the contract to show the first leg, which takes place in Gothenburg next Wednesday.

Scottish Television will be responsible for screening the Tannadice tie on May 20.

The games are likely to be shown in Scotland only.

The S.F.A., which ran into controversy when it tried to curtail screen time for United's last two ties against Borussia Moenchengladbach, have this time given their blessing for two live matches.

A spokesman said yesterday, "The B.B.C. have approached us for permission to screen the first leg live, and this has been granted.

"STV have still to register their application to cover the second leg live. But I don't foresee any problems in permission being granted."

On the flights front, D.P. & L. Travel in Dundee have another 30 places still to be claimed on a charter.

A.A. Travel, Overgate, Dundee, have a scheduled flight to Gothenburg from Aberdeen on Wednesday morning costing £165.

COUNTDOWN TO NEXT WEEK'S ENCOUNTER IN GOTHENBURG

English hooligans make fans suffer

RIOTING ENGLISH football fans are to blame for Dundee United supporters having to face 10 extra gruelling hours on the buses to Gothenburg next week for the first leg of the UEFA Cup final.

Sealink have "reluctantly" refused to allow the United coaches on their Harwich-Hook of Holland ferry, sending them instead to cross from Dover to Calais.

The switch in arrangements means the fans will travel through no fewer than eight separate countries by the time they reach Gothenburg.

It also deprives them of a 10-hour break from coach travel which they could have enjoyed while on the Harwich ferry.

A spokesman for Sealink in Harwich said yesterday, "We're very sorry, but we can't make an exception to our policy.

"At the start of the season, there were riots on the Harwich-Hook ferry by a large number of English football fans. A great deal of damage was caused, and every ferry company had to look anew at its policy regarding football fans."

The incidents in question, caused by West Ham and Manchester United fans, resulted in one ferry actually turning back.

Rioters wrecked thousands of pounds worth of furnishings, and one seaman was stabbed.

The spokesman went on, "Because of this, the seamen at Harwich have refused to take other football fans.

"This in no way reflects on the behaviour of Dundee United fans, who I'm told have conducted themselves in exemplary fashion all season.

"United fans sailed to Calais earlier in the season. The captain of that ferry tells us they were model customers, and the trip was a great success."

Those fans travelling by D.F.D.S. ferry direct to Gothenburg will not be affected. Mr Gordon Easson, manager of Bell Travel which had organised two coach-loads of fans to travel on the Harwich-Hook route, said Sealink's decision was a "disgrace."

Demand for information

GOTHENBURGERS ARE becoming increasingly eager for information about Dundee United—its team, its fans, its city and its ground.

They were eager, therefore, to hear this week what policing arrangements are being made for the second leg and how Tannadice copes with crowds.

The man they came to see was Chief Inspector Ron McBean, in charge of Monday night's game against Hamilton, who spoke afterwards to sports reporter Staffan Lindeborg of Swedish Television.

'It was an informal discussion on the forthcoming game," said Mr McBean, "and most of it was routine stuff.

"But the Swedes did seem a bit taken aback at the fact there's no fence ringing the ground—I gather that's a standard feature in Swedish grounds.

Mr McBean said he was satisfied there would be "no worries" about crowd behaviour on May 20.

Banks cleared out of kronor

EAGER DUNDEE United supporters cleared out the entire stock of Swedish kronor at the Reform Street, Dundee, branch of the Bank of Scotland yesterday—over £1500 worth exchanged by mid-afternoon.

Obviously undaunted by the high prices in Sweden, such as £3.50 for a pint of beer and £6 for a small whisky, the fans look set to spend, spend, spend next week.

Around 15 people visited the bank throughout the day and, by late afternoon, staff were even refusing to take any orders, unsure if new supplies would be available from Glasgow.

A spokesman for the bank said that, as well as exchanging money, many of the fans were also taking travellers' cheques.

"We have had quite a few phone calls asking about the availability of kronor and our other branches in the city have been asking if we could supply them with quite sizeable amounts, but we had none to spare.

"Normally we have about £300 worth in stock. "Hopefully more kronor will be coming through from Glasgow this morning."

He warned that anyone intending to exchange money at the Bank of Scotland should do so today, since the bank will be closed on Monday, and Tuesday will probably be too late for most fans.

Tribute to Dundee United fans

AS DUNDEE UNITED fans set off on yet another trip as Scotland's ambassadors abroad, glowing praise has come, entirely unsolicited, from someone involved on their last sortie overseas.

A total of 180 fans stayed at the Dutch National Sportscentre at Sittard, on the Dutch/German/Belgian border, 10 days ago when United were playing Borussia Moenchengladbach.

They left, elated, after a memorable match and an enjoyable stay in Sittard—and that, they thought, was the end of it.

Now, however, Mr Hendrick Femer, director of the centre, has been moved to put pen to paper, so impressed were he and his colleagues by the Dundee visitors.

Writing to Mr David Ben-Areyah, director of Dunedin Travel of Edinburgh, who arranged the trip, Mr Femer says:

"After the Scottish Dundee United fans left early morning of April 23, I felt that I had to write this letter to you.

"I must give the fans and you my compliments about how everything was arranged and the fine way everyone behaved.

"When I got your reservation I was called by the local police department who asked me if I realised what risks I took to do so.

"They almost forced me to cancel everything because of security reasons."

He got in touch with Mr Ben-Areyah, however, and was given a categorical assurance that United fans would behave impeccably.

He then managed to persuade colleagues and police chiefs that United fans were different from others. "So, finally, they accepted."

He continues, "As the fans of your country have a bad reputation, this group proved that there are also fans who don't make troubles.

"Before the arrival of the group everybody was excited what would happen, but afterwards everybody said that this group was a very fine group to handle both here and in Maastrict.

"I will ask you to do me a favour to hand over a copy of this letter to the board of Dundee United Football Club."

The National Sportscentre is a multi-million pound complex covering an area of two square miles, with probably among the best facilities in Europe.

According to Mr Ben-Areyah yesterday, Mr Femer and his colleagues "really stuck their necks out" to get the United fans booked there.

Last night United chairman George Fox was "very happy" to hear of the letter.

He said he was as proud of the fans as he was of the players.

The letter was much appreciated, too, at Dundee United Supporters' Association Social Club.

A committee spokesman said last night, "There was no trouble at all on that trip—the whole thing was great.

"This isn't the first praise we've had, though—the captain of the ferry across to Calais came up to personally thank us for our behaviour!"

A welcome indication of the changing attitude of fans was given, too, when the spokesman remembered the coach trip down to the south of England.

"There were four people on board then that could have caused trouble," he said, "but we actually put them right off the bus when we reached Carlisle."

UEFA tickets go on sale today

IT'S UEFA CUP final (second leg) ticket time at Tannadice, starting today (writes THE SPORTS EDITOR).

The game against Gothenburg isn't until May 20, but early indications are that the demand will be heavy.

First to get their chance of tickets will be those with a voucher from the semi-final with Borussia Moenchengladbach (Tannadice, 9 a.m. to 5 p.m today).

Those who can't make it today can call between 9 a.m. and 3 p.m. tomorrow.

On Sunday, the remaining tickets go on sale to the general public between 10 a.m. and 4 p.m. and will continue to be sold during normal office hours from then until sold out.

As United's fans won more praise from another batch of new European friends, local firms were looking for ways to cash in on "final fever".

6000 United fans get second leg tickets

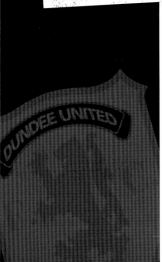

OVER 6000 people headed for Tannadice Park yesterday as tickets for the home leg of Dundee United's UEFA Cup final went on sale. Staff at the Tannadice sales office were kept busy from 9 a.m. when the doors opened on a patient line of fans already 100 strong.

The May 20 game will decide the issue between United and their cup rivals Gothenburg—who meet in Sweden next week—and local fans were obviously keen to book their place at United's finest hour and a half.

Only those holding the special ticket vouchers from the Borussia game at Tannadice four weeks ago were entitled to buy a cup final ticket yesterday, but demand remained high.

One of the first to emerge with a ticket was unemployed David Patterson of Craighill Place, Dundee, who had queued from 7 a.m. "There's just no way I could afford to go to Gothenburg," he said, "but I was determined to see United in the final . . no matter what!"

The Tannadice staff reported late yesterday afternoon that the day's lengthy queues had dispersed satisfied but a steady stream of callers kept them busy throughout the rest of the day.

Malpas now looks 'odds-on' to make squad for Gothenburg

Maurice Malpas—back in training.

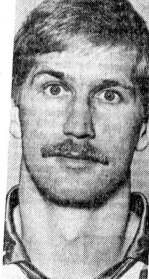

Lennart Nilsson—scored Gothenburg's winning goal

WIN OR LOSE, Taysiders are certainly going to be able to taste the sweet flavour of Dundee United's success over the next couple of weeks.

As the Tangerines prepare for the Scottish and UEFA cup finals, Andrew G. Kidd outlets throughout the region are clearing the shelves for a special Dundee United cake which they are sure will score heavily with the fans, United followers or not.

The sponges, decorated of course in United colours, will roll out of the oven in time for United's Scottish final on May 16, and then again for the UEFA second leg a few days later.

Origianlly the intention had been to sell the cakes only in Dundee but with almost the whole nation caught up in the 'final-fever' the firm feel that hungry supporters throughout Tayside and Fife will be keen to get a slice of the cake as well as the action.

● PICTURE.—Maureen Thomson with one of the cakes.

DUNDEE UNITED boss Jim McLean yesterday returned from his Swedish spying mission, in which he saw UEFA Cup final opponents Gothenburg beat Hammarby 3-2 on Thursday night, to encouraging news on the injury front.

Scotland defender Maurice Malpas, sidelined since sustaining a foot injury at Parkhead on April 18, has restarted light training.

"Maurice has begun running again, is looking better and now appears odds-on to be included in the squad for Gothenburg," revealed McLean.

The pool for Sweden, however, isn't being announced until after today's match with Hibs.

"There are still a couple of places in the squad up for grabs and I want to see how certain players perform against Hibs before making up my mind," said the manager.

Having seen the Swedes in action, McLean now has a better idea of the task confronting his side in the Ullevi Stadium on Wednesday night and, though giving little away, he still clearly rates United's chances of lifting the trophy.

"We have no reason to lack confidence, particularly in view of the results we've already achieved in the competition," he commented.

United fans can purchase tickets for the game in Gothenburg, from the Tannadice office as of 9 a.m. today.

Tickets are priced, £7.20 (ground), £15 (stand).

Meanwhile, United will decide this weekend whether or not to accept an invitation to participate in a six-club tournament in America next month.

121

United set sights on booking Euro place

By Steve Bruce

DUNDEE UNITED can today book their place in next season's UEFA Cup competition.

To be assured of European football—regardless of how they fare in the Scottish Cup final—the Tannadice side actually require three points from their three remaining Premier League matches.

However, such is the healthy state of their goal difference, victory over Hibs at Tannadice this afternoon would all but guarantee them the top four finish needed to secure a UEFA Cup spot.

And if either of their Euro rivals, Aberdeen or Hearts, drop any points today it will definitely be sufficient.

While keen to have a place in continental competition secured before tackling Gothenburg in the UEFA Cup final, first leg, manager Jim McLean intends resting several players today, with Sweden in mind.

He said, "One or two looked a wee bit tired against Hamilton on Tuesday night and will be left out to freshen them up."

Midfielder Ian Redford, having completed a two-match suspension and now recovered from a calf muscle strain, returns to the side.

Youngsters Billy McKinlay and Gordon McLeod are also set to play and they could be joined by left-back Harry Curran.

Those first-team pool members who aren't to feature in this afternoon's action, are reporting to Tannadice in the morning for a light training session.

Hibs will have Gordon Hunter and Tommy McIntyre at full-back.

Winger Mickey Weir is fit again and former United player Eddie May should be available if required.

"Courier" readers going to Gothenburg

TWO DUNDEE UNITED fans have won the chance to follow the team abroad for the very first time when they fly out to Gothenburg next week.

Mr Graeme Bowman, an architectural technician who lives in Symers Street, and Mr Alistair Roy, of Bellefield Avenue, won the trip by entering the recent "Courier"/V.G. Food Stores word square competition. The prize includes travel to and from Sweden and two nights' accommodation.

Mr Bowman admitted that Manchester was the farthest he'd ever travelled to watch United and Mr Roy joked, "As I'm still a student, winning a competition like this is the only possible way I could afford to go to Sweden."

The two men set off from Tannadice on Monday. They received their tickets yesterday from United players Billy McKinlay and Jim McInally. From left—Billy McKinlay, Alistair, Watson & Philip divisional director Mr Eddie Thompson, Graeme Bowman and Jim McInally.

Fans queueing outside Tannadice.

Tannadice UEFA Cup tie a sell-out

THE DUNDEE UNITED-Gothenburg UEFA Cup final second leg at Tannadice in 16 days' time became a sell-out yesterday after fans queued all night for tickets. By the time the office gates opened at 10 a.m. a huge queue of cold but eager supporters snaked the ground.

A total of 30 enthusiastic and hardy supporters began their weary and chilly vigil late on Saturday night—a dedicated effort which was later rewarded by the office staff at the United ground.

"When we arrived at the office shortly before 10 a.m. the queue stretched from the ground up and around the edge of the play-park and into Sandeman Street," explained club secretary Mrs Ann Diamond.

It was originally hoped that general public ticket buyers would be allowed to purchase two tickets each. "But when we saw the extent of the queue I realised there would not be enough to go round," she added.

Over the previous past two days, the United faithful with vouchers from the semi-final home leg against Borussia were given first chance of the United-Gothenburg tickets and took the vast majority of them.

With the capacity of Tannadice Park only 22,310, a mere 3500 tickets were left on sale to the general public yesterday after the complimentary, Press, U.E.F.A. voucher and Gothenburg supporters' tickets (1700) were taken into account.

Said Mrs Diamond, "I had to make the decision to allocate only one ticket each to anyone in the queue—with the only exception being the first group of 30 which had been outside overnight.

"It was only right to reward their dedication—it was one awfully cold night."

Once the initial queue had dispersed at about 11 a.m., only 700 tickets were still to be sold and they soon quickly disappeared as late arrivals snapped them all up by 1.30 p.m.—two-and-a-half hours before the ticket office was due to close.

"It has been a terribly busy weekend and we are all just going home now to rest," said Mrs Diamond.

The first group in the hordes of Dundee United supporters intent on their general public tickets arrived at Tannadice Park at 10.30 p.m. on Saturday—nearly 12 hours before they were due to go on sale.

Complete with sleeping bags, groundsheets, woolly jumpers and flasks of hot drinks, the first hardy trio arrived determined to overcome the inclement conditions.

Dundee women Alyson Westwood (21), 83d Hilltown, and Christine Hart (24), 7 Southampton Road, who are both unemployed, met up with their new friend, Andy Barber (35), of Ingliston Farm, Eassie, as they all approached the entrance to the ticket sales office.

"We all knew right away that we shared a common purpose. The final will be well worth a sleepless night," said Alyson.

As the night progressed, the trio were joined by a further 27 United supporters—some equipped with other fluids to keep off the chill!

From left—Christine Hart, Robert Wilson, Lorraine Wilson and Christopher.

Christine's wait worthwhile

THE ENDURING task of securing her position at the head of the overnight queue was well worth the effort for 24-year-old Christine Hart.

"My sister and brother-in-law, who is a fanatical United supporter, are flying from Canada to spend just one week here so he can see both the UEFA Cup final and the Scottish Cup final," explained a tired Christine last night.

"I just would not like to think what would have happened if they had travelled 3000 miles only to find out I could not get them tickets.

"Being first in the queue was the only way to make sure I did not let them down," added Christine.

In fact, Christine's sister Lorraine (27) and brother-in-law Robert Wilson (31) last visited Dundee only five months ago when they spent three weeks here over Christmas with their 10-month-old son Christopher.

"Robert phoned my mum from Ottawa as soon as the semi-final in Germany was over—despite the time difference," added Christine.

"As soon as he heard the score he insisted we get tickets for both finals and he said then he was going to go straight out to book tickets for the flight to Prestwick."

Robert and Lorraine emigrated to Canada six years ago after Robert, a marine draftsman, was made redundant from the Caledon Shipyard in Dundee.

"Robert is such a United fanatic that he even got a special sports channel installed into his television so he could occasionally watch Dundee United on the football highlights," she said.

However, his avid determination to see both cup finals threw up an unfortunate clash with his mother-in-law's forthcoming five-week holiday in Ottawa.

"I was due to leave from Prestwick on May 20," explained mum-in-law Mrs May Hart at her home in Southampton Road.

"But Robert arranged their trip so they would leave Scotland on May 21. He said that it did not matter and that I should just rearrange my flight no matter the cost," said Mrs Hart.

"After the cost of their flights and then my rearranged flight I cannot help thinking that he has more money than sense," joked Mrs Hart.

All credit to physios for Malpas recovery

By the Sports Editor

TAKE A bow physiotherapists Jim Joyce and Andy Dickson.

As late as the middle of last week, Dundee United's Maurice Malpas was still "favouring" the ankle badly damaged in a tackle against Celtic the previous Saturday.

As I saw him limp away from the ground, my thoughts were that he would be lucky to be ready for the Scottish Cup final on May 16!

Now the report is that, because of constant care and attention by the physios—and, of course, his own hard work—the Scotland man isn't only in the United party for the UEFA Cup final (first leg) in Gothenburg on Wednesday night, he actually has a chance of playing.

Gothenburg's Glenn Hysen knows how to celebrate a goal in style but United will be hoping he isn't given the chance to do so in the tie.

COUNTDOWN TO WEDNESDAY'S ENCOUNTER IN GOTHENBURG

It will be treatment and training up to the very last minute, but the damage to the ankle joint has improved so much already that Malpas has rejoined the running side of training. Work with the ball will follow.

The party for Gothenburg is —Billy Thomson and Scott Thomson; Holt, Kirkwood, McInally, Hegarty, Narey, Ferguson, Bowman, Bannon, Sturrock, Redford, Clark, Gallacher, McGinnis, Beaumont, Gordon McLeod, Malpas, Page.

Scott Thomson suffered a knee twist on Saturday, but was passed fit yesterday and Gordon McLeod has a stiff calf muscle, but will also travel.

Several players trained yesterday and there will be another work-out before departing today.

Iain Ferguson is included though suspended for the first leg—an extremely wise decision, as he can weigh up the opposition at first hand with the second leg in mind..

Gothenburg manager Gunder Bengtsson was extremely polite but non-commital after watching United in action on Saturday.

He knew they had a lot of good players and appreciated that many of them had not played against Hibs.

He knew particularly of Paul Sturrock, a very, very good player indeed as he had shown many times at club and international level

The UEFA Cup final would be "very, very difficult for us."

He added, "I did hear on the radio this morning that United are favourites. It was, of course, Scottish radio."

During the game, I had been incessantly questioned by two Swedish journalists over United's likely team for Gothenburg.

When I kept repeating there were so many alternatives it was impossible to forecast, I felt they thought I was trying to hide something.

They tried again with the Gothenburg boss, who turned the question on me, getting the same reply—that there were so many alternatives . . .

Gunder Bengtsson.

Later they tried again. This time the questions were aimed at United manager Jim McLean who was to tell them, as politely as the Gothenburg manager had been with me, that it was more than likely there would be no team announcement until just before the game!

I believe they are still unconvinced.

The key to any uncertainty there might be is Malpas.

If he is fit—and he will have to prove this beyond any shadow of doubt whatever—he will be in. But where?

In his normal left back slot? At right back? In midfield?

It's wait-and-see time, with the manager the one who knows his alternatives should Malpas be fit, or unfit.

● **Exclusive interview with Dundee United chairman George Fox—see News Spotlight on Page 8.**

Fans' Swedish cash delayed

A LARGE number of Dundee United supporters about to embark on the marathon journey by coach to Gothenburg may have to travel without ready cash.

Such has been the overwhelming demand for Swedish currency that banks and travel agents have rapidly sold out their quotas of kronor—placing desperate orders for more.

Further problems have arisen for Dundee travel agents Thomas Cook after an alleged slip-up by the Post Office.

"Apparently the Post Office 'lost' seven bags of registered mail on Wednesday night—and we had four packets of Swedish currency ordered in these bags," said the firm's City Square office manager Mr Richard McKenna.

Altogether, thousands of pounds' worth of kronor were contained in the packets and until the mix-up is sorted out, some United fans are worried they may arrive in Sweden without the appropriate currency.

"The Post Office say they are completely in the dark about the whole situation. They do not even know where the mail is meant to be," added Mr McKenna.

His office was cleaned out of kronor within an hour of opening on Saturday morning and the awaited currency could have been sold out easily.

Mr McKenna is also anxious from a purely financial point of view—"If the kronor does not turn up until later in the week it will be too late for the fans and the travel agents will have trouble selling thousands of pounds of Swedish notes."

A Post Office spokesman has admitted that one mail was "outstanding."

"Investigations are taking place," he declared. He would not confirm or deny whether the missing mail had been registered.

Nor could he say whether the mail had been lost or stolen. He could not comment on a report that the mail had been left in a locked P.O. van at Gatwick.

Last-minute United supporters can still take up the opportunity of travelling to Gothenburg by taking up some of the eight available seats on a Dundee United Social Club coach.

The coach leaves the club's Victoria Street premises tonight at 10 p.m., returning to Dundee at 8 a.m. Friday, costing £90.

Anyone interested in taking up the vacant seats should contact Findlay McKay or Peter Sime at the club by 6.30 p.m. tonight.

Malpas keen to be part of the "buzz"

THE KEY to team selection this trip is definitely going to be the fitness of United and Scotland full-back Maurice Malpas **(writes The Sports Editor)**.

As I said yesterday the players and the United physios Jim Joyce and Andy Dickson have done a remarkable job in getting him fit enough even to come here.

The "time out" Maurice had between getting the ankle injury at Celtic Park and turning up for training as opposed to treatment last week was the longest he has had since becoming a senior player.

"And it was definitely not pleasant," he tells me.

"You go into the ground, you see the bustle around you as your mates get ready for the training—then they are gone and you are lying on the treatment table with the physios working on you.

"I'm used to being involved. It was like I was cut off from everything.

"One thing I can say though. Being, as it were, off to the side, I was able to judge how things were going, maybe even better than if I was completely involved.

"And there is a definite buzz with the lads, a really great feeling.

"You'd think it was the beginning of the season, not nearly the end. Everyone really is looking forward to the three cup final games. The mood is right."

So, if the result matches the mood . . .

Maurice Malpas.

United were setting off for Sweden, and it seemed everyone wanted a piece of the action.

Not even a minor currency crisis could wipe the smiles off the faces of fans heading for Gothenburg.

Some of Dundee United's well-travelled fans who set off for Gothenburg from the supporters' association social club in Victoria Road at 10 last night. Two coaches carrying 100 fans will travel through France, West Germany and Denmark with three ferry crossings before arriving in Sweden tommorow morning.

NEWS SPOTLIGHT

TODAY Dundee United leave for Sweden to play I.F.K. Gothenburg in the first leg of the UEFA Cup final on Wednesday.

Here, on the eve of this historic occasion, the chairman Mr George Fox talks to a "Courier" reporter about his long association with the club.

WHEN DUNDEE UNITED jet off to Scandinavia today they leave behind them the club's most ardent fan and faithful servant—chairman George Fox.

Angina has meant that Mr Fox's travelling days are over.

He will of course watch the game live on television with his wife Violet in their Carnoustie home, fingers nervously crossed.

His association with the club stretches back over 30 years to a time when Dundee United were in the then second division and a league win was a cause for major celebration.

Today he is tasting success the like of which he could hardly dream in the mid 1950s.

"When I think back to the days when the late Mr Johnston Grant and I joined the club, if he'd been alive we would be saying we couldn't believe this was happening," he said.

"Because when we joined the board the club was in the lower regions of the second division as it was at that time.

"There was a bank overdraft of £4500, £2300 was due for terracing work and there was nothing on the field in the way of players."

In fact Mr Fox, an accountant who retired in 1979 after 48 years in the profession, was appointed to the board mainly to look after the financial side of the club.

And tracing the history of the club one can see how his sure financial guidance provided the platform for on-field successes of recent years.

Today thoughts of a few thousand pounds' debt are far from Mr Fox's mind.

Recently the club has made a lot of money from transfer fees, although one suspects that Mr Fox would rather have kept the players.

As it is Dundee United are one of those rare clubs enjoying the best of both worlds—money in the bank and success on the field.

And as the old adage goes, success breeds success.

"Success on the field has meant success in financial terms, most definitely," said Mr Fox.

"Plus, we have the best part of £1 million in transfer fees . . . unwillingly. I say unwillingly because this is as a result of players being bought by other clubs against our wishes.

"But we are in the black and most clubs would be envious of our position."

Becoming a multi-million £ industry did not happen overnight. United were not always thought in six and seven figures.

When Mr Fox came to Tannadice there was only a small rickety stand and the directors sat at one end of the field in a run down pavilion. The

Mr Fox surveys Tannadice, a stadium which today is vastly different from the way it looked when he first joined the club.

Mr Fox is United's greatest fan

dressing rooms he remembers as "appalling."

The board heard about a pools system being run successfully by Nottingham Cricket Club and a staff member was sent down to find out about it.

From that emerged Taypools, which over the years has raised over £1 million for the club.

The sale of player Ron Yeats in the early 1960s raised £34,000 which when combined with the Taypools revenue was enough to build the stand and offices.

Although a more solid financial foundation improved the infrastructure at the club, Mr Fox suggests that good managers rather than bulging coffers have brought success on the pitch.

Ironically one of the early signings that signalled an improvement in the playing staff was a winger called Orjan Persson, who came from Gothenburg (although not I.F.K. Gothenburg).

"Mr Grant and I travelled three times to Gothenburg before we could sign him," Mr Fox recalls.

There then followed a number of other Scandinavian signings who

brought a degree of success to the club.

When Jerry Kerr resigned Jim McLean was appointed to the job towards the end of 1971.

Mr Fox was impressed with the then Dundee F.C. coach and over the last 16 years that admiration has grown.

COUNTDOWN TO WEDNESDAY'S ENCOUNTER IN GOTHENBURG

"Jim McLean was coach of Dundee at that time and we had always admired the fitness of the Dundee players and we decided we would give Jim McLean a go," he said.

"And Jim McLean is THE reason for our success."

Describing the relationship with his manager Mr Fox said, "Jim McLean and I have had an excellent understanding.

"We give him carte blanche really."

Mr Fox said that the only time he and Mr McLean had not seen eye-to-eye was when £600,000 was offered for a United player.

"I said to him at the time, it's people on the field our supporters come and look at not pound notes stewn around the track.

"He has later agreed we were right. Basically we couldn't afford to lose the player. Mr McLean didn't want to sell the player but thought that the offer was too good to refuse.

"We have never wanted to sell a player."

A month ago Mr Fox signed a new contract with the manager which takes him up to 1992.

"I was delighted because I think probably by that time he will have had enough," said Mr Fox.

"His is the most stressful occupation that anyone could undertake.

"And I have said often that I wouldn't be a football manager for £1 million a year.

"The stress of the job is really tremendous."

Mr Fox was quick to point out that also in his capacity as a director Mr McLean makes a major contribution to the running of the club.

"He contributes a great deal to the practical side of the running of the club," he said.

"His was the idea to install executive boxes.

"On the field he is a brilliant coach obviously, and a brilliant tactician."

It may surprise United fans to know that Mr Fox was once a Dundee supporter, although he claims he was never really an avid follower. In fact he only followed the Dark Blues because a relative took him to Dens Park as a child.

Reaching the final of the UEFA Cup is in his view the pinnacle of United's history.

The importance of the club's success to the city from which it takes its name is not lost on the United chairman.

"Well I think we reflect what the people of Dundee are," he said.

"They are very peaceable and I think this goes a long way to making firms abroad look towards Dundee as a possible base to get good workers."

Mr Fox confesses that he may get a bit emotional if and when Dundee United win the UEFA Cup, a feat he describes simply as "something that when I first came here was beyond my wildest dreams."

Team still buzzing from a glorious Dundee send-off

AS THE FIRST wave of the Dundee United invasion, including the team and their wives, flooded into Gothenburgh last night, they must have been still buzzing after the send-off they received in Dundee.

A large crowd of well-wishers and autograph hunters cheered the United squad on to their

The biggest cheers were reserved for the manager, but also for international full-back Maurice Malpas, who had fought back from a savage foot injury which required several stitches, to make the team.

Tayside Police Assistant Chief Constable Mr Jim Cameron and Chief Superinten-

COUNTDOWN TO TOMORROW'S BIG MATCH IN GOTHENBURG

"Courier" competition winners Graeme Bowman and Alistair Roy at Tannadice yesterday before leaving for Gothenburg.

United manager Jim McLean signs autographs at Tannadice.

luxury bus, bound for Glasgow Airport, outside Tannadice yesterday morning.

On the bus as well as manager Jim McLean, training staff, club officials and players—accompanied by their wives—around 70 lucky fans who managed to secure tickets on the club's charter flight.

dent David Chalmers travelled with the team. Their mission is to meet their Swedish counterparts in Gothenburg, primarily to discuss crowd arrangements for the second leg.

"It will be well-remembered the criticism given to the Brussels police authorities following the Heysel Stadium

disaster," explained Mr Cameron.

"By making this trip we will discover exactly how many Swedish fans are coming to Dundee for the second leg and how we can make proper arrangements to handle them," he said.

The "official" party was followed by the vanguard of the Tangerine hordes who faced a gruelling 26-hour journey.

Some 78 fans, packed into two coaches, departed at 10 a.m. from Lindsay Street, heading south for the 10-hour trip to Dover.

From there, they were ferried across to Calais and after another marathon journey, they should arrive in Sweden today.

Some fans are slightly apprehensive about the length of the journey and for many this will be their first time abroad to see United.

According to one ardent fan, Jim Moonie, of Forthill Road, Broughty Ferry, most have saved up on the gamble that Dundee United would win through to the final, rather than go to the games with Barcelona or Borussia.

"I could only afford to go to one game and I kept hanging on hoping they would go all the way. Now my gamble seems to have paid off."

Later, another two coachloads left Tannadice bound for Glasgow and a leisurely flight across the North Sea.

Also congregating at Tanna-

dice were those, unable to go to Gothenburg, who simply wished to cheer their heroes as they left.

Customers at Crawford the baker, 4 Murraygate, Dundee, yesterday morning could have been forgiven for thinking they had stepped into the Tannadice dressingroom by mistake when they were confronted by four shop assistants wearing the complete Dundee United strip.

The four, manageress Irene Shearer and assistants Karen Cairnie, Amanda Morgan and Jacqueline Garthley, will remain in the strips until the first leg of the UEFA Cup final is played tomorrow.

According to Karen Cairnie, whose idea it was, the ladies quickly conquered their embarrassment at serving customers while clad in shorts.

Dressing up has proved quite a crowd-puller, with the shop surprisingly busy, although there is another attraction for United fans with a sweet tooth.

"We are running a prize draw for a huge cake which we have specially made to mark the occasion," said Karen.

"It is decorated with 22 model footballers painted in the proper colours and even has pitch markings and corner flags."

A bonus for the lucky winner will be a framed photograph of the United team which will be signed by them after their return from Sweden.

"The draw will take place on the day of the return leg at Tannadice, May 20," she said.

Billy Thomson signs autographs for youngsters at Tannadice.

Laughter all the way to Sweden

"THANK YOU, Glasgow Rangers, for travelling Servisair, and we hope your team has a good game in Sweden..."

It looked, at first sight, as if the Scandinavians had adopted the kind of ruthless tactics normally associated with the less reputable Iron Curtain countries—get the other team hopelessly demoralised before they even set foot in your country.

BY A "COURIER" REPORTER WITH THE TEAM IN SWEDEN

But stewardess Eva Holt's honest mistake was greeted with gales of forgiving laughter from Dundee United players as they unhooked safety belts and stepped into the Gothenburg sunshine late yesterday afternoon.

And their reaction was typical of the happy atmosphere that surrounded United and their entourage throughout yesterday, as the players, their wives and the vanguard of supporters landed safely in Gothenburg 50 hours before the first leg of the UEFA Cup final.

The whole day was a whirl of good-natured wisecracks between the three groups, from the howls over wives' passport photos to the jokes in the duty-free queue—Jim McLean at the head.

But it was an atmosphere of cheerfulness and quiet confidence, not loud over-confidence. United can do it, they know, but they're not going to shout it from the rooftops until they have the trophy in their hands.

The day started with a heartening send-off from Tannadice Street at noon, as the four coaches carrying team, officials, wives, supporters and Press left for Glasgow.

There were no pipes and drums to lift the team into the air at Glasgow—but nobody was complaining. Too many remembered Ally McLeod's 1978 World Cup departure, the "kiss of death" inspired by unthinking loyalty and supreme over-confidence.

Nor was there any great show on United's landing. Instead, the Swedes presented them with a culture shock.

Gothenburg is prosperous and spotlessly clean. The average taxi-rank looks like the car park of the Old Course Golf and Country Club on a good day. The Lord Provost's limo, TS1, would seem out of place.

The Ullevi Stadium, scene of United's battle tomorrow evening, is a triumph of money over engineering, and resembles the Sydney Opera House more than a football ground.

And most of the inhabitants seem to have been dressed straight from the catwalks of Paris.

Dundee United don't mind at all. Last night they relaxed in the opulent, marble-walled surroundings of the Sheraton Hotel's central covered courtyard, while a bevy of Swedish beauties paraded themselves on a centre dais during a fashion show marking the hotel's first birthday.

COUNTDOWN TO TOMORROW'S BIG MATCH IN GOTHENBURG

Their wives are esconced in the equally splendid Europa Hotel, and thouroughly enjoying every minute—although they admit their purses won't last long this morning.

But it will be a different story for the fans, due to arrive in bulk tomorrow.

Last night there were only a handful to be seen around Gothenburg, most of them passengers on the team flight.

Accommodation has been no problem for them, although difficulties are foreseen for the newcomers.

But entertainment might prove hard to find. Drink is laughably expensive, and an hour's foot-slogging by our reporter—purely on behalf of arriving fans—unearthed the sorry total of two pubs in the whole city centre.

Tomorrow's game will undoubtedly provide all the entertainment anyone could ask for.

But in the meantime it looks as if fans will have to content themselves with the game being played yesterday by most of the male members of the Scottish party—find the one ugly woman in Gothenburg. So far, none has succeeded...

● Regulars at Dundee's Rendezvous in Union Street should keep their eyes glued to TV-am over the next couple of days, if they can rise in time.

Davie Young, mine host at the popular music-goers' pub, was one of a group of fans grabbed eagerly by the London-based TV team as yesterday's plane landed in Gothenburg.

Davie doesn't know when his interview is to be broadcast, but the national camera team thought this morning.

TV-am is only one of six TV and radio crews to have arrived in Gothenburg already. The interest the game has attracted is phenomenal, and the Ullevi stadium is expected to be awash with cameras and microphones from over a score of European stations by tomorrow night.

The United players arrive at their hotel in Gothenburg.

A Sturrock winner?

PAUL STURROCK leaned back in the chair and considered the question (writes The Sports Editor).

"You want a scoreline?" he queried, then, after a pause, "A 0-0 draw here on Wednesday night and a 1-0 win for us at Tannadice in a couple of weeks."

Might the goal be scored by Paul Sturrock, I questioned.

A long sideways look was followed by "Now that WOULD make a change!"

Personally I have great respect for Gothenburg and feel the best two teams in the competition are meeting in the final, which as I have said before is not always the case in Europe.

I don't see a no-scoring draw here, rather a scoring one 1-1 or 2-2, and a 2-1 victory for United at Tannadice.

And you can still send your complaints on £5 notes if I am wrong!

The trip to Gothenburg was a real family affair for the United squad, while fans who had shelled out to get there faced "laughably expensive" prices for quenching their thirsts.

Some of the players' wives outside Tannadice before the departure to Sweden. From left—Glen Kirkwood, Linda Hegarty, Maria Malpas, Louise Thomson, Janine Redford, Norma Narey, Helen Beaumont and Linda Holt

No team hints but the target is quite clear

"A WIN FOR us or any scoring draw."

That is manager Jim McLean's target for tomorrow night's UEFA Cup final, first leg, against IFK Gothenburg in this lovely city.

He made this clear as we settled down after another perfect flight from Glasgow.

It was bright sunlight at what will be kick-off time tomorrow but for people flying out later for the game I would advise some warm clothing as the temperature is rather similar to that we left behind.

The only doubt for United is whether Maurice Malpas will be fit after his ankle trouble.

The manager isn't certain the player will be there, Malpas himself is determined he will be.

"We will give him up to the very last minute before we make a decision," said the manager, adding that the full-back had kicked a ball for the first time in training since his injury just before we left.

"He must be back in full training tomorrow to have any chance of playing," manager McLean continued, so it will be all eyes on the player when the massive media corps of an

estimated 80 plus (there were only three Press representatives on the first round tie) assemble for the impressive Ullevi Stadium this morning.

Said Maurice as he and I left the plane together, "I honestly thought over a week ago that I was going to make it, then the wound turned septic and held back my progress.

"I kicked a ball today though and am feeling no reaction and don't forget there are 48 hours to go."

The manager made it clear that this being an away game he wants his full defence in action.

It had to be appreciated how much of the success so far this season had to be attributed to the consistent qualities of Billy Thomson and Malpas at the back.

Both Dave Narey and Paul Hegarty had been out for

By THE SPORTS EDITOR

lengthy spells—over 30 games between them—whereas, until this injury, Malpas and Thomson had been there more or less all the time.

He wasn't discussing tactics and didn't want his comments misinterpreted but it was obvious that if you had to be short of a defender this was best at home and if you had to be short of an attacker, as he is because Iain Ferguson is suspended for the first leg, it is better away.

Could it be assumed that Kevin Gallacher would be the Ferguson replacement, he was asked.

"It is likely the team announcement will be a last-minute thing and nothing can be assumed," was the smiling answer.

"Our confidence is as high as ever I have seen it," the manager went on.

"Apart from Ferguson being unavailable and the doubt over Malpas, we are at full strength."

In the last two games the situation he likes has been reversed with the home leg first, the away leg second ... but two magnificent away wins over Barcelona and Borussia Moenchengladbach maybe indicate that he could have changed his mind.

"No. We still want the draw

the way it is this time, with the first leg away," he said.

He had been disappointed with the first-half against Borussia at Tannadice.

"If we had gone away first and won 2-0 I don't believe we would have had that bad half," he said, adding, "Mind you, in a final, 45 minutes of poor play cannot be allowed."

Then it was off for another succession of interviews with waiting Swedish journalists.

As I have said over the last few European games I have never seen the United manager so relaxed, so obviously accepting, even maybe enjoying the spotlight that has fallen on himself and the club.

But there is one worry nagging him and coach Gordon Wallace.

I have disclosed in the past that a team of coaches including these two have played a Press team on the morning of the away leg in the past two European ties.

They claim the score stands at an aggregate 17-0 in their favour, though this is hotly disputed!

We are however improving steadily as a team and may unveil our new tactics tomorrow morning or may hold them back for the pre-second leg meeting of the two teams.

Whatever, this has them worried ...

COUNTDOWN TO TOMORROW'S BIG MATCH IN GOTHENBURG

Fans impress captain

IT EMERGED yesterday morning that United fans have won yet another convert—the captain of the D.F.D.S. ferry that brought 80 of them into Gothenburg.

The United fans that, late on Monday night, he told those 70 with accommodation problems that they could remain on the boat overnight if they wished.

No other fans in European football have been afforded that kind of privilege for many a long year, and it is seen as yet another sign that United's supporters are now as welcome throughout Europe as their team.

Colin Westwood, one of the 10 fans on last night's ferry that had already booked accommodation, said, "It was a great crossing, and the crew took to the fans right away.

"There was singing, dancing and jokes all the way, without a hint of trouble.

"The boys were delighted at the captain's offer, as it is getting harder and harder to find somewhere reasonably cheap to stay. They'll have to find their own beds tonight, but there's a chance we'll get to stay on the ferry on Wednesday night."

Accommodation is dear, undoubtedly—but it's not just the fans who are overawed by prices.

The team's wives yesterday enjoyed, if that is the word, a long, hot afternoon of pure window-shopping!

Some also enjoyed a boat trip around the nearby islets, in gloriously hot sunshine which had the temperature nearing the seventies.

The one shadow over the morning's activities came when the team officials inspected the pitch—far below the standard of the rest of the stadium, and indeed the standard of most other parks in the city.

"It's more like Gussie Park than Gothenburg," muttered Jim McLean as he scanned the torn turf.

The pitch's condition is a legacy of a pop concert held last year which turned the whole of the ground to mud and has taken almost 12 months to repair.

One of its sternest critics yesterday was Nestor Larurem, the Swede who has already been dubbed Scotland's No. 1 fan in Scandinavia. Nestor is a veteran of countless trips to see Scottish clubs in action at home and abroad, despite being a born-and-bred Gothenburger.

A long-standing friend of Jock Wallace, he has helped organise many trips by Scottish clubs to Scandinavia, and there's no doubt where his affections lie.

"I've always preferred to watch Scottish clubs in action," said Nestor, one of the thousands in the city who work for Volvo.

"There's something different and exciting about the attitude to the game.

"I'll be backing United all the way tomorrow. I know they can do it."

ABOVE—These United fans have no doubt who their favourite is—Paul Sturrock. Pictured with Paul are (from left) Bob Paul, Gary Ross, Rab Paul, Simon McGilchrist and Innes Edwards.

LEFT—Relaxing in the town centre (from left) Paul Hegarty, John Holt, Dave Bowman, Kevin Gallacher and Jim McNally.

129

Tonight's the night!—and Jim McLean keeps Swedes guessing

Goalkeeper Billy Thomson being put through a training routine by understudy Scott Thomson.

Maurice Malpas (right) and Billy Thomson hard at work during training.

Casting an appraising eye over the United squad at training yesterday was Gothenburg manager Gunder Bengtsson (right).

ON THE eve of the first of the three biggest games in the history of Dundee United Football Club—the two legs of the UEFA Cup final and the Scottish Cup final—the report from Gothenburg is that the mood is right, the players' fitness is right, everything, in fact, is the way a club would want it at such a time.

It only needs now for the result to be right for Scottish football.

In the centre of things is United manager Jim McLean giving more interviews than the Prime Minister and Ronald Reagan put together—and enjoying it.

He knows with certainty the line-up he will be putting on the field if the one doubt, the absolute fitness of Maurice Malpas, is proved today.

However he refused to divulge it either at a general Press conference in the morning or at a private interview later.

What he has given is the list of 13 players from the 19 here (including the suspended Iain Ferguson) from whom the team will be chosen.

It is—Billy Thomson; Malpas, Kirkwood, Holt, McInally, Hegarty, Narey (captain), Bowman, Gallacher, Bannon, Sturrock, Redford, Clark.

He denied it was as simple to work out as saying "Gallacher for Ferguson and the rest as expected."

He hid the serious side of this vital selection behind the light-hearted comment that his wife hadn't yet told him who was to take goal ace Ferguson's place.

"It is," he said, "a lot more complicated than people think when you are faced with a problem like this.

"John Clark has done exceptionally well as a striker in a couple of recent outings and always puts pressure on you to choose him even if only because of his goals and his value at set pieces.

"So it isn't automatically Gallacher. I know he seems the obvious choice, but then what about Malpas, if he is fit, Kirkwood, Holt, Clark?

"Who do you fit in? Where?"

It was pointed out that Eamonn Bannon had been a striker in an earlier Euro tie this season.

"Correct," was the reply, then, with a smile, "but we don't have anyone else who plays as badly down the left as Eamonn!"

The Malpas ankle injury stood up to the punishing practice game in the morning with the only flaw in the form of the Scotland man the fact that he missed a couple of sitters.

"But," he said quickly adapting to the famous striker's excuse, "I was there to miss them . . . that's the important thing."

Joking apart, there is still "a slight problem" with the injury so the morning's final tests will be rigorous.

M. Johansson, Tord Holmgren, M. Andersson, Tommy Holmgren, Petterson, Nilsson.

Yes, that is a full strength line-up and the one which destroyed Swarski Tyrol in the semi-final.

The Swedish manager also admits he has been "boxing clever" over his knowledge of Dundee United.

He says, "We had them watched against Moenchengladbach and also have a complete video of the game against Barcelona."

In addition to this United were studied recently against Falkirk by assistant coach Kjell Pettersson (40) and, though he saw more or less a reserve team against Hibs on Saturday, the manager "noted the size and quality of the pitch and the surroundings and learned something about the style of play of United."

THE SPORTS EDITOR PREVIEWS UNITED'S BIG GAME IN GOTHENBURG TONIGHT

I don't believe the starting line-up will be far removed from: Thomson; Kirkwood, Hegarty, Narey, Malpas, McInally, Holt, Bannon, Redford, Gallacher, Sturrock.

If Malpas is unfit, it could be Holt at left-back with Bowman in midfield.

But I add the usual cautionary note that I wouldn't bet too heavily—in kronor this time—on that!

WHILE THE Malpas injury problem and the absence of Iain Ferguson poses United problems, 41-year-old Gothenburg manager Gunder Bengtsson is very likely to field the following team in the final—Wernersson; Carlsson, Hysen, Larsson (available after injury) Frederiksson,

United's success, he believes, is based on the fact they are two teams.

They are expert at playing as a Continental team when away from home, but have all the fire and passion of a British team when they are at home, aggressive and professional.

It was difficult to compare the Gothenburg team which won the UEFA Cup with the present one, as outstanding players had left and his only regret at getting this far was that his team could be broken up again.

Scouts from the multi-millionaire clubs of Italy and Spain will be with us in the Ullevi Stadium and at Tannadice, weighing up the players and getting ready to bid for any they fancy.

The Swedish players are, of course, part-time and find it difficult to resist any offers from the Mediterranean countries or such as Germany and Holland.

The most special of occasions, and The Courier marked it with what in 1987 was a very rare phenomenon — colour photography!

Meanwhile, the "new" Jim McLean reflected on how a transitional season had turned into an unforgettable one.

Good luck, UNITED!

The heroes of Tannadice are all set for tonight's UEFA Cup Final first leg in Gothenburg and so is "THE COURIER"

SOUVENIR FULL COLOUR PICTURE OF THE SQUAD ON BACK PAGE

Plus all the latest news and pictures from Sweden

"New" Jim tackling media presence well

By THE SPORTS EDITOR

I HAVE SAID again and again recently that a "new" Jim McLean has emerged lately.

I do not mean that in the football sense, but in the sense of his association with the media, his public face, if you like.

Where before question and answer sessions were edgy, fraught with the possibility of a wrong question causing an upset, he has taken the massive media presence in his stride as his beloved United have pushed ahead in Europe and in domestic competition.

While his players have got on with their job and coped with reasonable pressure from the Press, radio and television, his time away from training ground and actual game has been almost entirely devoted to answering questions in front of cameras, into microphones, in front of Press conferences and in more selective interviews.

Some of the answers to the change emerged in a conference yesterday, with questions being asked that simply would not have been tolerated by the manager not all that long ago.

The harmony within the club had, he insisted, always been "great" but was even better this time because the success of being third in the league and in two cup finals, "an incredible achievement for our club" has been a tremendous boost for everyone connected with the club.

Dundee United had to build on concrete foundations, not sand, otherwise the path would be downward.

"And we have been fortunate such as David Narey and Paul Hegarty have given us that foundation," he said.

"There is nothing personal in what I am saying, but it would have been easy for such as these two to more or less opt out this season as they watched lesser players than themselves make more money by leaving.

"But they are here and we are doing well.

"It's harder to be loyal at Dundee United than at Rangers or Spurs. It is easier with us than with, say, Albion Rovers.

"Our first team is important to us; our reserves are important, our youths are important.

"Success," he insisted, "is all down to players. I am delighted for those who have come in, I am even more delighted for those who have been here for many years."

Having said that he made it clear that winning things was success to him—and there were still games to be won!

Admitting, "I have changed", he said he had realised it was no longer his responsibility to force his players to play, "which I did in the past".

"But it is rubbish to think that change in me has made the difference to us doing so well this season."

"At the end of the day players either play out there or they don't. They win things by their performance, no one else's.

"Where I have changed is in getting to know people better.

"I was," he said, talking of the media, "judging everyone on some I did not trust. Getting to know people better has made me realise this was not right."

Gothenburg pitch worry

THE STATE of the pitch in the Ullevi Stadium is worrying everyone here, even though both managers were extremely diplomatic in their comments on it (writes The Sports Editor).

Said Jim McLean, "What ground at this time of the year is in perfect condition? It's the same for both teams. The goal areas are O.K."

Said Gunder Bengtsson, "This is Sweden. It has been a long winter. We have just started playing."

I walked over the pitch, and while accepting the McLean comment on certain areas found that, overall, it was like walking on soft sand with grass growing in it.

Fortunately the sand IS soft, so it isn't like there are ankle-twisting holes—but even at that I know that every United player with any ankle problem whatsoever, was well "strapped up" by physiotherapist Jim Joyce before they took the field for their training session and will be the same for the actual game.

There is, I feel, a deep respect between the two managers for one another.

The Gothenburg boss was their No. 2 when they won the UEFA Cup exactly five years ago this month. Jim McLean's career has peaked in the eyes of the world of football outside Scotland for his achievements this season.

They are both boxing clever.

Both use the word "respect" when referring to the other's team.

Both talk of the ability of individuals in the other team. Both believe their team can win, but don't shout about it.

This is best summed up by the McLean comment, "Our opponents' record is exceptional, but, then, Dundee United didn't get to the final without having a good record also."

The tactics of this twosome over 180 minutes are going to be as intriguing as the actual play.

Paul Sturrock puts in a bit of heading practice.

Bad start could end up best ever season

By THE SPORTS EDITOR

WHEN ASSISTANT manager Walter Smith left to join Rangers, Richard Gough was transferred to Spurs, on top of Davie Dodds being transferred and later Ralph Milne, not to mention Hamish McAlpine moving to Raith Rovers and such things as Derek Stark having to give up the game because of injury, there were predictions that Dundee United would have it really tough this season—and for some time to come.

As it is, they could, in the next 15 days, establish 1986-87 as the club's greatest ever season.

Yet manager Jim McLean admitted yesterday, "I would have settled at the start for being clear of the bottom lot in the Premier League at the end, having had a reasonable season of reorganisation."

He went on, "Don't take from that that we are satisfied. We are still overhauling. Don't forget Hegarty, Narey, Malpas and very few others are the only ones left from before.

"I have never promised anyone anything.

"Ten years is a long time for a provincial club to be doing as well as we have.

"It may be that one reason is our players are paid for winning, not simply appearing!"

He emphasised that United would never lose sight of that fact and, though the club is now in a good financial position, they would not be competing with the likes of Rangers and Spurs on wages.

Having said that, he added that "our players play for bigger bonuses than most in Scotland."

They would also get more in their pockets than their opponents in the UEFA final.

But, he finally emphasised, "Finance is not the important issue with our players tomorrow night . . . winning is."

Continuing on the theme of the game, he expressed his delight at the way people had got behind United.

"We have had messages from all over the place, including one from St Mirren wishing us success in the UEFA final . . . but not for the Scottish Cup final!"

United one down at half way—but all to play for at Tannadice

IFK GOTHENBURG 1, DUNDEE UNITED 0

NOT THE best of United's European performances, but the fact still remains that there is half of this final to go on their own ground and they are only one goal behind.

Manager Jim McLean maybe didn't get his wish for either a victory or any scoring draw, but the way it stands it isn't all bad, even though it is their first European defeat away since Craiova!

First half, United never really got into their stride and their hesitancy was punished by a goal in 38 minutes from the ever-dangerous Petterson.

If Billy Thomson seemed a bit slow to move off his goal-line on this occasion he totally redeemed himself later on with a succession of outstanding dives and clutches to defy the frequent Gothenburg scoring attempts.

It was the kind of game which makes you wonder if two-leg finals are a good thing.

There was an obvious fear for a long time by both sides of making a mistake rather than pushing forward, but once the goal went in it seemed to relax everyone and led to much more open play.

Dave Narey was an inspirational captain for United, making countless superb interceptions and Maurice Malpas, doubtful almost up to the last minute with an ankle injury, had a great second half.

In midfield, the control was mostly won by the Swedes, with Jim McInally, Eamonn Bannon, Dave Bowman and Billy Kirkwood battling hard, but never really taking over.

Ian Redford was mostly in his attacking role and very, very nearly got the goal United wanted in the 63rd minute.

Paul Sturrock was all the Swedes expected—a danger to them almost every time he got the ball. But they managed to cope and he never got that final pass or shot in.

John Holt started shakily but settled as the game progressed. When Paul Hegarty went off injured after playing well, John Clark took his place and looked completely comfortable.

The United players are doing their warm-down as I write and their fans are still there singing "You'll never walk alone."

They certainly won't if they can triumph at Tannadice in two weeks' time.

The Swedes are good in a solid, if unspectacular way and there is little doubt their ability to get Pettersson and Nilsson into scoring positions will have to be watched carefully on May 20.

However, though their defence is good, I felt when United stepped up the pace it looked stretched and though Wernerrson had that great save from Redford, it will be interesting to see how he reacts to what is likely to be a much more hectic evening at Tannadice.

Manager Jim McLean said afterwards, "We are disappointed we didn't get an away goal, but we still have a great chance now.

"They are a tremendous team."

He disclosed that Billy Thomson had five stitches inserted in an ear wound at half time and that Paul Hegarty had a pulled muscle.

"We could not play our normal game on that pitch," he ended.

Scorer Stefan Pettersson then made what could be the most significant remark of the evening.

"I do not think one goal is enough," he said.

There are a lot of people in Scotland hoping he is right!

A "tremendous" Swedish team and a dry, slow pitch meant United failed to hit their usual heights in the first leg.

However, 1-0 was by no means a disaster and the prospect of a famous Tannadice comeback was very much alive.

Erik Frederikson belts the ball clear to thwart Dave Bowman (No. 8).

A look of confidence as Paul Sturrock takes the field.

Eamonn Bannon (No. 9) watches Paul Hegarty rise above Larsson and Andersson to bullet a header at the Gothenburg goal.

Thomson stars after injury

UNITED LOST the toss and were facing the sun and a strong wind. It was Malpas at right back, Holt left back and Kirkwood in midfield.

The early sparring almost took a dramatic turn in two minutes when Sturrock sent Bannon away on the left and his cross was met by Redford.

But that was not the real drama of the opening spell because, two minutes later, a bad Holt pass went straight to Tord Holmgren, who immediately got Nilsson away down the right.

As he raced in on goal, Thomson advanced and, as the striker shot, threw himself bravely towards him.

In clutching the ball for a magnificent save he swirled round and Nilsson smashed into him.

Thomson was knocked out and was immediately surrounded by a posse of United pl~yers, with Kirkwood racing off the pitch to bring on Jim McLean.

After anxious moments while physio Jim Joyce treated the big keeper, he got to his feet and, even though he looked groggy,

> **❝** *I had to get five stitches put in the wound and it left me with a splitting headache for the rest of the game. However, it was all worthwhile.* **❞**
> —Billy Thomson

took two high balls and a long-range shot within a minute to prove—hopefully—that he wasn't too affected.

It was mostly the Swedes pushing forward, but a United break engineered by Sturrock was only halted when Bannon moved fractionally offside.

Next, Redford crossed high and behind to encouraging roars from the 2000 or so United fans to my left when he might have been better to let the ball run for a corner.

Thomson seemed fully recovered and calmly dealt with a couple of shots and a cross, but it was at the other end that the real action happened.

First Sturrock went down after a Hysen tackle and McInally's free was just too high for Hegarty, running in from the right, to reach.

Then, in 20 minutes, Sturrock beat off three Carlsson tackles

and whipped over a great cross which Redford just couldn't get to.

When United won a corner it looked good but was easily cleared and Holt again was in trouble when he set Tord Holmgren up with a sloppy pass.

Fortunately, the burly, blond-haired midfielder was as poor with his pass, which went for a throw-in.

Redford and Sturrock set up a shooting chance for Kirkwood, bursting through from midfield, but as he tried to connect he was tackled and went down injured, recovering after treatment.

They tried an obviously planned move but couldn't get Hysen on the end of the cross.

After half an hour it was still more a sparring match than a thriller.

Neither goalkeeper had been really threatened, except for that breakthrough in which Thomson was injured, but overall United had moved in on Wernersson more purposefully.

Typically, the moment that was written, Gothenburg made their best chance.

When Bannon and McInally failed to stop Tord Holmgren on the right, he got in a cross.

The ball bounced and swirled around the United box and, just as Frederiksson was about to lash in a shot, Narey belted it off his toes and high upfield.

You could almost hear the collective sigh of relief from the United support.

When Narey fouled Nilsson, he paused to shake hands. The free kick was taken quickly and a corner conceded—and it was a disaster for United.

As the ball was crossed by Andersson, Thomson stayed on his line when it seemed from our angle in the Press box that he should have come off it.

Petterson rose high beyond the keeper's left-hand post to head powerfully downwards. The ball hit the ground then rocketed upwards into the roof of the net. Time 38 minutes.

United tried to strike back quickly through Sturrock, but first he failed to get through, then a corner he created was cleared.

An uphill battle was now on and it could have been more uphill when Narey hesitated in clearing and nearly let Petterson in again. Fortunately, he recovered in time to clear.

The half-time reflection that it was an edgy game as most two-leg finals are and that Goth-

Gothenburg's scorer, Stefan Pettersson.

enburg were slightly ahead on points as well as goals in the territorial sense was abruptly shortened within a minute of the restart.

Dave Narey could only deflect the ball into Petterson's path when a dangerous swirling ball arrived in the penalty area.

The striker steadied and shot and Billy Thomson made a truly magnificent dive high to his right to turn the ball away when a goal looked certain.

Hardly had the roars for that

near thing died than there was more danger for United.

This time Malpas and Hegarty failed to stop Frederiksson who drifted into a dangerous position in the box and was only stopped by a truly great tackle by Narey.

It was getting tougher for the United defence and when Hegarty went down injured he didn't rise, but immediately signalled that it was a bad one.

In an instant he was off and John Clark went on to partner Narey in 54 minutes.

More pressure from the right and a high swirling cross from

Johansson was clutched brilliantly by Thomson—fortunately, as three Gothenburg players were racing in to meet the ball.

United moved forward via Sturrock and though the linesman gave a corner, the referee overruled him.

United were finding it hard to string their passes together and when Bannon went on a solo run it petered out for lack of alternatives to give the ball to.

They were attacking more though and, in 63 minutes, it almost paid off.

Sturrock twisted and turned his way down the left before delivering a great cross.

Bowman controled it beautifully and crossed again, this time from right of the goal. Redford leaned back and smashed in a great shot with his right foot.

Wernersson did well to leap high and turn the ball over the bar. Clark got in a header from the corner but it was cleared.

This was definitely more like it from United and when Redford was fouled 33 yards out, a Clark blockbuster was scooped away for a corner by the keeper.

Immediately afterwards, R. Nilsson went on for Johansson.

Malpas was maybe fortunate in 69 minutes that the nearside linesman obviously didn't understand his Fife accent as he claimed a corner, but it was all part of a more positive approach by United.

Narey was in with another great tackle which sent Bowman and Sturrock away on the right, but the threat that Gothenburg posed in "sucking in" the opposition then striking back quickly showed when L. Nilsson burst through.

Thomson had to dive out to beat the ball away.

The danger was again evident in 75 minutes when Pettersson got in a looping header—yet

again brilliantly saved by Thomson.

L. Nilsson burst through on the right a minute later and a not-too-well-hit shot somehow swirled off Thomson and across the gapingly empty goal.

It had been a clean game, well refereed until this point but, suddenly, when the ball was away and a free kick given for a tackle by Larsson on Redford, the big blond centre-back lashed out and kicked the United man.

The referee, close by, did nothing.

It was a faster, more open game now and though United

had improved, the Swedes were still causing major problems on the break.

When Tord Holmgren swirled in a cross from the right, it was headed down by Hysen and an overhead kick by Nilsson was saved by Thomson.

That was in the 81st minute and though the battle raged back and forth until the end, it was the last chance at either end.

In the very last minute, Sturrock went off and Dave Beaumont took his place, obviously a tactical ploy as a corner had been awarded and Gothenburg were trying to end things in style.

Attendance—50,023.

IFK Gothenburg—Wernersson; Carlsson, Hysen, Larsson, Frederikson, Johansson, Tord Holmgren, Andersson, Tommy Holmgren, Petterson, L. Nilsson. Substitutes—Tobiasson, Mordt, R. Nilsson, Zetterland, Rantanen.

Dundee United—B. Thomson; Holt, Malpas, McInally, Hegarty, Narey, Kirkwood, Bowman, Bannon, Sturrock, Redford. Substitutes—Gallacher, Clark, Beaumont, G. McLeod, S. Thomson.

Referee—Siegfried Kirschen (East Germany).

THE AGONY OF DEFEAT

● *A downcast Billy Thomson with blood trickling from the ear injury which needed five stitches.*

133

UNITED FANS ARE STILL CONFIDENT

A MEMORABLE performance in Sweden last night took Dundee United halfway towards their greatest-ever triumph and set the scene for an historic occasion at Tannadice in two weeks.

Before the eyes of Europe, United managed to contain IFK Gothenburg to only a one-goal lead in the first leg of the UEFA Cup final.

One scrambled goal was conceded in the first half, but United took everything else the Swedes could throw at them, and at the same time threatening the home goal on a few thrilling breaks.

It is not over yet, by any means. The Swedes were the toughest proposition United have met in this campaign, and

BY OUR MAN WITH THE TEAM IN GOTHENBURG

Billy Thomson had to pull off some tremendous saves to keep his team in the game.

But confidence is high. United know they can win the cup—and, if they do, it will be before the roar of an ecstatic home crowd on May 20.

The day was a triumph for football. The Swedes gave a great display of ball skills, while United's defending prowess once again came into its own.

United fans, too, continued to give a tremendous display of what good supporters should be.

The 2500 or so travellers, whose behaviour has now won them friends all around Europe, stayed on for the best part of an hour in the chill Gothenburg stadium to sing and cheer their team.

And the biggest roars of the night came from the Tangerine faithful after the game was well over—the first for Jim McLean as he came on the pitch for an interview, and the second for the team who rewarded the fans' loyalty with a lap of honour.

Last night the city of Gothenburg was thick with atmosphere.

Many of the United fans had to leave after the game for transport home, but those remaining made up for their absent friends as singing and dancing went on well into the night.

The fans have loved their time here, regardless of prices. Gothenburg has welcomed them with open arms and they have responded in kind.

The police have already sung their praises. And last night the British Vice-Consul in Gothenburg described them as "a credit to Scotland."

Even though the rivalry is fierce, United and Gothenburg have proved together that friendship and fair play, both on and off the park, still have their place in football.

The day was one to remember. United fans entertained the city all through the afternoon and Gothenburg put on a show of marching girl bands, flyovers and bunting for the game.

The carnival atmosphere continued for hours after the game.

Both sets of fans had enjoyed a thrilling game, and while they know the fierce rivalry will reappear in a fortnight's time they were able to settle their differences, swap colours and disappear, singing, into the night.

Tayside Region Convener John McAllion said after the game, "It was a tremendous match in the end.

"That was a silly goal to lose, you have to admit—very strange. But United's defending was great and there were some great pieces of football by everyone.

"I'm sure, quite sure now, that United will do it at Tannadice. That will be some game.

"The fans, of course, were once again wonderful. No praise can be high enough for what they're doing for the name of Dundee—and I was delighted to hear about the two getting medals from the police!

"The city has a lot to thank both team and fans for."

His sentiments were echoed by Lord Provost Tom Mitchell, who, like Mr McAllion, was bedecked in United colours over his suit.

Wilson's defence of Scots fans

Mr Wilson

IT WAS QUITE wrong that Scottish—and particularly Dundee United—football fans should be tarred with the English brush and discriminated against when travelling abroad, Dundee East M.P. Gordon Wilson has told Foreign Secretary Sir Geoffrey Howe.

Mr Wilson said Scottish fans had proved to be gregarious, friendly and peaceable when abroad (writes Our Man At Westminster).

The hooliganism, violence and mayhem in recent years had been by English fans.

The M.P. pointed out that the past behaviour of English fans had caused problems for the Dundee United supporters travelling to Sweden for the UEFA Cup final first leg against Gothenburg.

There had also been earlier incidents where the Belgian government had banned Scottish football supporters from attending games.

Mr Wilson called on Sir Geoffrey to instruct his diplomatic staff to check cases of discrimination over the last two years prior to making representations to the European countries involved pointing out the difference in behaviour between Scottish and English fans.

Fans are still in optimistic mood

IN THE PUBS and clubs of Dundee last night, if it was not Swedish the United fans were muttering under their breaths at full-time, it was something pretty close to it.

The fans' verdict on the first leg of the UEFA Cup final ranged from the Tangerines getting a raw deal, to a suspect referee and a pitch looking better suited to army manoeuvres than a cup final.

Celebration may have been muted but, with typical optimism, the vast majority of stay-at-home fans remained convinced their heroes would come up trumps in the second leg at Tannadice.

United chairman George Fox, who watched the match from his home in Carnoustie, echoed that view.

"That was murder watching it on TV!" he said.

"The goal would never have been scored at Tannadice and I thought, all in all, the Swedes had the luck on the night.

"Tannadice will be different. Multiply tonight's United support by 20 and we'll have the best inspiration we could hope for.

"We've got the best set of supporters in the country."

Pubs throughout Dundee were packed with fans hoping for a repeat of United's famous international forays.

It did not happen, but in the somewhat square-eyes of the hundreds of fans who followed every kick on the TV screen, United gave a good account of themselves.

"One-all would have been a fairer result on the night. The

Raymond and his girl friend Wanda decorated the outside of her house with banners, scarves and Tangerine rabbits and teddy bears.

"When the neighbours saw what I was doing they handed stuff in," said Raymond, who admitted the match was a disappointment.

"It was a bit scrappy but we've got tickets for the Tannadice match. I'm confident they can do it there."

Dundee East M.P. Gordon Wilson had his ear to a radio in London, where the match was not being televised.

Mr Wilson was pleased with United's performance. "It was a good result to get away from home.

"The cup is now up for grabs at Tannadice in a fortnight's time," he added.

boys were unlucky," said Mr John McKay, of Turnberry Avenue, in the Phoenix Bar, Nethergate.

Chambers Bar in Castle Street was also well populated.

Publican Ron Duncan, who had offered free beer every time United scored, found himself with a cellar full of German lager at full-time.

"It's a shame they lost the goal. They'll do the business at Tannadice, I know they will," he said.

Free drinks may have been a rarity in the city, but fans were more than ready to toast the future as muted celebrations continued well into the night.

United fanatic Raymond Langlands turned a house in Pitkerro Drive into a mini Tannadice last night as he settled down to watch the match.

Search goes on for identities of Gothenburg heroes

WHO WERE those heroes? That was the question being asked around Dundee yesterday as the search went on for the two Dundee United fans whose actions in Gothenburg have won them medals of commendation from the local police.

The pair won high praise from both Swedes and Scots after apprehending a would-be thief in the centre of the Swedish port on Tuesday night.

Unfortunately, it now looks as if it could be a few days before the pair can be officially identified.

Police are unwilling to give out their names until they have spoken to the men and this is proving difficult.

A spokesman said yesterday that one of the fans, who lives in Douglas, was still travelling home from Gothenburg.

He is driving through Europe but not with any of the official coach parties.

The other fan, who works for the R.A.F., is thought to have returned to his base in England.

"We expect to have some news next week," said the spokesman. "Until then, the identities have to be kept under wraps."

The only hope of finding out earlier is if friends of the pair come forward. Someone, somewhere, must know who they are . . .

Many of the fans who were in Gothenburg had arrived back in Dundee yesterday after a flight to Glasgow—happy to be back in a city where a beer doesn't cost an arm and a leg.

Fortunes were spent by hundreds of fans in the Swedish port and the vast majority will have to forego nights out for a long time before they reach solvency again.

Even if last night's scoreline wasn't all that could have been asked for, the fans have had a great trip.

The consensus of opinion from those back in the city—shared by those still travelling by coach, who will be arriving today—was that Gothenburg had been a memorable place to play—friendly and welcoming as well as being a beautiful city.

One supporter had his eyes opened by an act of honesty which, it was agreed, would be unlikely to happen elsewhere in Europe.

On Tuesday afternoon, the bottom fell out of Euan Henderson's world when he discovered his wallet was missing.

Euan, of Monifieth, was devastated. Everything he needed was in the wallet—air ticket, credit cards, passport and match ticket.

He and his friends were sure the wallet had been pickpocketed and held out little hope for its return but, nevertheless, began retracing their footsteps of earlier in the day.

They made a routine call to the police and after more fruitless searching returned to their hotel in black moods.

As soon as they arrived, however, they were told the police had made contact. Euan's wallet had been found and handed to a local bobby.

Euan raced to the station to collect it—and was delighted to find it intact. Not a penny had been taken.

"This says a lot about the Swedish," agreed the whole group. "They've been great to us all the time."

Heroic deed "no surprise" to have-a-go fan's mother

AS THE fever of Wednesday's Euro final first leg died down yesterday the mother of one of the two have-a-go citizens arrest heroes in Gothenburg said she was delighted, but not surprised, at her son's brave deed.

Alan Boath, a cook with the M.S.C.U. of the R.A.F., was one of the two Tangerine fans who tackled a would-be thief in the packed streets of the Swedish city on Tuesday night.

The pair were walking when they witnessed a local man trying to rob the local American Express centre, and raider had even managed to break the window of the shop when he was caught in the act by the two visitors.

Alan and his companion, who is believed to be still travelling back from Gothenburg and whose name has not been released by police, grabbed the man, and held on to him until police arrived, an act which earned praise from Tayside police, their Gothenburg counterparts and even United supremo Jim McLean.

At present Alan is stationed at R.A.F. Hullavington, Chippenham, Wiltshire, and last night his mother, Eleanor waited anxiously by the phone at the family home in Bankhead Terrace, Forfar to hear of her 22-year-old son's exciting week.

"It didn't enter our minds that it could be Alan who was one of the men involved in making the arrest," said Mrs Boath.

"Obviously we're delighted that he did, but I'm not surprised—that's the sort of thing he would do in that situation."

Already police in Tayside have been in touch with the Boath's in order so that Alan can receive the medals of commendation which the Gothenburg police chief, Nils Klanderson, has given to Tayside assistant chief constable Jim Cameron.

Mrs Boath is also delighted Alan has helped keep the United fans at the top of the good behaviour league.

"The two lads' action certainly hasn't done Dundee United any harm, so I'm obviously very pleased about that."

If the match in Gothenburg failed to provide too many highlights for United, once again the fans were on top form. Not only were they not causing crime, some of them even found the time to prevent it!

Medals for arresting fans

TWO UNITED fans are to receive medals of commendation from Gothenburg's chief of police after making a citizens' arrest on a would-be thief.

The whole travelling support continues to win glowing praise from all quarters, after an exemplary season.

But these two have proved once and for all that United's fans can lay claim to the title of best fans in Europe.

The two heroes have not yet been named by Swedish police, as it is thought they may be shy of publicity.

One is from the Douglas area of Dundee, and the other works for the R.A.F.

But they will be known soon enough, as Tayside Assistant Chief Constable Jim Cameron is to present them with the congratulatory medals soon after their return.

On Tuesday night, the pair were walking through the city centre when they came across a local trying to rob the main American Express centre.

The man had already broken the glass of the showroom when the two fans rounded the corner.

They immediately grabbed hold of him and held him on the premises until local police arrived.

Yesterday, Mr Cameron—who is in the Swedish city on a courtesy visit before the return leg—said he had now been given two medals by Gothenburg police chief Nils Klanderson to pass on to the pair.

Mr Klanderson was "absolutely delighted" by the episode, he said yesterday afternoon.

"It was a fantastic thing to happen," he said, adding that all the United fans had been a credit to their city.

Mr Cameron was yesterday "very, very pleased" to hear of the arrest.

"The fans have made a great name for themselves, but this kind of thing is super," he said.

"Unfortunately, I can't give away the lads' names yet. But they know themselves they've done Dundee a huge favour."

The news was welcomed, too, by Mrs Pat Doran, regional convener for fire and police, who arrived in Gothenburg with friends yesterday to see the match.

"It's news like that you love to hear," she said.

"These fans—and all the others across here—deserve every praise they get."

The news had even filtered down to those Swedish policemen working points duty yesterday evening, who were laughing about the whole affair.

"I had heard United had the best fans in Europe, and this proves it," said one.

"From what I've seen of your fans this afternoon, they deserve the title. It's been a pleasure to have them here."

Relaxed McLean looks back—and plans ahead

IN THE early hours of yesterday morning Dundee United flew back into Glasgow Airport after the 1-0 defeat by IFK Gothenburg in the first leg of the UEFA Cup final.

As manager Jim McLean moved out into the concourse an elderly gentleman spotted him and advanced to deliver the comment, "You didn't do so well tonight, then."

There was a time this would have caused, for want of a better word, an explosion from the United manager. This time his reply was a mild, "It wasn't too bad."

It's indicative of the more relaxed mood prevailing at Tannadice these days—and it was again illustrated yesterday when, the morning after the UEFA Cup before, the manager was intently working on his

By THE SPORTS EDITOR

reserve team line-up for last night's "little local derby."

Once that was out of the way it was on to thoughts of Gothenburg—and ahead.

"Do you know physiotherapist Jim Joyce stopped counting the stitches in Billy Thomson's ear injury when he got to five?" said the manager.

"The club doctor (Dr Harry Leadbitter) doesn't yet want to take away the hardened blood to see how many stitches there are. It is a really bad one.

"The cartilage was showing, the ear nearly ripped off when he clashed with Lennart Nilsson after only minutes of the game.

"I was glad I was so slow between dug-out and Thomson.

"All the way I was worrying over how serious the injury was, who was to go in goal if we had to take him off, who would then take that player's place, how we would shuffle the team."

Billy Thomson

"It was a tremendous relief to see Billy get to his feet again and I have to pay tribute to his bravery, not only in going for the ball, but also in carrying on."

Said the big keeper, "I was groggy for 15 minutes and felt sick at half-time, but that save had to be made. It was no use them going ahead so early in the game."

Actually there was another off-field drama because of the injury.

The doctor, and physiotherapist Andy Dickson, were in seats on the opposite side of the park to the dug-out where the manager was.

He wanted them beside him in case of further accidents to Thomson. At half-time they hustled round the underground track to the dug-out side.

Without tickets, they weren't allowed to sit beside the manager and, in fact, spent until the end of the game standing behind the dug-out.

The immediate result is that young Scott Thomson, who played against Hibs last Saturday, seems certain to be in after an impressive display then.

Paul Hegarty will be another absentee over a weekend when United face games against Motherwell and Hearts, both away.

His problem is the hamstring strain which saw him leave the field second half.

Maurice Malpas isn't likely to play tomorrow—though with his recovery rate I wouldn't say it is impossible—because of more trouble below the ankle which nearly caused him to miss the Gothenburg game.

Note, below the ankle.

This time it was that shocking pitch which caused the problem, though there is little doubt it is connected with the original injury.

By the way, the Malpas comment on the game was, "I felt a bit out of condition, but got better as the game went on.

"They are a good team, but we can beat them all right."

Ian Redford has a knock, but should be fit.

The manager described as "ludicrous" the programme expected of teams like themselves who reached finals and did well in other competitions.

Paul Hegarty

He reiterated the fact that 70 games would be played by United this season and wondered at European Cup ties and Scottish Cup ties being a mere four days apart.

"It all happens at the end of a season—with the exception of the League Cup final, of course—yet we have this pile-up of fixtures."

Then there was a glance back at the actual result on Wednesday night.

If, he commented, someone had told him the game was cancelled and that it had been decided United would be considered to have lost 1-0, he would have settled for that.

"Don't forget we lost 1-0 to Lens in the first round and won through 2-1," he said.

Already the letters and calls of congratulation have poured in to Tannadice.

Not for the result as much as for the great show United are putting up.

One of them is from manager Jim Smith of Queen's Park Rangers.

"For the size of the country, our record is good in European

football," said manager McLean.

"As far as Gothenburg are concerned, of course I respect them. They have two excellent centre-halves and two good players up front.

"But they are definitely beatable."

He then described himself as always having been fortunate in the type of player at Tannadice, but felt the togetherness of the present group was the best yet.

"No-one is a loner," he commented.

Then he disclosed that he is still worrying over the situation "up front" in his team.

"I will be experimenting on Saturday with a pairing who could play themselves into two Cup finals.

"We simply must get more goals from up front.

"You can get a wee bit slack in any walk of life when some success comes your way, but it is when you think you have made it that you land in trouble.

"In the case of Dundee United we are looking for more mountains to climb."

Maurice Malpas

Ian Redford

Jim McLean arrived back in Scotland broadly satisfied with the first-leg result.

However, he was clearly concerned about the "ludicrous" number of games United had played and the hectic schedule they still faced at the most critical stage of the season.

Ann looks after the United 'machine'

IN 1982, a part-time secretary by the name of Mrs Ann Diamond joined the office staff at Tannadice Park, home of Dundee United.

For Ann, it seemed at the start like just another office job, even though she had always enjoyed football. Little did she realise that five years later she would be guiding United through the bureaucratic minefields of Europe on their way to the biggest match in their history, the UEFA Cup final.

The players have already been feted throughout their campaign, and more glory

> *The job takes over your life, to a certain extent*

awaits them if they manage to pull off the big one in a week's time against Gothenburg at Tannadice. And, in between times, there's the Scottish Cup final against St Mirren at Hampden on Saturday!

But long-overdue credit must go to the backroom staff who, with Ann at the helm, have cleared a smooth path for every trip abroad and liaised with hundreds upon hundreds of European visitors and news teams back at Tannadice—while still keeping the team's home schedules running as smoothly as clockwork.

Ann's time at Tannadice has always been hectic—but even more so since she became full-time club secretary after the retiral of Ella Lindsay.

And this last season, already hailed as United's finest ever, has been one long whirl of activity of the like never before seen in Tannadice Street.

Ann yesterday managed, with difficulty, to take a few minutes to talk to "The Courier" about her time with United.

And one of the points she stressed was her huge debt to others associated with the club—fellow office staff, club directors and manager Jim McLean.

"They've all been an invaluable help," she said. "I couldn't have done it without them."

It must be fairly true, however, to say that the club couldn't have done it without Ann either.

Over the past season, mail to Tannadice has trebled, the phones never stop ringing and the office reception has been subjected to non-stop bombardment by national and international Press and fans.

"It's certainly been our busiest season ever," she smiled. "But it's also been our best, of course—it's hectic, but exciting!

"When I came here, I took an interest in the team of course, but nothing like this.

"The job takes over your life, to a certain extent. There's no way you could treat it like a 9 to 5 office job—you have to get involved, you have to work late and you find yourself thinking about United all the time."

It's easy for the fans to forget the work that goes on behind the scenes.

In European competition, for example, the draw is announced and the public sits back waiting for the game. But that's just when Ann and her team get down to their hardest work.

Every detail of a tour abroad has to be worked out well in advance. Schedules, itineraries, bookings, insurance, coach transfers, passports—all have to be checked and double-checked before the team sets off.

It is a huge responsibility. With the team playing before the eyes of Europe, it is imperative that all runs smoothly; the slightest hiccup in arrangements will not only inconvenience the team but be picked

Ann busy in her office

up, too, by the hordes of newsmen who have followed United around the continent.

Often, Ann's call to her counterpart in the various European cities visited by United is the first contact of any kind between the two clubs.

"It can be a bit difficult," she smiled yesterday.

"You're phoning somewhere thousands of miles away, where nobody talks English. The communication problems have begun already—and there are hundreds of details to be gone into as soon as possible.

"Fortunately, however, this hasn't happened too often—normally it's just the Iron Curtain countries.

"This UEFA season has run fine, although we're experiencing so much more interest all the time.

"The mail coming in here is three times what it was. All in

> *I'm making sure I'm upstairs for the second half.*

all, you could say we've dealt with hundreds of thousands of tickets over the campaign.

"The main problem was Gothenburg. We had only two weeks to get everything organised. There wasn't much room for error."

But Gothenburg, as everyone now knows, was organised and

run with the same precision as every other trip abroad.

Once again, all the stops had been pulled out behind the scenes, leaving yet another successful journey which gave the entirely mistaken impression that it had been no trouble at all.

Added Ann, "We just got on with it—we knew it had to be done. In fact, I treated it just the same as any other European game—if I'd stopped to think of the importance, and the responsibility, I don't think we would have got there!"

After all her efforts, Ann won't even be able to watch the whole of the Tannadice match next Wednesday. She and the other office staff have to take it in turns to man the office during the game to cope with the inevitable host of callers—ranging from international Press to locals wondering what the score is.

But she's determined to see some of it. "I'm making sure I'm upstairs for the second half," she grinned. "Nothing's going to stop me being there."

If United do lift the UEFA Cup, it will be no more than their magnificent efforts deserve. Their fans, too, are likely to win high praise again, after an exemplary season.

But those fans celebrating afterwards should spare a toast or two for Mrs Ann Diamond and her backroom team who, catapulted into the glare of top-class European football, have come through the test with flying colours.

137

NEWS SPOTLIGHT

DUNDEE UNITED are anticipating the greatest moment in the club's 64-year history. On Saturday they play St Mirren in the Scottish Cup final, and on Wednesday they take on IFK Gothenburg in the second leg of the UEFA Cup final.

No one doubts that the architect of this achievement is manager Jim McLean. Here, in a revealing interview, he talks exclusively to a "Courier" reporter about his life both in and out of the football spotlight.

Jim McLean—the man behind the football mask

As Dundee United prepare for two cup finals within the next week, the club's mainspring, manager Jim McLean, has given an exclusive, enlightening interview to "The Courier."

- Read about Jim McLean, husband and father.
- The stress of life as a top manager and how he copes with it.
- His hopes and ambitions —and a frank look at the future.

Read this revealing insight into Jim McLean, the man behind the football mask

in TOMORROW'S

COURIER

Days before United faced their two cup finals, The Courier secured a rare in-depth interview with the manager.

JIM McLEAN does not suffer fools gladly, nor does he mince his words, and so it is with some caution, and not a little trepidation, that one sets out to interview him.

I found the Dundee United manager in his modest office at Tannadice Park tracksuited, in stockinged feet, and in reflective mood.

He stands today a giant in the game of football, the man of the moment, a manager two short steps away from the pinnacle of an already distinguished career.

During 16 years as manager Mr McLean, who is 48, has had a slice of the cake—a Premier League title, two League Cup wins and 12 seasons in Europe—but is now anticipating the icing of sweeter success.

> ❝ The crunch time comes now. We've been too often in finals and not won. ❞

There is no doubt he wants that success now. Referring to the fact that Dundee United have been runners-up in the Scottish Cup three times and runners-up in the League Cup twice, Mr McLean said, "The crunch time comes now. We've been too often in finals and not won. We've got to win at least one to have any tangible reason to be happy with the season."

And if he had to choose . . . "The European one, no doubt. It most certainly is the more important of the two.

"We've won the League Cup and we've won the league in the time I have been here. It would be nice to win the Scottish Cup as well, but there is no doubt in my mind that Europe is the one that people will remember you for winning."

In a recent interview, Dundee United chairman Mr George Fox told me that he would not swap places with his manager for £1 million. The stress is just too great.

Jim McLean is feeling the pressure and admits that he is not sure for how much longer he will take it.

"I think that the stress is easier to handle when you are younger, when you are fitter," he said.

"Without doubt the best part of the job is being out with the players and seeing younger players getting better, but I don't know whether I'm getting too old for that too.

"The younger players of today, too many of them, disappoint me with their attitude. They want something handed to them on a golden plate and don't really want to graft and work for it."

Is that a product of society more than football?

"Yes, beyond a shadow of a doubt. It's just the modern way. We are just far, far too good to our kids and protect and hand them things without them earning them.

"We are to blame as parents. The attitude really is very, very disappointing for me personally.

"In life I don't think you get anything other than working for it."

At the beginning of the season Mr McLean lost several key players and his assistant Walter Smith, making team selection particularly difficult.

This factor, plus an exceptionally large number of "crunch games," has put him under tremendous pressure and he admits to feeling "extremely tired."

Teetotal and a non-smoker, Mr McLean perhaps finds it harder than some to let off steam. Indeed, his only relaxation is a rare game of golf.

It is impossible to be as successful a manager as Jim McLean without attracting the attention of other football clubs and over the years there have been numerous attempts to lure him away from Tannadice.

Has he ever been tempted?

"Every time someone comes along I am tempted," he said.

"But in some ways it is very upsetting because you go through days and weeks wondering what you should do.

"In most cases everybody thinks the grass is always greener on the other side but fortunately for me I have decided I have too much that is important to me here and I am completely satisfied that the decisions I have made are the right ones for me and my family and what I want out of life."

What has kept Mr McLean at Tannadice is, firstly, his love of Dundee and its people, and the support he has enjoyed within the club.

"We have loved living in Dundee since we moved here 21 years ago. My wife was saying the other day that she has lived longer in Dundee than anywhere else.

"We love the people of Dundee and that more than any other single factor has tied me to Dundee United as well as obviously the backing I have had from everybody on the staff.

"I thought I was fortunate to have a relationship with Johnston Grant (the late United chairman) which in my opinion was unique.

> ❝ Everybody thinks the grass is always greener on the other side but fortunately for me I have decided I have too much that is important to me here. ❞

"I am very, very difficult to work with and I am really pleased that Mr Fox has been able to handle me in exactly the same way and that the relationship with him is just as good.

"Honestly, if it's not right at the chairman/manager level, it will never be right anywhere down. Players cannot do it on their own.

"Johnston Grant and George Fox, in my opinion, deserve more credit than they get."

And money? "I could have been other places for more money, quite considerably greater money in some cases.

"But Dundee United have paid me as well as they possibly can and I have been happy with that.

"And money is most certainly not anywhere near the most important factor."

However, there is a question mark over how much longer Dundee United can keep Jim McLean as their manager.

Recently he signed a new contract up to 1992, but what is not widely appreciated is that Mr McLean can quit before that date if he so chooses. Will he?

"I don't foresee me being team manager of Dundee United up to that date," he said.

"It's always bad at the end of the season because you are tired, but I honestly do not want the pressure and I do not want the amount of work that I have got to do and I am a bit scared to be handling it.

"I'll be in my fifties at that time the new contract expires and I do not want as much responsibility at that time.

"And before that contract is out somebody else will most certainly be in charge at Dundee United as team manager."

Although he would not speculate, Mr McLean did not rule out the possibility of him staying at Tannadice in another role. However, United fans can be reassured that this is not Jim McLean's swansong season, but in some ways he wished it was.

"I would honestly love it to be in as much as I would rather enjoy life, play golf a lot more than I do and would rather have more time to spend with my family than I do," he said.

"But I feel I will have to work the way I do for a wee while yet."

It is clear that Mr McLean deeply regrets the amount of time spent with footballers that he, looking back, wishes he had spent with his family, particularly his two sons Colin (24) and Gary (18).

"It's a disgraceful statement to make, but I spend more time with young boys coming here than I have spent with my kids," he said.

"As a father that has been a disgraceful part in my life in that my two sons have grown up and I have hardly ever contributed anything to their upbringing.

"It's too late now in my opinion, now that they are hopefully going their own way anyway, but it disappoints me that part of it.

"It's a price that everybody in this type of game has to pay. The treatment of your wife is to me an absolute utter disgrace. She cannot open her mouth if you get beaten, she's scared to speak to you or decides it's better not to speak. And there are plenty of defeats.

"I don't know why the wives stick it so long. Some of them don't, but fortunately mine has."

> ❝ It's always bad at the end of the season because you are tired, but I honestly do not want the pressure and I do not want the amount of work that I have got to do and I am a bit scared to be handling it. ❞

Although Mr McLean clearly has the deepest respect for his players, he never allows himself to get close to them. The player/manager relationship tends to be strictly professional.

"Definitely I am a wee bit distant from them, I don't relax with them. Basically it's because I have a job to do," he said.

"A lot of them would be far happier if I patted them on the back when things weren't going well but I feel I would be cheating them.

"I have got to fall out with them, too often for my liking, but I am better doing that then cheating and conning them.

"If I pat them on the back and say 'sorry it's not going well' and the next day sign somebody else, I don't think I would be doing my job.

"It's got to be complete honesty all the time. If you do one dishonest thing you will never be trusted again."

If success is founded on the will to win and dedication to the job, then a deserved historic double awaits Jim McLean.

Plans for returning heroes

DUNDEE UNITED will receive a heroes' return to the city if they are successful in their quest to win the Scottish Cup at Hampden Park this afternoon.

Tayside police said yesterday that plans have been made for the team to make a victory procession through the city, but these do not include any City Square celebrations.

The occasion clashes with the annual fiddlers' rally in the Caird Hall, which traditionally chokes the city centre streets with parked cars as almost 3000 people turn out for the concert.

"The team bus will not be stopping in the city centre," emphasised Chief Superintendent David Chalmers, the man in charge of arrangements.

He is hoping the team's arrival will be timed some time after 7 p.m., when all the concert-goers will be inside the Caird Hall.

Weather permitting, the team will make the journey back to Tannadice in an open-topped bus.

After arriving on the outskirts of the city, they will travel along Perth Road, down Nethergate, into High Street, past the City Square to Commercial Street, Albert Square, then up Victoria Road, Dens Road and Provost Road, before turning into Tannadice Street and their home ground.

The streets are expected to be mobbed by cheering fans, who will just have to pick a spot and wait for their heroes to arrive.

If the unthinkable happens and United lose to St Mirren, there will be no trip through the city and the team will simply return home quietly.

A big year for quiet man Dave

MANAGER JIM McLEAN has never made any secret of the fact that he rates Paul Hegarty, Dave Narey and Paul Sturrock as key figures in the development of Dundee United.

Sturrock is the confident, talkative type, the other two much quieter—with the quietest of all three, team captain Dave Narey.

Despite this, he has firmly held views on the game in general and specific games in particular.

"What I am most of all is delighted that we are in the Scottish Cup and UEFA Cup finals," he said.

"We are a good team and this proves it."

Then, turning to today's final, he expressed disappointment . . . that United are favourites!

"I can see WHY it has happened—because we are doing well in Europe and have finished third in the league.

"But if I have a choice I always like to 'come from behind' as it were.

"We have got used to doing that over the years!

"What we also have is a thorough knowledge of never becoming over-confident about second favourites if you are the favourites.

"We have learned that from experience of being second favourites ourselves—and winning.

"All that said, I am confident.

"I believe this is our year and that we will start tomorrow by winning the Scottish Cup."

The cup finals are the biggest dates in the immediate future for Dave, but it is fitting that this season, rated by many his overall best, marks his testimonial year with, still ahead, a major celebrity golf tournament at Letham Grange in early June, a prize draw car competition, a testimonial game (probably against English Cup finalists Spurs) and a dinner-dance to round things off.

With the World Cup last summer, the season at club level peaking with two cup finals, a place in the Scotland pool for the England and Brazil games, plus the work involved in his testimonial year, it's certainly a busy time for Narey, but, as he says, "It's a lot better this way than not being involved."

United's "Euro" form enough to bring the cup home—McLean

DUNDEE UNITED manager Jim McLean is convinced that if his men give a repeat of their recent performances in the Nou Camp and Bokelberg stadiums, they will lift the Scottish Cup for the very first time at Hampden this afternoon.

The Tangerines' supremo said yesterday, "I've been hammering home to the players that if they go out and express themselves as they did against Barcelona and Borussia, that will be enough to win the trophy given a fair share of the breaks."

This is the seventh Hampden final United have reached under McLean's leadership and they have yet to leave the national stadium with a cup in their possession but confidence is high that today is their day.

"We have definitely been in too many finals and not come away with silverware," admitted the manager.

"The players are as aware of this as I am, however, and know this is their big chance.

"Looking at some of our recent results, we cannot be anything other than confident."

The United boss also dismissed suggestions that his side's defeat at the hands of St Mirren in a league match last month would have any relevance to this afternoon's proceedings.

"I've read a few interviews with Frank McGarvey in which he has talked about them beating us 2-1 but I would point out that we were without Dave Narey, Paul Sturrock, Iain Ferguson and Billy Thomson and lost Billy Kirkwood through injury in the opening minutes that day," said McLean.

"It is also the case that we have won the other three games between the sides this season but as far as I'm concerned past results mean nothing—it's all about what happens on the day."

United's starting line-up will come from a pool of 14 players. Missing from the original 16-strong cup final squad are back-up keeper Scott Thomson and utility player Dave Beaumont although the latter may still be named as a substitute because of his versatility.

In the running for places are—W. Thomson, Holt, Malpas, Kirkwood, McInally, Hegarty, Narey, Ferguson, Bowman, Gallacher, Bannon, Sturrock, Redford, Clark.

"Everyone is fit which gives me a pleasant headache over team selection," commented McLean.

"I have to decide whether to play the side which beat Dundee in the semi-final or the one that triumphed over Barcelona or the line-up that won in West Germany."

Opposite number Alex Smith is giving even less away about his team choice.

The St Mirren manager, apart from declaring a clean bill of health, is masking his plans behind a pool of 17.

Smith announced the team to his players in a Glasgow hotel last night but won't go public until just before kick-off time today.

"If our younger players don't freeze and play to their potential we can have no fears," said the Paisley boss.

"Both sides play with a lot of flair, therefore this promises to be a really entertaining cup final."

St Mirren from—Money, Wilson, McWhirter, D. Hamilton, Fitzpatrick, Abercrombie, Godfrey, Winnie, Cooper, B. Hamilton, Ferguson, McGarvey, McDowall, Cameron, Chalmers, Lambert, Speirs.

No team likes to tempt fate by planning victory parades, but the need to be prepared for a Scottish Cup party meant arrangements had to be made in advance.

United's "Dutch" connection arrive

IT IS estimated that 10,000 fans will travel to Hampden today to see in the flesh for the first time a United captain lift the sought-after trophy aloft.

Many diehards have crossed the globe at considerable expense from Hong Kong, the United States, Canada and Europe, but perhaps the title for total Tangerine fanaticism deserves to go to a pair of Dutchmen.

Last night, two Dutch fans from the "Dundee United Supporters Club, Nederland" arrived in the city for the week's events—the first time either of them has ever been in Scotland!

Jos Koemeester (26) and Peter Berkvens (27), both engineers from Alkmaar, became friends with several home-based United supporters on the team's earlier UEFA Cup visits to Lens, in France, and at the semi-final in Moenchengladbach.

According to the pair, there are actually 60 members of the supporters' club in their native city with an even split between actual Dutch football fans and expatriate Dundonians.

"There is quite a mixture of Dutchmen who work offshore in the North Sea who follow Dundee United as well as men from this city and Forfar who live in Alkmaar," explained Jos.

"Both Peter and myself go to the pub in Alkmaar where the club members meet and over the years our interest has grown and we became members."

Their enthusiasm for United's Continental style of play has been fuelled by the fact their own local team has languished in the Dutch lower divisions for several years.

"When we met up with the United supporters in France and Germany they were very open and friendly to us," added Jos.

"There have been many people who offered to get us tickets for both finals and to give us accommodation.

"I can tell we are going to enjoy our stay very much."

On Monday, both Jos and Peter will present United's team captain David Narey with their club's player-of-the-year award at Tannadice Park.

"It would be good if United can join Ajax in winning a European cup this season," added Peter.

As they both predicted Ajax's win in the European Cup Winners' Cup earlier in the week, perhaps their forecasts for United's fortunes will be blessed.

"United will win 3-1 tomorrow and 5-0 on Wednesday," predicted Peter.

● Pictured (from left) are Peter, friend George Kettler and Jos.

Gavin wishes now he'd bought a ticket

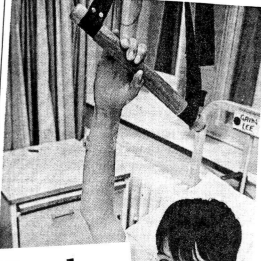

GROVE ACADEMY boy Gavin Lee reckons he's the unluckiest Dundee United fan in the whole of the city.

Gavin (13), of Ballantrae Road, Douglas, was over the moon when he was one of the 10 youngsters chosen to be ball boys for United's most important game ever—the UEFA Cup final second leg at Tannadice next Wednesday.

But yesterday morning, football-daft Gavin's dream crashed when he broke his left arm playing football with his mates.

Now he will have to pull out of ball boy duty—and he risks missing out on the Tannadice game altogether.

"If I'd known something like this was going to happen I'd have bought a ticket for the match," said a glum Gavin from his hospital bed in the Royal Infirmary.

"But as it is I'm going to miss the game altogether."

Gavin's mum, Mrs Violet Lee, says her son is "United daft."

"I don't think he realised at first what breaking his arm was going to mean.

"But when it sank in he was very upset about the whole thing," said Mrs Lee.

Though he'll miss the game Gavin, who plays for Monifieth Under-13s, has absolutely no doubt about who's going to win the UEFA Cup on Wednesday.

"Dundee United, of course," he asserted bravely.

"And they'll win the Scottish Cup, too."

● Picture shows a disconsolate Gavin in Ward 16 at Dundee Royal Infirmary.

Vital Paul undaunted by myths

WHEN THE history of Dundee United's rise to power in Scottish and European football comes to be written, many names will be involved.

There will be Jerry Kerr, who set the ball rolling, Jim McLean who built so magnificently on that start, and many players.

One of the main chapters will surely be devoted to Paul Sturrock.

This striker-winger has scored many goals himself, created many, many more. He has delighted with his skills both in a United and a Scotland jersey.

Injury has taken its toll in recent seasons, but he is still, in the view of experts up and down the land, the man who can turn a game in United's favour with one flash of genius.

United fans at the game today and on Wednesday night will be looking for that—no, expecting it.

In conversation the player displays the confidence which makes him such a dangerous opponent on the field.

"There will," he says, "be one goal in it—in our favour."

He and I have had this forecasting thing running throughout the season. He has yet to get the score right, but he has always been spot on with the result, so, on that basis, we can expect United to win . . . by more than one goal!

What surprises Paul is that United have been installed as favourites.

"We have been battling away in Europe and catching up on our league fixtures and there is our supposed lack of form at Hampden.

"They have been coasting along steadily with no pressure and no publicity and—even though it was a long time ago—have won the cup at Hampden."

Then he changed direction.

"But the fact is we have been turning over myths about ourselves all year—and that one about Hampden is due to be next.

"This is a one-off game and we are supposed to be only at our best in two-legged games. That is another myth to be smashed.

"I am looking forward to the game. We all are. Hampden is a great stage and I can see a great game ahead—with that one goal in it for us, as I have said."

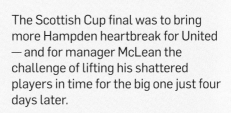

The Scottish Cup final was to bring more Hampden heartbreak for United — and for manager McLean the challenge of lifting his shattered players in time for the big one just four days later.

One United fan with something to smile about

DESPITE THE disappointment of Saturday's Scottish Cup defeat being firmly fixed in the minds of most Dundee United supporters, at least one—David Wilkie, of Westbank Farm, Longforgan—has something to smile about.

David (pictured) will be starring in the UEFA Cup final second leg match against Gothenburg at Tannadice on Wednesday—but as a mascot, not a player.

Among the many United fans who went to Hampden on Saturday to see the cup final against St Mirren were the six lucky winners of the "Courier" wordsquare competition and their guests.

The fortunate few received as their prize two stand tickets for the game, luxury coach travel to and from Glasgow, and lunch at a first-class Dunblane restaurant on the way.

For one of the six—Michael Souter, of Main Street, Invergowrie—disappointment turned to delight when he found that, although his entry had not been chosen as a winner, he was nominated to go when one of the successful entrants had to pull out.

Family friend Leanne Fenwick (10), of Morris Place, Invergowrie, had sent in the winning entry but could not take advantage of the prize as it clashed with a school trip to Holland.

Said Michael, "I had planned to go to Hampden anyway, but this is an added bonus."

Michael did get the competition answers right, but his entry was not one of the first six opened.

The other five winners were—Stephen Coope, c/o 70 Lamond Drive, St Andrews; G. Fraser, 409 Brook Street, Broughty Ferry; H. Gallacher, 33 Scott Street, Perth; D. Hamilton, 2-Glenmoy Place, Arbroath; and Albert Lorimer, 37 Wellington Square, Dundee.

We can bounce back—Narey

AS THE still stunned Dundee United players, staff and supporters were trying to pick up the pieces yesterday, team captain Dave Narey and I talked . . . briefly, because the losing of a cup final was still too fresh in his memory (writes The Sports Editor).

"Murder," was his first comment. Then, "I still can't really believe it.

"I'm still expecting to wake up and find it didn't happen.

"I was saying to my wife on the way back from Hampden that that's four times we have played there and we still have to get a result. It's ridiculous.

"On the way back, we were passing cars and buses with our supporters in them. I feel genuinely and sincerely sorry for them. They travelled with high hopes and we didn't win the cup.

"I know how the players are feeling now and how we felt when that final whistle blew. It must be twice as bad for our supporters.

"I honestly could not see St Mirren scoring and, without wishing to get involved in controversy, could see nothing wrong with the goal scored by our Iain Ferguson.

"I was so shattered by it all I was in bed by ten o'clock on Saturday night.

"Now we have to lift ourselves for the game on Wednesday night—and I firmly believe we can do it.

"We have had disappointments before and bounced back. It is up to us."

Then he was away, still obviously hardly believing the Scottish Cup was lost.

Now they must pick themselves up

HAVING CLIMBED the mountains of reaching two cup finals in one season, Dundee United fell off the first one with a resounding crash when they went out of the Scottish Cup to a goal in the sixteenth minute of extra time by St Mirren's Ian Ferguson, at Hampden, on a glorious day and in front of a wonderful crowd of 51,782.

Now, they have to, as the old song has it, pick themselves up, dust themselves down and start all over again, before meeting

IFK Gothenburg in the second leg of the UEFA Cup final at Tannadice on Wednesday night.

It is going to be a terrific task if the evidence of Saturday is anything to go by.

Success is punished fiercely in our domestic football.

While St Mirren have been coasting along steadily recently, their end-of-season involving only five league games in the 35 days since their semi-final defeat of Hearts, United have played two away European ties in Germany and Sweden and seven league games in exactly the same period.

So, Saints played once every seven days, United once every three-and-a-half, with two lengthy journeys midway through. Saints' total number of games in league, League Cup and Scottish Cup is 51, United's 66 in the same competitions, plus Europe.

I am not putting forward excuses, just getting in early my total opposition to talk of keep-

ing the current Premier League card of 44 games. That is a nonsensical burden if we want our most successful clubs to be in with a chance at the tail end of a season.

Almost from the off on Saturday, United looked to be struggling.

The cylinders that have kept them pounding along so often, Jim McInally, Ian Redford and Eamonn Bannon, never really fired together and service to the front, and problems for the men behind, grew.

United played, basically, 4-4-2. When Bannon was at his peak that could become 4-3-3 in a twinkling as he thrust from deep on the left to the opposing bye-line and even 4-2-4 if another midfield man burst through with him.

But Eamonn's below-par season hit a low on Saturday and seldom did he make one of those famous surges and equally seldom did anyone else back up the strikers or get to the bye-line, or near it, for cut-backs or crosses.

The one occasion this did happen brought the only really explosive moment of a disappointing game.

As John Holt nodded the ball forward, Dave Bowman got to it and threaded it through to Ian Redford on the left. With both Bowman and Iain Ferguson looking anxiously to see if the linesman thought, as many did, that Redford was offside, Redford controlled the ball and hit a powerful low drive across the face of Campbell Money's goal. The linesman's flag stayed down.

A flick of the keeper's glove saw the ball 'break' slightly.

The inrushing Kevin Gallacher would assuredly have scored but for this. As it was, the ball went between his legs.

His impetus carried him forward to within inches of the goal-line as Iain Ferguson, who had been following in, connected left footed with the ball and smashed it high into the net.

Within seconds, the leaping, hugging, cheering United players and their 20,000 or so fans were the very opposite—angry, bitter and, in the case of one or two players, lucky to stay on the field after violent verbal protests as Referee Kenny Hope, of Clarkston, chalked off the goal (Ian Redford was booked).

Was Gallacher offside? The

BY THE SPORTS EDITOR

Laws of the Game state that "a player is off-side if he is nearer to his opponent's goal-line than the ball . . . unless there are at least two of his opponents nearer their own goal-line than he is."

There is also the question of him interfering with play or seeking to gain an advantage by being in a certain position.

On the second point, Gallacher was certainly not interfering with play because he was out of line of the Ferguson shot; keeper Money was well out of his goal and left-back Derek Hamilton only got to Gallacher (and sent him crashing, incidentally) after the ball had hit the back of the net. He equally certainly, was not seeking to gain an advantage.

But was he offside? It is a question of millimetres. Smack

on the goal-line, which extends from corner flag to corner flag remember, were Hamilton, actually in the goalmouth, and right-back Tommy Wilson, off to the right of the goal and not mentioned in the many arguments so far.

It was not a goal because the referee decided it was not a goal. I believe it could just as easily be proved that it was if there was a right of appeal.

If you are a Dundee supporter and have stayed with the report this far let me ask you this. If this was not a goal, why was the one Davie Cooper scored against the Dark Blues at Ibrox recently allowed to stand?

On that occasion, Ally McCoist was lying on the goal-line when the ball went in the net to open the scoring, yet wasn't given offside and wasn't, according to Referee Doug Yeats of Perth, interfering with play.

But back to the final. From that sickening blow, United never recovered and were hit by an even more positive one exactly five minutes later.

As the ball was lobbed forward to Saints' Ian Ferguson, John Clark was in close attendance.

My mind immediately switched back over 30 years to a great St Mirren centre-half, Willie Telfer. In an international, he was chasing Wales' centre-forward John Charles, bursting through and eventually scoring.

The letters' columns in newspapers were filled for weeks

with arguments over whether he should have committed what is nowadays called a professional foul and taken him down from behind. He didn't . . . neither did Clark.

Instead, the United man tried to hook the ball away, it hit Ferguson and bounced ahead of him as Clark fell.

As John Holt rushed to cover and Billy Thomson advanced to put the youngster off, he ham-

mered in a left foot shot which went into the narrow gap between Thomson and his right hand post.

A great goal marvellously struck by one of several outstanding youngsters in this St Mirren line-up.

In fact it might have been 2-0 four minutes later when a brilliant Ian Cameron dipping shot was equally brilliantly turned over by Thomson.

Incidents were few and far between in a final which (apart from the 'no goal' incident) was the "friendly and family affair" expected and only boiled over at that incident and when the goal was scored.

On Saturday I said I expected Saints' Alex Smith to become an outstanding manager in the years ahead.

He has sneaked up on me. He is now an outstanding manager, even if only for the Cup win in his first (part) season in charge. But it isn't only that.

The sheer talent at his disposal must excite even this most controlled of characters. Imagine having Paul Lambert on your staff. A 17-year-old with a 27-year-old football brain.

That doesn't take into account rock solid Campbell Money (26) in goal, fronted by a group of players with Tony Fitzpatrick and the ageless and elusive Frank McGarvey, at 31 the oldest.

There is plenty of "mileage" left in 28-year-olds Derek Hamilton and skipper Billy Abercromby. The others are 26 and under—considerably under in the case of Brian Hamilton (19), Dave Winnie, Ian Ferguson and Ian Cameron (all 20). That and Lambert too! Some line-up.

I rated Winnie and Cooper Saints' best and delighted in the touches of Lambert until he went off in 88 minutes, and Brian Hamilton.

The immaculate Dave Narey was again . . . immaculate for United and for most of the time John Clark did well, as did Ian Redford, Jim McInally and Dave Bowman in midfield from the point of view of effort.

What was lacking from them was the control they normally exert, the openings they normally create—and often use themselves.

Gallacher took the place of Sturrock in 76 minutes, Hegarty went on for Redford in 88. Saints had Cameron on for McDowall in 73 and Fitzpatrick for Lambert in 88.

Iain Ferguson joined Ian Redford in being yellow carded.

Saints' Neil Cooper won the Mr Superfit award.

Phone message from Jim McLean turns Gavin's despondency to joy

A YOUNG Dundee United fan's dream has come true, thanks to a "marvellous gesture of generosity" by team manager Jim McLean.

Thirteen-year-old Grove Academy pupil Gavin Lee thought he had endured the cruellest day of luck when, after being selected as one of the ballboys for tomorrow night's UEFA Cup final second-leg tie between United and IFK Gothenburg at Tannadice, he broke his arm when he fell during a playground kickabout with school pals.

That was on Friday and, as he spent that night laid up in the Royal Infirmary with his left arm which, had suffered a double fracture, encased in plaster, he felt nothing could relieve his despair.

Being allowed home at noon on Saturday raised his spirits slightly, but, after watching his heroes fail against St Mirren in the Scottish Cup final on television, he was back down in the dumps.

When Grove rector Kenneth Anderson answered his first telephone call of the day at 9 a.m. yesterday, however, Gavin's luck changed for the better.

The caller was none other than Jim McLean, who inquired if the young-ster was out of hospital and, if so, if he would be able to be at Tannadice on Wednesday as a V.I.P. guest.

Mr Anderson continued, "Mr McLean said he would arrange for Gavin to meet the players before the match and then he could watch the match.

"I thought it was a marvellous gesture of generosity by the manager. He is clearly under a great deal of pressure between the two big matches on Saturday and Wednesday, yet he found the time to ask about Gavin first thing on Monday morning."

Mr Anderson immediately notified

Gavin's mother, Mrs Violet Lee, who said her son had recovered to a sufficient extent and would be able to take up Mr McLean's offer.

Speaking from the family home in Ballantrae Road, Gavin said last night, "I'm absolutely delighted to get the chance of going to Tannadice. It was very kind indeed for Mr McLean to think about me when he's got so much else to think about.

"I very much want United to win the UEFA Cup and being a ballboy would have made me feel a real part of things. I thought I'd lost that chance but now this has happened and I'll feel I will be part of the big night again."

Gavin Lee

The captain's day of many duties

WHILE THE newly-arrived Gothenburg team enjoyed a restful day in and around St Andrews yesterday their opponents' captain was busy in Dundee fulfilling the never-ending stream of duties that come over and above his back-breaking playing schedule.

David Narey sped round town in a number of guises—player, celebrity, team ambassador.

After treatment at the ground for an ankle knock picked up in Saturday's Scottish Cup defeat he arrived in Reform Street to perform the opening ceremony at the new Britannia Building Society.

He found time to chat to officials and staff, all keen to offer both sympathy and encouragement, before moving on to his next stop—a date with two members of Dundee United's Dutch supporters' club, Jos Koemeester and Peter Berkvens.

The club—composed of exiled Scots and Dutch fans—have nominated David as their player of the year and Jos and Peter presented him with their award at a special ceremony at Tannadice.

"It's always great to see fans like this," said David. "These boys have taken the trouble to travel all the way across here. I'd like to thank them very much."

Adopted fans apart, how had home-based supporters been reacting to Saturday's result?

Half-joking, he answered, "To tell the truth, I've been hiding from them. But, seriously, there have been mixed reactions. There's disappointment, obviously, but some are showing it more than others."

Jos and Peter declared themselves very impressed with what they had seen of Dundee so far, on what is their first visit to the country.

They are staying with their friend George Kettles, one of United's most loyal supporters.

For George tomorrow night will be the culmination of a long, enjoyable but rather expensive European season.

As he explained yesterday, "After seeing all the European games there's one thing I remember very clearly . . ."

He found himself in Spain for the Barcelona game along with three mates—and a king-sized transport headache.

The four were staying in Benidorm and could not find transport to Barcelona for love nor money. Trains and buses were full or left too late, and they were not allowed to hire cars.

Eventually they realised that the only way to see the match was by taking a taxi from Benidorm to Barcelona. The cost? £230!

Peter (left) and Jos (right) after presenting their trophy to David Narey

There was no time for United to lick their wounds. It was straight into Gothenburg build-up — although, even amid the hysteria, McLean still made the time to ensure one young fan's bad luck was put to a stop.

Angry" United keen to make up

IT WAS a relaxed, though still bitterly disappointed Jim McLean who yesterday looked back to the trauma of the 1-0 Scottish Cup defeat and ahead to tomorrow's UEFA Cup final second leg at Tannadice (writes THE SPORTS EDITOR).

The look ahead had a straight-from-the-shoulder start.

"There is no sign of any enthusiasm for Wednesday about the place this morning," he said, then added, "but that will definitely be different tomorrow, I am sure.

"The players are absolutely shattered at the result on Saturday but there will be 11 angry men out there on Wednesday night determined to make amends.

"We have a wonderful opportunity to make up to our supporters.

"Normally, we would have had to wait until next season, but here we have a second final only four days later. What a chance that gives us!"

The players were given a day off if they wished yesterday, "if we had won on Saturday they

would have been celebrating and training would have been needed, but now there will be little training up to the game."

However, most turned up and the manager took the opportunity of going over Saturday's poor showing.

He didn't want to lambast players, but Dundee United needed nine of them playing well together because they played it as a team game and only four performed to their own high standards on Saturday.

"Against Barcelona and in the second half against Borussia over there we actually had 11 playing well," he mused.

He didn't absolve himself

from blame for Saturday, saying, "the performance we gave, myself included with the substitutions and the way the tactics were interpreted, was very, very disappointing."

The question of the goal-that-never-was, scored (?) by Iain Ferguson and which would have put United one up, kept recurring, but was always followed by the remark that his team shouldn't really have needed to be worrying about that—the conclusion being that they should have put the issue beyond doubt without the arguments over a disputed goal.

"People say going out in semi-finals is a terrible thing," said the United manager.

"I'll tell you something—and I

am speaking from a whole lot of experience—going out in a final is a whole lot worse."

He described Saturday's performance as "the worst we have ever turned on at Hampden, even allowing that we have never played particularly well there," but didn't put it down to tiredness, even though the World Cup men had all been short of top form this season.

Though the club had played some 70 games most players, because of injuries, had played many fewer.

He aded, "We let our supporters down badly. They were there in numbers, they gave us great backing, but we let them down."

The aftermath of Saturday is

a certainty that there will be team changes for tomorrow night.

For a start, Eamonn Bannon has Achilles tendon trouble, though the groin cramp which affected him late on seems to have cleared.

The only other casualties at the moment are Dave Narey, who went over an ankle in training, and Maurice Malpas, who got a stud in his foot, but both should be fit.

The manager is still convinced he made the right team choice on Saturday . . . the team that beat Dundee in the semi with the exception of John Clark for Paul Hegarty, which he explained by referring again to the excellent game Clark had

against Hearts last week and the fact Hegarty had not completed the games against Gothenburg and Hamilton Accies.

Now he had to think on Wednesday's team. Would he introduce fresh legs? Would he stand by the men who, mostly, have done so well that they have got the club to the stage of two finals?

My overall impression yesterday was that everyone connected with the club is 'down' at the moment over the Scottish Cup final, but that, in the growing anger at their own performance, there could be the inspiration for a totally different outlook on Wednesday night at Tannadice, "where," as the manager commented at one point, "a lot of our players definitely play better than they do away."

EAST GERMAN Gunter Schneider will present the UEFA Cup to the winners at Tannadice tomorrow night. Schneider is a member of UEFA's executive committee and vice-president of its organising committee.

Tannadice pair out talent spotting in Fife

WHILE EUROPE waits to see whether or not Dundee United can pull back that one goal advantage held by IFK Gothenburg, United's managerial team were last night out searching for new talent.

Manager Jim McLean and coach Gordon Wallace watched separately the England v.

Italy and Scotland v. Netherlands semi-professional games at Dunfermline and Kirkcaldy respectively.

Meanwhile, reports from England of a United interest in Swindon Town's 22-year-old Stranraer born centre-half Colin Calderwood are denied.

Back in town for the UEFA Cup final is a man who went the other way, Richard Gough of Spurs, still "sick" at losing in the F.A. Cup final to Coventry City.

"It will help a bit if my old team take the cup on Wednesday night" he said. "They are good enough to do it."

'Consolation prize' which will have to be fought for

"NEITHER GOTHENBURG nor the UEFA representative is going to hand the UEFA Cup to us because of our disappointment at losing the Scottish Cup on Saturday.

"We have to face up to the fact that we have to help ourselves in this situation, because there is absolutely no chance of anyone else helping us.

"It is down to the players' performance, contribution and attitude . . . plus, hopefully, that share of luck that can happen in every game."

Dundee United manager Jim McLean summing up the situ-

> *We have had some great experiences this season, but you don't remember them when things go against you*

ation for his club as they face the UEFA Cup final (second leg) tonight and after a 20-minute talk-in behind closed doors with his players yesterday morning.

He then named a pool of 15 players. It is—

Billy Thomson, John Holt, Maurice Malpas, Jim McInally, John Clark, Dave Narey (captain), Iain Ferguson, Dave Bowman, Kevin Gallacher, Paul Hegarty, Billy Kirkwood, Dave Beaumont, Paul Sturrock, Ian Redford, Scott Thomson.

Eamonn Bannon has still to pass a fitness test this morning. If he is successful he will be added to the pool, if not it will be someone else, "a player who has played in games recently."

So the speculation starts. What will the actual TEAM be at kick-off time.

I would expect, with the manager saying, "it will be 4-3-3, because 4-4-2 would never do in this sort of situation," that it won't be far away from: Billy Thomson; Malpas, Narey, Clark, Holt; Bowman, McInally, Redford; Gallacher, Ferguson, Sturrock.

Then I will add my usual cautionary note—you never know with this manager. For instance he (and everyone else present) was mightily impressed by the performance of Dave Beaumont in midfield against Hearts in the last league game of the season.

There are so many alternatives it is ridiculous! Kirkwood in midfield, or at full back; Malpas used in his midfield role instead of full back. So it goes on, but I'll stick with the line-up I gave.

I do not believe, even if they are fully fit, that Bannon or Hegarty will start the game, but if they came on at some point it would be no surprise.

The manager admitted he hadn't expected the players to be as "down" as they were first thing yesterday morning, but a bit of horseplay when tennis coach Dave Gordon ended in a bath full of ice cracked the gloom and gave the boss a much more optimistic view of the attitude prevailing.

By THE SPORTS EDITOR

It is interesting that the instigators of the "ice-breaker" were Dave Bowman and Jim McInally, aided and abetted, it must be admitted, by many willing hands!

"He went in the bath in Gothenburg, but that didn't work. Hopefully this will," commented the manager.

Then he returned to the Scottish Cup final.

"Saturday was the worst experience we have ever had," he said.

"We have had some great experiences this season but it is amazing how you don't remember them when things go against you."

He was adamant that the crowd could play a vital part in a United performance worthy of the team.

"I hope our supporters can forget about Saturday and concentrate on getting together with the players," he said. "The atmosphere they create will bring out the best in the players, as it has done repeatedly in the past.

"This is the pinnacle of the players' careers so far and a pinnacle for the supporters. They want to win the UEFA Cup as much as we do.

"It was twice as bad on Saturday because we had twice the number of fans with us that we usually have on big occasions. It would be wonderful to do it tomorrow night in front of those fans on our own ground."

He then admitted that he had "swithered" over the idea of taking the pitch in by a yard at each side, but had rejected it.

"We have to get in behind them and width helps. Mind you the best solution would be to have it full width when we are attacking and narrower when they are!" he joked. "I doubt, though, if that would be allowed." He was delighted that Iain Ferguson was available for this second leg.

He was absent for the first because of suspension, "and it is better that we didn't have him there than here."

He concluded with, "On Saturday, the players had something to fall back on with this second final to be played.

"Now it is down to the one game, the last chance of a trophy this season.

"We always need nine to eleven players playing as they can. As I have said, we had only four upon Saturday. It must be back to at least nine tomorrow night.

"Whether I believe they will do it or not do it is irrelevant. What matters is that they have to go out there and do it themselves. I honestly do not know if it is there any more. We will find out with the game.

"It is about enthusiasm and appetite. On Saturday there was no zest or enthusiasm. Tomorrow there must be both."

Very serious looks on the faces of the United players as they got down to training at Tannadice yesterday morning

The eyes of Europe turn to Tannadice Park tonight

The UEFA Cup final officials were shown around Tannadice yesterday by Dundee referee Bob Valentine. From left—Dan Petrescu, Bob Valentine, referee Ioan Igna and Radu

TONIGHT AT Tannadice Park the city of Dundee hosts the biggest football occasion in its glamour-game packed history (reports THE SPORTS EDITOR).

At 7.45 p.m.—note that time because it says 8 p.m. on the tickets—Dundee United are hosts to IFK Gothenburg in the second leg of the UEFA Cup final.

United are one goal down from the first leg and it is all to play for, with extra time scheduled if it is a draw at the end of 90 minutes then the nerve-shattering climax of a penalty shoot-out should there still be no decision after two hours of football.

So, at the earliest, by 9.25 p.m. and the latest by 10 p.m., we will know whether or not the UEFA Cup has come to Scotland for the very first time.

The game is being beamed live by television to (at least) 19 countries, including England, where they have tended to feel other issues more important so far this football season, despite the fact United have been the only British team competing in Europe for several months now.

So the eyes of millions will be on the Tannadice team and their supporters.

It will be the highest profile exposure the City of Discovery, Dundee, has ever had.

Yesterday, as the minutes to the big occasion ticked away, both managers, Jim McLean of Dundee United, and Gunder Bengtsson of Gothenburg, and several of their players, had their pre-match say.

"The Courier", as it has been all the way along this lengthy European trail, was there to note and relay . . .

We can bring back the smiles, says Jim

"I HAVE never played in a Cup final before and have never felt like I felt after Saturday.

"I wasn't just upset for me, but for the supporters I saw standing about or sitting in their cars and buses completely stunned.

"I slipped away to Glasgow at the week-end. I would have gone mad staying at home.

"I felt that way right up until this morning, then I saw the cameras and the reporters and felt the interest rising as it always does before a big game.

"There was nothing different about preparation or our approach on Saturday, but things simply didn't happen for us.

"I believe we are over that now. I believe we can win the UEFA Cup and bring back the smiles to those faces that have been so glum since the week-end."—Jim McInally.

United can do it, with a little help—Narey

By The Sports Editor

Dave Narey

"I KNOW what the betting odds say, that we are favourites for this game, but I prefer to think on the general view, that we are the underdogs.

"As you know I have always been happier in that situation and believe we can come from the back and give ourselves and our supporters something to celebrate late tomorrow night."

The view of Dundee United team captain Dave Narey, who believes the Scottish Cup defeat has created the opinion that United won't overcome the one-goal deficit they face in the second leg.

"They are a good team, they cannot be anything else having got to the final of this tournament," he went on, "but by the same token, we must be good, too.

"Of course we have to lift ourselves after the Scottish Cup final defeat, but I believe we will do that—and I ask again for the backing of the fans.

"I have said before that whatever we as players felt on Saturday, they must have felt too—only more so.

"Now, with their encouragement and support I believe we can do it on the night.

"Certainly, that encouragement and support will improve our chances."

"So near, yet so far". How else could The Courier put it? A season of unimaginable highs ended with the most crushing of lows for the United players, who had given their all over the course of 73 matches.

Expecting a hectic evening

GOTHENBURG GOALKEEPER **Thomas Wernersson** anticipates having to earn his money at Tannadice this evening (**reports STEVE BRUCE**).

"I think I'll be in for a busy time of it," said the 32-year-old part-timer yesterday.

"Being a goal behind from the first game, Dundee United have to attack, and I expect them to come at us at great speed early on."

Wernersson, who denied the Tangerines a vital away goal with a brilliant save from Ian Redford in the Ullevi Stadium a fortnight ago, has a healthy regard for them.

"No side has attacked us more at home in the competition than United did and I know we still face a hard 90 minutes," he commented.

"If I do my job, the 1-0 lead we established in Sweden will be enough," he smiled, adding, "But, seriously, I feel we will need to score at Tannadice, and if we do that the cup will be ours, for I do not believe United can score three times."

The Swedes strongly fancy their chances of netting this evening. Striker **Stefan Pettersson**, who scored the only goal of the first leg, claimed, "If I do not score in this match I feel one of my colleagues will get the crucial away goal that will secure the cup for us.

"The United defence is hard, but fair, and even when you get past them the positional play of Billy Thomson is excellent.

"However, we are on a high at present and can win the UEFA Cup."

The man United must find a way past tonight—Gothenburg goalkeeper Thomas Wernersson at the Old Course yesterday.

Hysen a man in demand

THE SWEDES were yesterday trying to play down the transfer speculation surrounding skipper Glenn Hysen (writes STEVE BRUCE).

The 28-year-old central defender is interesting clubs throughout Europe, including Manchester United, whose manager, Alex Ferguson, met with Gunder Bengtsson at the weekend.

However Bengtsson yesterday claimed the subject of Hysen never arose during his conversation with Ferguson.

"Being part-timers we have to accept the fact that players will be lost to other clubs in other countries, it happened last season and will happen again this year," conceded the Gothenberg coach.

"However, Alex Ferguson and I have not discussed Hysen and our club president, who deals with transfer negotiations, says that he has not been approached with regard to the player."

Hysen though is well aware of the attention he is attracting and admitted, "Manchester United are a good team and joining them would appeal to me."

Any transfer however—a fee of around £500,000 is being mentioned—would almost certainly be delayed until the Swedish season ends in November.

A Hysen move could be followed by a bid for Celtic's Brian McClair, though talk of this has been "suspended" until after the Scotland v. England and Scotland v. Brazil games at Hampden.

Striker Steffan Pettersson is also being linked with a move to Italy.

Transfer talk swirling round the Gothenburg camp will do no harm to Dundee United's chances tonight!

UNITED'S GREAT FIGHT FOR UEFA GLORY

Full reports and pictures of last night's game

So near, yet so far, as United battle to the final whistle

Clark goal raises hopes

AT KICK-OFF, a strong wind was blowing straight into the Arklay Street end, Billy Thomson's charge.

The crowd had arrived early and it was the noisiest Tannadice of the season—even allowing for Old Firm games, with the shed at the Dens end ahead on points in the decibel stakes.

The ground was a blaze of tangerine with a defiant blue and white corner, the IFK colours, to my left.

United lost the toss and kicked off, with the actual event delayed to allow for the television cover—beaming out to 21 countries.

Kirkwood, playing up early, caused the first kerfuffle when he went in low on Wernerrsson

and the keeper, untouched, fell as if poleaxed.

It was Kirkwood again in five minutes. When Gallacher got the ball over from the right, he and the keeper clashed and the ball spun out for a fruitless corner.

It was 4-3-3, with Kirkwood ready to burst off the middle three to make it 4-2-4 with the other front men, Gallacher, Ferguson and Sturrock, at every opportunity.

The Swedes were concentrating on defence at this stage, but proved their ability on the break when first Petterson fed Lennart Nilsson and Clark had to make a brilliant interception to save the day, then Lennart Nilsson let go with a 30-yard shot which took a deflection and had Thomson reaching full stretch to take the ball.

After a promising start, United had become careless with the final pass and the crowd had quietened considerably!

And they were really worried when Clark conceded a corner. Holt headed it out and Petterson lashed in a great shot which Thomson cleared with his feet.

United's reply on the quarter hour was a shot by McInally, well taken by Wernerrsson. Petterson replied with a 35-yard

shot which Thomson gathered at the second attempt.

Redford was looking good as the game slowed down to a hard slog with both teams working for a break but making sure they kept a firm hold at the back.

He set up a neat move with Malpas and Sturrock, ruined when Sturrock fell over near the bye-line.

But, in 22 minutes, came the moment all Scotland had been dreading.

Sturrock appeared to be obstructed on the edge of the Gothenburg penalty area. It wasn't a penalty and Tord Holmgren sent a 40-yard pass away to the left. It was picked up by Lennart Nilsson, who turned inside Clark and lashed a great shot past Thomson.

That was the away goal the Swedes wanted and United knew could be fatal . . . and the whole Swedish team fell on the scorer as if he had won the Cup . . which he well might have done with the goal!

It now needed three from United, even allowing that the Swedes didn't score again.

A McInally shot gave the fans momentary hope but, over-all, United were finding the going tough, though again hopes were raised in 32 minutes.

Malpas and McInally combined to get Sturrock free on the left. His instant cross was head flicked by Ferguson . . . agonisingly on to the top of the crossbar and into the crowd behind the goal.

The Swedes were controlling the game and there was another dangerous moment for United when Narey had to concede a corner which was headed in by Carlsson and taken low down by Thomson.

United were still trying though and when Gallacher brilliantly went past two defenders on the right to get in a great cross, Hysen took it off Ferguson's head when the striker was perfectly positioned in the goalmouth to equalise.

Three to get, only 45 minutes to get them in. It was the toughest task of their football lives that faced United.

The interval thought was of the physical strength of the Swedes, which didn't stop them being good on the ball. They seldom lost a tackle that mattered.

Hegarty was on for Holt, with Clark moving up front, but the first attack was by Gothenburg.

Andersson seemeed surprised he wasn't offside and hesitated before shooting weakly and off the outside of the post.

The game had opened out and Sturrock buzzed three times in succession down the left wing, being heavily upended for his pains in 49 minutes.

A fruitless corner followed the free kick and, though it looked as though manager Jim McLean's half-time comments had sparked new life into his team, IFK's danger on the break was proved when McInally got a toe end in to stop Petterson when he was all but through.

The award of a free kick against Hysen for hands 25 yards out had the crowd roaring again as Clark got ready to take it.

His tremendous drive beat the wall, but Wernersson was perfectly placed to take it cleanly in the midriff.

Next it was Clark again, muscling through three tackles but

finally shooting weakly when Ferguson was free on his right.

And yet again it was Clark in 60 minutes—and this time it was glory, glory all the way for the big young giant!

When Ferguson sent a low cross from the right, Clark twirled inside Tord Holmgren like a ballet dancer and left-footed a great shot past Wernersson.

Was it possible? Could the cup yet come to Tannadice? All of a sudden there was hope.

The suspect handling of Wernersson hadn't been evident up to now but in 63 minutes he completely lost a McInally free from the right. Sadly for United, no one was in the right position to take advantage.

There was a flashpoint when Gallacher charged in on the keeper and Hysen took exception, but things didn't spill over in a game which had never gone beyond being hard.

The pressure was on Gothenburg now and their nerves were fraying. When Clark bundled Wernersson into the net he was

jostled by four Gothenburg players as the keeper again made a meal of what wasn't too serious a knock.

It still wasn't the smooth United it can be, but this was the fire and the effort that had been so sadly lacking at Hampden on Saturday.

Still, there were those two goals to get—and the minutes were ticking steadily away.

One of them oh so nearly came in 70 minutes. A Narey free, a Clark header and Gallacher in to beat the keeper to the ball—but only to send it over the bar.

Then Hegarty got in a great header in 69 minutes, but it went just past and three minutes later Redford went off and Bannon on

I·F·K

GOTEBORG

and Tommy Holmgren went off for Mordt.

Redford had been slipping out of the game after a great early spell and it was a logical move.

The final pass was still not quite on, though, as first Sturrock, then Malpas proved when promising moves broke down.

Clark again won a ball in the air to raise hopes, but it was desperately scrambled clear.

Thomson was practically unemployed, but the minutes were stil ticking away and there were those two goals needed . . .

Next substitution was Johannson for Roland Nilsson.

United were still trying, but a bit of the edge had gone off their play. In one thrust into the penalty area, though, Narey was sent crashing and, though Petterson looked guilty, the referee waved away penalty claims.

Again and again Clark got headers in and Malpas a shot but this was in the last few minutes and there simply wasn't time to get the goals that mattered.

Dundee United—B. Thomson; Holt, Malpas, McInally, Clark, Narey, Ferguson, Gallacher, Kirkwood, Sturrock, Redford. Subs: Bowman, Bannon, Beaumont, Hegarty, S. Thomson.

IFK Gothenburg—Wernersson; Carlsson, Hysen, Larsson, Fredriksson, R. Nilsson, Tord Holmgren, Andersson, Tommy Holmgren, Petterson, L. Nilsson. Subs: Tobiasson, Mordt, Johansson, Zetterlund, Rantanen.

Referee—Iona Igna (Rumania).

An acrobatic leap by Ian Redford in a bid to score.

The goal that rekindled United's hopes. John Clark's rocket shot flashes past Gothenburg keeper Wernersson and into the net.

DUNDEE UNITED 1, IFK GOTHENBURG 1 (aggregate 1-2)

FOR THE second time in five days Dundee United were shattered and stunned by defeat in a Cup final.

On Saturday it was the Scottish Cup at Hampden, last night the UEFA Cup on their own Tannadice Park.

There is absolutely no one with even the remotest connection with or loyalty to United who will, right now, appreciate my comment that the achievement of getting to the two finals was alone a remarkable one.

Both have been lost. Disaster is all and no consoling words from anyone will be accepted for the foreseeable future. But achievement it was.

While I was shocked by the ineptitude of the United team on Saturday, I was equally impressed by the 13 men who gave their all here and were cheered back on to the ground after 15 minutes in the dressing-room by a crowd that simply wouldn't be satisfied until they returned.

Jim McLean and coach Gordon Wallace joined them, but they left centre-stage to the players.

Maybe the first half per-

formance bore the hallmarks of Saturday's disappointment, but after the interval United more or less threw caution to the winds at two goals down—the one in Gothenburg and Lennart Nilsson's counter here—and got a reward on the hour when John Clark scored his fourth European goal of the season.

For a spell hope flared. They pounded in on Gothenburg, but the two goals that would have created history

with them being the first Scottish club to win the UEFA Cup didn't come.

It was never going to be easy. Starting one down against a top European club even at home is the equivalent of shaving blind with a cut-throat razor!

The men in tangerine last night made sure no one could criticise them on the

score of effort, however, especially in that second half.

Over the two games, Gothenburg deserved their honour—their second UEFA Cup triumph of the 1980's.

They can make mistakes, but they are not frightened when they happen to battle their way out of them.

And their danger on the break was amply illustrated with their goal.

As I finish this report, the

with a chance of two cups.

Now they have none, but I repeat that it was an achievement to get there.

Kevin Gallacher worked hard throughout, Dave Narey was his immaculate self yet again, Ian Redford started well and Jim McInally proved what a tremendous acquisition he has been for the club.

Then there was John Clark. That second half in the striker's role might have ended in even more glory than the single goal.

On Saturday, you would have been hard pushed to find those earning pass marks. Last night—on the score of effort alone, especially second half—I refuse to criticise anyone no matter what the technical "experts" might say.

The Swedes were good, with Hysen, likely to be Manchester United bound, commanding at the back, Tord Holmgren getting in vital passes and Petersson always willing to seek out the half chance.

A great night, a great season . . . but oh the cruelty of the game when you are a loser!

THE SPORTS EDITOR REPORTS ON DUNDEE UNITED'S BID FOR UEFA CUP GLORY

crowd has only slightly thinned from the attendance of 20,911 and they have sportingly applauded the award of the UEFA Cup to Gothenburg as the United players file up for their losers' medals, their tears shed, their misery complete and a quiet lap of honour completed.

It doesn't seem only five days ago that they were in

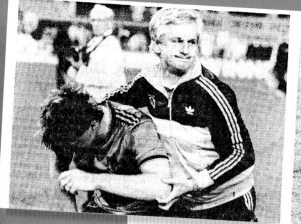

An agonising end to the game and, indeed, the season, for the brave men in tangerine. Our strip of pictures shows the level of despair as John Clark (helped to his feet by coach Gordon Wallace), Maurice Malpas and Paul Hegarty realise their great efforts have gone unrewarded.

AGONY AS UNITED'S DREAM TURNS SOUR

THEY'RE BRAVE, they're sporting and they've done the city proud. But they're not UEFA champions—yet.

The prayers of Dundee, the goodwill of Scotland and the magnificent skills of Dundee United went for nothing at Tannadice last night, as Gothenburg striker Lennart Nilsson shattered the Tangerine dream with a vital first-half goal.

All over the city—all over Scotland—the heads went down. Dundee United, who had toppled the mighty Barcelona and Borussia on their way to European glory, had fallen at the final hurdle and lost their second cup final in the space of five days.

Despite a glorious second-half fightback, which had United fans screaming themselves hoarse as they began to believe a miracle could happen, the game ended in a 1-1 draw. The Swedes lifted the UEFA Cup thanks to a 2-1 aggregate over the two-leg final.

But every cloud has a silver lining—or rather tangerine.

The thousands of fans who stayed behind to roar their appreciation made it clear that United would always be winners in their eyes.

So the team had fallen—but to one of the strongest sides in Europe, and after a long, backbreaking season both at home and abroad.

And on the way they had made friends throughout the Continent, they had established themselves as a world-class team and they had given notice, in no uncertain terms, that a new force had arrived to challenge the very best.

The fans' loyalty managed even to lift the almost tangible cloud of depression that settled over the heads of the exhausted United players as they sank to their knees in despair at the final whistle.

For forty minutes the supporters sang, cheered and whistled their appreciation—and out came United, heads once again held high, to salute their faithful.

And the biggest cheer of the night—apart from that which greeted John Clark's thrilling second-half goal—was for manager Jim Mclean, who came on not once but twice to wave his thanks to the terraces.

The result was a cruel, cruel blow. To have come so far... But although there were grown men in tears at the end of the

game, even they realised that United had done all they could, and knew that the disappointment was magnified a hundredfold for the players, whose slow, bowed shuffles off the pitch told their own story.

In stark contrast to Saturday's Scottish Cup defeat, however, there were no harsh words for the players. Sympathy, yes—and congratulations for a fighting second-half performance that had the Swedes badly rattled despite their very comfortable goal cushion.

United, it was widely acknowledged, had still done the city proud—and the 86/87 season won't be forgotten for a long, long time.

The team had lifted the city into headlines all over Europe, and had joined with their various opponents to serve up a series of thrilling, and sporting, games.

The fans, too, had worked wonders, bringing friendship back into European football and winning accolades in all corners of the Continent.

As both Scottish and Swedish fans headed off to the city's hostelries, many were swapping colours and flags.

The fans, in fact, came in for high praise from Chief Superintendent David Chalmers, head of Tayside Police's central division. "They were absolutely excellent. We had no trouble and no arrests were made during the game. It is a great tribute to them. We asked for them to behave and they did us, themselves and the city proud."

Despite the bitter pill of defeat, United supporters were still friendly enough to congratulate their opposite numbers—as they cheered the Gothenburg team on the presentation of the magnificent UEFA Cup.

There were a few cynics, as ever—the

ones who said United could never have done it. But they were the ones saying the same thing before both Barcelona and Borussia games.

And there were others, too, who made mention of the great British trait of sportsmanship in defeat—"the best losers in the world, that's the British," said one.

But he forgot the message coming from all over town last night. We're not just British—we're Scottish. We don't like losing, and we'll be backing United again and again until they lift that Cup. This is just the beginning...

More than 60 pubs throughout the city had been granted late licences in anticipation of a United victory.

However, when Gothenburg scored an eerie silence fell upon the bars in contrast to the scenes of wild excitement which greeted the successes of earlier rounds.

Typical of the city centre bars where fans thronged around television screens was Frames in Castle Street.

Manager Peter Rose summed up the anti-climax of the evening when he said, "We had the fancy hats and everything out for a celebration but I've had to put them away. I feel for the fans. It's a big disappointment and United deserved to end the season with some trophy."

Ged McColl, barman at the Chelsea Lounge, said, "It was a superb performance in the second half and we were unlucky on one or two occasions.

"Overall, though, I thought Gothenburg deserved to win the cup. This is one night where it's fair to say we're all as sick as parrots."

● Match report and more pictures on pages 14 and 15.

The UEFA Cup is held aloft by the triumphant Gothenburg players

Gothenburg "too good"

DUNDEE UNITED manager Jim McLean was an understandably disappointed man (writes STEVE BRUCE).

"Considering what United are capable of, the performance wasn't all we would have expected, but the players gave every ounce they had," he said.

"Unfortunately, there wasn't enough left when we needed it most," he added, clearly referring to the demands that a 70-game season had placed on his players.

"The problem was that we asked players to peak twice for the two cup finals in a matter of days and that crucified us.

"We started really well but they got the goal at an important time.

"You could look back at important decisions during the game and make excuses, but we got breaks against Borussia and Barcelona so we cannot complain.

"At the end of the day, the result is what it is and they honestly were too good for what my players had left to give.

"They had that bit more than us over the two games—the better team won the trophy.

"Most of all, I'm disappointed for the fans because at the end of the day we've given them nothing tangible.

"We've come so close . . ."

Not that the United supporters who were still inside Tannadice a full 45 minutes after the final whistle appeared to have been let down.

A group of around 200 fans occupied the middle of the shed end of the ground refusing to leave.

They only did so when the United boss set aside his own disappointment and went to talk to them.

Those same supporters then made their way to the main entrance at Tannadice, where they greeted the United players as heroes as they left the ground.

Winning manager Gunder Bengtsson commented, "We played a perfect first half and the goal came at the right time.

"After we'd scored, my players believed they had won the trophy, thinking United could not score three, and that caused us a few problems.

"It wasn't a great football match but it was some fight.

"The only difference between the teams was that we were physically stronger."

The Gothenburg boss also praised what he termed "the fairness" of the supporters.

United chairman George Fox said afterwards, "I thought that was the most sporting crowd I have ever seen and our players played their hearts out.

"Both were a credit to this club and Scottish football."

Among the crowd was former Dundee manager Archie Knox who said, "Not that it will be any consolation to United, but they were up against one of the top sides in Europe.

"It's hard to peak twice in four days, especially after losing the Scottish Cup final.

"That said, United didn't get a break when they had Gothenburg under pressure during the second half, but what a marvellous achievement for them reaching the final."

Another spectator was Manchester United boss Alex. Ferguson, who is poised to move for Gothenburg defender Glenn Hysen later this week.

"I thought United were very unlucky in the second half," said Fergie.

While United's exhausted players fell to the ground amid the pain of defeat, viewers around the world also witnessed something truly extraordinary — the home fans overcoming their disappointment to applaud the Swedish stars and cheer them on a lap of honour.

Gothenburg "heroes" honoured

WHEN DUNDEE UNITED supporters visited Gothenburg for the first leg of the UEFA Cup final on May 6, they gained the support of the public for their exemplary behaviour.

One incident highlights the bond which accrued between Swede and Dundonian.

Two United supporters, walking in Gothenburg city centre, came across a local man trying to rob the main American Express centre.

The two, James Stewart, of 42 Balmerino Road, Dundee, a window cleaner and R.A.F. cook Alan Boath, of 16 Bankhead Terrace, Forfar, grabbed the culprit and held him until the police arrived.

Neils Klintelberg, chief of Gothenburg police, was "absolutely delighted" with their action and arranged for Gothenburg medals to be presented to the heroes at Tannadice last night.

● Pictured from left are— George Fox (chairman of Dundee United), James Stewart, Alan Boath and Chief Superintendent David Chalmer, of Tayside Police, who made the presentation.

Fans may have done the British game a lot of good

THE MAGNIFICENT behaviour of the Dundee United fans last night and throughout the competition, could open the door for English clubs to once again take their place on the European stage—that's the view of one of the many English journalists at the match.

He talked of his pride at seeing a British club (we'll accept its usage just this once) and its fans, contesting a European football final with only good-natured, sporting rivalry.

And of seeing happy Swedes sitting alongside diehard United fans without a hint of the trouble which has seen English football teams banned indefinitely from European competitions.

Handshakes rather than fists were exchanged at the end of an emotional 90 minutes.

As an advertisement for the changing face of the British game in the eyes of European football autocrats, it could have done English clubs seeking a passport back to European competition no harm, he felt.

Those lucky enough to get inside the ground, were watched on television by hundreds of millions more, reflecting on the football rather than the bloody scenes of carnage which accompanied Liverpool—the last British club to contest a European final, two years ago.

This was indeed a night when Scottish, and yes British football won, even though one of its best teams suffered defeat.

One of the proudest men last night was Dundee Lord Provost Tom Mitchell who was at the game and had nothing but praise for the team's efforts.

"They worked very hard indeed and although the result was a disappointment the attitude of the fans at the end made up for this.

"They behaved impeccably and cheered both teams at the end. I honestly don't think you would find such a response from fans who had lost such an important trophy anywhere in Europe," he said.

"The team performed very well and I would also like to say that I am proud of the two Dundee United fans who were presented with plaques after the game in token of their law-abiding act in Gothenburg when they apprehended a would-be thief.

"Tonight I was very, very proud to be associated with the city of Dundee."

Tayside Regional Council convener John McAllion, said, "I thought the team fought magnificently in the second half and their performance was matched by the fans' behaviour throughout and after the game.

"I was filled with emotion when I saw the way the fans responded to Gothenburg after the match.

"These people were an absolute credit to the city and their country. Both they and their team will be back next season, there can be no doubt about that."

McLean is named top manager

DUNDEE UNITED'S achievement in reaching the final of both the UEFA and Scottish Cups has been recognised in the Scottish Brewers Annual Football Personality Awards.

Tannadice boss Jim McLean has been voted Manager of the Year after taking United to the verge of a dream double.

McLean won the near-unanimous vote of a panel of top sports writers and broadcasters.

It's the second year in succession that the Tayside club has figured in the awards for 12 months ago Richard Gough was named Personality Player of the Year.

Succeeding Gough is Rangers skipper Terry Butcher who this afternoon plays for England in the Rous Cup clash with Scotland at Hampden.

Butcher wins the award after helping the Ibrox men lift both the Skol Cup and Premier League title.

McLean and Butcher will each receive cheques for £1000 and special commemorative trophies at a lunch to be held in their honour on Monday.

There was a manager of the year award for Jim McLean, but the greatest sense of achievement came from reflecting on how his club, and its fans, had won friends around the world for their efforts and sportsmanship.

Smiling, in spite of it all

LOOKING AT our pictures, you might find it hard to believe that Dundee United manager Jim McLean was smiling the morning after his team had lost out in their second final in a matter of days (writes The Sports Editor).

But no matter the deep hurt he must have been feeling, McLean mixed many a smile with serious comment as he faced a cross-section of the British Press in the Tannadice boardroom yesterday.

The final picture is of the consolation prize that is little consolation—the plaque for appearing in the UEFA Cup final.

The letter is one of well over 1000 which poured into Tannadice Park before United's two cup finals, and now the post-bag is full of those expressing disappointment at the results, praising the supporters, and wishing United better fortune in the days ahead.

Only a small proportion bear local postmarks—and one came from a Rangers supporters' club in Melbourne, Australia.

"I will try to answer every letter," Mr McLean said.

● Scottish Secretary Malcolm Rifkind yesterday added his tribute to Dundee United and their sporting fans.

"They are to be congratulated on their keen work and sportsmanship."

A success in failure for Dundee—and publicans

A DEGREE OF normality finally returned to Dundee yesterday evening after one of the most astonishing nights the city's publicans have ever witnessed.

The 20,000 Dundee United supporters at the UEFA Cup final continued, throughout yesterday, to win glowing praise for their behaviour both nationally and internationally (see Page 13).

But the bar staff in the city centre did not need to read of the fellowship shown between United and Gothenburg fans—the tills told their own story yesterday morning.

All over town, after the game, bars were stacked six or seven deep with United fans determined to make the best of it—and Swedes celebrating their 2-1 aggregate victory.

But there was no trouble in any part of the town.

In every corner of the city Dundonians were welcoming their Scandinavian friends and congratulating them on their success.

The signs could be seen right after the match at Tannadice, when a couple of dozen Gothenburg supporters lined up in Sandeman Street and refused to let the home fans past until they had shaken hands.

Then it was on to the town centre, with both groups singing all the way.

An estimated 300 fans from both sides of the North Sea were still gathered in City Square at 2 a.m., swapping scarves, flags—and girl friends.

It was, all in all, an extraordinary night—made all the more so by the fact that United had fallen at the final hurdle.

● Our picture shows the Tannadice team which is not in the public eye but without whom the United machine would grind to a halt.

A big hand for the backroom staff, from left—Jim Young, head groundsman Jimmy Fox, Evelyn Fiddes, Susan Penman, Ann Diamond, Gail Sutherland, Priti Trivedi, Gillian Mason, Angela Old, John Monks, Beth Gibb, and Val Petrie.

Our supporters did untold good, says Jim

By THE SPORTS EDITOR

ON MONDAY I said that the hottest hot seat in football was the one the losing manager occupies after a Cup final. I was wrong. The hottest hot seat is the one that manager occupies after TWO losing Cup finals in four days.

Dundee United manager Jim McLean was in that double hot seat in the Tannadice Park boardroom yesterday, less than 12 hours after his team had gone out of the UEFA Cup final the previous night, drawing 1-1 with IFK Gothenburg, but losing 2-1 on aggregate.

The questions were muted, the atmosphere subdued, but he fielded every query and answered honestly, although he must have been hurting deep inside . . . and it was amazing how much optimism he drew out of the situation in matters other than the result.

For example, "It may be my lowest moment as a manager, but our supporters did British football untold good," he began. "It was a truly incredible display by them. I was genuinely worried about people, maybe coming from outside our support, encroaching on the park because we have no fences, but everyone stayed where they were.

"And they not only cheered and applauded us, they cheered and applauded the team which had beaten their team.

> **❝ . . . the city of Dundee should be proud of them. ❞**

"I know I am repeating the word, but it was an incredible display of what football supporters should do and the city of Dundee should be proud of them.

"At the end of the game my wife and the wives of several of our players couldn't get out of the main door. I went to the supporters and said I would appreciate it if they could go

and have a couple of ginger beers and thanked them for their support throughout the season."

He did the same to a wedge of supporters behind the Dens end goal and, in both cases, the crowd quietly dispersed.

Which makes him completely entitled to say, as he did next regarding the frightening night at the Heysel Stadium in Belgium which got English clubs banned from Europe, "UEFA

Jim McLean making a point on Wednesday night.

must look at the situation again. "There is no way English clubs should be banned after what our supporters did last night. Surely that display by them must go some way towards getting English clubs back into Europe.

"I believe if you give the fans responsibility, there are more good than bad. Nothing will ever make up for the Heysel, but we must look ahead.

"I know they have a problem in England. Maybe we are fortunate in Scotland with, to me, the banning of drink a key factor. Equally there must be clubs in England with support like ours."

Then firmly, "It may be thought that I am looking for the straws of consolation for our defeat. Not really. What I AM looking for is the improvement

of the game. What happened on the terracing and in the stand at Tannadice last night, was the good part of the game for us."

The talk turned to United's future.

He had always said and still said, the team lacked quality. It had some quality, but not enough. There was also money available, but not as much as some people thought.

Players start on a low basic wage at Tannadice, but international honours and such like could push them through quickly—and, of course, bonuses for success were good.

Players like Narey, Hegarty and Sturrock were on life contracts. Eamonn Bannon and Ralph Milne had been the only two players who had turned down long contracts.

He illustrated the point about pushing through by saying Andy Gray had gone from ground staff boy to top contract in six months.

"A team would be unstoppable today with two wingers," he said, enlarging to make the comment that strikers take a lot of criticism today, but, more' often than not, the service to them isn't what it should be.

> **❝ We do not need a top-class signing just now. ❞**

But where were they?

There were around 25 players at Tannadice of first team quality. Only half a dozen were exceptional, which, he emphasised, was no criticism of others.

Around 30 players had been used this season and the plus from that was that they had been seen on first-team duty and tested.

"We do not need a top-class signing just now. We needed one when Richard Gough went," he continued.

"Even yesterday morning (the morning of the UEFA final) and the night before, I was talking to people about certain players.

"We need a Mark Hateley (of

Inter-Milan and wanted by Rangers) definitely. We don't need a centre-half like a Mick McCarthy, who was signed by Celtic for a reported £500,000.

"But if we did, and I am certainly in no way running down Dundee United, and he had a choice of a club like Celtic, we wouldn't be at the races.

"I want five players. I would have been happy with three," he said.

> **❝ . . . there will be players added during the close season. ❞**

"There is no way I can guarantee that players of the quality needed will be coming in but there will be players added during the close season.

"We have a better chance of getting players like Ian Redford and Iain Ferguson, who are maybe in a wee bit of a rut—as some players here are in a rut—and would be better elsewhere."

Making the point that he had had to use as strikers players like Bannon and Redford this season, he made the point that he had not written off John Clark as a striker.

His ability and physical presence could cause any defence problems and maybe, with the confidence born of his run at centre-half, he could still become a striker.

"If we want to win Scottish cups and European trophies, we need players who can score against the Rangers, Celtics and Aberdeens of this world as well as lesser teams. We also want chances created for them to take.

"We had a time when, from our youth policy, we got through Milne, Malpas, Narey, Holt and many others. It hasn't been so good lately, although it is better now. It is still the way we have to develop, along with the correct buying-in."

After expressing admiration at the way Bertie Auld, when with Partick Thistle, Benny Rooney, when with Morton and, especially, current St Mirren

manager Alex Smith, when with Stirling Albion, had run their clubs financially, he said a manager had two sides to his thoughts—what is best on the playing side, what is the bank balance?

United had to look at a loss of £150,000 annually. The only ways round it were to sell players or get into finals.

Finally, he talked first of Andy Roxburgh and the Swedish season, then of a vital decision he had made when he got home after the UEFA final.

"I am not having a go at Andy Roxburgh when I say Scotland doesn't struggle because we don't score goals, but because we don't create goals . . . the Swedish season is perfect for Europe. While we are at the end of our long season, they reach the finals nicely into the start of theirs."

Then the decision. "I am superstitious, One of those superstitions is that I wear the same short stockings, underpants, tie—washed after every game, I add—when we are on a good run.

"The lot went out last night.

"And while I am at it. When we won the Premier League I had a checked sports jacket. My wife put it away. I couldn't half do with that back. It might change our luck."

Then it was into his office . . .to start checking on players, reading letters, answering phone calls.

It is over for United in the playing sense now until the June 12 start to a close-season trip to Los Angeles and games against Roma and Guadalajara.

But it never stops for the Boss . . .

Jim pays tribute to "united" effort

DUNDEE UNITED boss Jim McLean yesterday picked up the Scottish Brewers Personality Manager of the Year award but in so doing declined to accept all the credit for the Tangerines' magnificent season (**writes STEVE BRUCE**).

The Tannadice supremo paid tribute to his chairman George Fox and right hand man Gordon Wallace and praised the efforts of the United players, during his acceptance speech at a special lunch in Glasgow.

"I receive this award on behalf of everyone connected with Dundee United," said McLean afterwards.

"It wasn't a one-man oper-

ation achieving what we did," he continued.

"The chairman, my assistant Gordon Wallace, the office staff and most of all the players, deserve credit."

The United boss received a commemorative trophy and cheque for £1000 from Mr Tony Belfield, managing director of Scottish Brewers.

Over the course of the season just ended, during which United reached the final of the UEFA and Scottish Cups and finished third top of the Premier League, he also collected three Manager of the Month awards.

Rangers' skipper Terry Butcher received his award as Personality Player of the Year at the same gathering.

Proud to be there, says Narey

By THE SPORTS EDITOR

"I BELIEVE we partly redeemed ourselves with that second half performance—and that magnificent support of ours certainly deserved it."

Reflective thoughts yesterday from Dundee United team captain Dave Narey.

"We are down, who wouldn't

be after two losing finals, but we aren't as down as we were after Saturday," he went on.

"I was proud to be out there for United that second half, though.

"And I have to say it again about our supporters. They just wouldn't go away, would they? We needed a lift and they gave it to us. We would have loved to

make it the perfect night for them."

Kevin Gallacher, back at his sharpest on the night, looked back on two of the nearest of the near things—the ball he sent over the bar and the one which tipped the top of the crossbar from Iain Ferguson.

"I hit my one too well," he said. "If I had sclaffed it the ball

would have dropped into goal, but I got it perfectly with my instep and it lifted over.

"I didn't actually see it go over, but if that gave people the same feeling the attempt by Iain gave me, then it was one of the big disappointments of the night.

"We were both so near. What a difference it would have made if they had gone in."

An example to the world

Every football fan believes their club is special.

Those who follow the richest sides have long lists of titles to remember and the promise of more to come, but those who choose to support smaller clubs like Dundee United do so in the knowledge that trophies will come around less often — and that the greatest moments may not always be measured by silverware.

United fans, of course, do have a list of honours to celebrate. The Premier League title of 1983 may be the club's greatest single achievement, but there have been League Cups and they finally banished the infamous Hampden hoodoo in 1994 to claim the first of two Scottish Cups so far.

Nevertheless, it is the European campaigns, and the swashbuckling football played during them, that many United fans continue to hold dearest of all.

And while there were many famous occasions before — Barcelona in 1966, AS Monaco and Borussia Moenchengladbach in 1981, Werder Bremen in 1982 and reaching the 1984 European Cup semi-final — 1987 stands out as the year world football formally recognised the special nature of this outward-looking club from Scotland's east coast.

December brought the news that FIFA had bestowed its very first Fair Play Award on Dundee United to honour the remarkable show of sportsmanship by fans throughout the UEFA Cup run, culminating in that unforgettable ovation afforded to Gothenburg.

It is a moment remembered just as fondly in Sweden. The IFK Gothenburg website still declares: "These two final matches have gone down in history for the total fraternisation between the teams' supporters.

"The scene where the whole of Tannadice Park gives the blue and white players of Gothenburg a standing ovation during the lap of honour with the trophy is still jaw-dropping and brings a tear to the eye."

United would put the FIFA money towards a new stand, the Fair Play Enclosure, as a physical reminder of what was achieved in 1987.

Although it was later replaced as Tannadice was redeveloped to meet modern standards, the memory of that year, and the manager who inspired it, is recorded in the new name: The Jim McLean Fair Play Stand.

For The Courier, the fans' achievement far outshone the disappointment of defeat. Following confirmation of the FIFA award, the paper paid fitting tribute:

It is almost impossible to estimate the power for good or bad that football can wield today ... In simpler past days, the money in football was not enough to warp standards or character. Success was only a cosy warmth. Failure did not distort lives or careers.

These days aren't likely to come again. But that sporting virtue can be its own reward was vividly demonstrated by Dundee United's supporters...

Ask any Dundee United supporter who cheered Gothenburg the night his team lost to them. Ask any amazed Gothenburg fan who stayed to see his team applauded by the fans whose team they had just beaten.

These were moments those present will never forget. They lifted football to a plane long but a memory.

United's fantastic fans have lit a torch of example for football worldwide.

F.I.F.A. new award goes to United for fans' sporting display in Euro final

THAT MAGNIFICENT May night at Tannadice when Dundee United supporters, despite their team having lost 2-1 on aggregate (1-0 away, 1-1 at home) cheered champions Gothenburg on a lap of honour after the U.E.F.A. Cup final (second leg) has brought an unprecedented benefit.

Football's world ruling body F.I.F.A. has awarded the club £20,000 because

By The Sports Editor

of their supporters' conduct, principally on that unforgettable night but also in Europe generally, where they are recognised as being an example to supporters everywhere because of their impeccable conduct.

The award—the first ever and to become an annual event—will be spent on the supporters, which probably means ground improvements.

When I contacted manager Jim McLean late yesterday for a comment, he couldn't keep the emotion from his voice as he said. "It is thoroughly deserved and a tremendous boost and tribute to our supporters.

"It is equally important to Scottish supporters generally, who are the best in the world anyway, but it is the Dundee United supporters in particular who must get top billing."

He went on, "For the first time this season they have got what they deserved"—an obvious reference to a spell in which, after the magnificent achievements of last season, results haven't gone the way anyone connected with the club would have wished.

He then made the point that while everyone had been talking about the performance of the supporters, F.I.F.A. had done the right thing "and is thoroughly justified" in tangibly recognising the event.

He ended, "The money is obviously important, but even more important is the encouragement the award gives the fans.

"That night at Tannadice was the greatest display by supporters I have seen in all the time I have been in football."

I second that.

I was in the ground long after the

game ended and will never forget the reaction of the Gothenburg team, officials and supporters.

They could not believe that, having beaten the home team, they had been accorded a lap of honour during which they were cheered to the echo every step of the way.

I recall, Mrs McLean, the manager's wife, and a group of players' wives trying to leave Tannadice an hour after the game and having to return to ask the manager to help them get through the crowd. He did—and a

passageway was made without the slightest bother.

So many fans stayed behind in the ground chanting his name that he finally had to go out and ask them to disperse. Again they did without a problem.

Tales were to be told later of parties that went into the wee sma' hours involving United and Gothenburg supporters and of the Swedish contingent departing for home over the next few days telling tales of hospitality such as they had never before experienced.

Now, fittingly, a marvellous exhibition of football support the way it should be has been rewarded.

Scottish League secretary Jim Farry said, "Naturally we are delighted that a Scottish club is the recipient of such a high award. It not only reflects well on Dundee United but also on the growing stature and resurgence of Scottish football.

"It also proves that when it comes to putting on a show, Scotland and the fans of Scottish clubs can match the very best of anywhere in the world."

> "It is thoroughly deserved and a tremendous boost and tribute to our supporters. It is equally important to Scottish supporters generally, who are the best in the world anyway . . ."

Dundee United's triumph of sportsmanship was formally recognised on August 19, 1988, when a FIFA delegation visited the City Chambers to present the Fair Play Award to representatives of the club and supporters' groups.

A United fan's banner at the final said it all.

Acknowledgements

The publisher wishes to thank those who helped to bring this book to reality:

Original project team members John Anderson, Ewan Cameron, Nadine Hawkins and Richard Rooney.

Business consultant Clare Moore.

DC Thomson Archives.

DC Thomson Enterprise.

Photographers Kris Miller and Kim Cessford.

Paul Hegarty.

Dundee United Football Club.

Leisure and Culture Dundee / Central Library.

DUFC Archive (*dufcarchive.co.uk*).

And, finally, all of those who wrote, photographed, edited and printed The Courier's original coverage.